# Microsoft Office 2010 and 2007 for SENIORS

Studio Visual Steps

# Microsoft Office 2010 and 2007 for SENIORS

*Practical applications for every day usage*

*Visual Steps*™

*www.visualsteps.com*

This book has been written using the Visual Steps™ method.
Cover design by Studio Willemien Haagsma bNO

© 2011 Visual Steps
Edited by Jolanda Ligthart, Rilana Groot and Mara Kok
Translated by Chris Hollingsworth, *1<sup>st</sup> Resources* and Irene Venditti, *i-write* translation services.
Editor in chief: Ria Beentjes

First printing: Februari 2011
ISBN 978 90 5905 177 5

**Do you have a suggestion or would you like to ask a question?**
**E-mail: info@visualsteps.com**

**Would you like more information?**
**www.visualsteps.com**

**Website for this book:**
**www.visualsteps.com/officeseniors**
You can also register your book here.

**Register your book**
By registering your book, you will be kept aware of any important changes that are necessary to you as a user of the book. You can also take advantage of our periodic newsletter informing you of our product releases, company news, tips & tricks, special offers, free guides, etc.

# Table of Contents

**Bonus Chapters**

At the website that goes with this book you will find bonus chapters. In *Appendix C Opening the Bonus Chapters* you can read how to open the bonus chapters.

# Foreword

Dear readers,

In this book you will learn how to use three of the most popular Office applications: *Word*, *Excel* and *PowerPoint* to accomplish common everyday tasks. For instance, you can compose and format professional looking documents in *Word*. You can use *Excel* to help keep your accounts in order by maintaining a household budget or create a database for your CD or DVD collection. With *PowerPoint* you can create an attractive presentation showing off pictures from a recent vacation or family event, including sound effects, illustrations, video clips and voice messages.

I hope you have lots of fun with this book!

Yvette Huijsman
Studio Visual Steps

P.S. Feel free to send us your comments and suggestions regarding this book.
The e-mail address is: info@visualsteps.com

# Visual Steps Newsletter

All Visual Steps books follow the same methodology: clear and concise step-by-step instructions with screen shots to demonstrate each task.
A complete list of all our books can be found on our website **www.visualsteps.com**
You can also sign up to receive our **free Visual Steps Newsletter**.

In this Newsletter you will receive periodic information by e-mail regarding:
- the latest titles and previously released books;
- special offers, supplemental chapters, tips and free informative booklets.
Also, our Newsletter subscribers may download any of the documents listed on the web pages **www.visualsteps.com/info_downloads** and
**www.visualsteps.com/tips**

When you subscribe to our Newsletter you can be assured that we will never use your e-mail address for any purpose other than sending you the information as previously described. We will not share this address with any third-party. Each Newsletter also contains a one-click link to unsubscribe.

## Register Your Book

When you can register your book, you will be kept informed of any important changes that are necessary to you as a user of the book. You can also take advantage of our periodic Newsletter informing you of our product releases, company news, tips & tricks, special offers, etc.

## Introduction to Visual Steps™

The Visual Steps handbooks and manuals are the best instructional materials available for learning how to work with computers and computer programs. Nowhere else will you find better support for getting to know the computer, the Internet, *Windows* or related software.

Properties of the Visual Steps books:
- **Comprehensible contents**
  Addresses the needs of the beginner or intermediate computer user for a manual written in simple, straight-forward English.
- **Clear structure**
  Precise, easy to follow instructions. The material is broken down into small enough segments to allow for easy absorption.
- **Screen shots of every step**
  Quickly compare what you see on your own computer screen with the screen shots in the book. Pointers and tips guide you when new windows are opened so you always know what to do next.
- **Get started right away**
  All you have to do is switch on your computer, place the book next to your keyboard, and begin at once.

In short, I believe these manuals will be excellent guides for you.

dr. H. van der Meij
Faculty of Applied Education, Department of Instruction Technology, University of Twente, the Netherlands

# What You Will Need

In order to work through this book, you will need a number of things on your computer:

The most important requirement for using this book is to have the English version of **Microsoft Office 2010** or **Microsoft Office 2007** installed on your computer.

Apart from that, your computer should run the English version of **Windows 7**, **Windows Vista** (including *ServicePack 1*), or **Windows XP** (including *ServicePack 3*). You can check which version you have by starting up your computer and viewing the opening screen.
The screen shots in this book have been made on a *Windows 7* computer. If you are working on a *Windows Vista* or *Windows XP* computer, you may see slightly different windows when compared to the *Windows* screen shots shown in this book. However, this will not affect the operations that are explained in this book.

In order to download the practice files and the bonus chapters from the website that goes with this book, you will need an active **internet connection**.

Finally, you will need a printer, a CD-rw, CD-r, USB stick or other type of external storage device. If you do not own any of these items, you can skip the exercises in which these items are used.

# Website

On the website that accompanies this book, **www.visualsteps.com/officeseniors**, you will find practice files, bonus online chapters and further information. This website will also keep you informed of any errata, recent updates or other changes you need to be aware of, as a user of the book.
Don't forget to visit our website **www.visualsteps.com** from time to time to read about new books and other useful information such as handy computer tips, frequently asked questions and informative booklets.

# How to Use This Book

This book has been written using the Visual Steps™ method. You can work through this book independently at your own pace.

In this Visual Steps™ book, you will see various icons. This is what they mean:

**Techniques**
These icons indicate an action to be carried out:

 The mouse icon means you should do something with the mouse.

 The keyboard icon means you should type something on the keyboard.

 The hand icon means you should do something else, for example insert a CD-ROM in the computer. It is also used to remind you of something you have learned before.

In addition to these icons, in some areas of this book *extra assistance* is provided to help you successfully work through each chapter.

**Help**
These icons indicate that extra help is available:

 The arrow icon warns you about something.

 The bandage icon will help you if something has gone wrong.

 Have you forgotten how to do something? The number next to the footsteps tells you where to look it up at the end of the book in the appendix *How Do I Do That Again?*

In separate boxes you will find tips or additional, background information.

**Extra information**
Information boxes are denoted by these icons:

 The book icon gives you extra background information that you can read at your convenience. This extra information is not necessary for working through the book.

 The light bulb icon indicates an extra tip for using the program.

## Prior Computer Experience

If you want to work through this book successfully, you should be able to do the following things:
- start up and close *Windows*;
- click, right-click, double-click and drag the mouse;
- open and close programs;
- execute commands.

If you do not have these skills, it is a good idea to read one of the following books first:

**Windows 7 for SENIORS**
Studio Visual Steps
ISBN 978 90 5905 126 3

**Windows Vista for SENIORS**
Studio Visual Steps
ISBN 978 90 5905 274 1

**Windows XP for SENIORS**
Addo Stuur
ISBN 978 90 5905 044 0

## Test Your Knowledge

Have you finished reading this book? Then test your knowledge with a test. Visit the website: **www.ccforseniors.com**

This multiple-choice test will tell you how good your knowledge is of the *Office* applications covered in this book. If you pass the test, you will receive your free *Computer Certificate* by e-mail.

## For Teachers

This book is designed as a self-study guide. It is also well suited for use in a group or a classroom setting. For this purpose, we offer a free teacher's manual containing information about how to prepare for the course (including didactic teaching methods) and testing materials. You can download this teacher's manual (PDF file) from the website which accompanies this book: **www.visualsteps.com/officeseniors**

# The Screen Shots

The screen shots in this book were made on a computer running *Windows 7 Ultimate* edition. The screen shots used in this book indicate which button, folder, file or hyperlink you need to click on your computer screen. In the instruction text (in **bold** letters) you will see a small image of the item you need to click. The black line will point you to the right place on your screen.
The small screen shots that are printed in this book are not meant to be completely legible all the time. This is not necessary, as you will see these images on your own computer screen in real size and fully legible.

Here you see an example of an instruction text and a screen shot. The black line indicates where to find this item on your own computer screen:

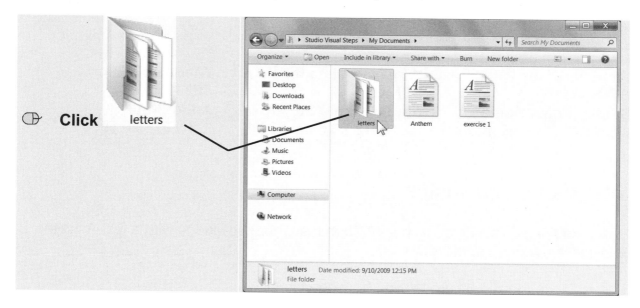

Sometimes the screen shot shows only a portion of a window. Here is an example:

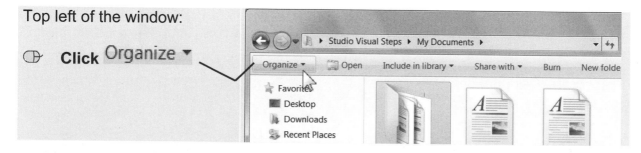

It really will **not be necessary** for you to read all the information in the screen shots in this book. Always use the screen shots in combination with the image you see on your own computer screen.

# 1. The Office Programs

This book will familiarize you with three programs from the well-known *Microsoft Office* suite: *Word*, *Excel* and *PowerPoint*.

*Word* is an all-round text editor. You can choose from a wide variety of options available to create your documents, insert pictures and edit or format the text. The program also provides various options for printing your documents.

*Excel* is a spreadsheet program that lets you store, organize and manipulate data. For example, a list of addresses, a list of your CD collection, or your book collection. There are formulas and functions built into the program that will allow you to perform many types of calculations.

*PowerPoint* is a program for creating presentations. Use it to prepare a speech or a lecture for your company or club, or create a slide show of your favorite holiday snapshots and videos.

The most powerful feature of the *Office* suite is the similarity between the windows of the various programs. For instance, each program uses the *ribbon*, the toolbar shown in the top of each window. The ribbon contains the commands and options you need for executing specific tasks, such as editing a document. These commands are grouped into tabs, in a logical way. You can adjust the existing tabs or even create a custom tab of your own with the commands you prefer.

Furthermore, all *Office* programs display the *Quick Access* toolbar. This toolbar can contain the commands you use most often and it is easy to customize. The *Quick Access* toolbar lets you execute these commands with just one click.

In this chapter you will learn how to:

- open the *Office* programs;
- use and customize the *Quick Access* toolbar;
- open the *Backstage* view;
- customize the ribbon.

 **Please note:**

This book has been written using the *Office 2010* suite of applications. These applications do not differ substantially from the *Office 2007* applications. This means you can use this book with the *Office 2007* suite. We will explain how to execute specific tasks in *Office 2007* as needed.

# 1.1 Opening the Office Programs

You can open any of the *Office* programs such as *Word*, *Excel* or *PowerPoint* in the same way. Try it now with the *Word* program:

☞ **Click**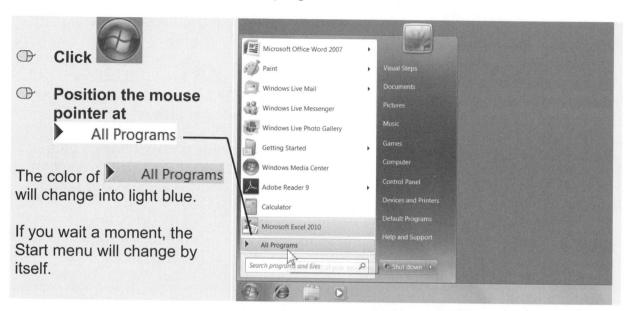

☞ **Position the mouse pointer at**
▶    **All Programs**

The color of ▶ **All Programs** will change into light blue.

If you wait a moment, the Start menu will change by itself.

☞ **Click**
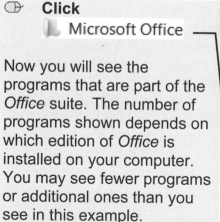   **Microsoft Office**

Now you will see the programs that are part of the *Office* suite. The number of programs shown depends on which edition of *Office* is installed on your computer. You may see fewer programs or additional ones than you see in this example.

To open the *Word* program:

☞ **Click**
W **Microsoft Word 2010**

If you have installed *Word 2007*, you need to click
Microsoft Office Word 2007.

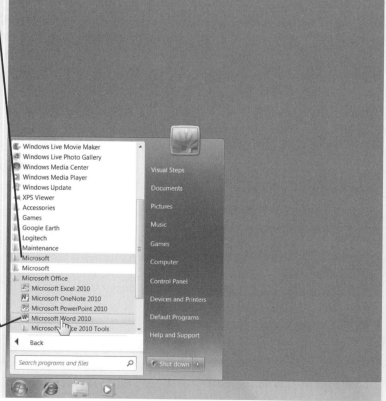

Now you will see the *Word 2010* startup window. A blank document is open:

At the top of the window you will see the ribbon:

The *Word 2007* window looks nearly the same.

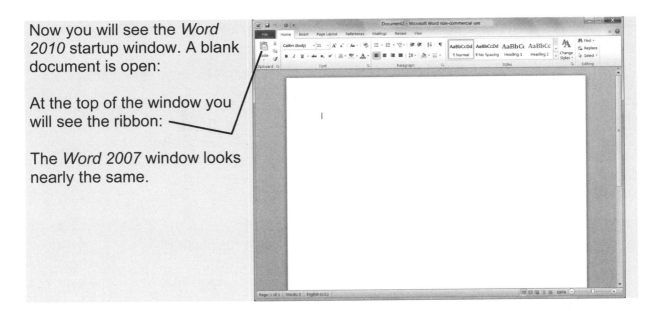

In the next section you will learn more about the ribbon.

# 1.2 The Ribbon

The ribbon is designed to quickly help you find the commands you need for creating and editing documents. Commands in the form of buttons, galleries, lists and other controls are organized into logical groups which are collected together under the tabs. Each tab relates to a type of task or activity such as writing or formatting a page. This is how the ribbon looks in *Word 2010*:

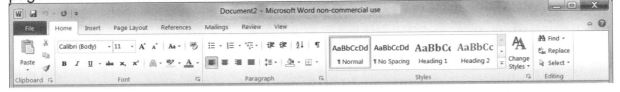

This is how the ribbon looks in *Word 2007*:

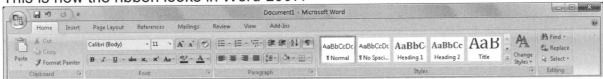

The ribbon consists of a number of tabs:

Each tab is task-oriented and contains logical groups of matching commands:

By clicking a tab you can display the corresponding groups and their commands.

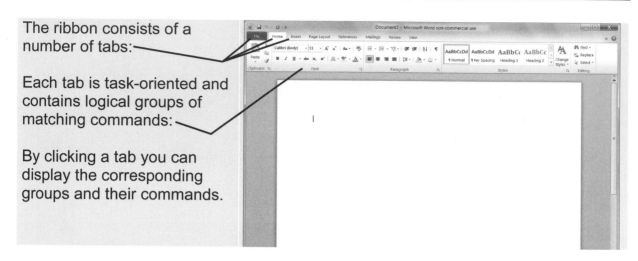

Take a look at the *Page Layout* tab, for example:

**Click the**

Page Layout **tab**

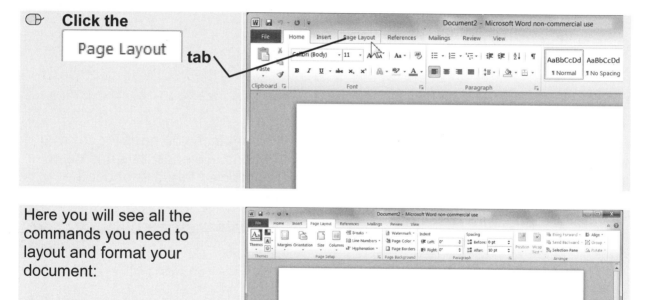

Here you will see all the commands you need to layout and format your document:

Now return to the *Home* tab:

**Click the** Home
**tab**

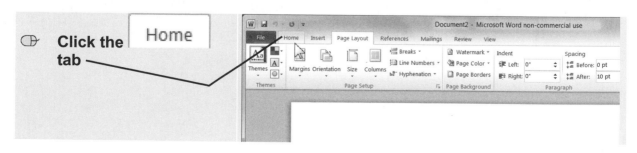

Here is the *Home* tab once again. If you need more working space, you can temporarily shrink the ribbon:

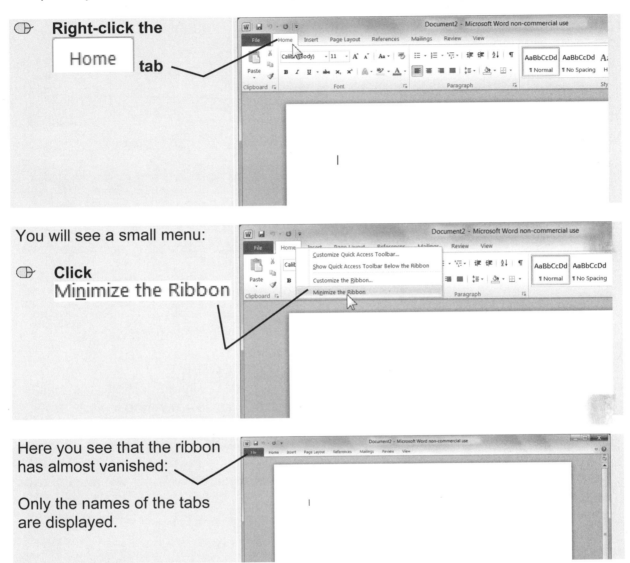

☞ **Right-click the**
  **Home** tab

You will see a small menu:

☞ **Click**
  Mi<u>n</u>imize the Ribbon

Here you see that the ribbon has almost vanished:

Only the names of the tabs are displayed.

You can restore the ribbon back to its normal size:

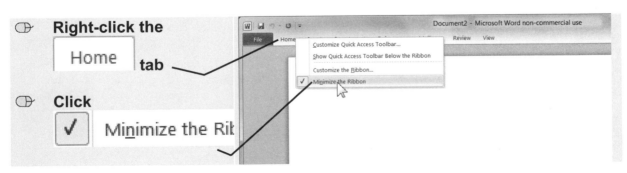

☞ **Right-click the**
  **Home** tab

☞ **Click**
  ✓ Mi<u>n</u>imize the Rib

**Tip**

**Minimize the ribbon with a different button**

You can also quickly minimize the ribbon by using the  button in the top right corner of the ribbon:

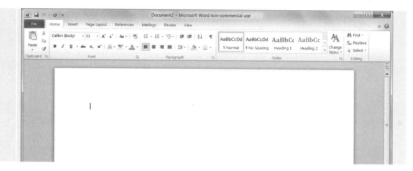

👉 **Click** ⌃

**Please note:** this option is not available in *Word 2007*.

Click once more and the ribbon returns to its normal size:

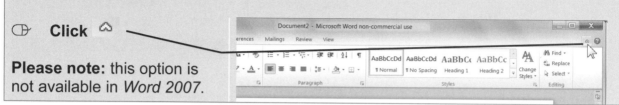

✕ **HELP! The ribbon looks different on my screen.**

The number of commands shown in the ribbon is automatically adjusted to the size and resolution of your screen as well as to the size of your *Word* window. The larger your screen and the higher the resolution, the more information the ribbon can display.

A wide-screen monitor – 1680 pixels wide – with a maximized window will display the entire ribbon:

On a smaller screen – 1024 pixels wide – the ribbon will look different:

*- Continue reading on the next page -*

On a small laptop computer with a screen resolution of 800 pixels, some of the information will not be visible:

You will still see all the tabs, but the groups of commands underneath are arranged differently. Some of the commands are hidden.

The screenshots in this book have been created on a screen with a width of 1280 pixels. If you are using a different resolution, your screen will also look different.

## 1.3 Customizing the Quick Access Toolbar

To execute a command on the ribbon, you usually need to click twice: first the tab itself and then the command. This is not very practical if these are the commands you use most often. This is where the special *Quick Access* toolbar comes in handy. Commands in this toolbar require just one click to carry out a specific action.

The *Quick Access* toolbar is positioned at the top of the *Word* window:

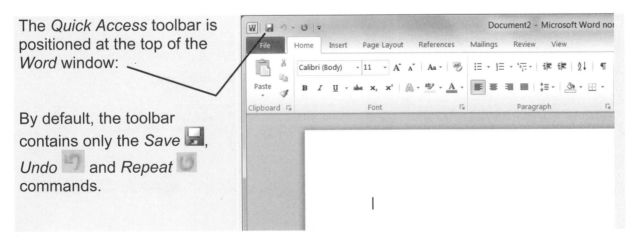

By default, the toolbar contains only the *Save*, *Undo* and *Repeat* commands.

You can decide yourself which commands to add or remove from the *Quick Access* toolbar. Here is how to remove a command from the *Quick Access* toolbar:

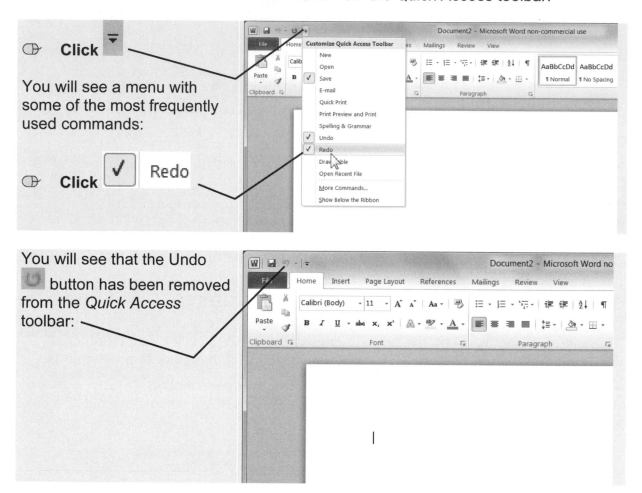

☞  **Click** ⬇

You will see a menu with some of the most frequently used commands:

☞  **Click** ✓ Redo

You will see that the Undo ↺ button has been removed from the *Quick Access* toolbar:

You can add a button to the *Quick Access* toolbar in the same way:

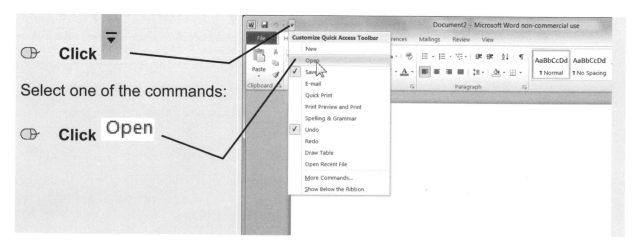

☞  **Click** ⬇

Select one of the commands:

☞  **Click** Open

Now the button has been added to the *Quick Access* toolbar:

You will see the new Open

button :

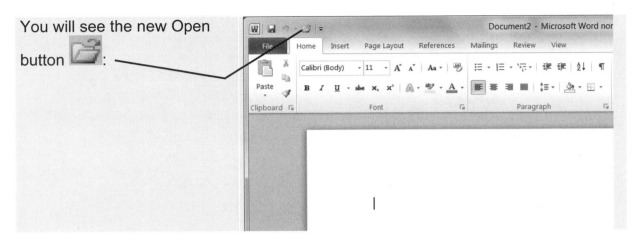

You can also adjust the position of the *Quick Access* toolbar, that is to say, you can position the toolbar above or below the ribbon:

☞  **Click**

Once again, you will see the menu:

☞  **Click**
    Show Below the Ribbon

Now the *Quick Access* toolbar appears below the ribbon:

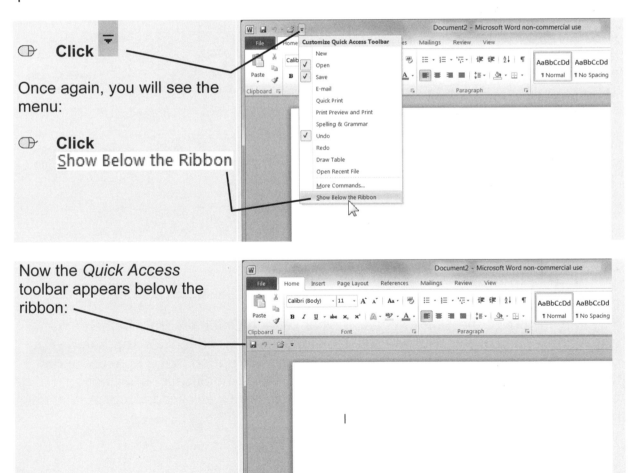

If you want to restore the *Quick Access* toolbar to its original position:

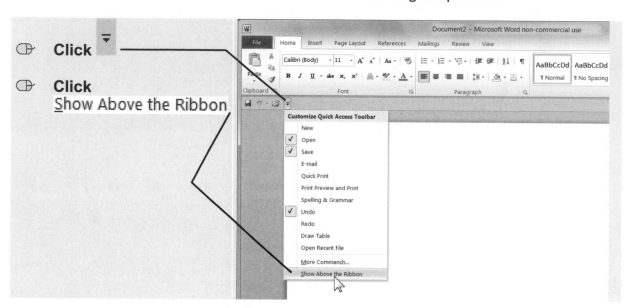

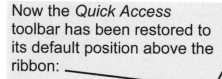

**Click** ▼

**Click**
<u>Show Above the Ribbon</u>

Now the *Quick Access* toolbar has been restored to its default position above the ribbon:

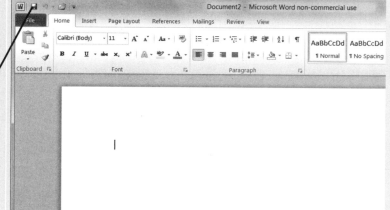

 **Tip**

---

**Customization of the Office programs**
You can customize the *Quick Access* toolbar in each *Office* program in the same way as described above. But you will need to customize the toolbar separately. For instance, if in *Word* you position the *Quick Access* toolbar so that it appears under the ribbon and you add various commands to it, these modifications will not be visible in *Excel* or *PowerPoint*. Any adjustments to the *Quick Access* toolbar in those programs must be done separately.

# 1.4 Customizing the Ribbon

You can also customize the ribbon. For example, you can create your own custom tab and add the commands you use most often to it.

 **Please note:**

You cannot customize the ribbon in *Office 2007*. If you are using *Office 2007*, you can just read through this section.

To do this, you will need to use the *Backstage* view:

**Click the**
**tab**

Now you will see a different view. This is called the *Backstage* view:

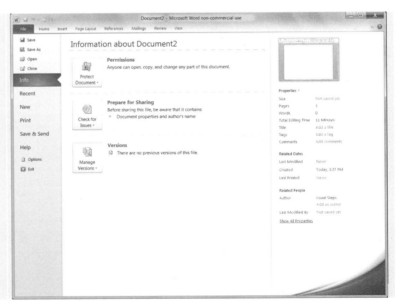

 **Tip**

**Backstage**
In essence, the *Backstage* view (or the *Out* feature set) hides your current document and gives you access to file-related activities. For instance, you can create, save, and print files and modify the settings. The other tabs on the ribbon give you all the necessary commands you need to do things *in* your document.

**Please note:**

In the *Office 2007* programs you will not see a **File** tab and there is no

*Backstage* view. Instead, you can use the *Office* button in upper-left corner of the window to execute similar tasks, such as creating, saving, and printing files.

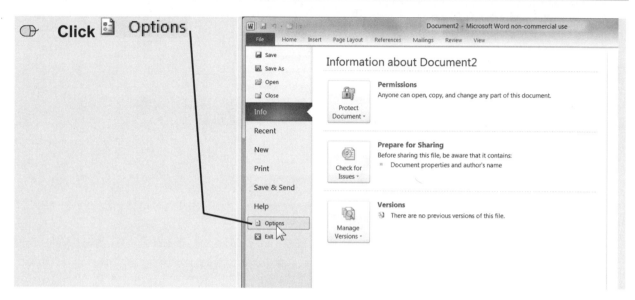

Now the *Word Options* window will be opened. In this window you can modify various settings for *Word*. Here you are going to modify the ribbon:

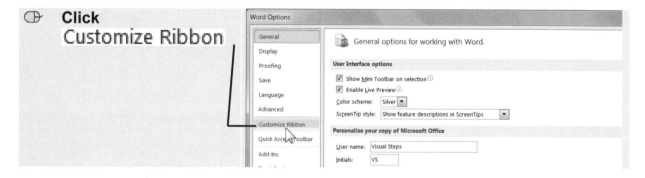

Here you see a list of popular *Word* commands: ─────

On the right side you see the tabs that are currently displayed on the ribbon. The ☑ Home tab has been selected: ─────

Now you are going to create a new tab:

👉   **Click** | New Tab |

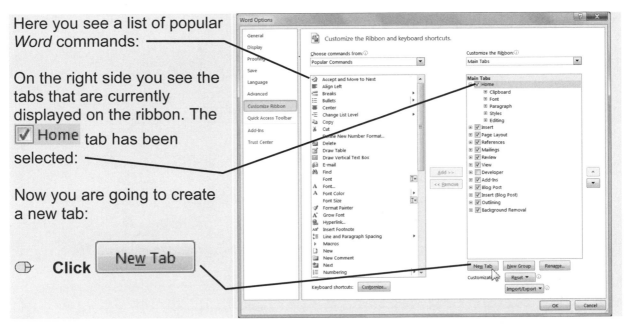

The new tab, called New Tab (Custom) has been added to the ☑ Home tab: ─────

This new tab also contains a new group, called New Group (Custom):

You can use the | Rename... | button to change the name of the selected tab: ─────
But for now, that is not necessary.

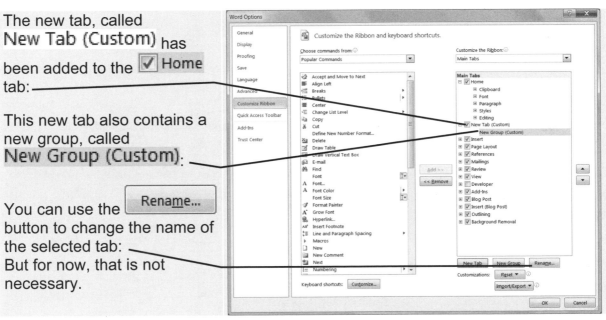

You are going to add a command to the new tab:

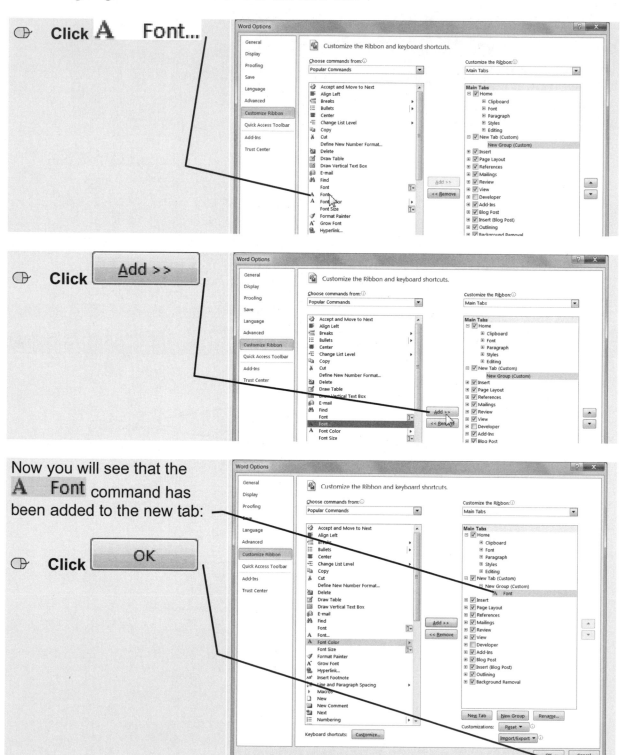

Click **A**    Font...

Click  Add >>

Now you will see that the **A** Font command has been added to the new tab:

Click  OK

The new tab has been added to the ribbon:

Click the tab | New Tab

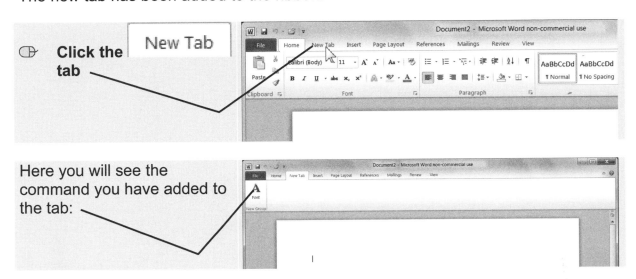

Here you will see the command you have added to the tab:

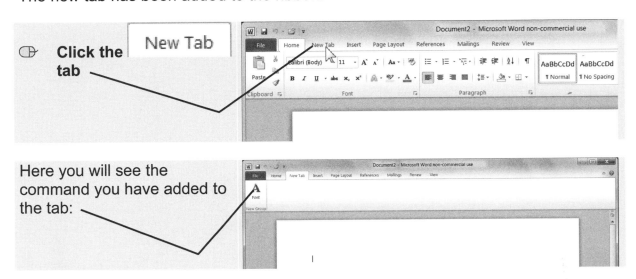

Now you are going to remove the new tab again. This is how you open the *Word Options* window:

**Right-click the** | New Tab | **tab**

You will see a menu:

**Click** Customize the Ribbon..

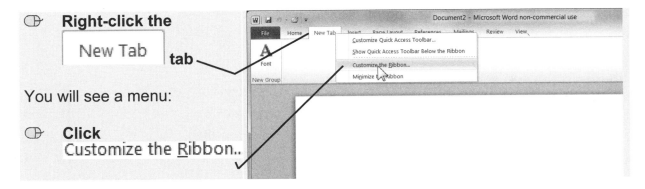

This is how you remove the new tab:

**Right-click** New Tab (Custom)

You will see a menu:

**Click** Remove

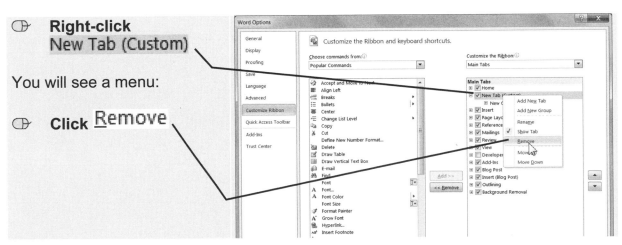

Here you will see that the new tab has disappeared from the list:

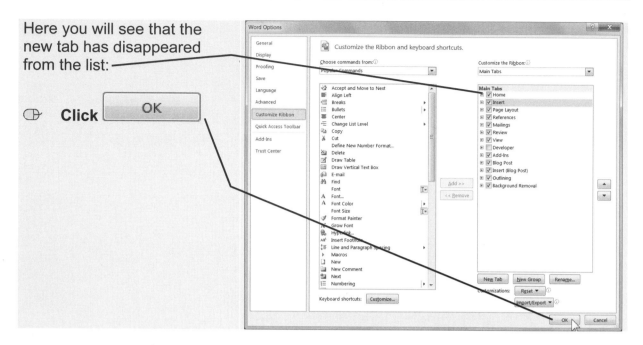

 **Click** OK

Now the ribbon has been restored to its original state:

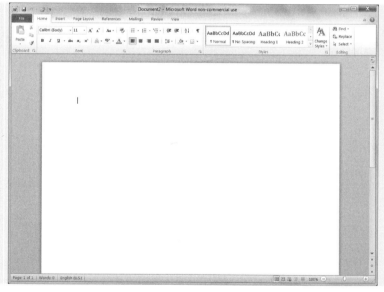

💡 **Tip**

**Customize separately**
You can customize the ribbon in each *Office* program in exactly the same way. But if you customize the ribbon in *Word*, these modifications will not be visible in *Excel* or *PowerPoint*. You will need to adjust the settings for those programs separately.

# 1.5 Closing Word

In this chapter you have become familiar with the ribbon and the *Quick Access* toolbar. These essential features can be found in *Word, Excel,* and *PowerPoint*. Now you can close the (blank) document. In *Word 2010* you do this in the *Backstage* view:

In *Word 2007* the window looks a bit different:

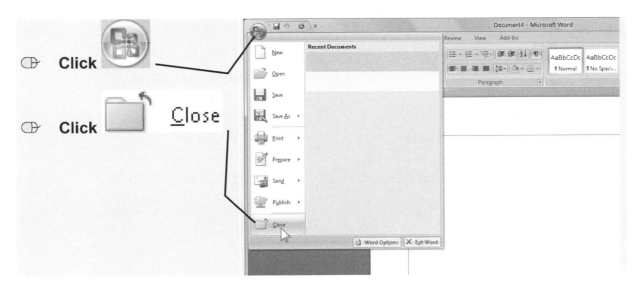

Now you can close *Word*. This is how you close the program:

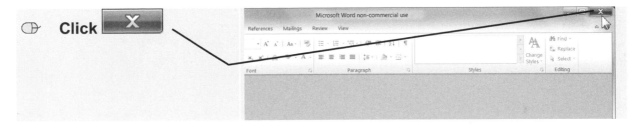

In the following exercises you can repeat all the commands you have learned in this chapter.

# 1.6 Exercises

The following exercises will help you master what you have just learned. Have you forgotten how to do something? Use the number beside the footsteps to look it up in the appendix *How Do I Do That Again?*

## Exercise: The Quick Access Toolbar

☞ Open *Word*. ⚇¹

☞ Position the *Quick Access* toolbar below the ribbon. ⚇²

☞ Add the *Quick Print* command to the *Quick Access* toolbar. ⚇³

☞ Position the *Quick Access* toolbar above the ribbon. ⚇⁴

☞ Remove the *Quick Print* command from the *Quick Access* toolbar. ⚇⁵

## Exercise: The Ribbon

**Please note:** some of the exercises can only be executed in *Word 2010*.

☞ Minimize the ribbon. ⚇⁶

☞ Restore the default view of the ribbon. ⚇⁷

☞ Add a new tab. ⚇⁸

☞ Add the *Copy* command to the new tab. ⚇⁹

☞ Take a look at the new tab. ⚇¹⁰

☞ Remove the new tab. ⚇¹¹

☞ Close the document. ⚇¹², ¹³

☞ Close *Word*. ⚇¹⁴

# 1.7 Background Information

| Dictionary | |
|---|---|
| **Backstage** | In essence, the *Backstage* view (or the *Out* feature set) hides your current document and gives you access to file-related activities. For instance, you can create, save, and print files and modify the settings. The other tabs on the ribbon give you all the necessary commands you need to do things *in* your document. |
| **Dot** | The smallest element of a digital picture. Also called *pixel*. |
| **Quick Access** | Toolbar that allows you to execute commands with a single mouse-click. You can determine which commands are located on the *Quick Access* toolbar. |
| **Resolution** | The definition and size of a screen. The resolution is determined by the number of pixels that compose the image. |
| **Ribbon** | A very extensive toolbar which contains a set of tabs and groups. Program options, commands, and tools are located on the ribbon. The ribbon replaces the menus in the older *Microsoft Office* programs. |
| **Tab** | A section of the ribbon. Each tab relates to a specific task or activity, such as writing or formatting a page. In order to preserve as much free space as possible, some tabs are only displayed when necessary. |

*Source: Windows Help and Support*

# Notes

Write down your notes here.

# 2. Writing and Printing a Letter

In this chapter you will start by typing a letter. You will learn how to use some of the many useful features in *Word* as you go along. For instance, you will learn how easy it is to insert the current date into your document as well as all sorts of different symbols. You will also learn how to use the automatic spelling checker and how to find synonyms for specific words.

You can modify the formatting of a letter in a number of different ways. For example, by adjusting the line spacing or the margins. You can use the *Print Preview* window to see how your letter will appear as a printed document.

When your letter is finished, you can decide if you want to print it. *Word* contains a handy option that allows you to print a matching envelope to go with your letter. You can choose from a large number of different envelope sizes.

In this chapter you will learn how to:

- draft a letter;
- change the line spacing for a paragraph;
- insert the current date;
- indent the text;
- use bullets;
- use the automatic spelling checker;
- look up synonyms;
- save the document while you are working;
- insert symbols;
- insert and delete hyperlinks;
- format the text;
- change the line spacing;
- undo the most recent operation;
- modify the page margins;
- view the print preview;
- modify the font size;
- print the letter;
- print a matching envelope.

# 2.1 Starting to Write a Letter

You can get started using *Word* by typing a letter. First, you will need to open *Word*:

☞ **Open *Word*** ¹

You will see the *Word* window:

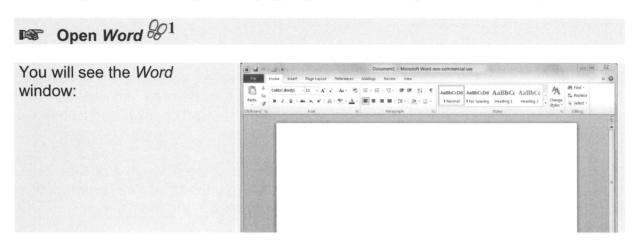

In this book we assume you are already familiar with the use of the keyboard and are able to:

Type letters, spaces and numbers.

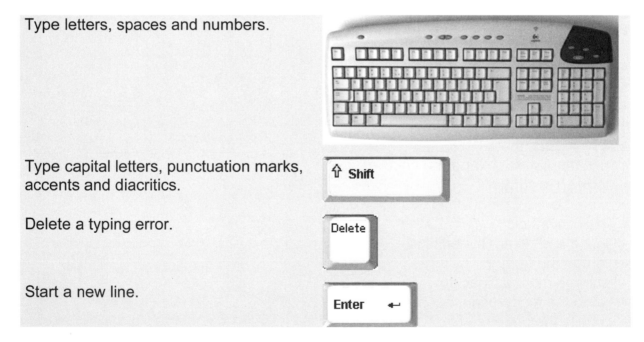

Type capital letters, punctuation marks, accents and diacritics.

Delete a typing error.

Start a new line.

➥ **Please note:**

If you have never used the keyboard for typing text before, please read *Bonus chapter 9 The Basics of Text Editing* first. The bonus chapter is posted on the website that goes with this book: **www.visualsteps.com/officeseniors**
In *Appendix C Opening the Bonus Chapters* you can read how to open this chapter.

Start your letter by typing your name and address:

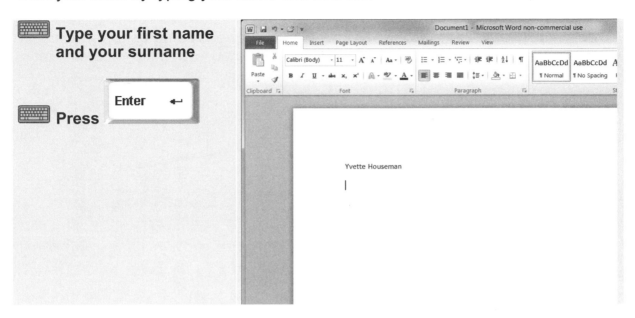

**Type your first name and your surname**

**Press** Enter ←

Now you can type your address:

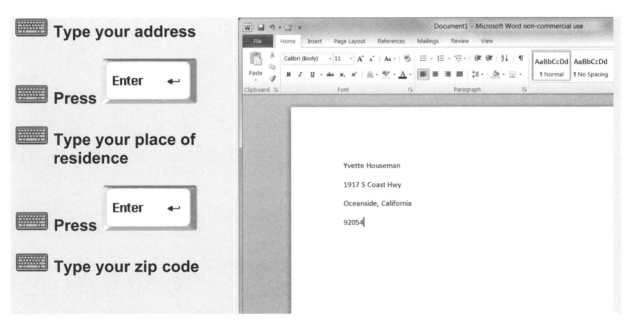

**Type your address**

**Press** Enter ←

**Type your place of residence**

**Press** Enter ←

**Type your zip code**

 **Please note:**

There are several ways to write down addresses. Feel free to use your own way.

You will see that *Word* inserts a blank line, every time you start a new line. In the next section, you will learn how to adjust this setting.

## 2.2 Change Paragraph Spacing

You can easily change the settings for the spacing between paragraphs, for example, when you want to prevent a blank line from being inserted each time you press Enter. First, you will need to select the text:

**Click** Select ▾

**Click** Select All

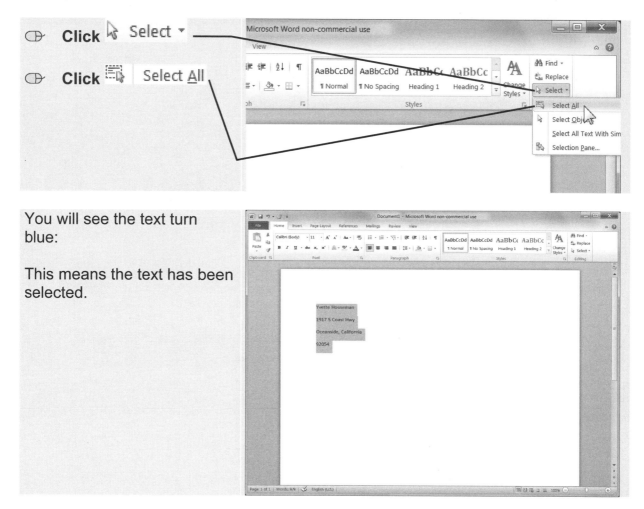

You will see the text turn blue:

This means the text has been selected.

In the *Paragraph* window you can set the space between the paragraphs. This is how you open the window:

**By** Paragraph **click** 

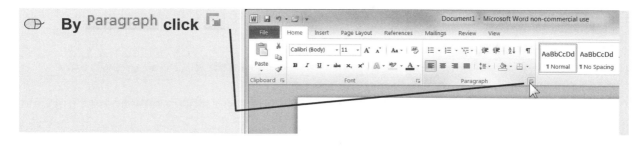

Now the *Paragraph* window will be opened:

Here you can see the setting that will be applied each time you press **Enter** ⏎ :

After: 10 pt

This means that after each paragraph a blank space of 10 points will be inserted.

The size of the letters and all other distances in a document are measured in points. The more points, the larger the letters become and the greater the distance.

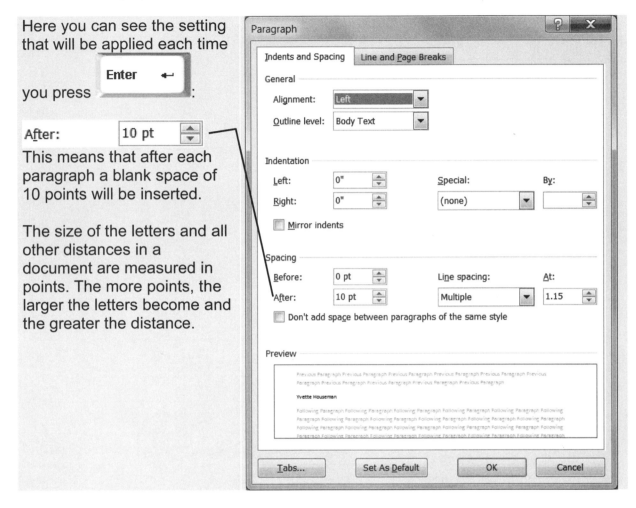

You can practice shrinking the spacing between paragraphs by setting it to 0 points:

By After: click ▼ twice

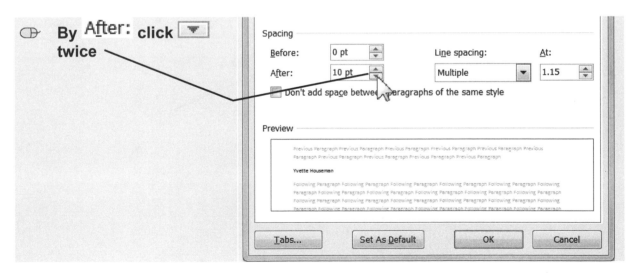

Now the spacing has been set to 0 points: ——

If you want to use this setting for every new document you create, you can click Set As Default.

For now, that will not be necessary:

☞ **Click** OK

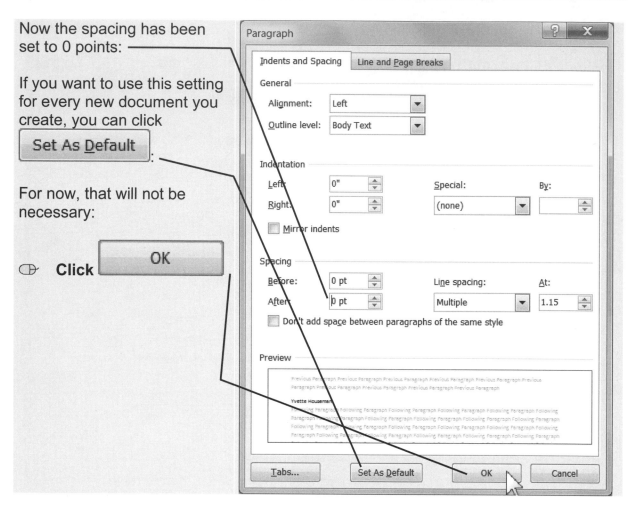

View the result in your letter:

☞ **Click an empty spot in the document** ——

You will see that the blank lines have disappeared:

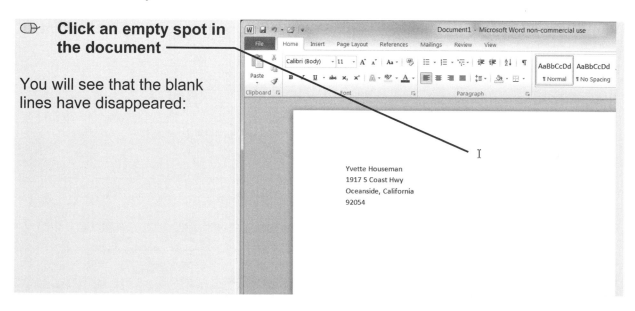

# 2.3 Insert a Date

*Word* has a built-in feature that will allow you to enter the current date into your document. First, insert a new paragraph:

**Place the pointer on the right side of the zipcode**

**Press**

Enter ⏎

**twice**

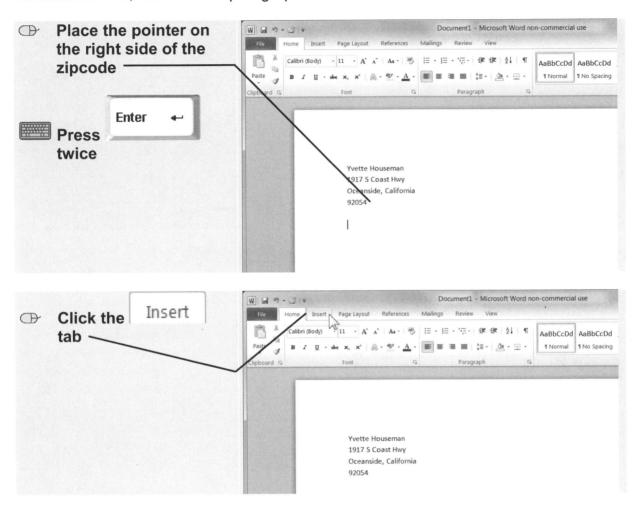

**Click the**  Insert  **tab**

Insert the current date:

**By** Text **click**
🕓 Date & Time

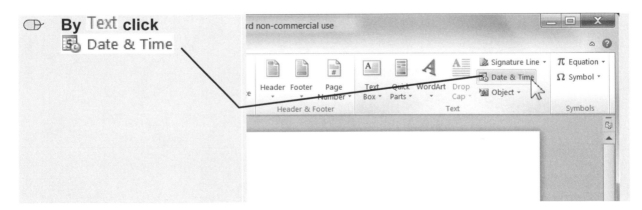

In the *Date and Time* window you can choose a format for the date and time:

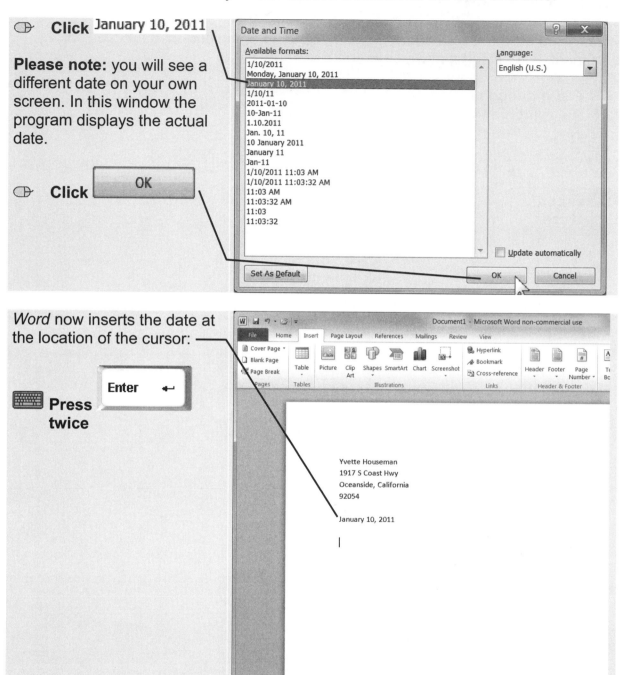

☞ **Click** January 10, 2011

**Please note:** you will see a different date on your own screen. In this window the program displays the actual date.

☞ **Click** OK

*Word* now inserts the date at the location of the cursor:

⌨ **Press** Enter ← **twice**

# 2.4 The Lay Out of a Letter

A formal letter is usually arranged in a specific way. You have started by typing the sender and the date. Now you can type the name and address of the recipient, the subject and the salutation:

**Type:**

John and Nancy Winter
1062 Mission Avenue
Oceanside, California
92057

Re: 5th Annual Bicycle
Rally and Scavenger
Hunt

Dear John and Nancy,

**Press twice** [Enter ↵]

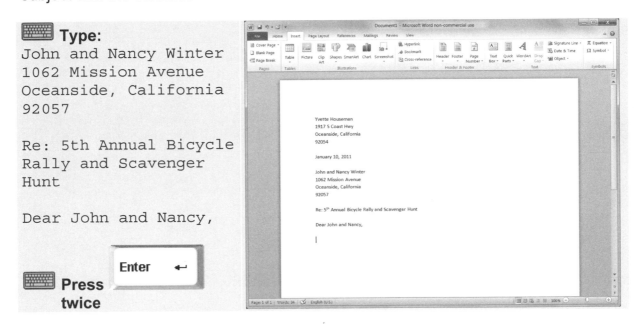

Continue with the content of the letter:

**Type:**

We are pleased to
announce that our
annual Bicycle Rally
and Scavenger Hunt are
scheduled for:

**Press twice** [Enter ↵]

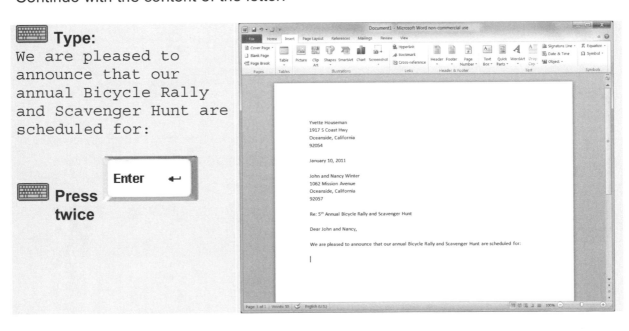

# 2.5 Indentation

If you want to emphasize an important sentence or paragraph, you can indent it. First, type the date and time:

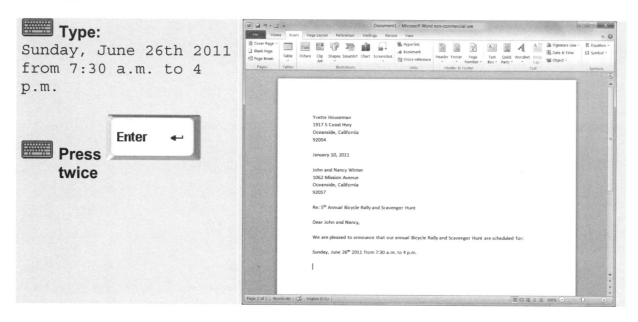

**Type:**
Sunday, June 26th 2011 from 7:30 a.m. to 4 p.m.

**Press twice**

To indent the date and time, you will need to select the line first. You can also do this by dragging:

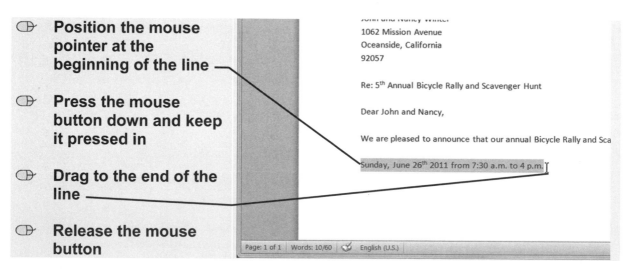

**Position the mouse pointer at the beginning of the line**

**Press the mouse button down and keep it pressed in**

**Drag to the end of the line**

**Release the mouse button**

The line is now selected and has turned blue. Next, you can indent the line. The indent command is located on a different tab:

**Click the** Home **tab**

**Click** ⬛ **twice**

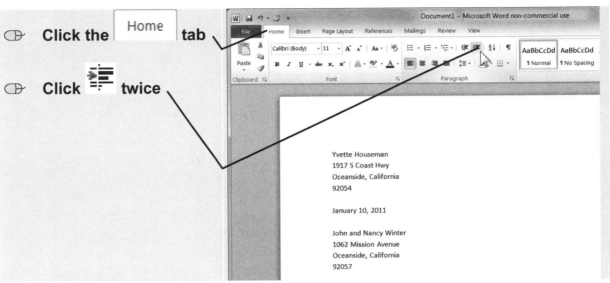

**Click the empty space below the letter**

You will see that the date and time have been indented:

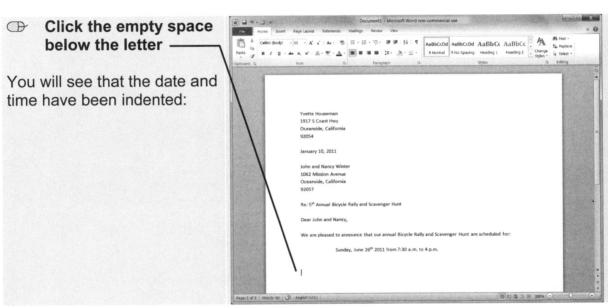

Now you can continue with the next part of the letter:

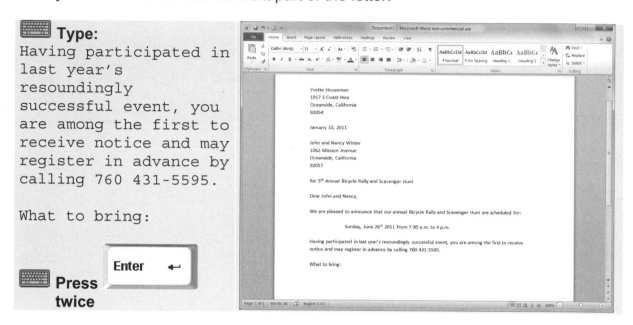

**Type:**
Having participated in last year's resoundingly successful event, you are among the first to receive notice and may register in advance by calling 760 431-5595.

What to bring:

**Press twice** [Enter ↵]

# 2.6 Bullets

Enter the necessary materials for the bicycle rally, in the form of a bulleted list:

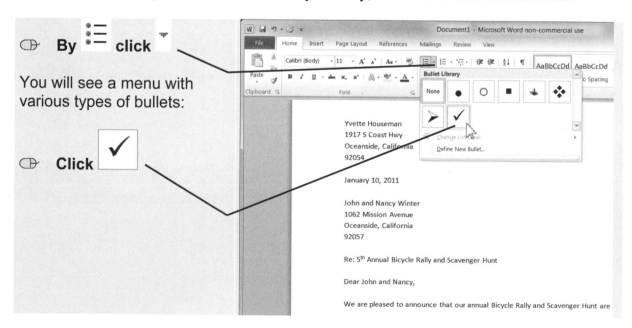

By [≡] **click** [▾]

You will see a menu with various types of bullets:

**Click** [✓]

**Type:**
`rain jacket;`

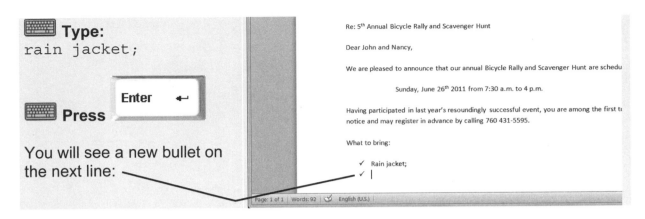

**Press** [ Enter ↵ ]

You will see a new bullet on the next line:

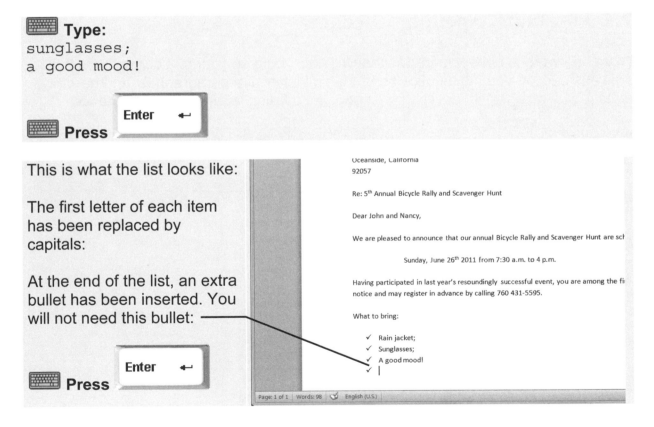

## ☛ Please note:

If you start the next line with a lower-case letter, *Word* will automatically replace this letter by a capital letter.

Now you can enter the other items:

**Type:**
`sunglasses;`
`a good mood!`

**Press** [ Enter ↵ ]

This is what the list looks like:

The first letter of each item has been replaced by capitals:

At the end of the list, an extra bullet has been inserted. You will not need this bullet:

**Press** [ Enter ↵ ]

Now the bullet has disappeared and the cursor is positioned at the beginning of the line:

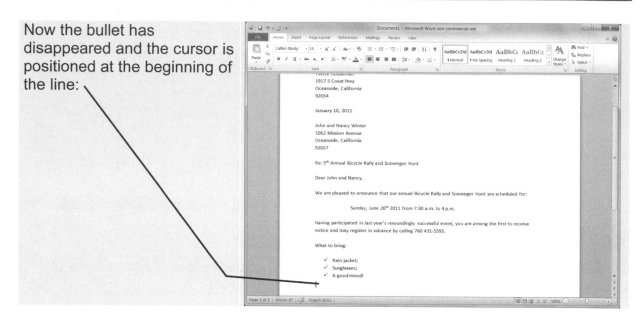

## 2.7 Automatic Spelling Checker

*Word* has various built-in functions that will help you type your text correctly. In the previous section you have noticed that the first letter of a paragraph is automatically replaced by a capital letter. The same goes for the first letter of a new sentence:

**Press** Enter ↵

**Type:**
There is no rain date for this event. rain or shine, the event goes on as planned, so be sure to pack a rain jacket or other rain gear!

You will see that *Word* immediately capitalizes the first letter in the second sentence:

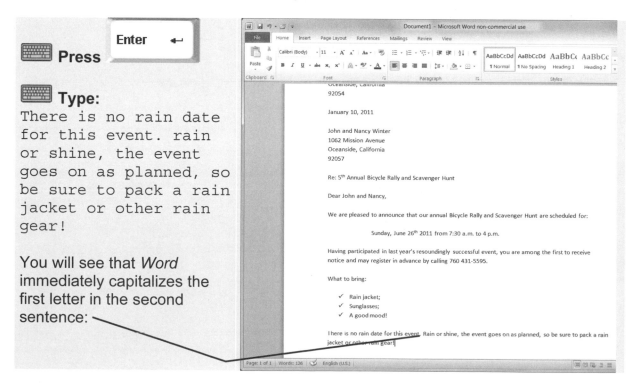

## HELP! No capitals.

If the first letter in your *Word* program is not automatically capitalized, then most likely the AutoCorrect option has been disabled. Here is how to reset it:

☞ **Click the** File **tab** (in *Word 2007* 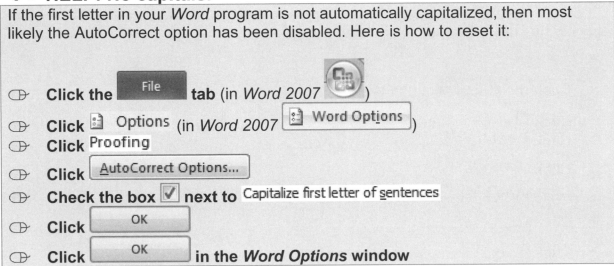 )

☞ **Click** ▣ Options (in *Word 2007* ▣ Word Options )

☞ **Click** Proofing

☞ **Click** AutoCorrect Options...

☞ **Check the box** ☑ **next to** Capitalize first letter of sentences

☞ **Click** OK

☞ **Click** OK **in the Word Options window**

 ## Tip

**Prevent a capital from occurring at the beginning of a sentence**
Do you want to start the sentence with a lower-case letter instead of a capital letter? Just delete the capital letter and replace it by a lower-case letter.

The text you have entered will be checked for spelling errors right away. Just give it a try:

⌨ Enter ↵
**Press twice**

⌨ **Type the next sentence, including the spelling error:**

```
Come and join us again
this year and help
your community's
efforts in becoming
the most bike frienly
city in California!
```

You will see that the incorrectly spelled word 'frienly' is underlined by a red wavy line :

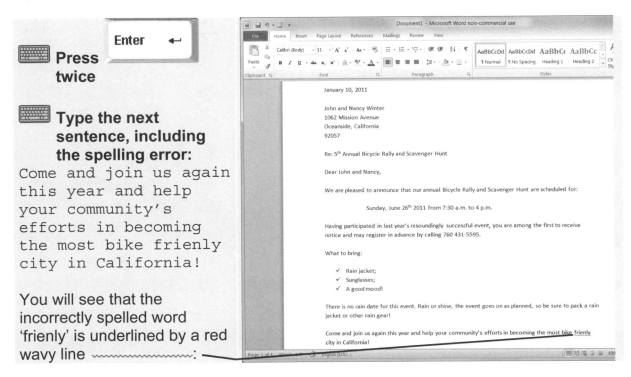

**HELP! No spelling checker.**

If the word 'frienly' is not flagged on your screen, then your automatic spelling checker has been disabled. Here is how to reset it:

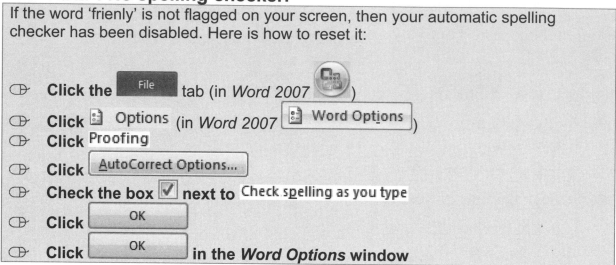

☞  **Click the** ▢ File ▢ **tab** (in *Word 2007* ▢ )

☞  **Click** ▢ Options (in *Word 2007* ▢ Word Options ▢ )

☞  **Click** Proofing

☞  **Click** ▢ AutoCorrect Options... ▢

☞  **Check the box** ☑ **next to** Check spelling as you type

☞  **Click** ▢ OK ▢

☞  **Click** ▢ OK ▢ **in the *Word Options* window**

If you see that a word is underlined by a red wavy line, *Word* will then provide a suggestion for a different spelling of the word. Just take a look:

☞  **Right-click** frienly

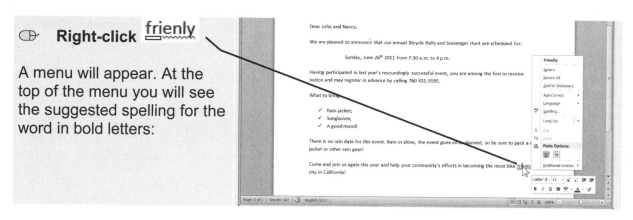

A menu will appear. At the top of the menu you will see the suggested spelling for the word in bold letters:

 **Please note:**

When you right-click the word, you will also see this tiny window:

This window contains a number of the most frequently used commands to format text.

Select the suggestion you want to use:

👉 **Click** **friendly**

The spelling error will be corrected:

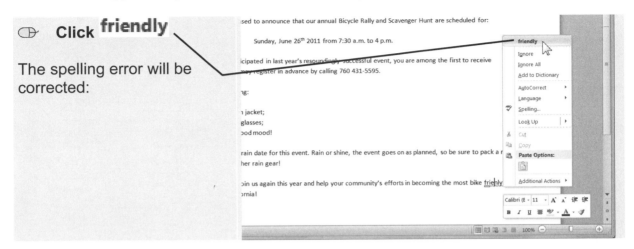

💡 **Tip**

**Spelling checker**
*Word* uses a list of English words to check the spelling. Your text will be compared to this list. But not all English words are included in this list. Words that are not included in the list will also be marked as an 'error'.

**Please note**: the spelling checker does not check if your English sentences are grammatically correct. The program only checks the spelling of each individual word. For instance, a sentence such as 'John's company offers a lot of scoop for one's abilities' would be allowed, when you really want to say 'scope' instead of 'scoop'. It is a good idea to proofread your text again after applying the spell checker.

## 2.8 Save a Document

It is recommended that you save your document at regular intervals. This will prevent you from losing your work, in case your computer crashes or stalls. Here is how to do that in *Word 2010*:

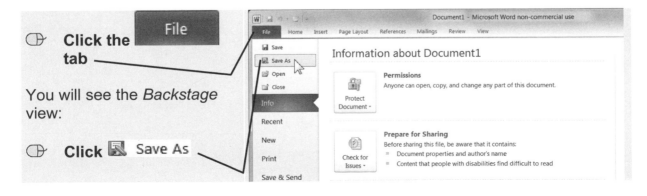

👉 **Click the** **File** **tab**

You will see the *Backstage* view:

👉 **Click** 🖫 **Save As**

In *Word 2007* you need to use the *Office* button:

Now the *Save as* window will be opened:

**If necessary, click Documents**

Enter a name that you can easily remember:

**Type:** letter bicycle rally

Save the letter as a *Word* document:

**Click** Save

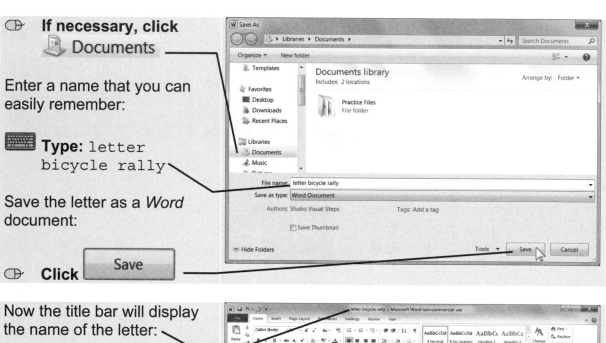

Now the title bar will display the name of the letter:

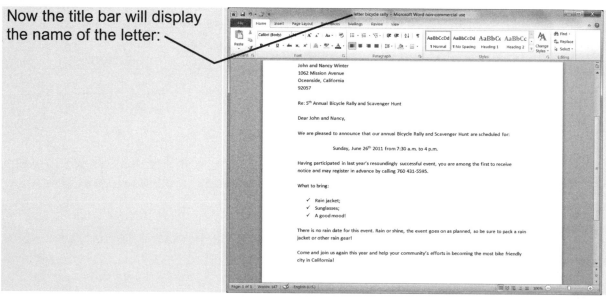

# 2.9 Synonyms

*Word* can also assist you in finding the right words for your text. For example, *Word* contains a list of synonyms to help you find an alternate to a word you just typed.

☞ **Right-click the word** *community's*

☞ **Point the mouse pointer to** Synonyms

You will see various synonyms for the word 'community's':

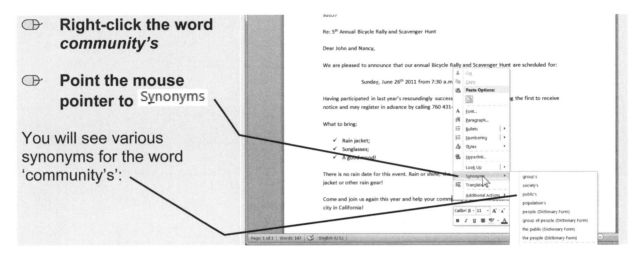

## HELP! I do not see synonyms.

It's possible you will not see synonyms for the word community's. In that case you can try this action with another word.

☞ **Click** group's

Now the word 'community's' will be replaced by the word 'group's'.

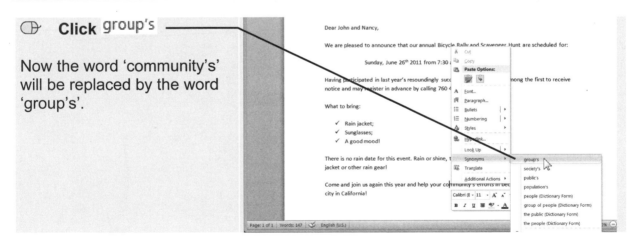

# 2.10 Inserting Symbols

*Word* makes it easy to insert symbols into your text. Add a new paragraph to the letter:

**Click at the end of the last sentence**

**Press twice** — Enter ↵

**Type:** Registration fees:

**Type a space**

**Click the Insert tab**

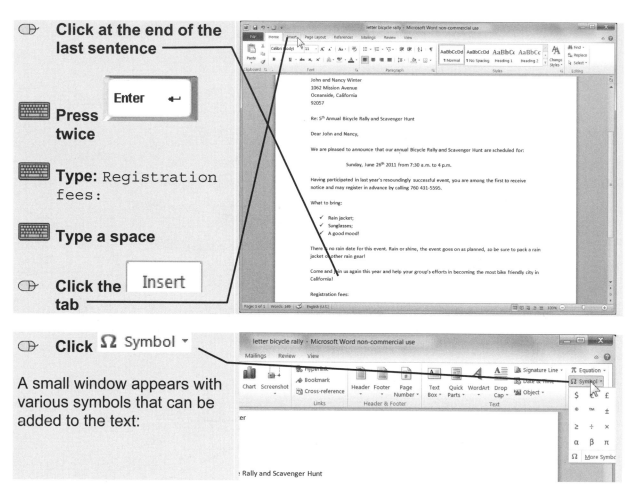

**Click** Ω Symbol ▾

A small window appears with various symbols that can be added to the text:

Insert the dollar sign:

**Click** $

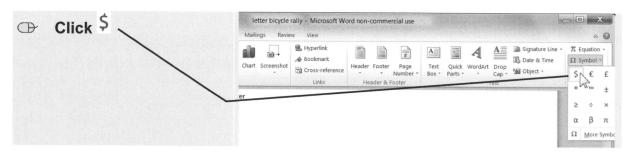

The dollar sign has been added to the text: ———

💡 **Tip**

**Additional symbols**
There are many other symbols you can use:

☞ **Click** Ω Symbol ▾
☞ **Click** Ω More Symbols...

The *Symbol* window will be opened:

Use the scroll bar to view all the symbols: ———

To insert a symbol from this window:

☞ **Click the desired symbol** ———

☞ **Click** [ Insert ]

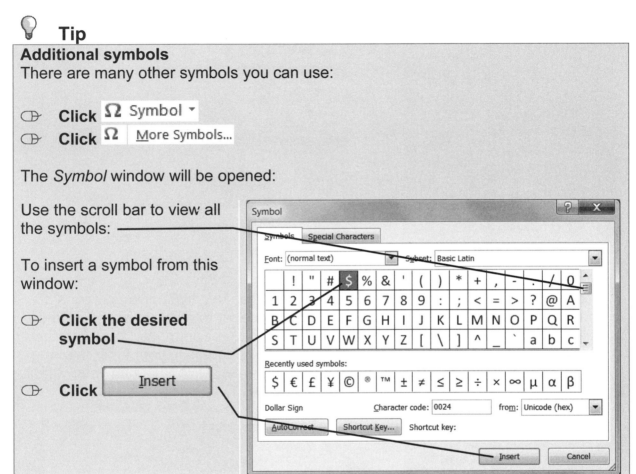

Now you can finish the letter:

⌨ **Type:**
7.50 adults and $5 for children aged 6-12.

For additional information contact our Rally Chairman, Yvette Houseman by e-mail at events@sanreyriverpark.com or by telephone: 760 431-5595.

Sincerely yours,

Yvette Houseman
Rally Chairman

You will notice that part of the letter extends beyond the first page:

Also, the e-mail address has changed into a *hyperlink*:

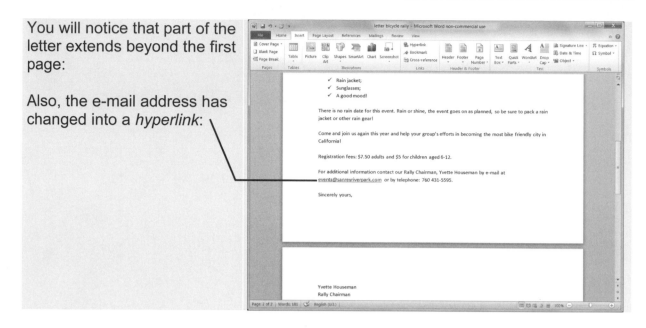

## 2.11 Hyperlinks

You may be familiar with hyperlinks. Nearly all websites use hyperlinks, portions of underlined text or images, as a way to connect the reader to other webpages. When you click a hyperlink, a webpage opens in *Internet Explorer* or another browser application. *Word* has automatically turned the e-mail address in your letter into a hyperlink. But this hyperlink is a little different. It will automatically launch your default e-mail program. See what happens when you click the hyperlink:

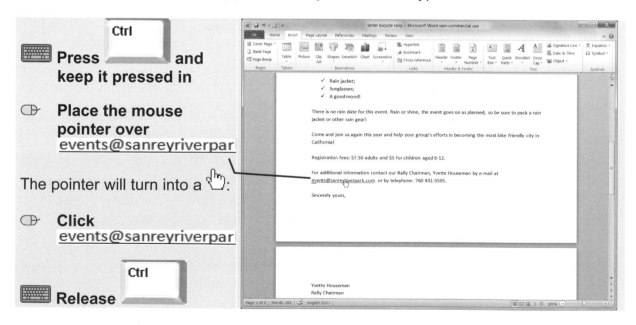

Press **Ctrl** and keep it pressed in

☞ **Place the mouse pointer over** events@sanreyriverpar

The pointer will turn into a 🖑:

☞ **Click** events@sanreyriverpar

**Release Ctrl**

A new message has been opened in your default e-mail program:

You can see that the e-mail address has already been entered by To...:

For now, you will not need to send this message:

☞ **Click** ✕

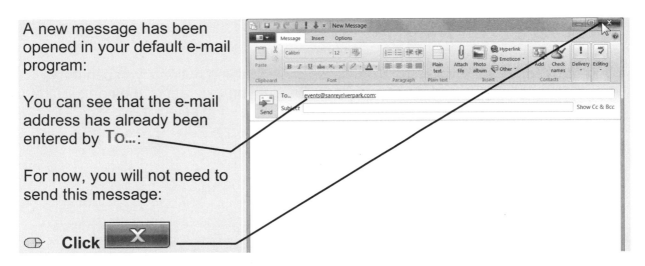

If you intend to send this letter by regular mail, the hyperlink formatting is useless. The recipient cannot click a hyperlink. Also, if you have a color printer, a hyperlink will be printed in color. It is better to remove the hyperlink before you print the document:

☞ **Right-click** **events@sanreyriverp**

You will see a menu:

☞ **Click** **Remove Hyperlink**

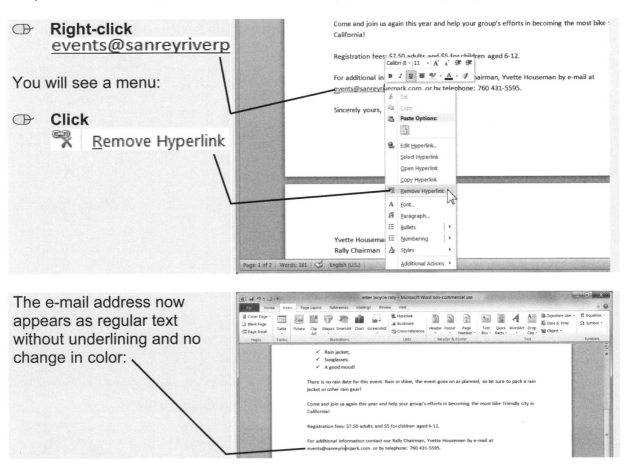

The e-mail address now appears as regular text without underlining and no change in color:

In the next section you will learn how to modify your letter further with some of the additional options available in *Word*.

# 2.12 Text Formatting

If you color your text or apply the bold, italics or underlining options, you can make certain parts of a document stand out. For example, you can render the name of the meeting place in a bold and italic font. First, you will need to select the text:

☞ **Drag the scroll bar up a bit**

☞ **Click the line 'Sunday, June 26th 2011 from 7:30 a.m. to 4 p.m.' three times**

The line is now selected and has turned blue:

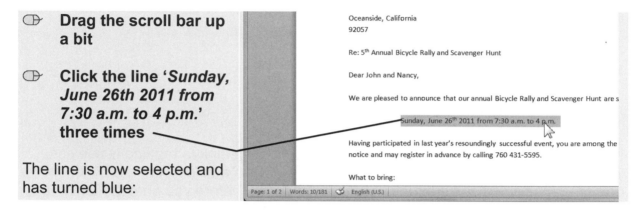

The *Home* tab contains all of the commands to format the text:

☞ **Click the** Home **tab**

☞ **Click** **B**

The text will become bold:

☞ **Click** *I*

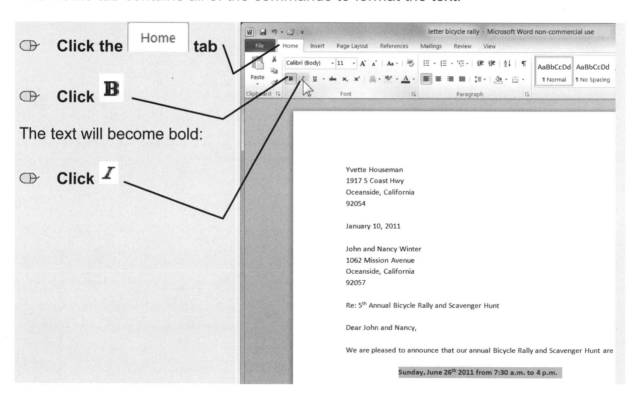

View the results:

 **Click an empty spot in the document**

The letters have already become bold and italic:

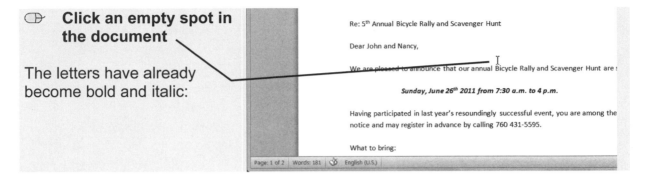

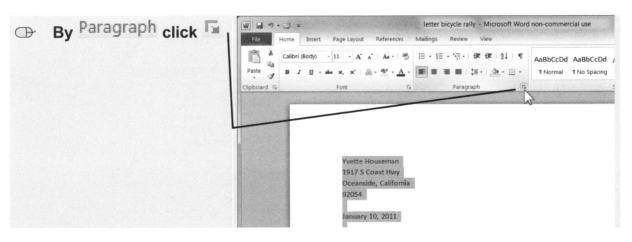

## Tip

**Text formatting**
Do you want to refresh your knowledge of text formatting? Then read *Bonus chapter 9 The Basics of Text Editing*. The bonus chapter is posted on the website that goes with this book: **www.visualsteps.com/officeseniors**
In *Appendix C Opening the Bonus Chapters* you can read how to open this chapter.

# 2.13 Changing the Line Spacing

The letter now extends to a second page. *Word* offers several ways to fit the text onto a single page. For instance, you can diminish the space between the lines. First, you will need to select the entire text:

☞ **Select the entire document** ⑮

You can set the line spacing in the *Paragraph* window:

By Paragraph click

The line spacing is currently set at 1.15:

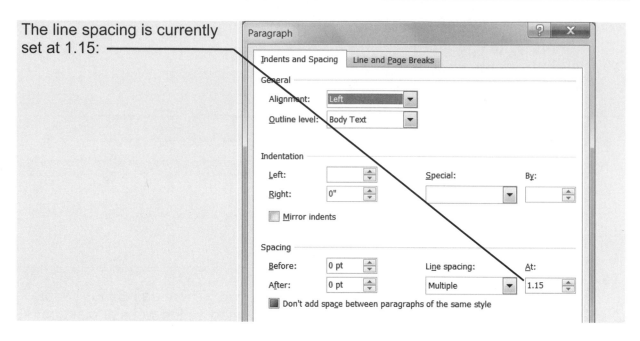

You can change the line spacing to 1 line, that is, a *single* line:

By Line spacing: **click**

**Click** Single

Confirm this setting:

**Click** OK

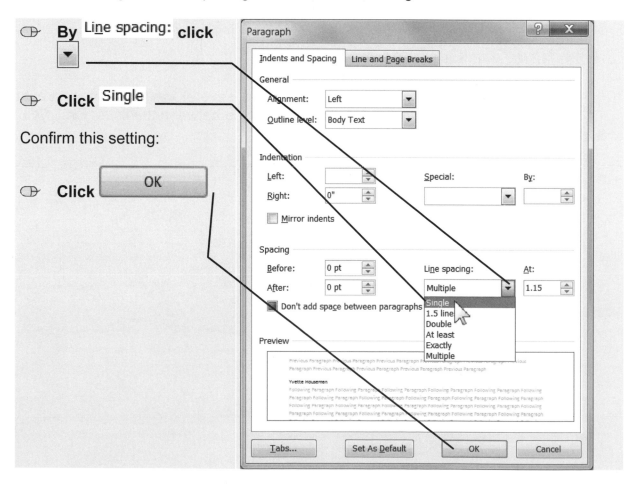

☞ **Drag the scroll bar all the way down** ————

Now you will see that the letter fits on one page:

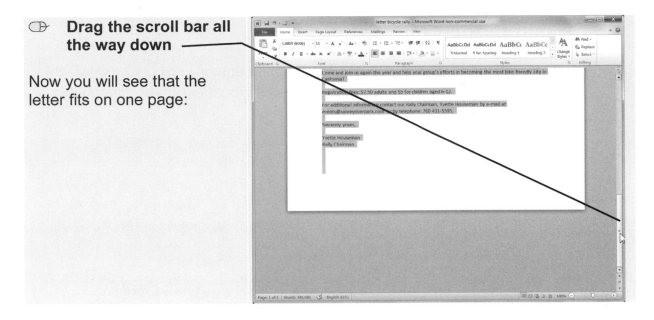

# 2.14 Undo

You may now feel the text is too hard to read as the lines are so close together. You can revert back to the original line spacing by *undoing* the last operation. Here is how to do that:

☞ **Click** 

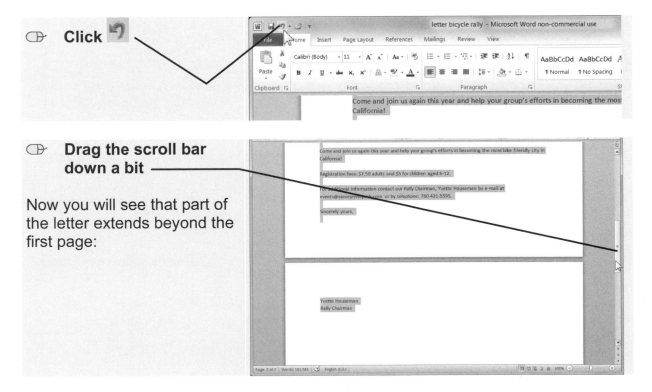

☞ **Drag the scroll bar down a bit** ————

Now you will see that part of the letter extends beyond the first page:

# 2.15 Changing the Margins

You can also try to fit the letter to a single page by changing the letter's margins. The margins are the blank borders that surround the text. If you diminish the margins, more text will fit on the page.

**Click the**

**Page Layout** **tab**

**Click** **Margins**

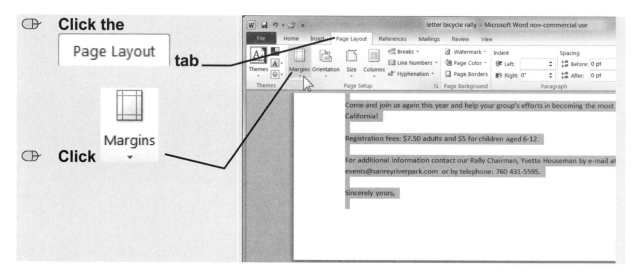

Now you will see a window where you can select among the various default settings for page margins. You can also customize the margins to fit your needs:

**Click** **Custom Margins...**

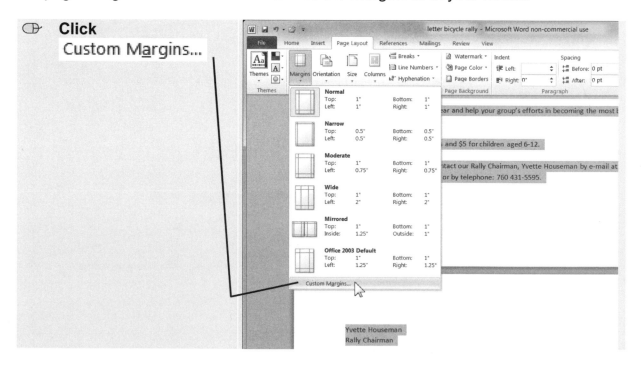

The *Page Setup* window will be opened:

Here you can enter the top, bottom, left and right margins:

Diminish all margins to 0.8 inches:

☞ **By** Top: **click** 🔽 **twice**

👉 **Do the same thing by** Left:, Bottom:, **and** Right:

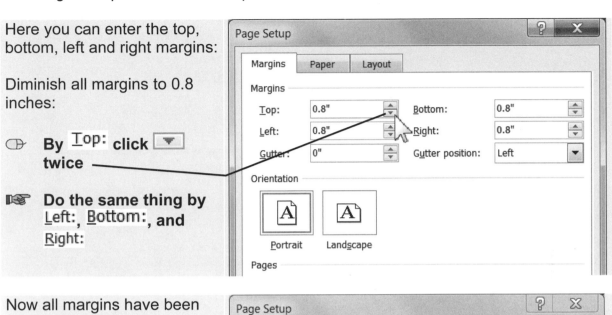

Now all margins have been set to 0.8 inches:

☞ **Click** OK

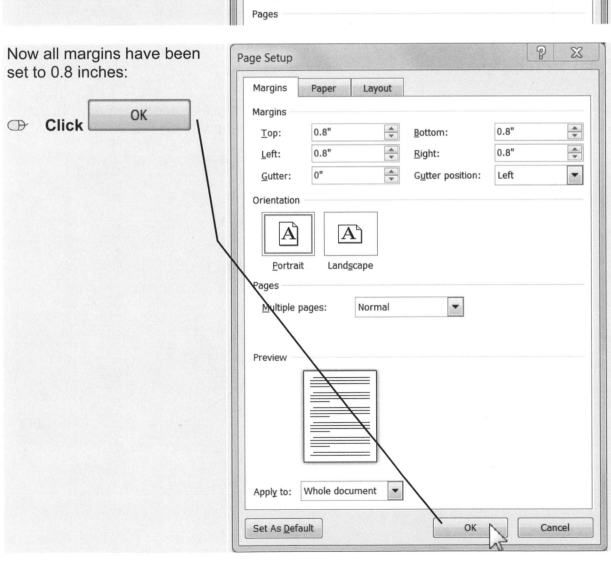

You will see that the letter still extends beyond the first page:

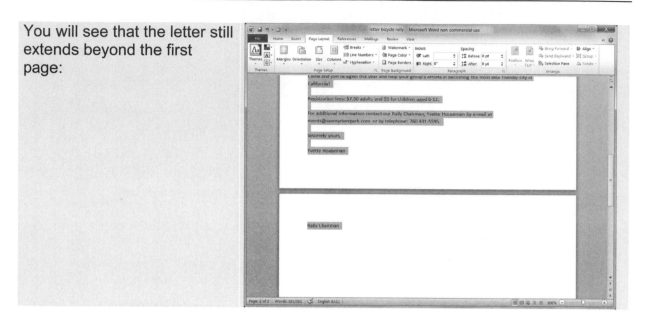

# 2.16 Print Preview

If you use print preview to view the letter, you will get a pretty good idea of what your formatted page will look like when it is printed. Here is how to do that:

**Click the** File **tab**

**Click** Print

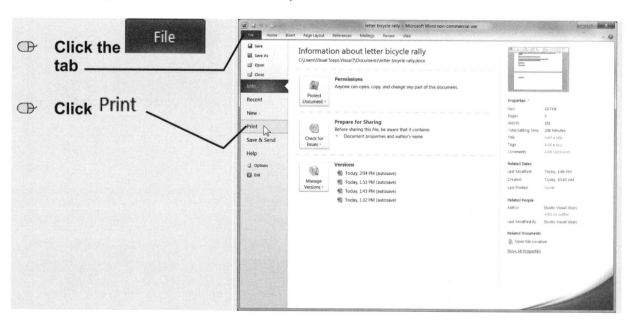

In *Word 2007* you do it like this:

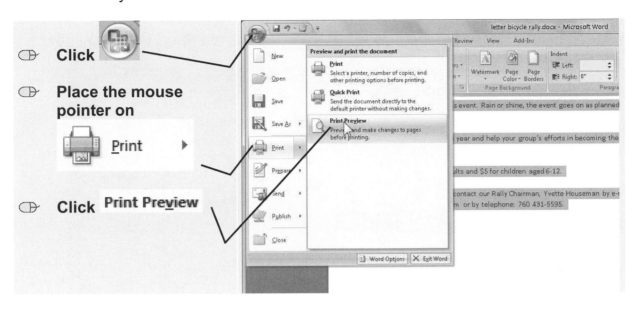

The window of *Word 2010*:

If you shrink the margins even further, the page may become a bit too crowded:

The addresses, date, subject and salutation are printed very close to one another:

In *Word 2007* your window looks a bit different.

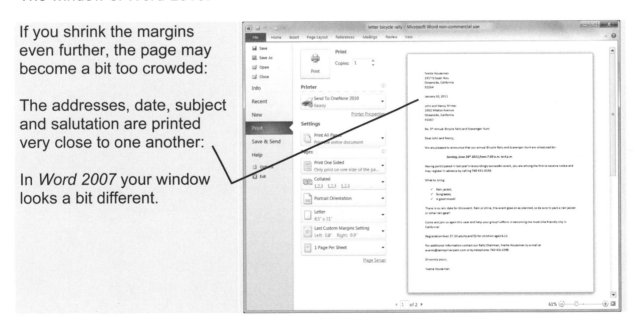

The letter will actually look better if you allow the text to extend beyond a single page and use a slightly larger font. By adding a few extra blank lines to the letter, it also becomes easier to read.

# 2.17 Changing the Font Size

You can easily change the font size in *Word*. First, close the *Print Preview* window:

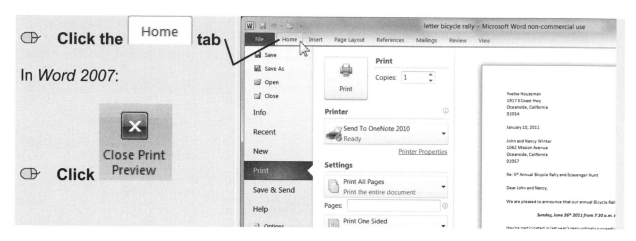

The text is still selected. You are going to enlarge the font size by one point:

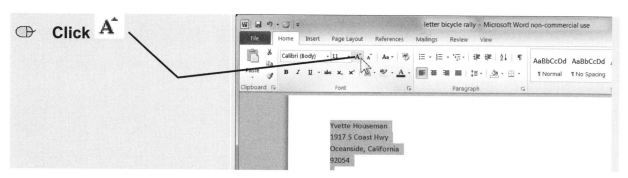

The letters are now a little larger:

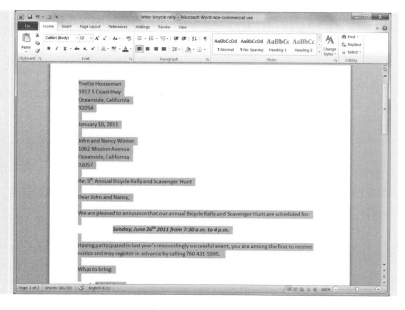

Now you can add some blank lines to the letter:

**Click a spot between your address and the date**

**Press** Enter ⏎

An extra blank line has been inserted:

☞ **Do the same thing here**

Now the upper half of the letter is much easier to read.

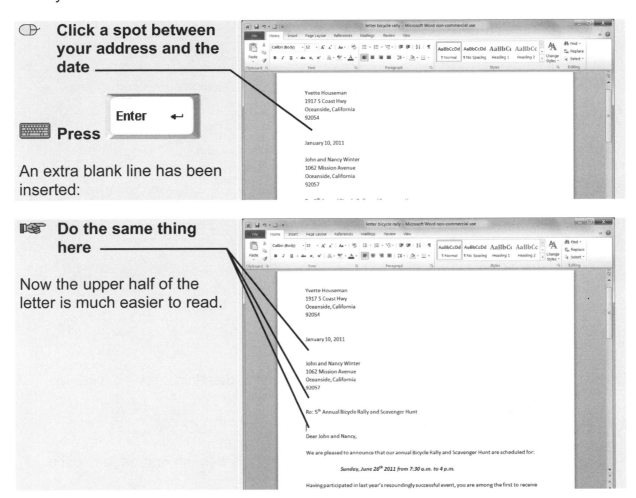

You can also reset the margins to their original settings:

**Click the** Page Layout **tab**

**Click** Margins

**Click**

**Normal**
Top: 1"
Left: 1"

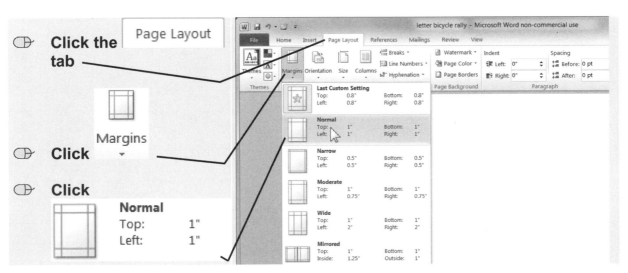

Leave some space open for your signature:

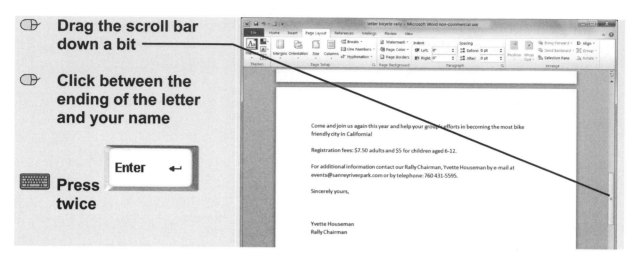

Now the letter is ready for printing and mailing.

# 2.18 Print a Letter

Before you print the letter, take another look at it first in the *Print Preview* window:

☞ **Open the print preview** 🦶 **16, 17**

You will see the second page of the letter. You can switch to the first page like this:

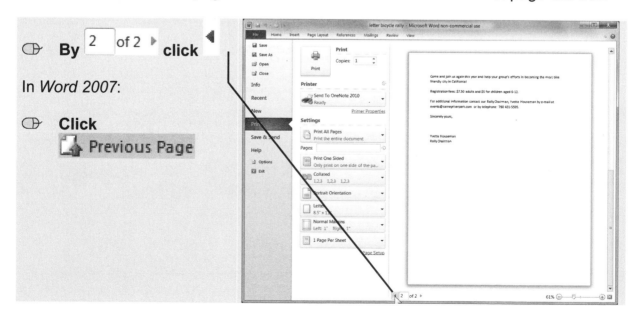

In *Word 2010*, all of the options available for printing a document are arranged here:

You can select the number of copies to print:

You can see which printer has been selected:

You can choose the default setting to print the entire document:

You can choose to print one sided or in duplex mode:

You can see the page orientation and paper size:

You can also change the margins, if you desire:

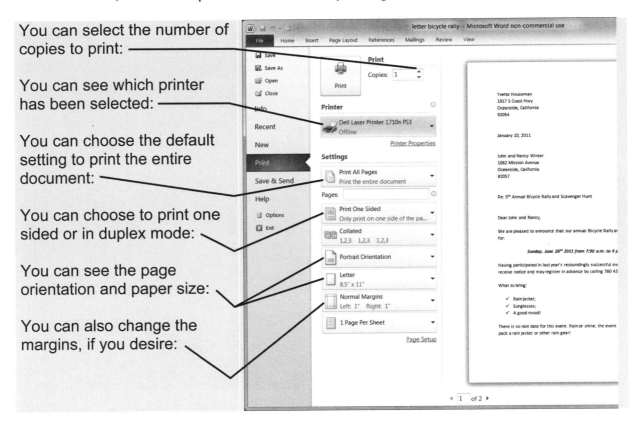

Now you can print the letter:

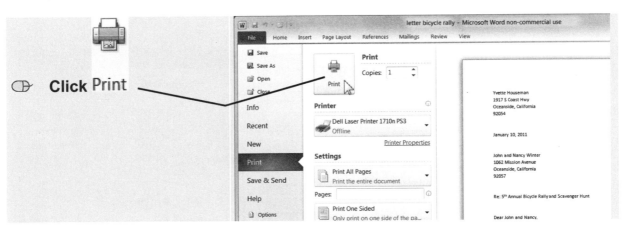

Click Print

The letter will be printed.

*Word 2007* offers the same printing options. Unfortunately, these options are not grouped together in the same window. You can find some of the functions in the *Print Preview* window:

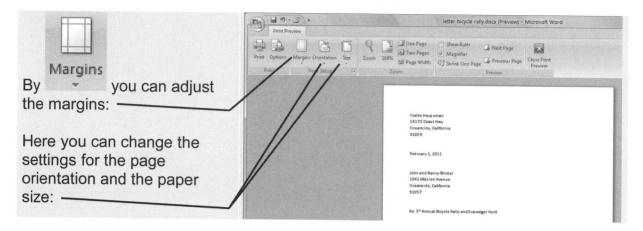

By you can adjust the margins:

Here you can change the settings for the page orientation and the paper size:

Now you are going to open the *Print* window:

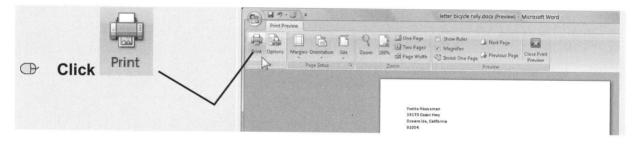

**Click** Print

In the *Print* window you will find the remaining settings:

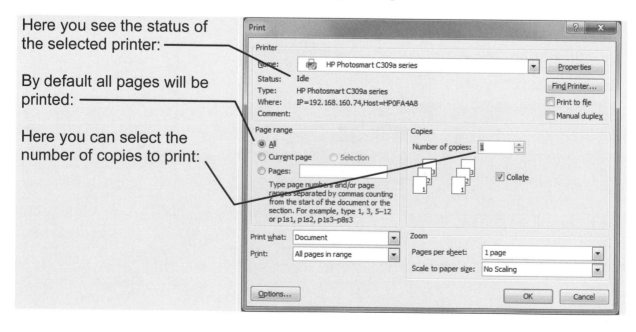

Here you see the status of the selected printer:

By default all pages will be printed:

Here you can select the number of copies to print:

Now you can print the letter:

In the bottom of the window:

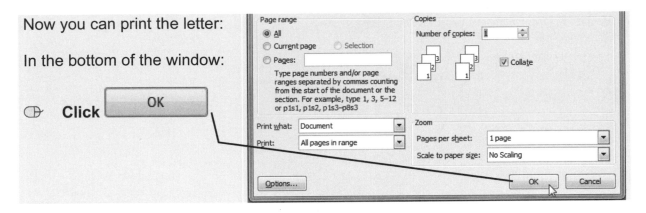

Click [ OK ]

Now the letter will be printed. You can close the *Print Preview* window:

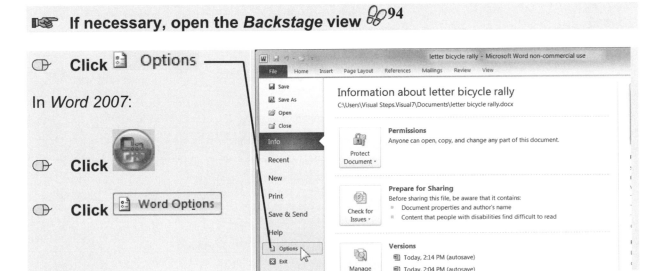

Click Close Print Preview

# 2.19 Print an Envelope

When you have taken all the time to carefully compose and print a document, it may seem kind of odd to send it in a handwritten envelope. In *Word* you can easily print an envelope with the name and address of the sender and the recipient. It is a good idea to set your own name and address as the default sender in *Word.* This will save a lot of time having to re-type this information over and over again.

☞ **If necessary, open the** *Backstage* **view** ✇**94**

Click 📄 Options

In *Word 2007*:

Click

Click [ 📄 Word Options ]

Now the *Word Options* window will be opened:

☞ **Click** Advanced

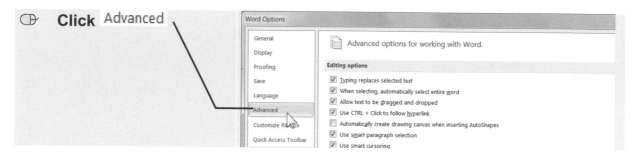

In the bottom of the window you can enter your name and address:

☞ **Drag the scroll bar down a bit**

☞ **By** Mailing address: **click the box**

⌨ **Type your name and address**

When you have finished:

☞ **Click** OK

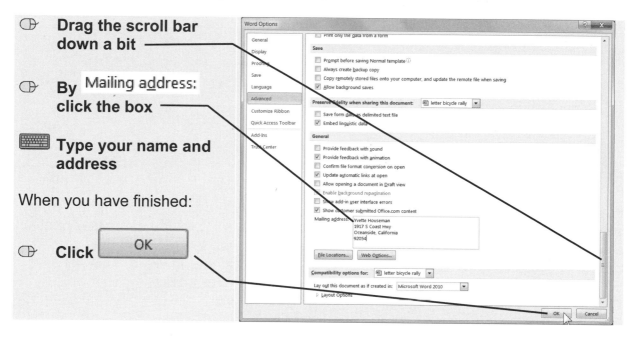

Now you can print the envelope:

☞ **Click the** Mailings **tab**

You want to display all the addresses:

☞ **Drag the scroll bar up again**

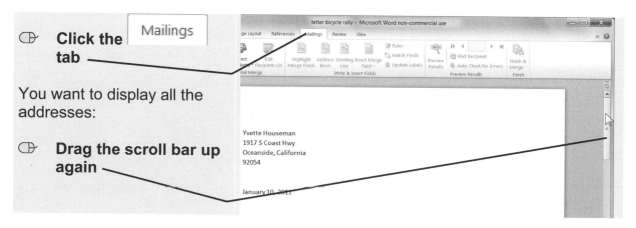

By default, *Word* will use the address on top as the recipient's address on the envelope. But you can decide for yourself which address to use:

⏏ **Click the recipient's name**

Now the cursor has moved to the line with the recipient's name:

⏏ **Click** Envelopes

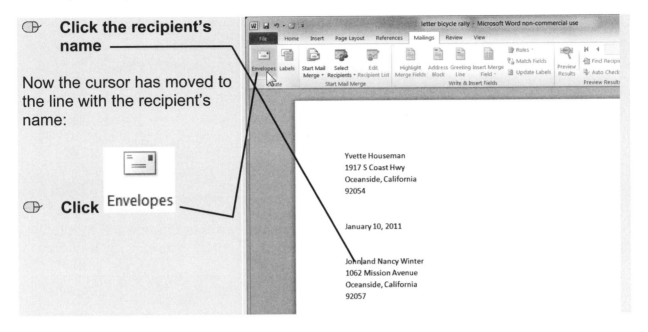

The *Envelopes and Labels* window will be opened:

You will see that the recipient and the sender have already been entered:

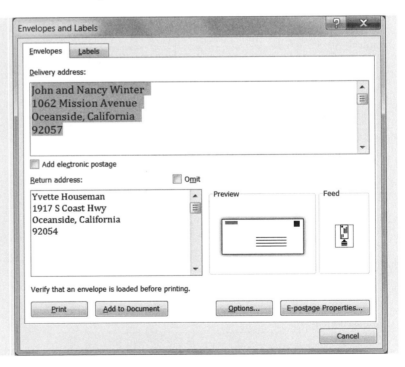

You can easily change the font for the recipient's and sender's names:

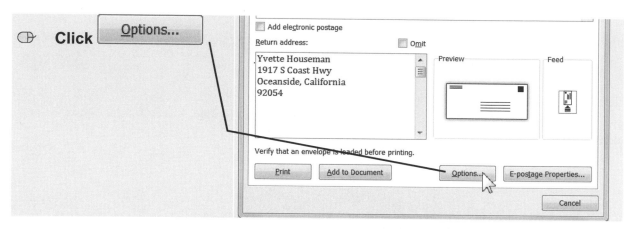

**Click** Options...

Now the *Envelope Options* window will be opened. You want to change the font for the sender's name:

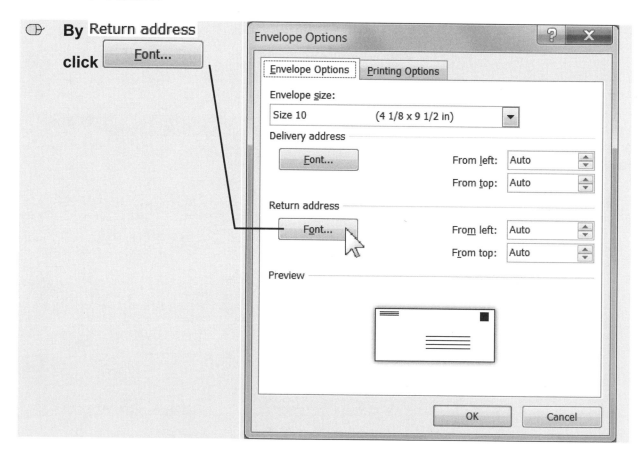

**By** Return address **click** Font...

Select the *Calibri* font:

 **Drag the scroll bar down a bit**

 **Click** Calibri

 **Click** OK

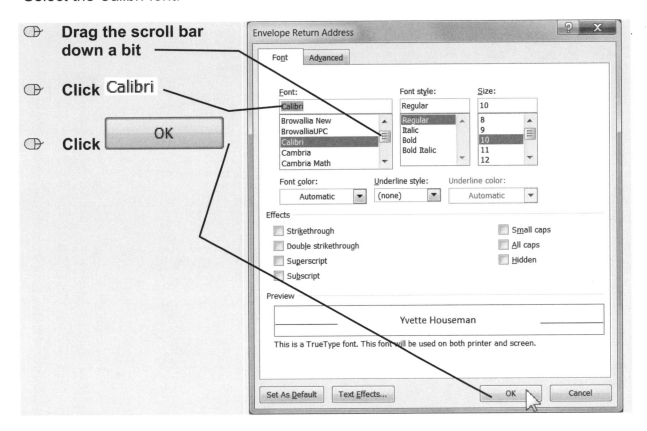

The font used for the sender's name has now changed.

Before you print the envelope, you will need to select the envelope size in the *Envelope Options* window.

## HELP! I do not have an envelope at hand.

This does not matter. Just follow the next couple of steps and print the text for the envelope on a regular sheet of paper.

In this example we have used the default DL envelope size of 110 x 220 mm:

By **Envelope size:**

click ▼

You will see a list with various envelope sizes:

**Drag the scroll bar down**

**Click**
DL     (110 x 220 mm)

**Click** OK

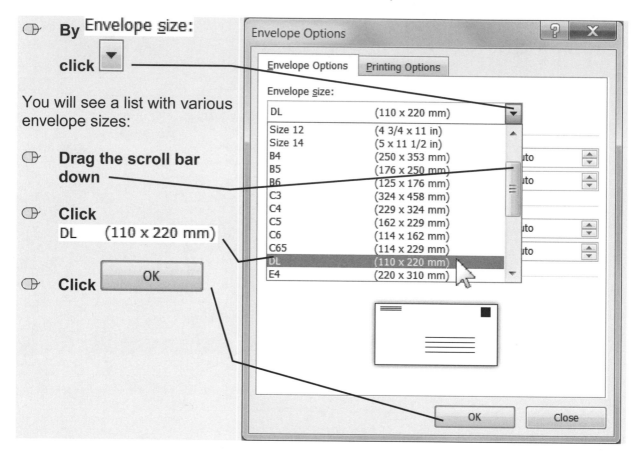

☞ **Insert an envelope in your printer's paper tray or input tray**

💡 **Tip**

**Loading envelopes**
There are many different methods for putting a single envelope or a stack of envelopes in a printer's tray. Some printers have a separate tray or opening for envelopes and smaller paper sizes. With other printers you may have to remove the paper from the tray first and then adjust the position of the media guides to the envelope's size.

☞ **For additional information on using envelopes, read your printer's manual**

Now you can print the envelope:

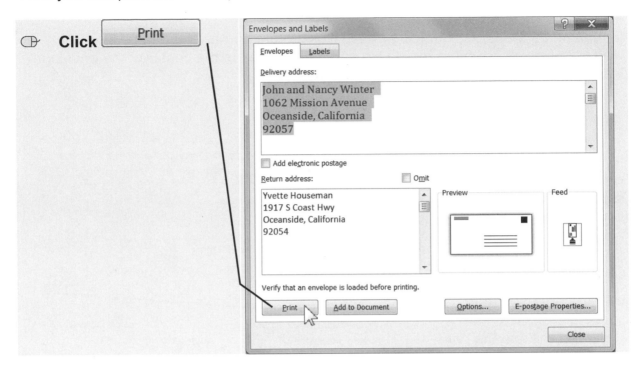

The envelope will be printed.

☞ **If necessary, close the *Envelopes and Labels* window** 🐾14

## Tip

**Formatting the envelope**

Is the sender's address bumping up too close to the border of the envelope? Or would you rather have the recipient's name positioned in the center of the envelope? Here is how to apply various options for envelopes:

☞ **Click** Options...

In the *Envelope Options* window you can accurately set the horizontal and vertical position of the addresses on the envelope:

Change the default settings with the arrow buttons:

Here you will see the print preview:

If you are satisfied with these settings:

☞ **Click** OK

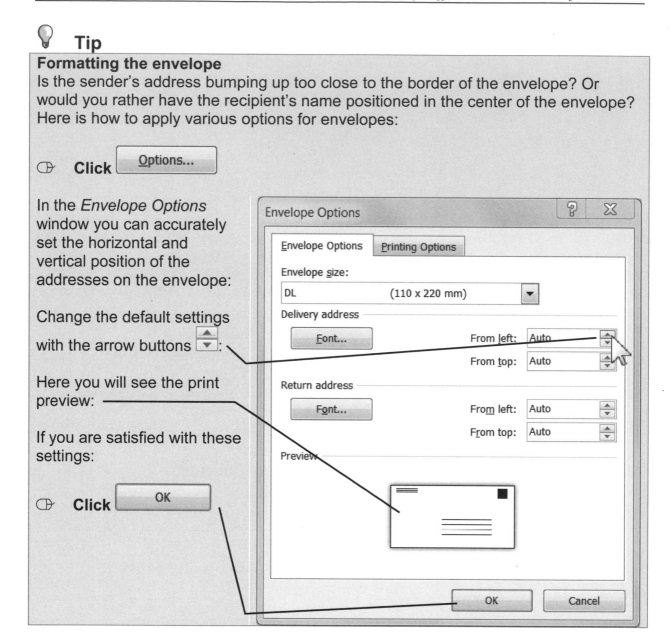

Now you have finished writing the letter and creating the envelope. Save the changes by using the *Quick Access* toolbar:

☞ **Click** 

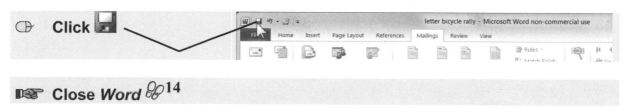

☞ **Close** *Word* 𝒶𝒷14

In this chapter you have written a lengthy letter and printed a matching envelope. In the following exercises you can practice the operations you have just learned.

## 2.20 Exercises

The following exercises will help you master what you have just learned. Have you forgotten how to do something? Use the number beside the footsteps to look it up in the appendix *How Do I Do That Again?*

## Exercise: Write a Letter

☞ Open *Word.* $\mathcal{B}^1$

☞ Type your own name and address one below the other.

☞ Select the entire text. $\mathcal{B}^{15}$

☞ Open the *Paragraph* window. $\mathcal{B}^{18}$

☞ Shrink the line spacing between the paragraphs to 0 points. $\mathcal{B}^{19}$

☞ Type the following text, including the spelling mistakes:

Boston,

Redwood Motel
36 Worcester Road
Charlton, MA 01507

Regarding: family dinnir

Gentlemen,

We would like to thank you for the great reception you gave us when we hosted our annual family dinner, last Satuday. The dinner was absolutely top class.

We would really like to visit you again sometime!

Yours truly,

Your name

☞ Insert the current date below Boston. $\mathcal{B}^{20}$

☞ View the spelling suggestions for 'dinnir' and 'Satuday', and select the correct spelling. 🐾21

☞ Change the top and bottom margins to 1 inch. 🐾22

☞ Undo the last operation. 🐾23

☞ Select the entire text. 🐾15

☞ Change the font size to 14 points. 🐾24

## Exercise: Print a Letter

☞ View the print preview. 🐾16, 17

☞ Print the letter. 🐾25

☞ In *Word 2007*: close the *Print Preview* window. 🐾26

## Exercise: Print an Envelope

☞ Open the *Mailings* tab. 🐾27

☞ Click the recipient's name.

☞ Open the *Envelopes and Labels* window. 🐾28

☞ Change the font for the recipient's name to *Calibri*. 🐾29

☞ Select the *DL (110 x 220 mm)* envelope size. 🐾30

☞ Print the envelope. 🐾31

☞ If necessary, close the *Envelopes and Labels* window. 🐾14

☞ Save the letter as family dinner, in the (*My*) *Documents* folder. 🐾32

☞ Close *Word*. 🐾14

# 2.21 Background Information

| | |
|---|---|
| **Dictionary** | |
| **Automatic spelling checker** | A feature that checks the spelling of words in a text document, immediately after the text has been typed. The spelling checker uses a built-in vocabulary. |
| **Cursor** | The blinking vertical line that indicates where the text will be inserted. |
| **Hyperlink** | A link to a different location. This might be a webpage, or part of a document. In *Word*, an e-mail address is automatically converted to a hyperlink. If you press the CTRL key and hold it down and then click the hyperlink, a new e-mail message will be opened in your default e-mail program. |
| **Indent** | Moving the paragraph(s) a little bit to the inside of the margins. This makes the text stand out. |
| **Margin** | Blank border surrounding a page. |
| **Page layout** | The ratio of the printed part of a page versus the margins. |
| **Print preview** | An option that displays a document on screen, instead of printing it. This way, users can see what the printed version will look like. |
| **Save** | Command to save a document to your computer's hard drive, or other storage medium. |
| **Synonym** | A word that has the same meaning. |
| **USB stick** | A little device which can contain data. A USB stick is connected to the computer's USB port. *Windows 7* will display a USB stick as a removable media disk. |

*Source: Word and Windows Help and Support*

# 2.22 Tips

  **Tip**

**Open a recent document**
If you do not finish a letter right away and choose to close *Word*, the next time you open *Word* you can quickly open this document:

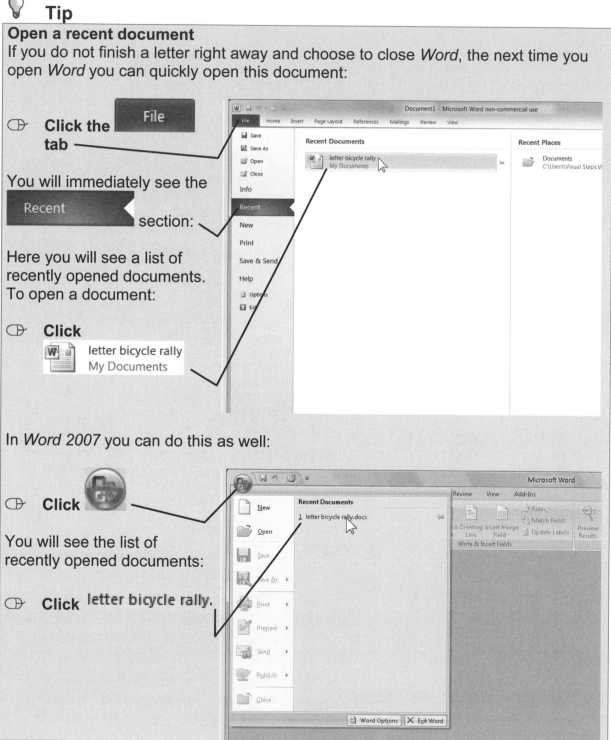

☞  **Click the File tab**

You will immediately see the **Recent** section:

Here you will see a list of recently opened documents.
To open a document:

☞  **Click  [📄] letter bicycle rally / My Documents**

In *Word 2007* you can do this as well:

☞  **Click  [🔵]**

You will see the list of recently opened documents:

☞  **Click  letter bicycle rally.**

**Tip**

**Save a document as a DOC file**

If you are familiar with older versions of *Word*, you will know that you could recognize the *Word* files by their .doc extension, for instance, *MyFile.doc*. In *Word 2010* and *2007* the extension is no longer called .DOC, but .DOCX. According to *Microsoft*, the *Word* manufacturer, the new file format offers quite a few advantages. For example, the files are automatically compressed, which means that they take up less space on your hard drive. When you open a file, it will be extracted at once. When you save a file, it will automatically be compressed again. Because the various components of the file are saved separately, DOCX files can easily be recovered and restored.

Saving a file in the .DOCX format is automatic in *Word 2010* and *2007*. But it is still possible to save files in the older *Word* file format. This can be useful if you want to send a *Word* document to someone who has not yet installed *Word 2010* or *2007*. This is how you save a file in the DOC file format:

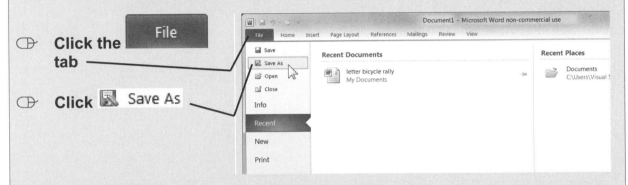

☞ **Click the** *File* **tab**

☞ **Click** *Save As*

In *Word 2007* you will need to use the *Office* button:

☞ **Click** [Office button] **,** *Save As*

*- Continue reading on the next page -*

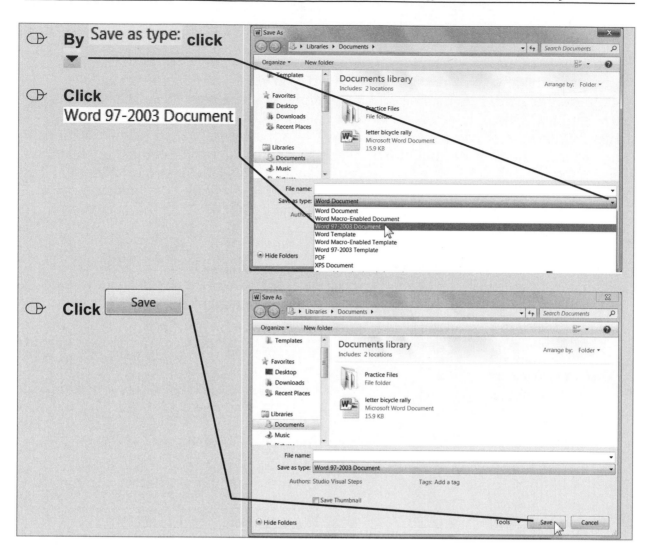

By Save as type: click
▼

Click
Word 97-2003 Document

Click   Save

**Tip**

**Open a Word attachment to an e-mail message**

Lots of letters these days are no longer sent by regular mail. You may receive a letter more often as an attachment to an e-mail message. This is how to open the attachment:

☞ **Click the e-mail message**

In the reading pane you will see the text of the message and the attachment:

☞ **Double-click the attachment**

You will see a warning message:

☞ **Click** Open

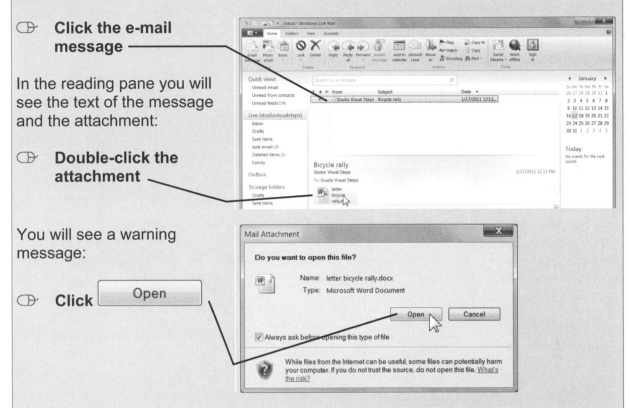

Now the attachment will be opened in *Word 2010*, in **Protected View**. This means that you will not be able to edit, save, or print the file right away. In *Word 2007* it is still possible to edit the document right away.

If you trust the sender, you can leave the protected view:

☞ **Click** Enable Editing

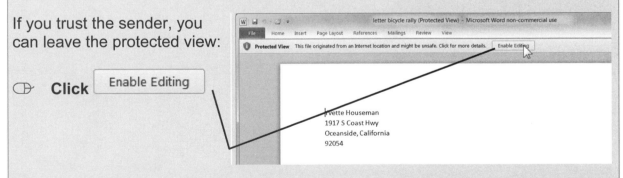

Now you can edit, save and print the *Word* document the same way as always, just as if you had created the document yourself.

**Tip**

**Send a document as attachment to an e-mail message**
In *Word* you can easily send an opened document as an attachment to an e-mail message. This is how you do it in *Word 2010*:

Click the File tab

Click Save & Send

Click Send as Attachment

In *Word 2007*:

Click

Click Send

Click E-mail Send a

A new e-mail message will be opened, and the *Word* document will be attached to it:

Now you can enter the e-mail address of the recipient, write a message and send the e-mail.

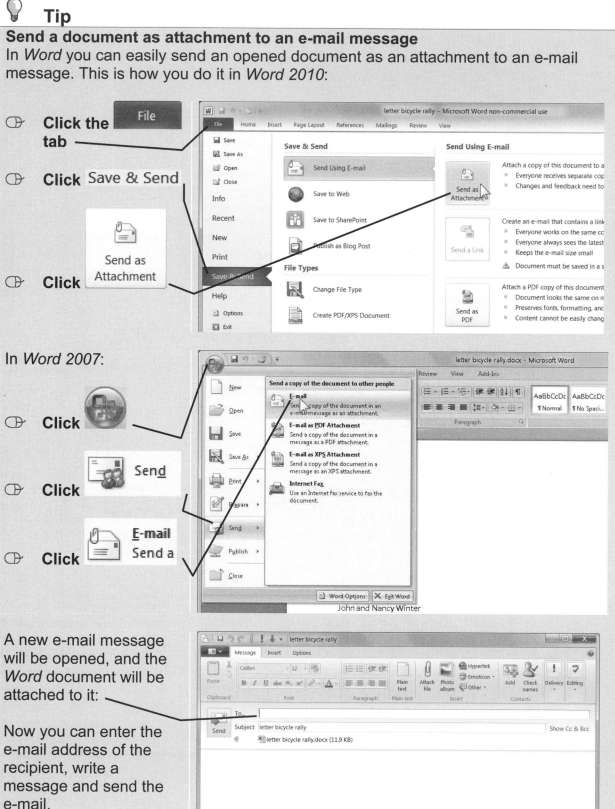

**Tip**

**Save a document to a USB stick or other external device**
In this chapter you have saved the letter to your computer's hard drive. If you want to transfer the letter to a different computer, you can also save the document on a USB stick. A USB stick is a small storage device with a large storage capacity, which you can reuse over and over again. This is how you save a document to a USB stick:

☞ **Connect the USB stick to your computer's USB port**

☞ **If necessary, close the *AutoPlay* window** 𝒢𝒢14

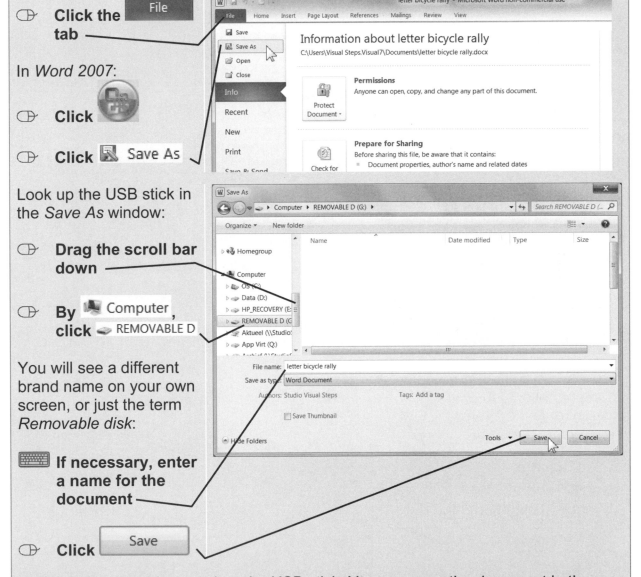

🖰 **Click the File tab**

In *Word 2007*:

🖰 **Click**

🖰 **Click 🔲 Save As**

Look up the USB stick in the *Save As* window:

🖰 **Drag the scroll bar down**

🖰 **By 🖳 Computer, click 💾 REMOVABLE D**

You will see a different brand name on your own screen, or just the term *Removable disk*:

⌨ **If necessary, enter a name for the document**

🖰 **Click Save**

Now the document is stored on the USB stick. You can save the document in the same way to other types of external storage devices such as a portable hard disk. This way you will always have a back-up copy of your file.

**Tip**

**Open a document from USB stick or external hard disk**
If you want to open a document that is stored on a USB stick, this is how you do it:

☞  **Connect the USB stick to your computer's USB port**

☞  **If necessary, close the *AutoPlay* window** ✇**14**

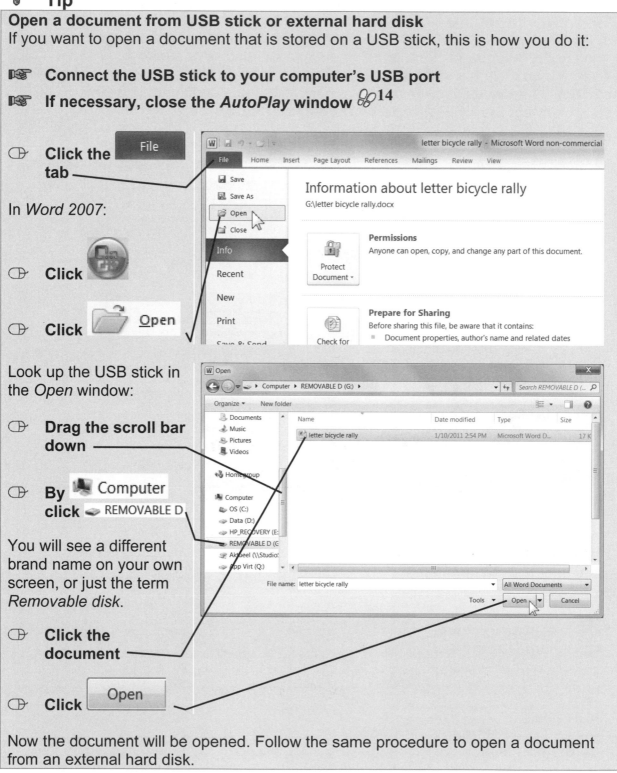

☞  **Click the** **File** **tab**

In *Word 2007*:

☞  **Click**

☞  **Click** **Open**

Look up the USB stick in the *Open* window:

☞  **Drag the scroll bar down**

☞  **By** **Computer** **click** ▭ REMOVABLE D

You will see a different brand name on your own screen, or just the term *Removable disk*.

☞  **Click the document**

☞  **Click** **Open**

Now the document will be opened. Follow the same procedure to open a document from an external hard disk.

# 3. Pictures in a Document

'A picture is worth a thousand words', is a well-known expression. Adding a photo or illustration to your text can do much more than just express your feelings. The text can become more attractive and clearer by adding pictures.

In *Word* it is very easy to add photos, illustrations and WordArt to your documents. You can edit the picture any way you want and make it match the text. You can change the size, the color and the position of a picture within the text.

In this chapter you will learn how to:

- open a sample text;
- insert a photo;
- enlarge and shrink a photo;
- change the position of a photo;
- move a photo by dragging it;
- set the text wrap;
- crop a photo;
- adjust the brightness and contrast of a photo;
- change the colors;
- add artistic effects;
- create a watermark;
- delete the background of an image;
- open a new document;
- insert WordArt;
- edit WordArt;
- find and insert an illustration;
- remove an illustration.

 **Please note:**

To work through all the exercises in this chapter, you will need to download the relevant practice files from the website to the (*My*) *Documents* folder on your computer. You can read how to do that in *Appendix A Downloading the Practice Files*.

# 3.1 Open a Sample Text

In this chapter you will need to open a practice file. Here is how to do that:

☞ **Open *Word*** 👣¹

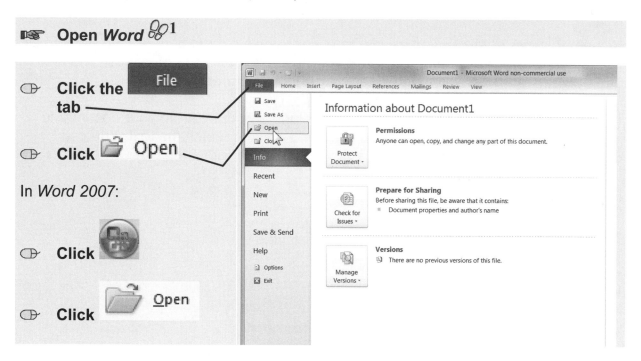

**Click the File tab**

**Click 📂 Open**

In *Word 2007*:

**Click**

**Click 📂 Open**

You will see the *Open* window. The folder containing the practice files has been stored in the (*My*) *Documents* folder:

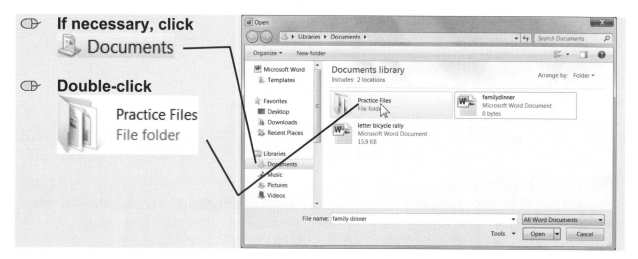

**If necessary, click 🗄 Documents**

**Double-click**

Practice Files
File folder

# HELP! The window on my computer looks different.

Perhaps the layout of your window looks a bit different. This is how to make your window look like the examples in the book:

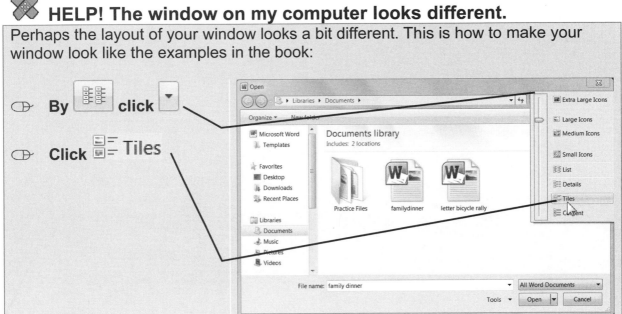

By click

Click Tiles

Open a sample text:

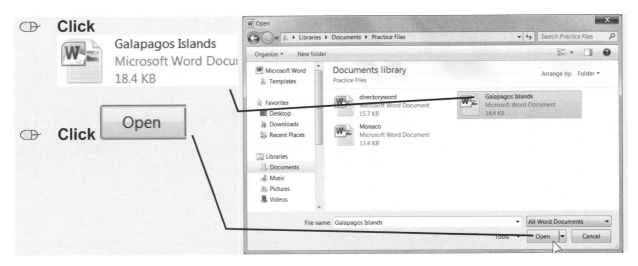

Click
Galapagos Islands
Microsoft Word Docui
18.4 KB

Click Open

You will see the sample text concerning the Galapagos islands:

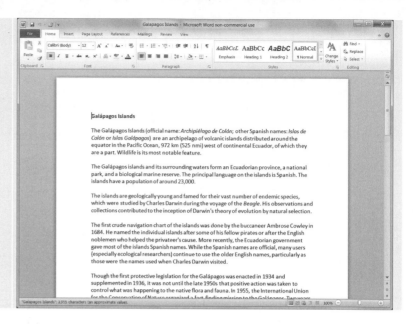

## 3.2 Insert a Photo

Now you are going to insert a photo into the text. First, move the cursor to the spot where you want the photo to be:

**Click the fourth blank line**

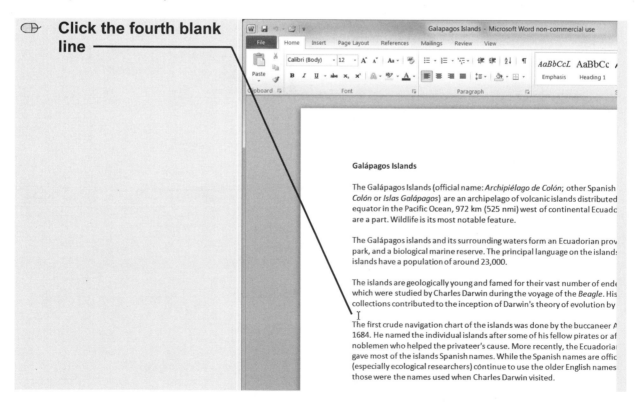

**Click the tab** *Insert*

**Click** Picture

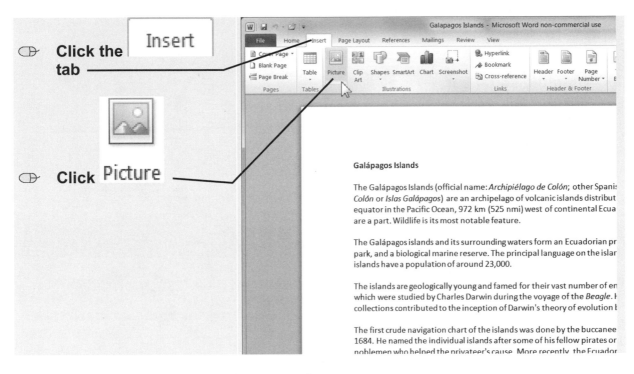

The *Insert Picture* window will be opened:

**Click** Documents

**Double-click** Practice Files File folder

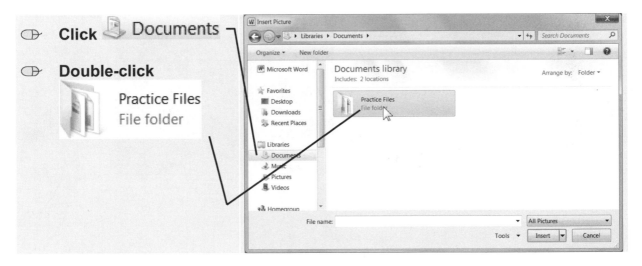

Now you will see several pictures:

 **Drag the scroll bar down a bit**

 **Click**

iguana
JPEG Image
98.9 KB

 **Click** Insert

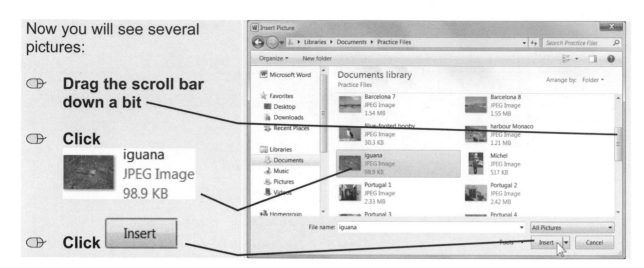

The picture of the iguana will be inserted:

You will see that the photo is quite large:

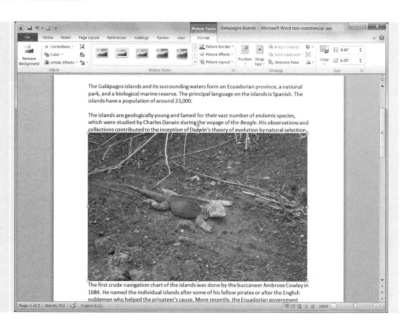

💡 **Tip**

**Large photos**
*Word* will always try to display the photos you insert as large as possible within the page margins. A portrait-oriented, high resolution photo will easily take up the entire page.

# 3.3 The Picture Tools

When you start working with photos, the Format tab in the Picture Tools will automatically be opened:

You will see the Picture Tools on the ribbon:

The Format tab with the relevant commands has already been opened:

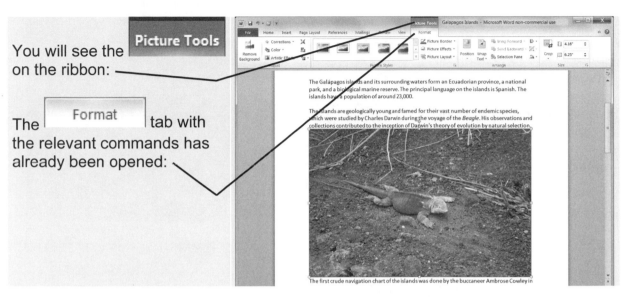

☞ **Click a spot next to the photo**

Now the *Format* tab has vanished:

☞ **Click the photo**

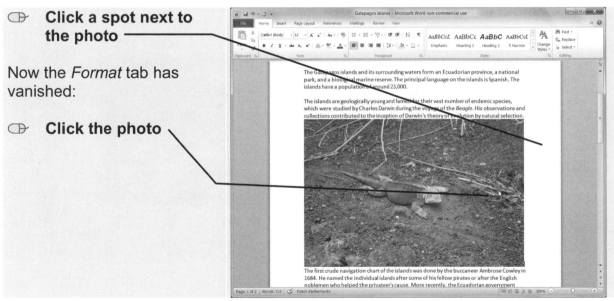

The Format tab is displayed once again. You will see this tab appear by itself, each time you select an image. As soon as you click a spot outside the picture, the *Format* tab will disappear again.

# 3.4 Resize a Photo

It is very easy to enlarge or shrink a photo by using the mouse.

The photo is still selected:

Along the edges of the photo you will see tiny circles and squares. These are the so-called *sizing handles*:

To enlarge or shrink a photo, you drag the *sizing handles* from the corners inwards or outwards.

☞ **Position the mouse pointer on the sizing handle in the lower right-hand corner**

The pointer will turn into ⬉:

☞ **Press the mouse button and keep it pressed in**

☞ **Drag the handle inwards towards the middle of the photo**

☞ **Release the mouse button**

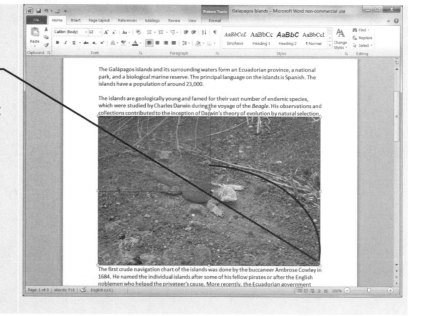

You will see that the photo has become much smaller:

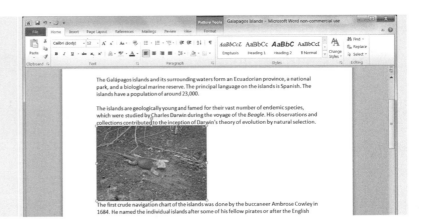

 **Tip**

**Other handles**

If you do not drag a corner handle, but one of the sizing handles from the side of the photo, it will become distorted. This is because you change the photo's current proportions (its aspect ratio). It will be stretched out or shrunk in a strange way.

See what happens if you drag the handle from the top or bottom inwards. The photo becomes 'flattened':

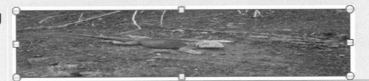

# 3.5 Text Wrapping

When you insert a photo into your document, you can set the text to wrap around it in a number of different ways. This is called *text wrapping*. Just try it:

☞ **If necessary, click the photo**

☞ **Click** Position ▾

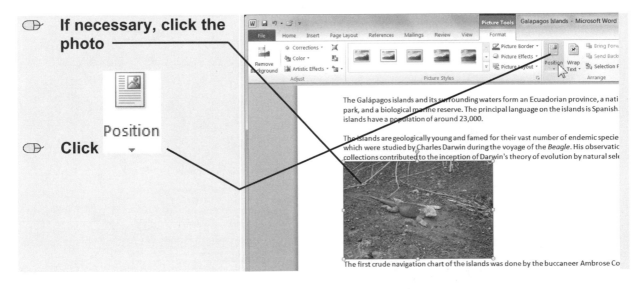

Now you will see the different placement options for your photo relative to the page.

👆 **Position the mouse**

**pointer over**

You will immediately see a preview of the page:

👆 **Click**

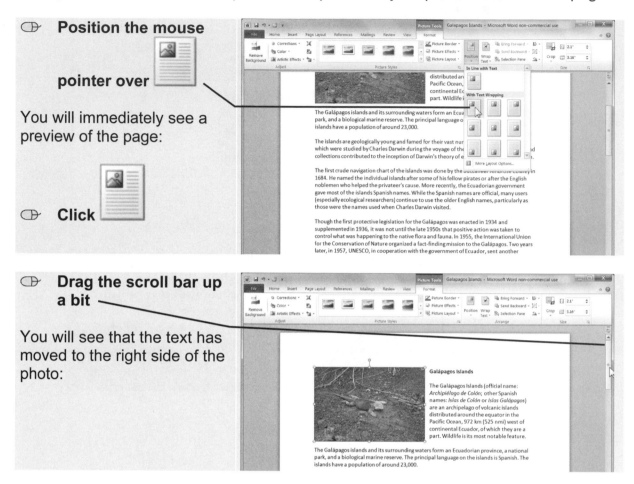

👆 **Drag the scroll bar up a bit**

You will see that the text has moved to the right side of the photo:

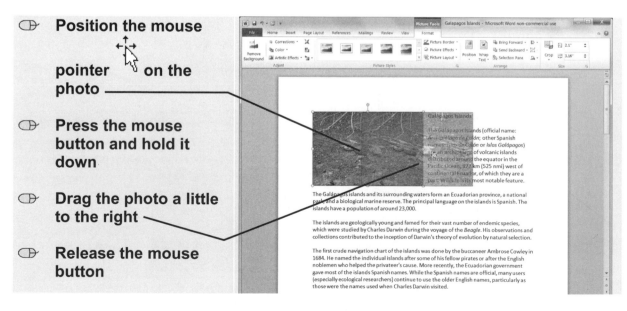

You can also use the mouse to move the photo by simply dragging it:

👆 **Position the mouse**

**pointer on the photo**

👆 **Press the mouse button and hold it down**

👆 **Drag the photo a little to the right**

👆 **Release the mouse button**

Now you will see that the text wraps around both sides of the photo:

This does not necessarily enhance the readability of the text, because the lines continue on both sides of the photo.

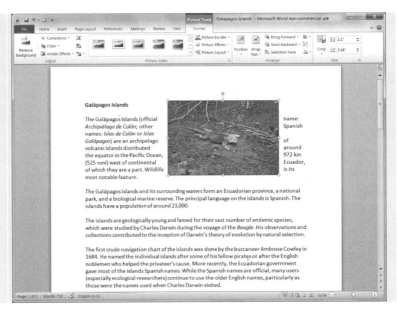

*Word* has several other ways to position photos. Take a look at some of these options:

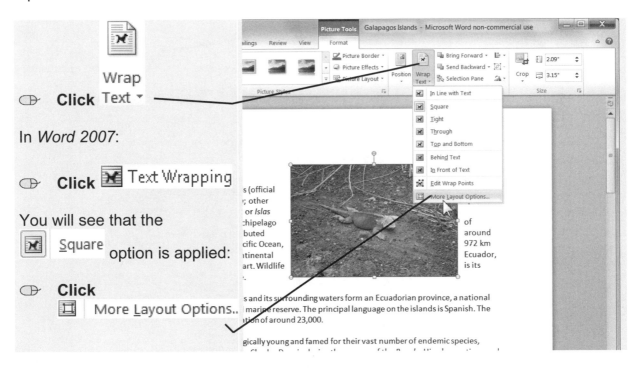

Wrap

☞ **Click** Text ▾

In *Word 2007*:

☞ **Click** 🖾 Text Wrapping

You will see that the 🖾 Square option is applied:

☞ **Click** 🔲 More Layout Options..

In the *Layout* window you can see the options for positioning text around the photo:

At this point, the text is displayed on both sides of the photo. You can change the position of the text to the left side of the picture.

☞ **If necessary, click the** Text Wrapping **tab**

☞ **Click the radio button** ◉ **by** Left only

☞ **Click** OK

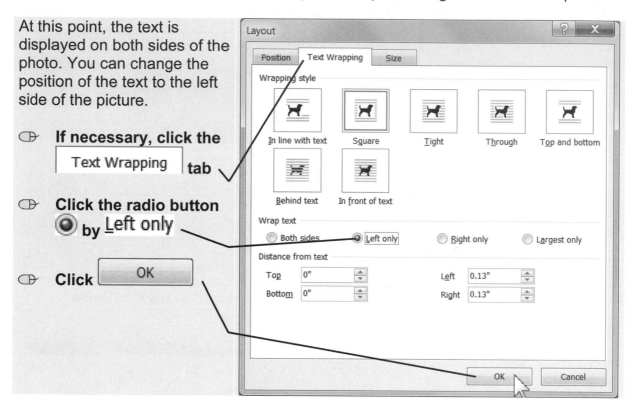

Now the text has moved to the left side of the photo:

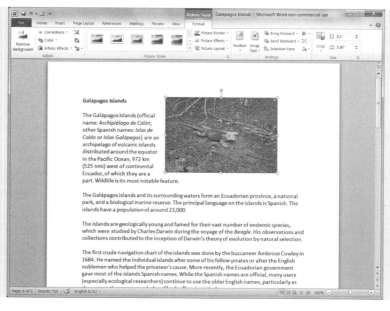

# 3.6 Crop a Photo

If you want to remove an unwanted area from your photo, you can cut a section of it off. You could crop the right side of the sample photo, for instance; then the iguana will no longer appear in the center of the picture. To do this, you need to select the cropping tool:

☞ **Click**

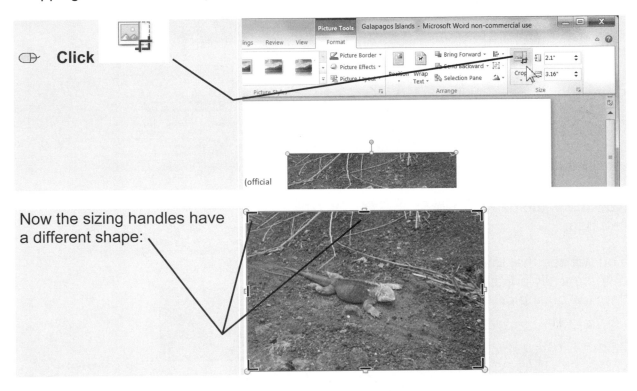

Now the sizing handles have a different shape:

You can cut off the right-hand side of the picture like this:

☞ **Move the mouse pointer to the sizing handle on the right**

**Please note:** the pointer should now have this shape ⌐.

☞ **Press the left mouse button and drag the handle to the left**

☞ **Release the mouse button**

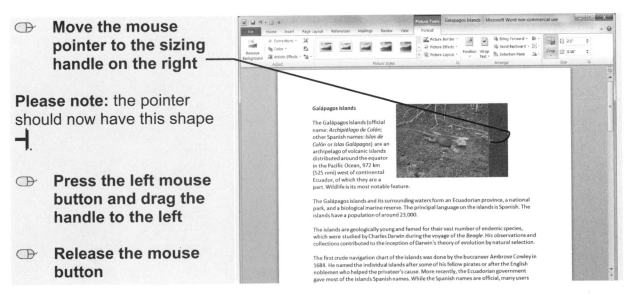

After cropping, in *Word 2010* the original photo will be visible as well:

In *Word 2007* the right hand side of the photo is cropped at once.

If you actually want to crop it,

disable the 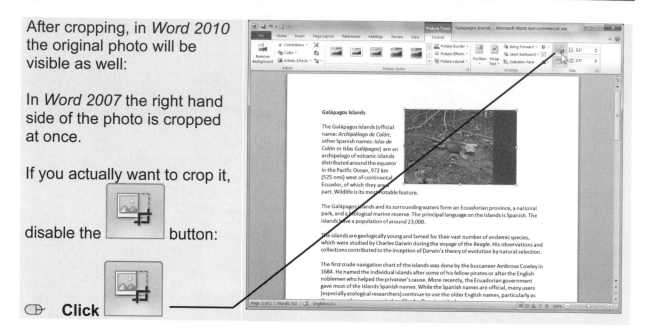 button:

⊙ **Click**

Now the photo has been cropped:

You will see that the text automatically adjusts itself to the new outline of the photo:

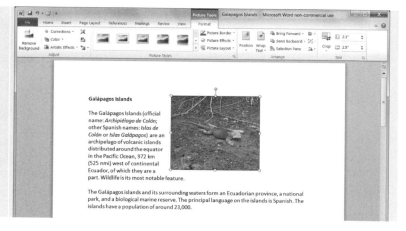

You can also crop the image to a specific shape. Here is how to do that:

 **Please note:**

The *Crop to Shape* option is not available in *Word 2007*.

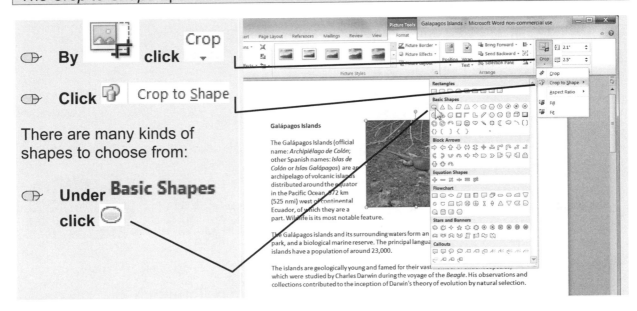

⊂▷ **By** click **Crop** ▾

⊂▷ **Click** **Crop to Shape**

There are many kinds of shapes to choose from:

⊂▷ **Under** **Basic Shapes**
click ⬭

The photo now becomes an oval:

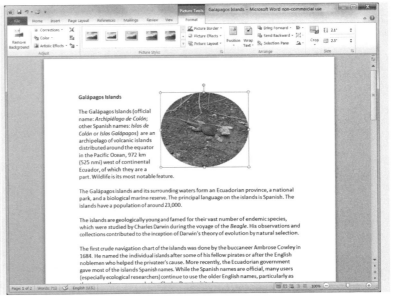

# 3.7 Reset Picture and Discard the Formatting

Once you have cropped a photo, you can always restore the original formatting like this:

The photo is still selected and the | Format | tab is still open:

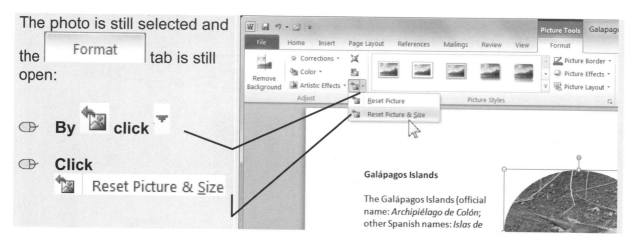

$\oplus$ **By**  **click** 

$\oplus$ **Click**
   Reset Picture & Size

**Please note:**

In *Word 2007* you will only see the Reset Picture button. If you click this button, the photo will be reset to its original size. The original photo is much bigger than the page which means that the page will merely display a patch of blue sky. Therefore, in *Word 2007* it is better to just undo the last operation.

In *Word 2010* you will see that the photo has been restored to its original size:

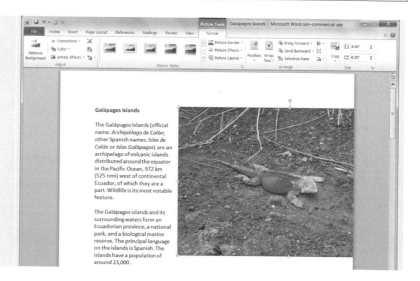

In *Word 2010*:

☞ **Shrink the photo to fit the page** &#x6067;44

☞ **If necessary, move the photo to the top right side of the page** &#x6067;46

# 3.8 Edit a Photo

*Word* continues to make improvements to its photo editing features. You can try some of these out with the *blue-footed booby* photo from the *Practice Files* folder:

☞ **Click the third blank line in the document**

☞ **Insert the *blue-footed booby* photo from the *Practice Files* folder** 👣33

Now the photo has been inserted:

☞ **Drag the scroll bar down enough so that you can see the entire photo**

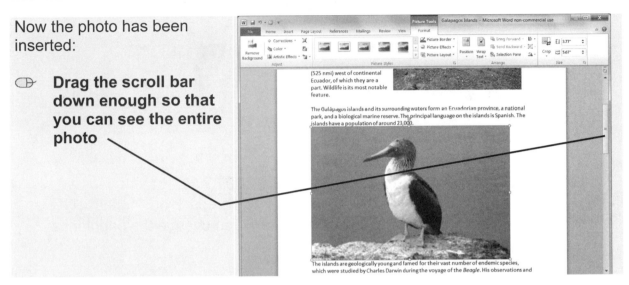

In the Adjust group, in the Format tab, you will find all the photo editing options. For instance, you can change the brightness and contrast of the photo. The photo selection is still active:

In *Word 2010*:

☞ **Click ⚙ Corrections**

In *Word 2007* see the *Help box* at the next page.

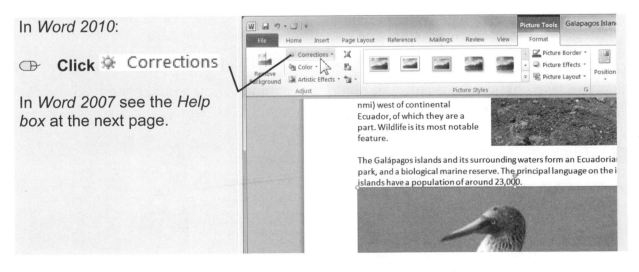

You will see a menu with the various corrections you can apply:

☞ **Move the mouse over some of the options**

You will see that *Word* displays the effect even before you have clicked.

☞ **Click**

> Brightness: +20% Contrast: +20%

The photo has become lighter.

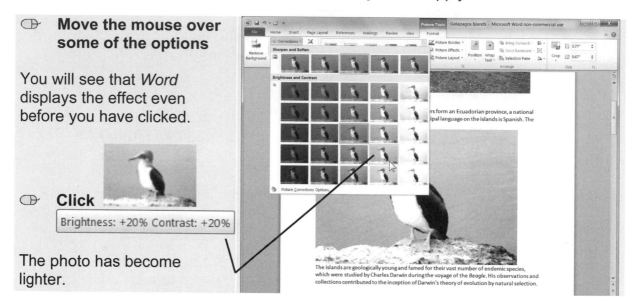

 **HELP! How Do I Edit Photos in Word 2007?**

In *Word 2007* you can apply the same correction in two steps, by using the ☀ Brightness ▾ and ◑ Contrast ▾ buttons. This is how you change the brightness:

☞ **Double-click the photo**

Now the | Format | tab will be opened:

☞ **Click** ☀ Brightness ▾ , ☀ +20 %

## 3.9 Changing the Colors

You can also change the colors of a photo. For example, you can apply an old fashioned sepia shade to the photo:

☞ **Click** 🖼 Color ▾

In *Word 2007*:

☞ **Click** 🖼 Recolor ▾

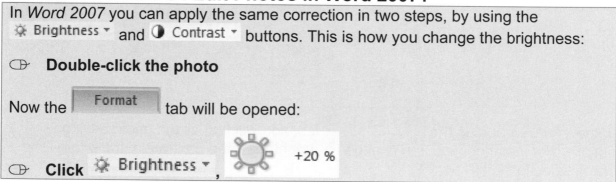

You will see various options:

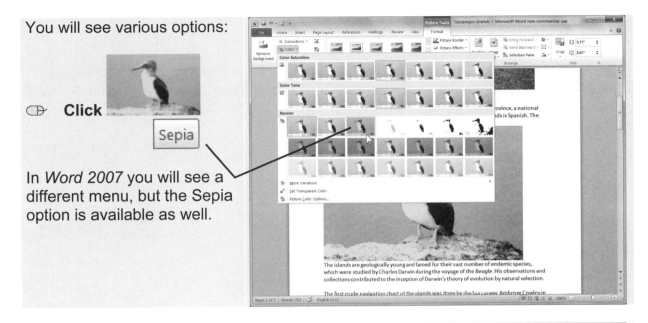

☞　**Click**

Sepia

In *Word 2007* you will see a different menu, but the Sepia option is available as well.

Here you see the result:

☞　**Undo the last operation** ✂️23

Now you will see that the photo has regained its original colors.

# 3.10 Picture Effects

In *Word 2010* you can apply a variety of artistic effects to a photo. Unfortunately, these options are not available in *Word 2007*. This is how you use the effects in *Word 2010*:

☞ **Click**

📓 Artistic Effects ▾

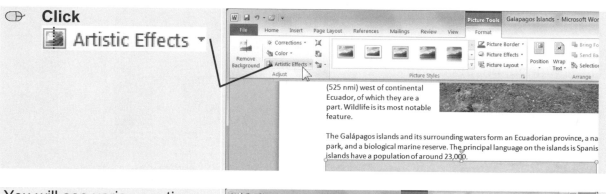

You will see various options:

☞ **Position the mouse pointer on**

Pencil Grayscale

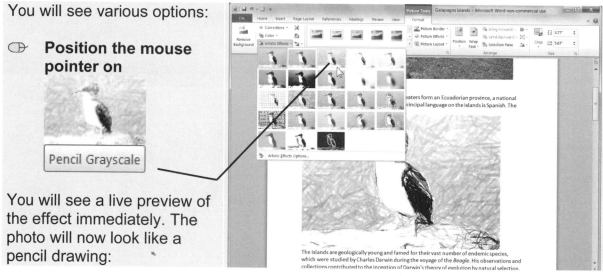

You will see a live preview of the effect immediately. The photo will now look like a pencil drawing:

You will see various other options:

☞ **Click**

Pastels Smooth

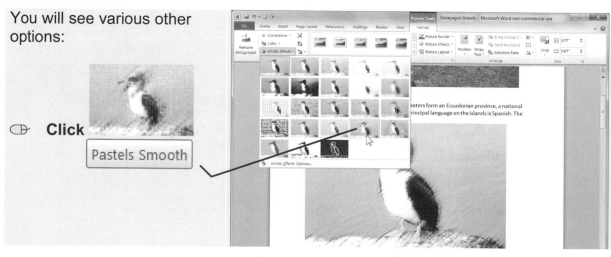

Now the photo has turned into a pastel chalk drawing:

## 3.11 Revert to the Original Picture Format

Earlier on, you have already reset a cropped photo to its original size. In *Word 2010* you have the possibility to reset the changes applied to the colors and effects only. Here is how to do that:

 **Please note:**

This option is not available in *Word 2007*.

The photo selection is still active and the | Format | tab is still open:

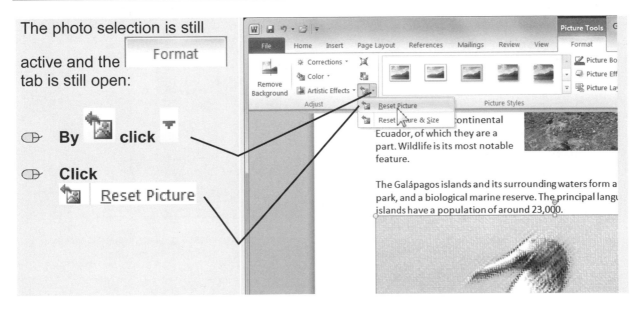

☞ **By** 🖼 **click** ▼

☞ **Click** 🖼 Reset Picture

Now you will see the original colors once more:

## 3.12 Washout effect

*Word* has a very nice effect which you can use to create a very faint 'watermark' of the selected photo. The *washout* feature lets you adjust the opacity of the photo. It can then serve as a faded background with the text appearing on top.

☞ **Click** 🖼 Color ▾

In *Word 2007*:

☞ **Click** 🖼 Recolor ▾

☞ **Click** Washout

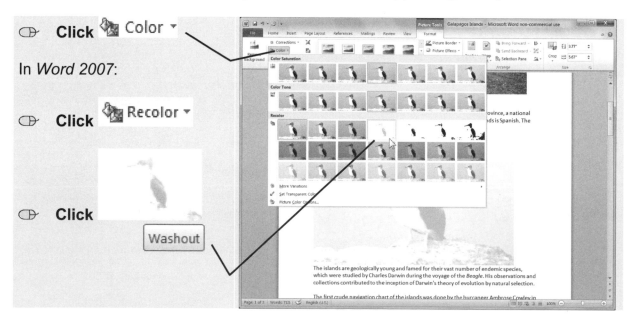

The photo is just as wide as the lines in the text. Now you can set the text wrapping, so that the text appears on top of the photo:

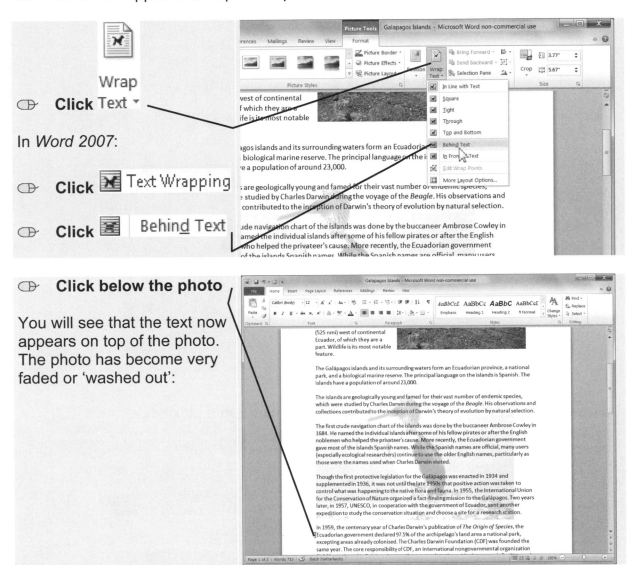

Wrap

⊕ **Click Text** ▾

In *Word 2007*:

⊕ **Click** ☒ Text Wrapping

⊕ **Click** ☰ Behind Text

⊕ **Click below the photo**

You will see that the text now appears on top of the photo. The photo has become very faded or 'washed out':

The photo is being used as a watermark. You can use a watermark to create nice looking stationary or perhaps a diploma or certificate.

☞ **Undo the last two operations** 🦶23

# 3.13 Automatically Deleting the Background

In *Word 2010* you can also delete a photo's background.

 **Please note:**

This option is not available in *Word 2007*.

The photo has been selected:

**Click** Remove Background

*Word* will look for the picture's background and mark it in a pink color.

You will see that not all of the area's have been marked correctly, such as the bird's head and feet:

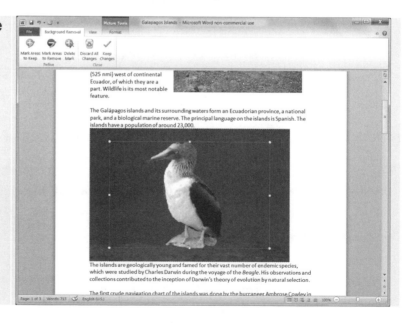

You can mark the area's you want to keep:

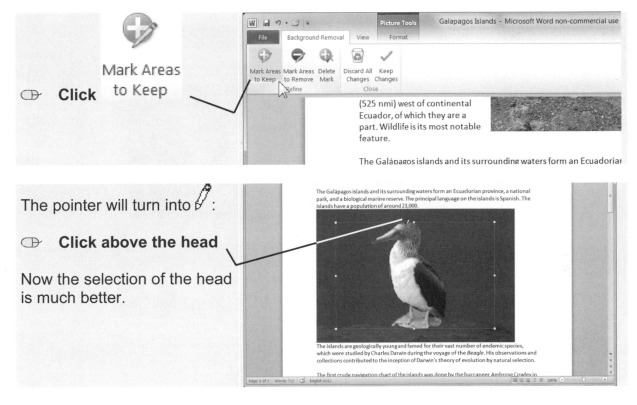

The pointer will turn into ✐ :

☞ **Click above the head**

Now the selection of the head is much better.

You can also remove a part that is currently selected:

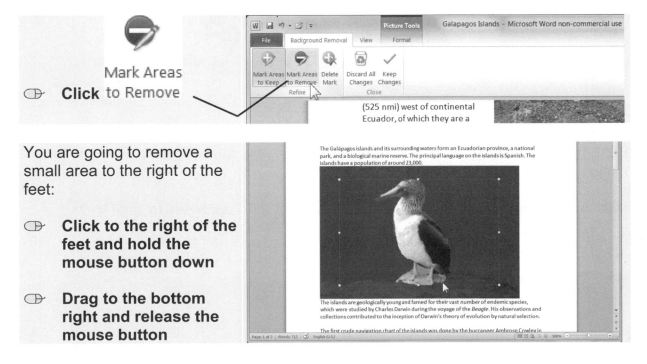

You are going to remove a small area to the right of the feet:

☞ **Click to the right of the feet and hold the mouse button down**

☞ **Drag to the bottom right and release the mouse button**

To apply the changes:

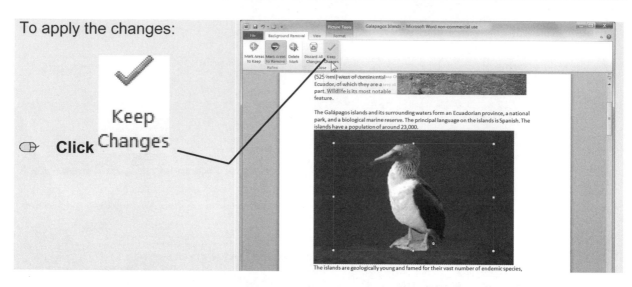

⊕ **Click** Keep Changes

Now the background of the photo has been deleted:

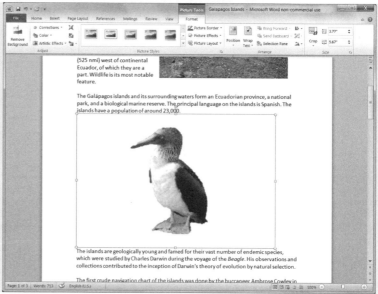

The *Remove Background* function does not always work as well as you would like. For optimum results, your photo should contain a good deal of contrast between the subject and the background.

☞ **Save the document as *Galapagos Islands with pictures*, in the (*My*) *Documents* folder** 🐾³²

☞ **Close the document** 🐾¹², ¹³

# 3.14 Open a New Document

Start the next exercise by opening a new, blank document. Here is how to open one:

**Click the tab**

**Click New**

In *Word 2007*:

**Click**

**Click** New

You can select the type of document you want to open:

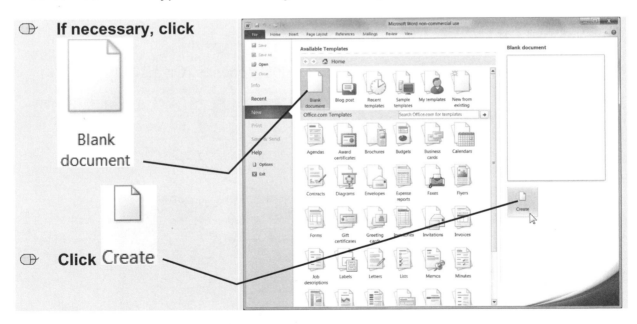

**If necessary, click**

Blank document

**Click Create**

Now you will see a blank document. In this document you are going to create a poster. This poster will be used to congratulate someone who has just turned 50. First, you are going to insert a picture:

☞ **Insert the *Michel* photo from the *Practice Files* folder** 🐾33

You will see that the photo
fills the entire page in this
document:

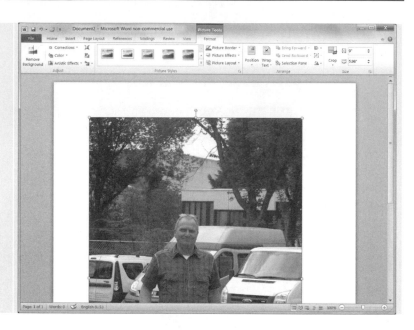

In the next section you can read how to use WordArt in *Word 2010*. If you are using
*Word 2007*, you can skip this section and continue with section *3.16 Insert WordArt in
Word 2007*.

# 3.15 Insert WordArt in Word 2010

You can use *WordArt* to add decorative texts in just seconds. Give it a try:

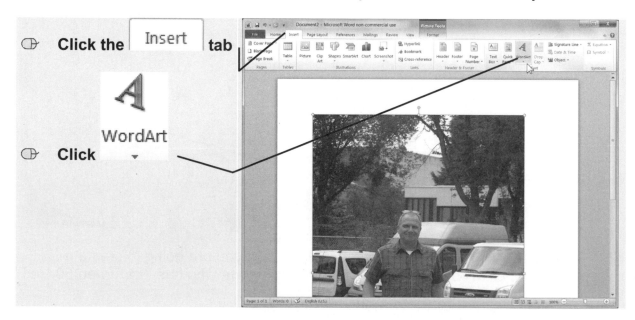

You will see a menu with various WordArt styles for you to choose from:

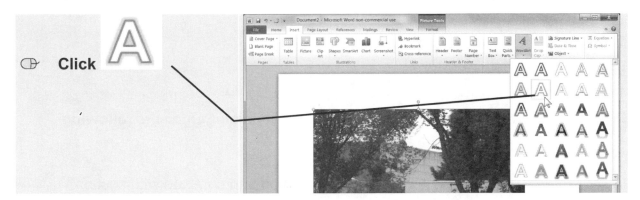

☞ **Click**

Now a text box will be opened, where you can enter your WordArt text:

⌨ **Type:**
Congratulations!

In the ribbon you will see the

**Drawing Tools** and the

Format tab:

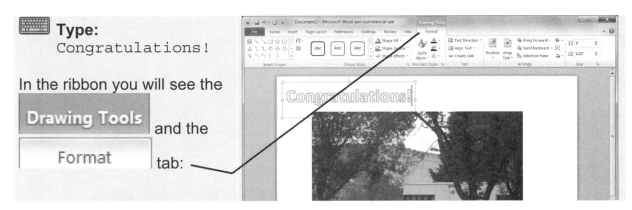

You can move the text box by dragging it:

☞ **Position the mouse pointer on the edge of the text box**

The pointer will turn into 🔀:

☞ **Press the mouse button and hold it down**

☞ **Drag the text box onto the photo**

☞ **Release the mouse button**

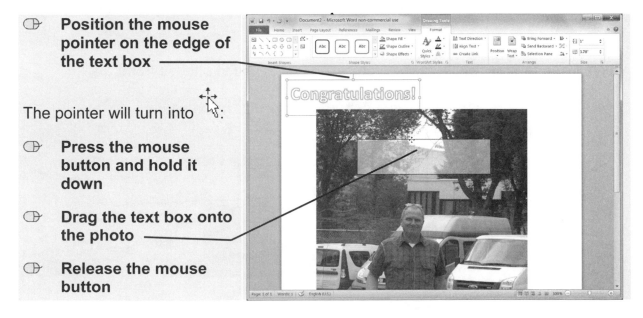

Next, you will add another WordArt text box. First, you will need to select the photo, otherwise the first WordArt box will be duplicated:

☞ **Click the photo**

☞ **Insert a WordArt text box in the** **style and enter the following text:** 50 years old! ✂️³⁴

For *Word 2010* users: you can skip the next section and continue with section *3.17 Zoom Out*.

## 3.16 Insert WordArt in Word 2007

You can use *WordArt* to add decorative texts in just seconds. Give it a try:

☞ **Click the Insert tab**

☞ **Click**

You will see a menu with various WordArt styles for you to choose from:

☞ **Click**

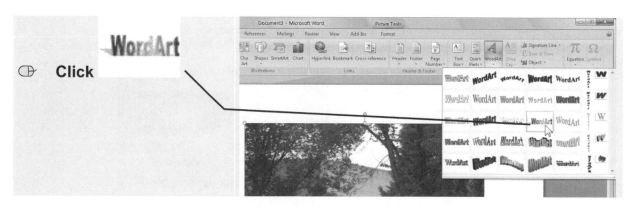

A window will be opened, where you can enter your WordArt text:

**Type:**
Congratulations!

Click OK

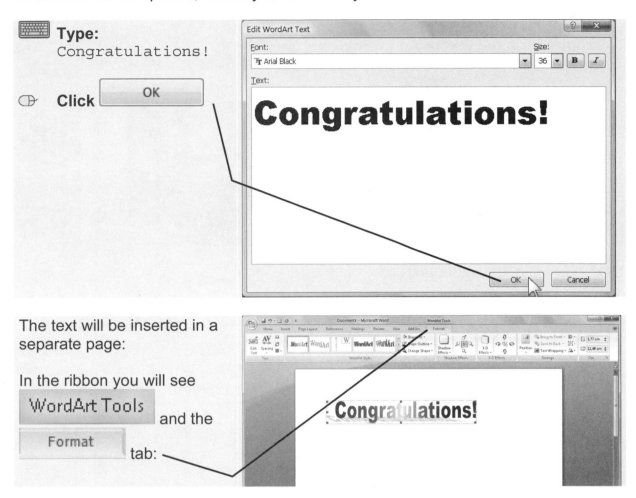

The text will be inserted in a separate page:

In the ribbon you will see

**WordArt Tools** and the

**Format** tab:

You can modify the text wrapping, so the text will print across the photo:

Click **Text Wrapping**

Click

**In Front of Text**

You can move the text box by dragging it:

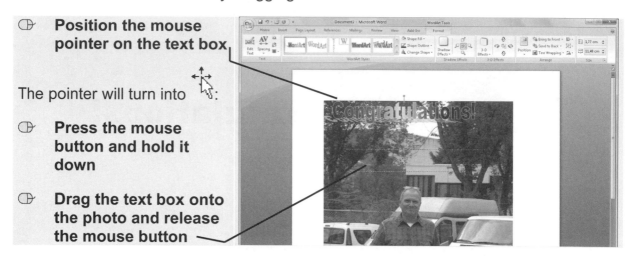

⊕  **Position the mouse
    pointer on the text box**

The pointer will turn into ⬄:

⊕  **Press the mouse
    button and hold it
    down**

⊕  **Drag the text box onto
    the photo and release
    the mouse button**

Next, you will add another text box:

☞  **Insert a WordArt text box in the** *WordArt* **style and enter the following
    text:** 50 years old! ✂³⁴

☞  **Change the text wrapping for the WordArt text box into** 🖼 In Front of Text
    ✂³⁵

## 3.17 Zoom Out

Now you will only be seeing the top section of the photo. If you want to position the
text boxes correctly, it will be easier to zoom out so that you can view the full page:

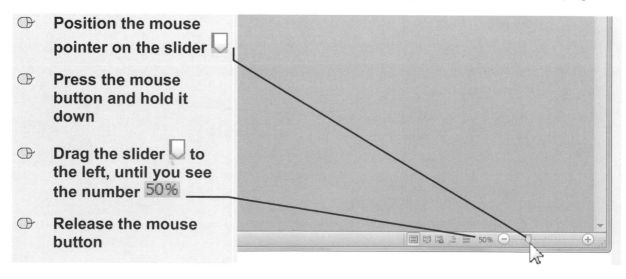

⊕  **Position the mouse
    pointer on the slider** ⬚

⊕  **Press the mouse
    button and hold it
    down**

⊕  **Drag the slider** ⬚ **to
    the left, until you see
    the number** 50%

⊕  **Release the mouse
    button**

Now you will see the full page. Next, you can position the second text box under the photo:

**Position the mouse pointer on the edge of the text box** ——

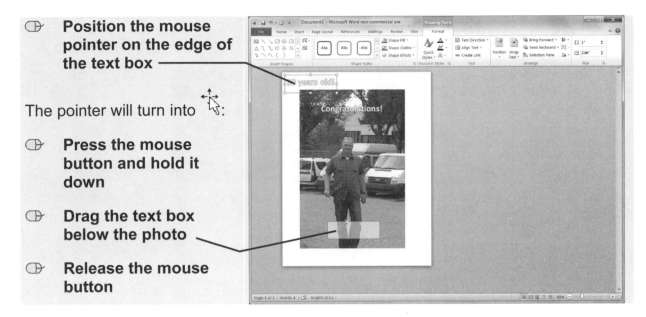

The pointer will turn into ⤧:

**Press the mouse button and hold it down**

**Drag the text box below the photo** ——

**Release the mouse button**

# 3.18 Edit WordArt

There are several ways to edit the WordArt text. This is how to make the letters larger in *Word 2010*:

**Click the uppermost text box three times** ——

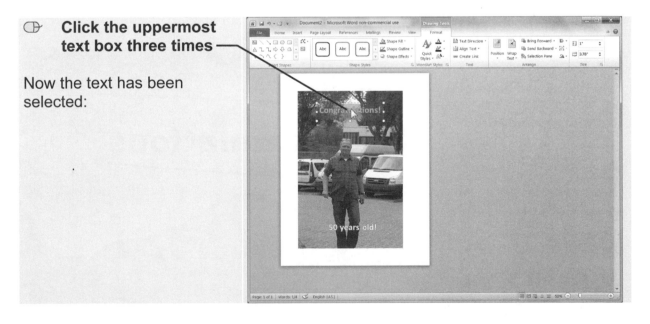

Now the text has been selected:

⊕  **Click the** Home **tab**

⊕  **Click** A⁺

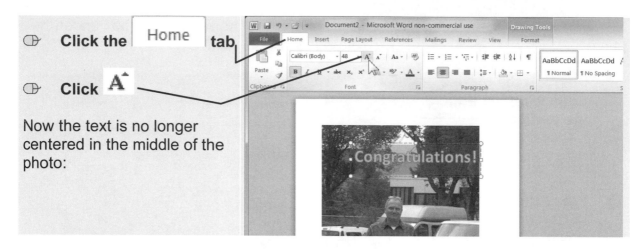

Now the text is no longer centered in the middle of the photo:

This is how you do it in *Word 2007*:

⊕  **Click the uppermost text box**

⊕  **Click** Edit Text

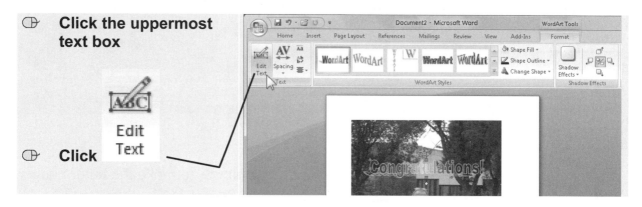

In the *Edit WordArt Text* window you can change the font size:

⊕  **By** Size: **click** ▼

⊕  **Drag the scroll bar down**

⊕  **Click** 44

⊕  **Click** OK

Now you are going to move the text back to the center of the picture:

☞ **Drag the text box to the left** ⚹⁰³⁶

You are going to do the same thing with the text in the bottom box. In *Word 2010*:

☞ **Select the text in the bottom text box** ⚹⁰³⁷

⊕ **Click the** | Home | **tab**

The text box selection is still active.

⊕ **Click** A⁺ **three times**

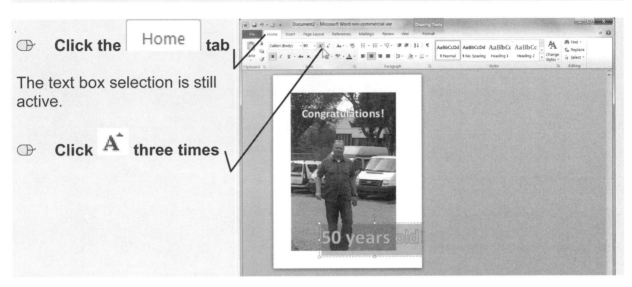

In *Word 2007*:

☞ **Change the font size of the lowest text box to 60 points** ⚹⁰³⁸

Move the text to the center of the picture:

☞ **Drag the text box to the left** ⚹⁰³⁶

If you are not satisfied with the WordArt style you have used, you can quickly select a different style in *Word*. To change the style, first select the WordArt text box:

⊕ **If necessary, click the bottom text box**

⊕ **By** `Drawing Tools` **click the** | Format | **tab**

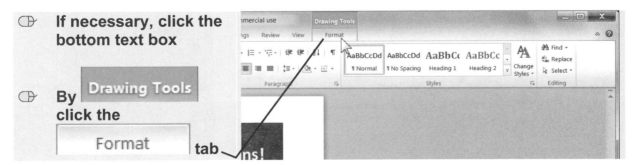

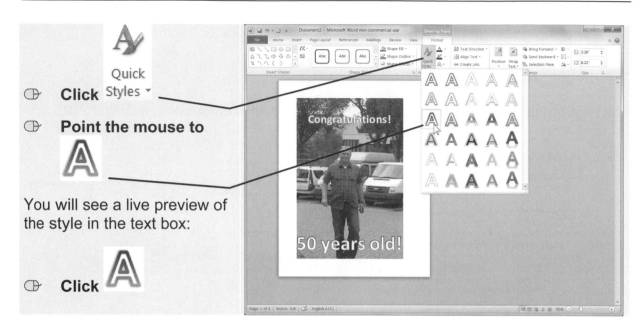

☞ **Click** Quick Styles ▾

☞ **Point the mouse to** 🅰

You will see a live preview of the style in the text box:

☞ **Click** 🅰

In *Word 2007*:

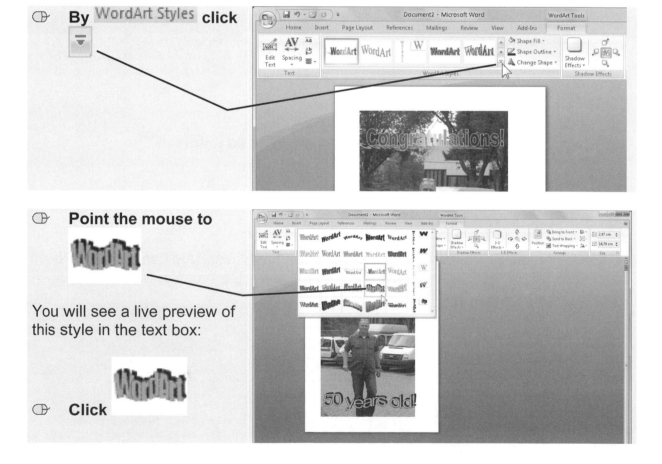

☞ **By** WordArt Styles **click** ⊽

☞ **Point the mouse to** WordArt

You will see a live preview of this style in the text box:

☞ **Click** WordArt

You can also apply a text effect. Here is how to do that in *Word 2010*:

You are going to select an effect from the *Transform* group:

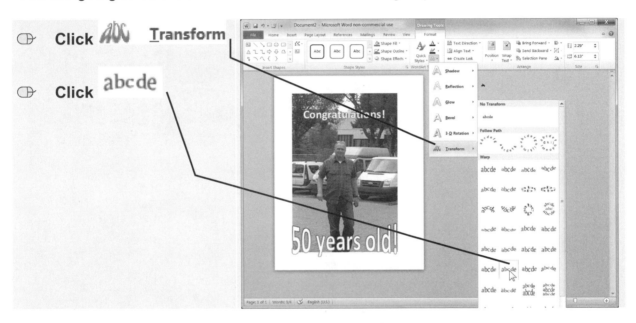

Here you will see the effect:

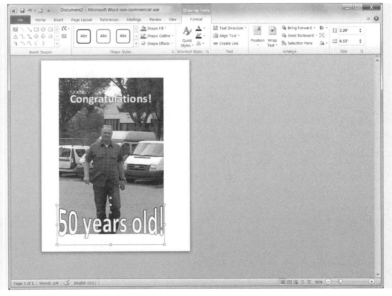

**Tip**

| **Lots of other effects** |
| You can select from a multitude of other effects for your WordArt text. For example, you can add shadow or mirror effects. Or you can apply a colored glow to the borders of the letters. |

In *Word 2007* you can use a similar effect:

Click **Change Shape**

Click

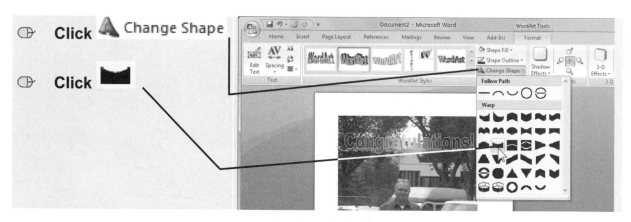

You will see this effect:

# 3.19 Add Illustrations

You can make the poster even more festive by adding colored illustrations. In *Word* you can find lots of free illustrations. Many of these have already been installed onto your computer with your *Office* program. You can download additional illustrations from the official *Office* website, www.office.com. Here is how to add an illustration:

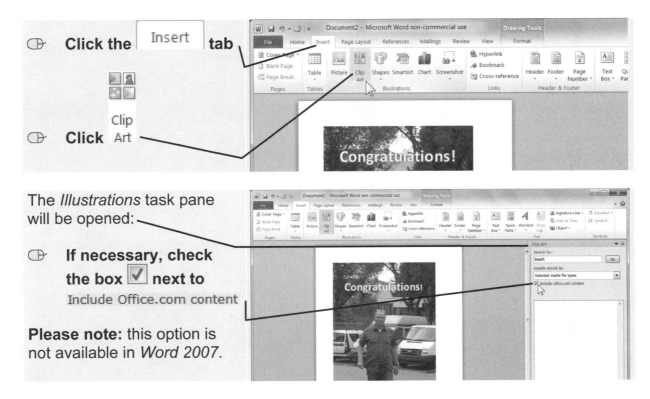

**Click the** | Insert | **tab**

**Click** Clip Art

The *Illustrations* task pane will be opened:

 **If necessary, check the box** ☑ **next to** Include Office.com content

**Please note:** this option is not available in *Word 2007*.

💡 **Tip**

**Downloading illustrations**
If you are connected to the Internet while you are searching for illustrations, you will also find additional illustrations that can be downloaded. Because these files are very small, you will hardly notice the difference between adding an illustration from your hard drive and downloading one from the Internet.

You are going to select an illustration from the birthday category:

👉 **Click the text box**

⌨️ **Type:** balloon

👉 **Click** Go

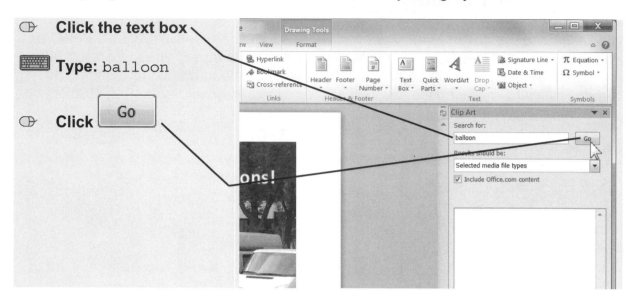

Now you will see the search results. You are going to select a balloon illustration:

👉 **Click the photo**

👉 **Click**

You may perhaps see
different illustrations on your
screen. This will not affect the
following operations.

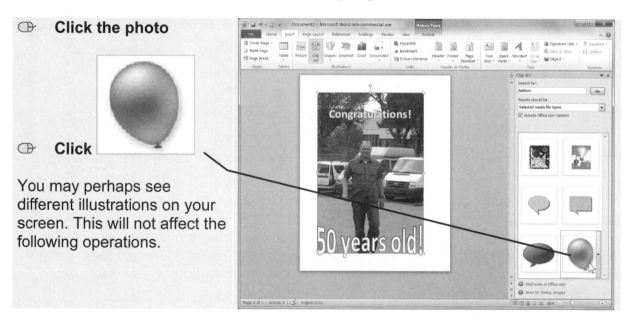

## HELP! In Word 2007 I see just one illustration.

In *Word 2007*, the *Office* collections on your computer will automatically be searched for illustrations. In some cases, there are not many illustrations to be found. You can look for more illustrations in the *Microsoft Office* web collection. Here is how to do that:

- By Search in: click ▾

- Check the box ☑ next to Everywhere

- Click Go

The illustration will be inserted on a separate page:

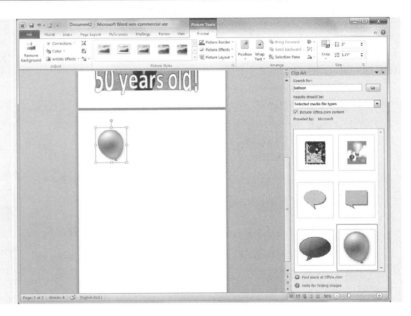

Next, you can change the text wrapping so that the illustration appears in front of the other images:

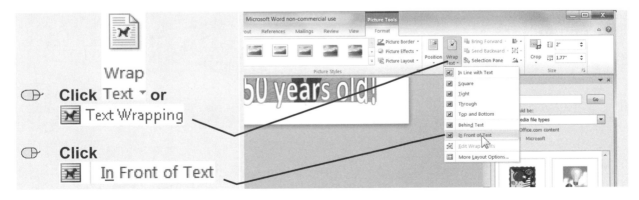

- Click Text ▾ or ☑ Text Wrapping

- Click ☑ In Front of Text

☞  **Drag the scroll bar up**

Now the illustration is shown in the top left corner:

You can close the *Illustrations* task pane:

☞  **Click** ✖

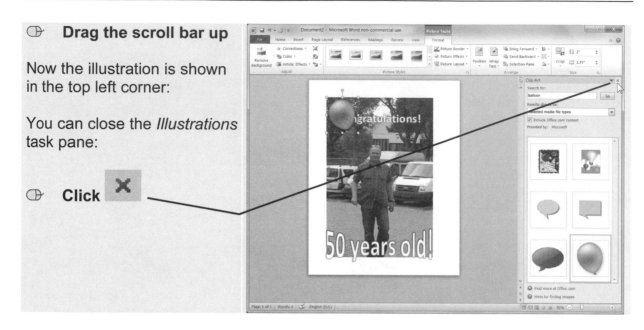

You can enlarge, shrink or move an illustration in exactly the same way as any other image or photo. Here is how to enlarge the illustration a bit:

☞  **Position the mouse pointer on the handle in the bottom right corner**

The pointer will turn into ⬂:

☞  **Press the mouse button down and keep it pressed in**

☞  **Drag the corner handle to the man's head**

☞  **Release the mouse button**

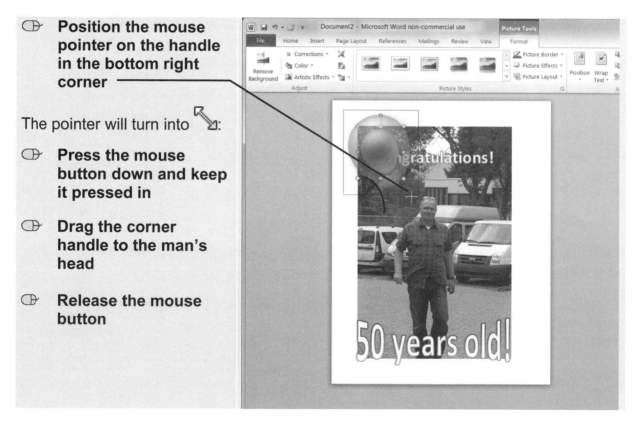

The illustration has become larger. You are going to move the illustration:

 **Position the pointer** on the illustration

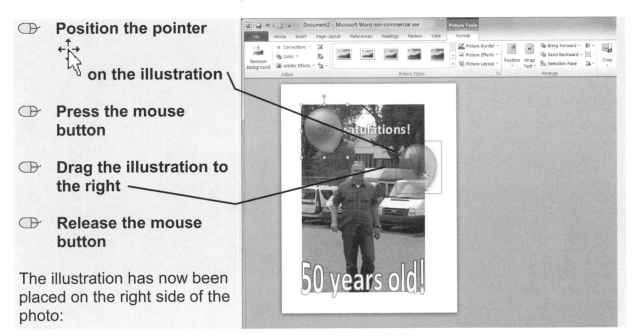

**Press the mouse button**

**Drag the illustration to the right**

**Release the mouse button**

The illustration has now been placed on the right side of the photo:

## Please note:

Do not place the illustration too close to the edge of the page. Otherwise the illustration may end up outside the printable margins of your printer. When you try to print such a page, you may get an error message or if the page does print, only a portion of the illustration shows up.

## 3.20 Delete an illustration

You can easily delete an illustration:

You will need to select the illustration first:

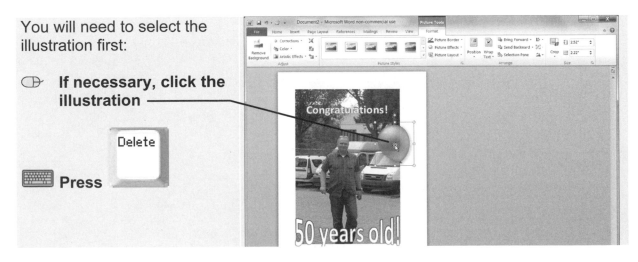

**If necessary, click the illustration**

**Press** Delete

Now the illustration has been deleted:

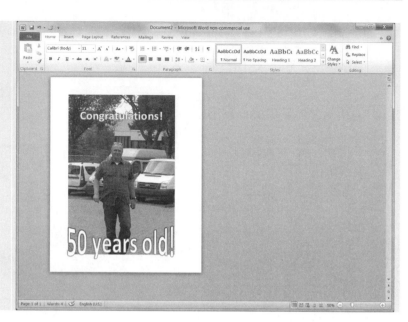

 **Tip**

**Delete a photo or a WordArt text box**
In the same way, you can delete a photo or a WordArt text box.

☞ **Close the document and do not save the changes** ᧚ ³⁹, ⁴⁰

In this chapter you have learned how to insert photos, illustrations and WordArt into a text. In the following exercises you can practice all the operations you have learned above.

## 3.21 Exercises

Have you forgotten how to do something? Then you can use the number next to the footsteps to find the information in the appendix *How Do I Do That Again?* at the back of this book.

## Exercises: Insert and Edit a Photo

In this exercises you will practice inserting a photo into the text and then editing it.

☞ Open the **Monaco** Microsoft Word 13.4 KB document from the *Practice Files* folder. 🐾**43**

☞ Insert the **harbour Monaco** JPEG Image 1.21 MB photo from the *Practice Files* folder. 🐾**33**

☞ Shrink the photo. 🐾 **44**

☞ Select the position at the top left corner. 🐾**45**

☞ Drag the photo to the middle of the text. 🐾**46**

☞ Wrap the text to the right of the photo. 🐾**47**

☞ Crop the bottom of the photo. 🐾**48**

☞ Undo the last operation. 🐾**23**

☞ Change the photo's brightness to +20, and the contrast to 0. 🐾**49**

☞ Render the photo in black and white. 🐾**50**

☞ Delete the photo. 🐾**51**

☞ Close the document, do not save the changes. 🐾**39, 40**

☞ Close *Word*. 🐾**14**

# 3.22 Background Information

**Dictionary**

| | |
|---|---|
| **Brightness** | The relative lightness of a picture. |
| **Contrast** | Difference between opposites, for example, between the lightest and darkest areas of a photo. |
| **Crop** | Making an image larger or smaller by cutting off a piece the image. |
| **Illustration** | A drawing from the *Media Gallery*. |
| **Image** | A synonym for pictures, such as illustrations or photos. |
| **Rotation handle** | With this handle you can rotate an image. |
| **Sizing handle** | The markers that appear at the borders of a selected image. You can enlarge or shrink the image by dragging the handles. |
| **Text wrapping** | The way in which a text is wrapped around an image. |
| **Washout effect** | Turn a photo into a very faint image. You can use the resulting image as a watermark which will appear in the background of the text. |
| **Web collection** | A collection of illustrations which is part of the *Office* program; additional images can be downloaded from the Office.com website. |
| **WordArt** | WordArt is a gallery of text styles. You can add these styles to the text in your documents to create artistic texts, such as shadow or mirrored effects. |

*Source: Word and Windows Help and Support*

# 3.23 Tips

 **Tip**

**Rotate an image**
Apart from moving an image in the text, you can also rotate the image.

To do this, you need to use the rotation handle at the top border of the selection frame of the selected image.

☞ **Position the mouse pointer on**

☞ **Press the mouse button**

You will see a black circular arrow.
Now you can rotate the image by keeping the mouse button pressed down and simultaneously dragging it a bit.

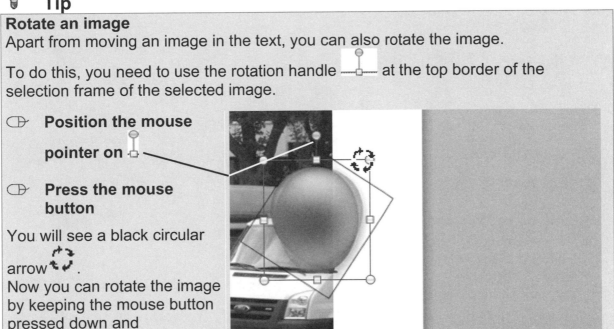

 **Tip**

**Picture styles**
After you have inserted an image, you can apply a special style to this image. You can find the commands on the *Format* tab:

☞ **Click the picture**

☞ **Click the** `Format` **tab**

In the `Picture Styles` group you will see many different kinds of effects that can be applied to the selected picture.

For instance, borders and frames and even three-dimensional shapes and shadow effects. Just try these options by yourself and experiment a bit, for example by creating a sample document and inserting a photo or illustration of your own.

**Tip**

**Inserting a screenshot**

*Word 2010* contains an option to create screenshots and insert them directly into your *Word* document:

☞ **Click the** Insert **tab**

☞ **Click** Screenshot

Now you will see all the opened windows on your desktop:

☞ **Click a window**

The window will be inserted right away:

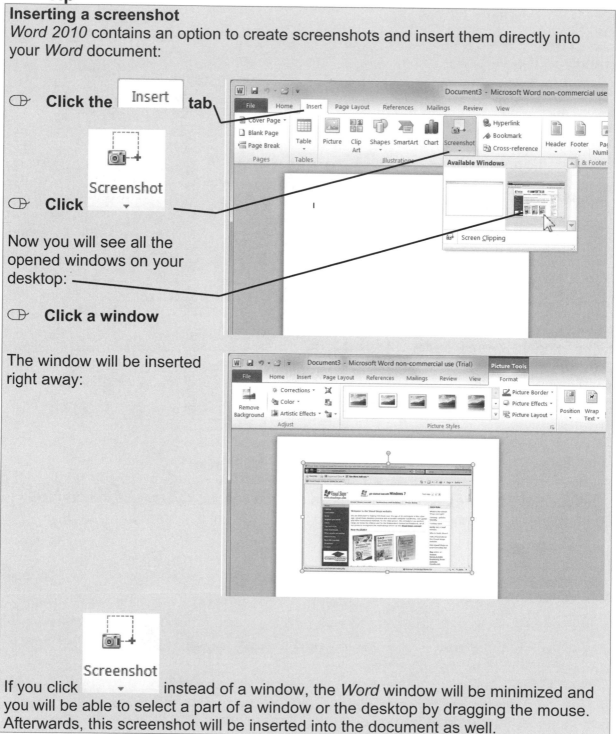

If you click Screenshot ▾ instead of a window, the *Word* window will be minimized and you will be able to select a part of a window or the desktop by dragging the mouse. Afterwards, this screenshot will be inserted into the document as well.

# 4. Using Templates

In *Word* you will find many useful tools. For instance, you can quickly and easily create letters and other frequently used documents by using *templates*.

A template is a sample document which contains a number of predefined elements. These elements may include the page layout, fonts, styles and margins as well as image formatting. When you compose a letter, for example, you can build in a predefined area for the address and salutation. You can edit a template yourself, which is usually less time-consuming then drafting an entire document from scratch.

Several templates will be installed automatically on your computer when you install the *Office* package. Many more templates are available for free from the *Office* website: www.office.com. You do not need to close *Word* to download these templates.

In this chapter you will learn how to work with various templates for drafting a letter, a greeting card, an inlay for a CD and a booklet. The actions you perform while working with these templates can be applied to each and every template you use in the future.

In this chapter you will learn how to:

- view the available templates;
- open a template;
- fill in a template;
- correct the data you have entered;
- record your name in *Word*;
- change the template's theme;
- download a template;
- insert a photo;
- delete a content box;
- print a greeting card on both sides;
- add a page to a template;
- paste copied text with the *Paste Special* function;
- create and print a booklet.

# 4.1 Open a Template

Each new document is based on a template. In this format the font type, font size, paragraph layout, and so on, are predefined. In the previous chapters you have worked with the *Normal* template. This is *Word's* default template that is applied each time you open a new blank document.

But a template can also contain text, images, or content boxes. You can choose from various templates for letters, greeting cards, newsletters, booklets, memos, faxes, and many other document types.

☞ **Open *Word* ⬿¹**

Take a look at some of the templates that are already installed on your computer:

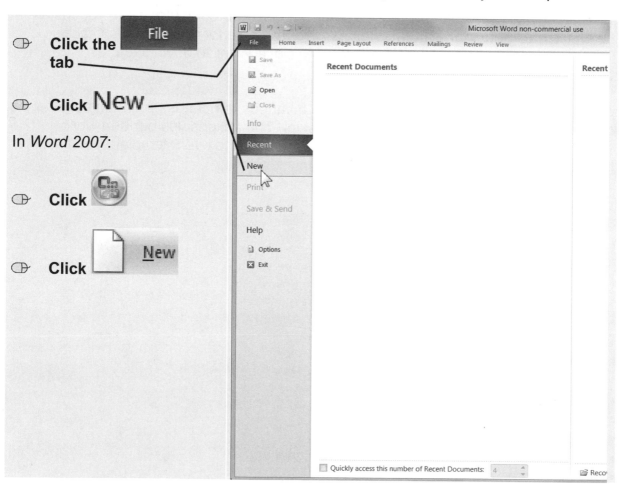

By default, *Blank document* is already selected. *Word* has set this template as the basis for a new document.

⊕ **Click** Sample templates

In *Word 2007*:

In the top left of the window:

⊕ **Click**
**Installed Templates**

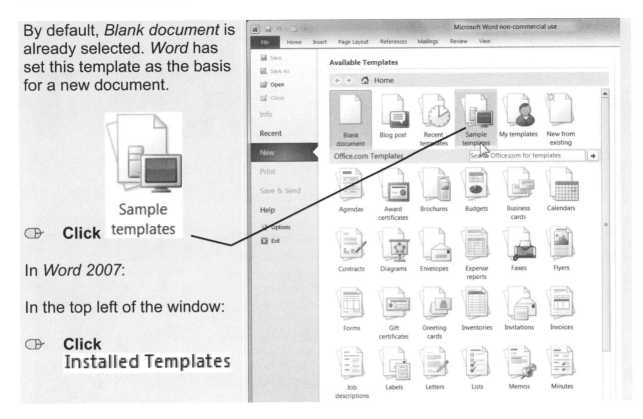

## 🢂 Please note:

The available templates may vary for each computer. This depends on the way in which *Word* has been installed. You may see more or fewer templates on your own computer.

You will see the available templates:

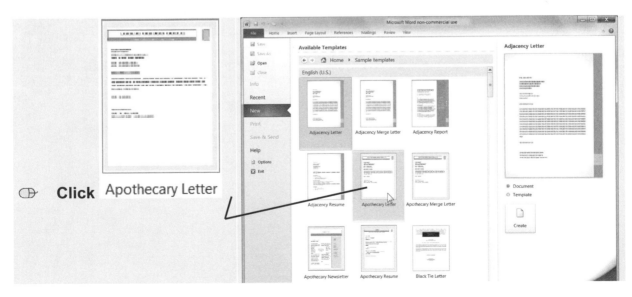

⊕ **Click** Apothecary Letter

**If necessary, click the radio button ⊙ next to Document**

**Click Create**

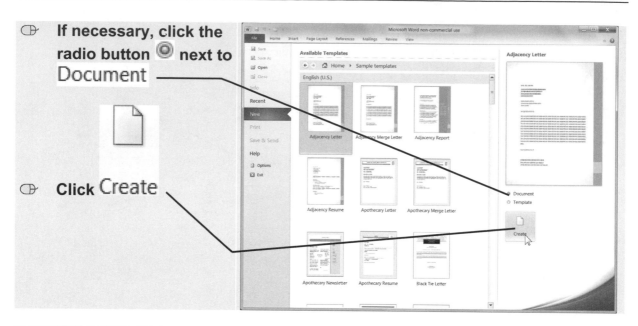

This neat and ordered letter will be opened in a new window:

In the text you will see a number of content boxes, between square brackets [ ]:

In these boxes you can enter your own data.

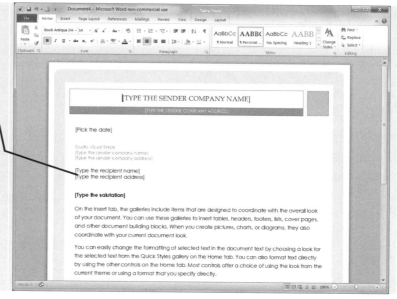

## 4.2 Fill in a Template

It is very easy to enter data in a document that has been created from a template. You are going to fill in the data in the letter. Start with the company or club name:

**Click**
[TYPE THE SENDER C

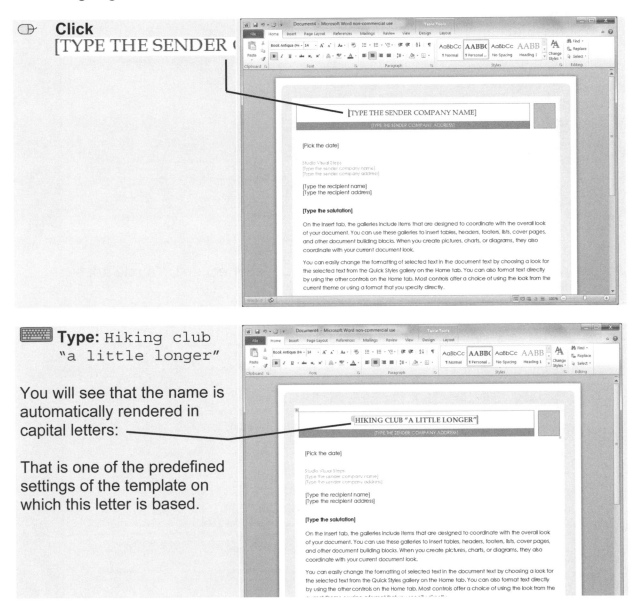

**Type:** Hiking club "a little longer"

You will see that the name is automatically rendered in capital letters:

That is one of the predefined settings of the template on which this letter is based.

 **Tip**

**Basic text editing operations**
Do you have problems typing quotation marks? Then read *Bonus chapter 9 The Basics of Text Editing*. You will find this chapter on the website that accompanies this book: **www.visualsteps.com/officeseniors** In *Appendix C Opening the Bonus Online Chapters* you can read how to open this file.

Type the club's address as well:

**Click**
TYPE THE SENDER COMPANY A

**Type this in one sentence:**
`98 Buchanan Place,`
`37924 New York`

The address in the header is also rendered in capital letters:

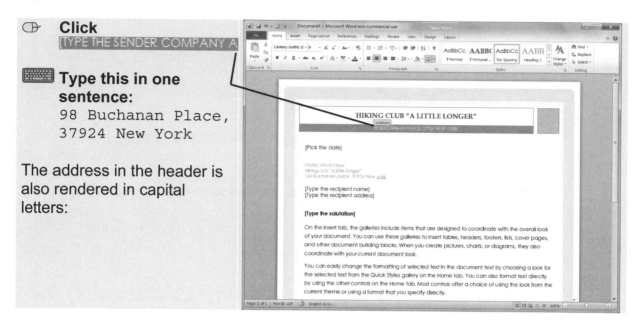

In this way you can click each [ ] box and enter the correct text. You do not even need to enter the date:

**Click** [Pick the date]

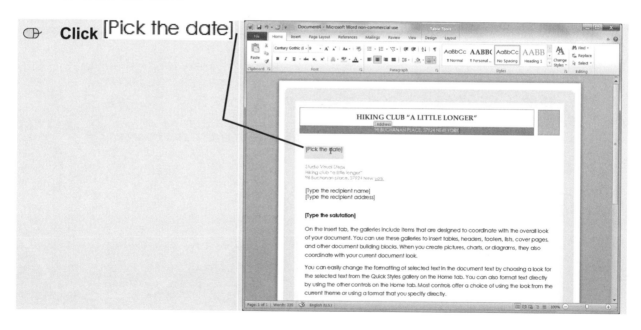

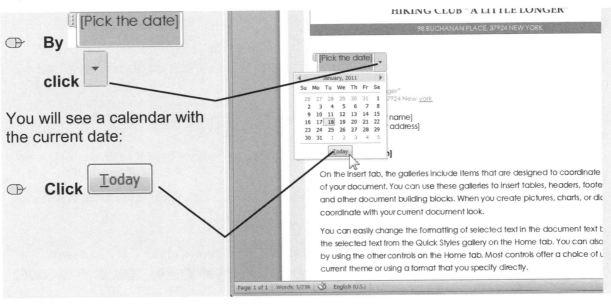

☞ **By** click

You will see a calendar with the current date:

☞ **Click** Today

The date has automatically been entered:

You will see a different date on your own screen.

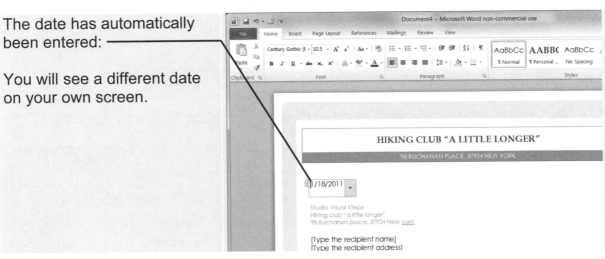

💡 **Tip**

**Select a different date**
With the calendar you can select any date you want:

☞ **Click ◀ or ▶ to select the desired month**

☞ **Click the desired day**

Now the date will automatically be inserted into the text.

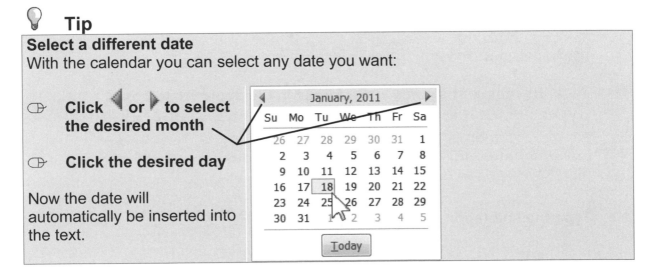

# 4.3 Correcting the Data

If you take a good look at the letter, you will see that a number of items have been entered automatically:

Here you will see a name, in this example it is Studio Visual Steps. You will see your own name, or a blank box.

Here you will see the text you have entered in the letter's heading:

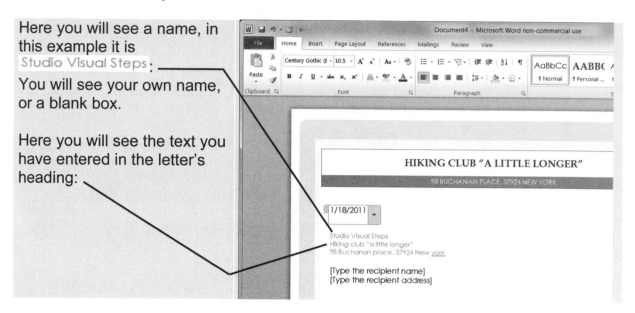

The hiking club's name is written in lower case letters. Here is how to correct this:

**Click** Hiking club "a little lon **three times**

Now the content of the box has been selected:

**Type:**
Hiking Club "A Little Longer"

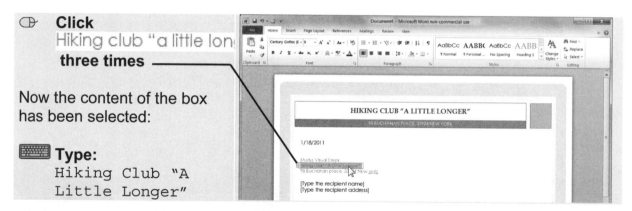

☞ **Type the recipient's name and address in the appropriate boxes**
[Type the recipient name] **and** [Type the recipient address] &52
Peter Johnson
160 Buchanan Place
New York, NY 37924

☞ **Type the salutation** Dear Peter, **in the** [Type the salutation] box &52

Now the letter looks like this:

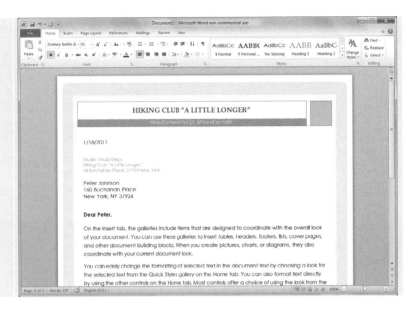

You have noticed that you can easily fill in and correct the content boxes. You can do the same thing with the main section of the letter:

☞ **Click the first paragraph**

The main section of the text will be selected:

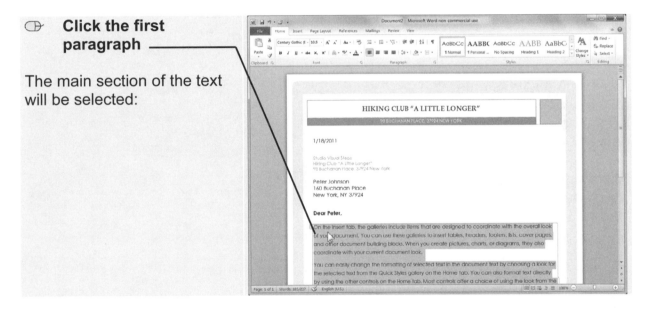

As soon as you start typing, the selected text will be replaced:

**⌨ Type:**
Following our
telephone
conversation, I am
sending you a map with
directions for a
stroll in Central
Park.

☞ **Drag the scroll bar down**

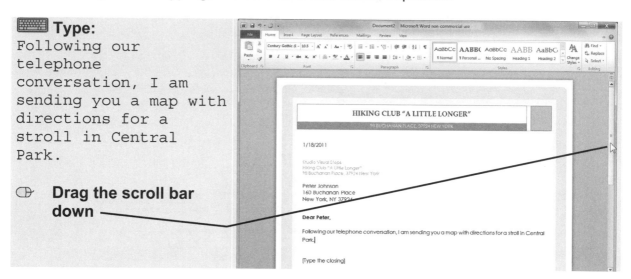

☞ **Type the conclusion for the letter:** With kind regards, **in the** [Type the closing] **box** 𝓰𝓸52

☞ **Type the title** Secretary **in the** [Type the sender title] **box** 𝓰𝓸52

The name that was entered as the sender's name in the letter's heading is repeated here: ——

The hiking club's name is also repeated (in capital letters): —

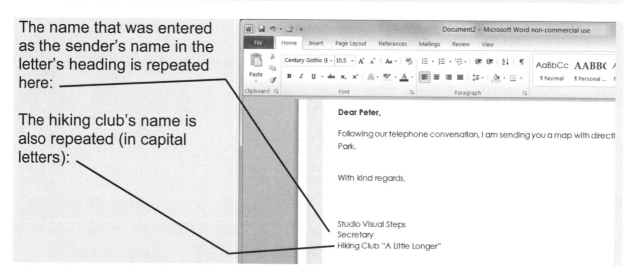

You have learned how to use a template to quickly and easily create a professional, clean-looking document. Now you can close the letter:

☞ **Close the document and do not save the changes** 𝓰𝓸**39, 40**

# 4.4 Add the Author Name in Word

You have seen that the template will automatically contain a name. If this is the wrong name, you can change it with the *Word* options. This name will then be entered correctly in all the subsequent templates you will be using.

**Click the** **File** **tab**

**Click** 📋 **Options**

In *Word 2007*:

**Click**

**Click**
📋 **Word Options**

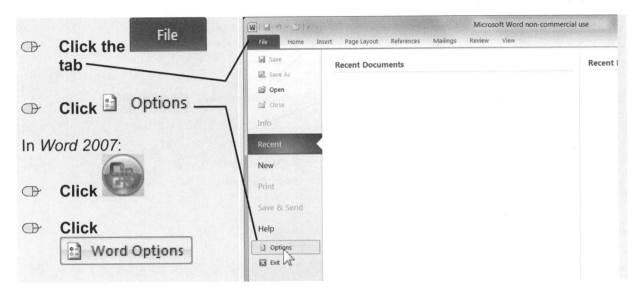

The *Word Options* window will be opened:

By **User name:** you will see the name that has been entered in the letter:

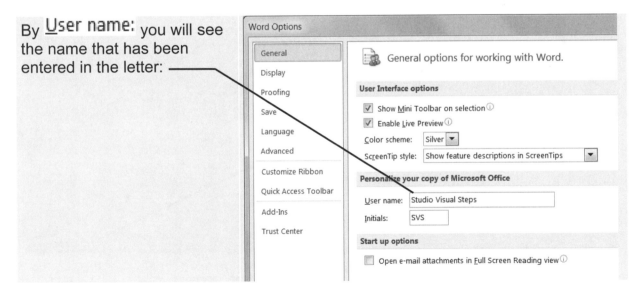

If the name in this box is incorrect, you can change the name:

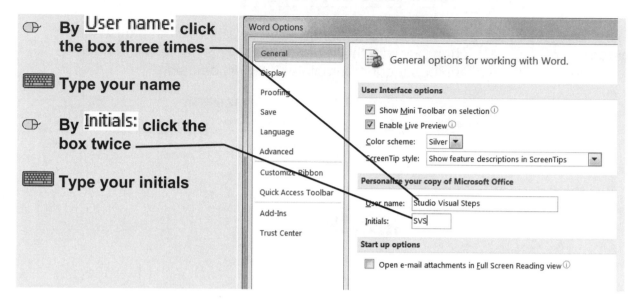

☞ **By** ~~**User name:**~~ **click the box three times**

⌨ **Type your name**

☞ **By** ~~**Initials:**~~ **click the box twice**

⌨ **Type your initials**

Now you can save the changes:

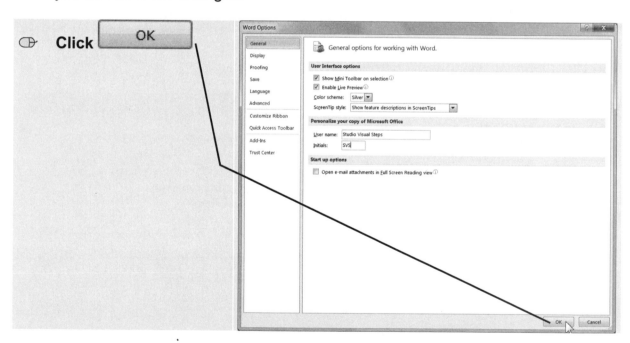

☞ **Click** [  OK  ]

Next time you use a template, your name will be entered correctly.

# 4.5 A Newsletter Template

Among the various templates installed on your computer with the *Office* package, are templates for letters, curriculums, faxes, reports and newsletters. Take a look now at a newsletter template:

☞ **Open a document based on the** Apothecary Newsletter **template** ✂53, 54

You will see a newsletter in the same style as the letter you have created previously:

All elements in this newsletter can be modified, in the same way as the letter you have typed.

The navigation pane on the left has been opened. You can close it now:

⌨ **Click** ✖

Just check if the correct name has been entered on the second page of the newsletter:

⌨ **Drag the scroll bar down** ————

Here you will see the name you have recorded in *Word*:

⌨ **Drag the scroll bar up again**

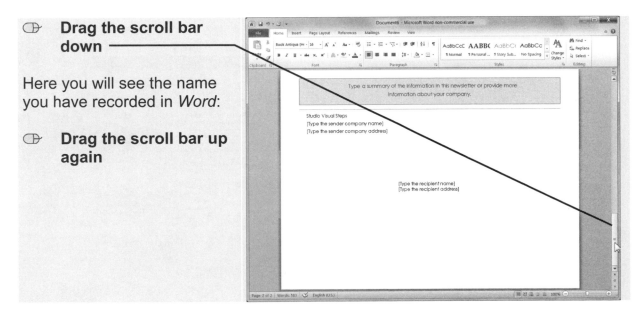

# 4.6 Change the Theme

If you are not entirely satisfied with the colors of your document, you can easily change the *theme*. A theme contains colors, shapes, and fonts. Just try it:

Click the

Page Layout **tab**

Click

You will see some of the available themes:

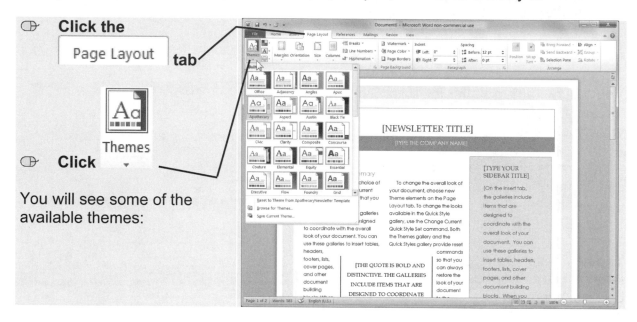

By selecting a different theme, the document will look totally different:

**Move the pointer over a few of the themes**

You will see a live preview of the theme in the newsletter:

Click **Angles**

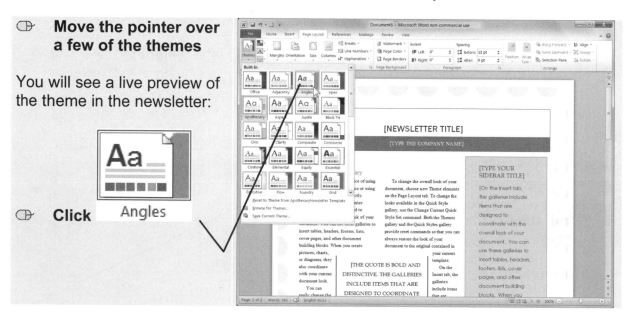

Now you will see the new look of the newsletter:

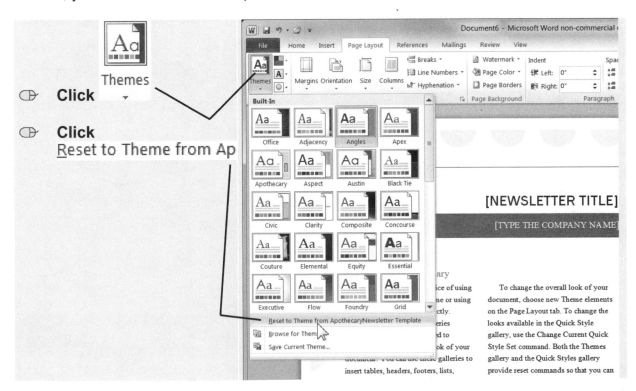

 **Tip**

**Change the theme afterwards**
You can also change the theme after you have completely filled in the template.

If you have tried out various themes and you want to return to the template's original theme, you can follow these steps:

☞ **Click** Themes

☞ **Click** Reset to Theme from Ap

You will see the original colors again:

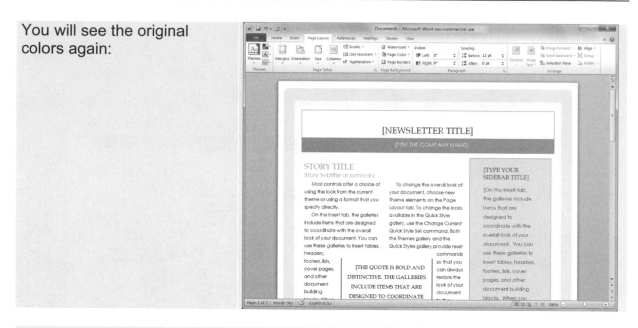

☞ **Close the document and do not save the changes** ✂️**39, 40**

# 4.7 Download Templates

The templates that are included in the *Office* installation on your computer are mainly intended for use in a business environment. But you can download other templates for personal use:

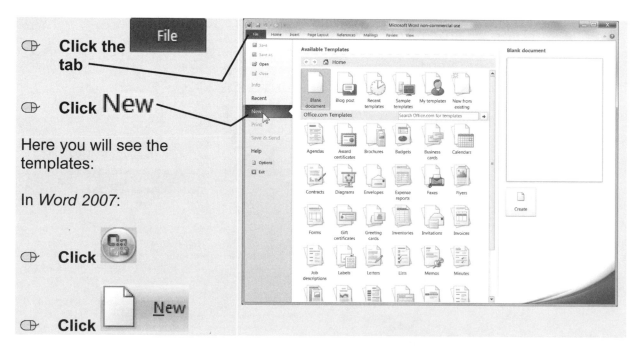

⊕ **Click the** `File` **tab**

⊕ **Click** New

Here you will see the templates:

In *Word 2007*:

⊕ **Click**

⊕ **Click** `New`

Take a look now at a template from the *Cards* category:

**Drag the scroll bar down**

**Click** Cards

In *Word 2007*:

**By Microsoft Office Onl** click Greeting cards

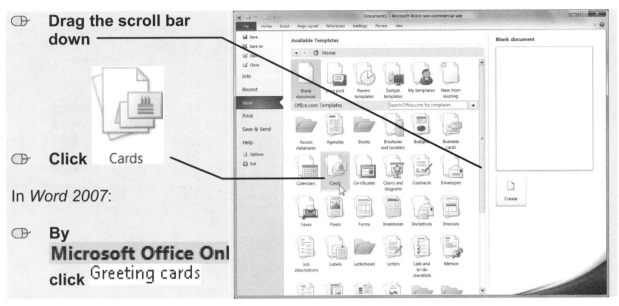

**Click** Thank you cards

In *Word 2007*:

**Click** Thank you cards

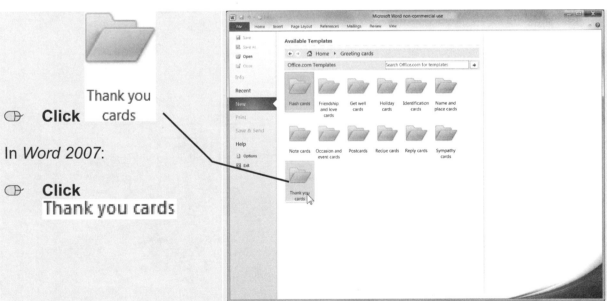

Now you will see the available templates. In this example, we will select the card with the tree design and photo:

**Click**

Photo greeting card (tree design, half-fold)

**Click** Download

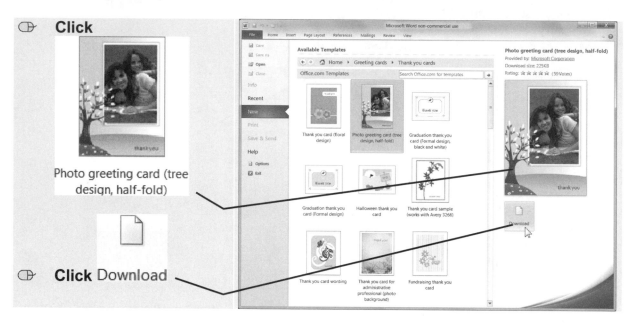

Now the template will be downloaded.

After a few seconds you will see the thank you card:

The card consists of two pages.

Here you see the instructions for printing and folding the card:

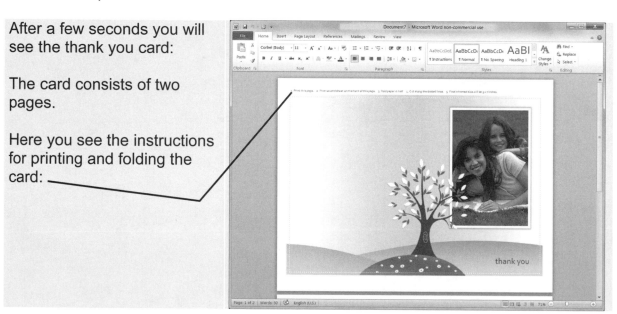

You can also replace the photo in the card with one of your own. Just try this with one of the sample pictures in the *Practice Files* folder:

☞ **Click the photo**

☞ **By** Picture **click**

Now the *Insert Picture* window will be opened:

☞ **Click** Documents

☞ **Double-click** Practice Files File folder

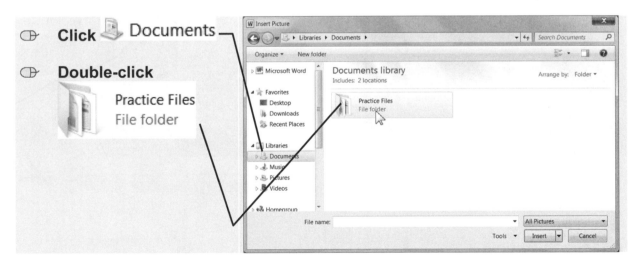

Select one of the sample photos:

 **Drag the scroll bar down** ——————

 **Click**

sisters

JPEG Image

3.24 MB

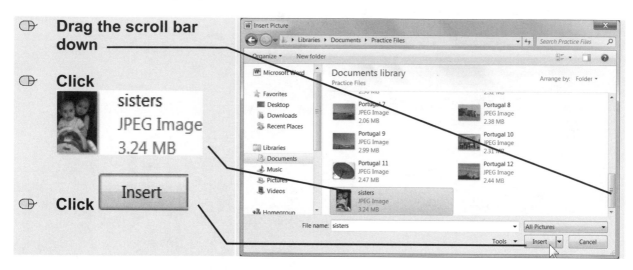

 **Click** Insert

The photo will appear almost immediately inside the card:

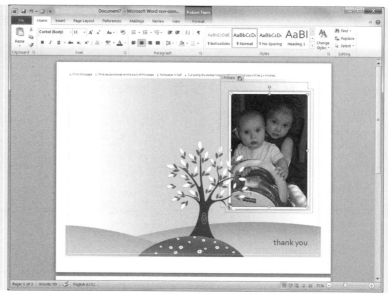

## 💡 Tip

**Change the theme**
If you feel the colors in the card do not match the photo, you can select a different theme that more closely matches the photo.

# 4.8 Delete a Text Box

You can type the data in this card in the same way as in the letter. If you want to write the inside of the card by hand, you can remove the text box on the inside:

☞ **Drag the scroll bar down** ⎯⎯⎯

You will see the card's second page:

☞ **Click the text** ⎯⎯⎯

You will see a frame around the text:

☞ **Click** 🔲 ⎯⎯⎯

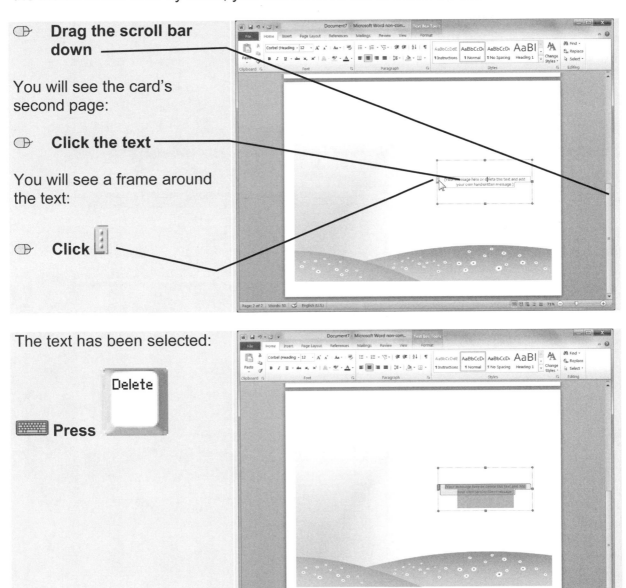

The text has been selected:

⌨ **Press** `Delete`

The text has been deleted:

Now only the text box is visible on the page. When you print the card, this box will not be visible. But if you want, you can remove the text box like this:

☞ **Click the edge of the text box**

The pointer will turn into :

The dotted line surrounding the text box has disappeared:

⌨ **Press** Delete

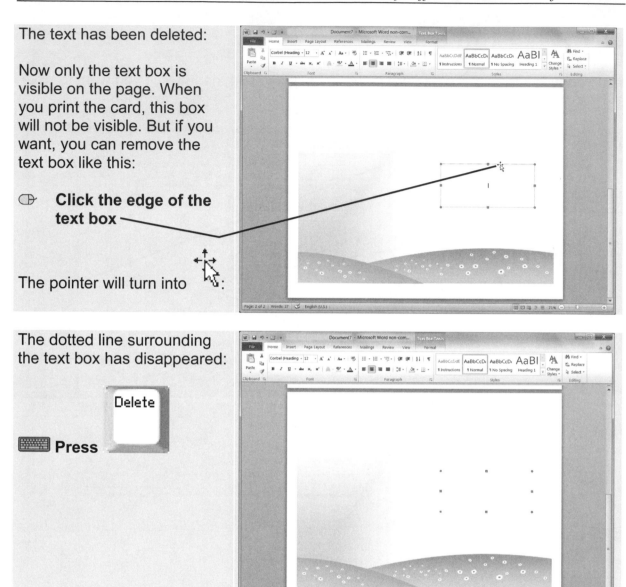

The text box has been removed.

## 4.9 Print a Greeting Card on Both Sides of the Paper

If you have finished with the greeting card, you can print it. Here is how to print the card on both sides of the paper:

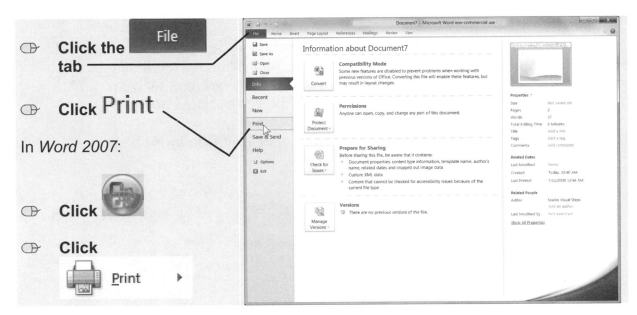

- ☞ **Click the File tab**

- ☞ **Click** Print

In *Word 2007:*

- ☞ **Click**

- ☞ **Click** Print ▸

You are going to change the setting to *Manually Print on Both Sides*:

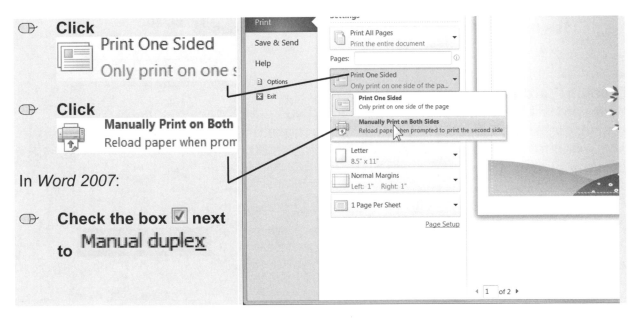

- ☞ **Click** Print One Sided — Only print on one s

- ☞ **Click** Manually Print on Both — Reload paper when prom

In *Word 2007:*

- ☞ **Check the box ☑ next to** Manual duplex

If you would like to print the card:

☞ **Print the card** ✂25

As soon as the first page has been printed, you will see this message:

 **Please note:**

Watch closely and check in which position the first page came out of the tray. With most printers, the second page will be printed correctly if you place the first page in the input tray in the same position as before. If this does not happen with your printer, you will need to experiment a bit, to find the correct input position.

☞ **Place the printed page in the printer's paper tray (the input tray)**

Now you can continue printing:

 **Click** OK

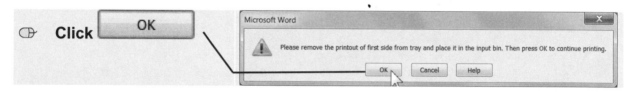

The second page will be printed on the back of the first page. When the page has properly dried, you can cut out the card along the dotted line, and fold it in the middle.

☞ **Close the document and do not save the changes** ✂³⁹, ⁴⁰

💡 **Tip**

**Greeting card paper**
Your card will become even more attractive if you print it on special greeting card paper. This paper is strong and shiny and suited for printing on both sides. You can also buy packages with both the paper and matching envelopes.

Photographic paper is less suitable, because you can only print on one side of this paper.

# 4.10 Inlay for a CD Case

Another useful template is the template you use to make an inlay for a CD case. If you regularly burn your own CDs, you can quickly and easily create a matching cover. This template can be found in the *Labels* folder:

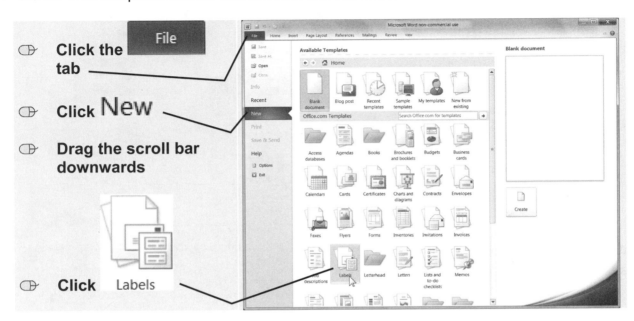

⊕ **Click the** **File** **tab**

⊕ **Click New**

⊕ **Drag the scroll bar downwards**

⊕ **Click** Labels

In *Word 2007*:

⊕ **Click** , **New**

⊕ **By Microsoft Office Online click** Labels

You are going to open the case inserts category:

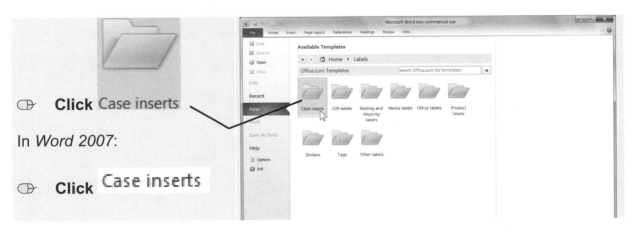

⊕ **Click** Case inserts

In *Word 2007*:

⊕ **Click** Case inserts

You will see the available templates. Select the first case insert:

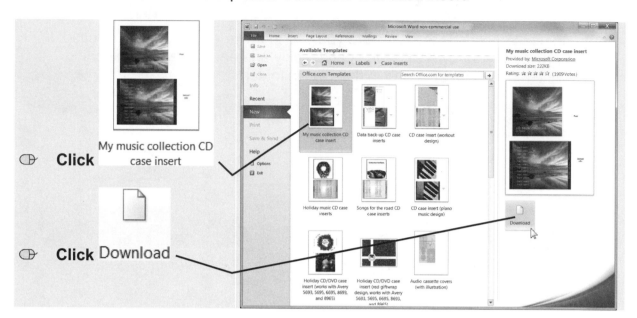

⊕ **Click** My music collection CD case insert

⊕ **Click** Download

After a few seconds you will see the front of the CD cover:

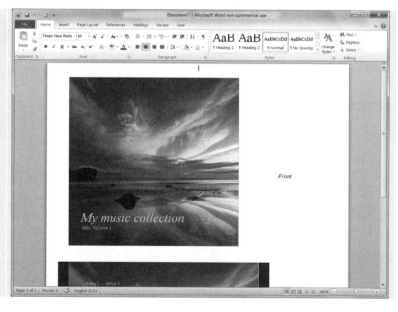

**Drag the scroll bar down**

Now you will see the back of the cover, where you can type the names of the songs and the artists:

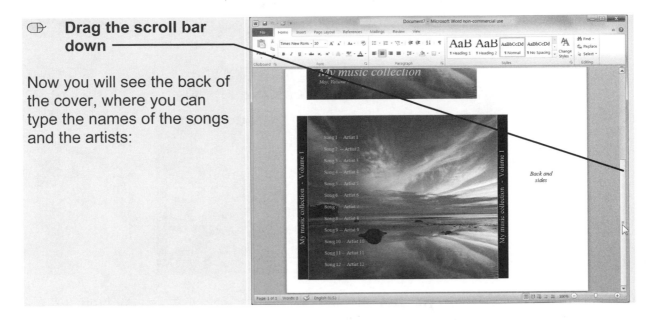

You can change the text on the CD cover in the same way you changed texts in other documents. This also goes for the vertical text on the side of the CD cover:

**Click** three times

**Type:** On the road music

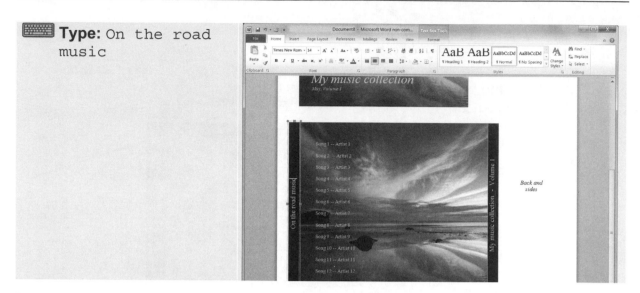

If you fill in the entire cover, you can print it, cut it out and fold it. This way, you can organize your entire collection of self-burned CDs.

☞ **Close the document and do not save the changes** ⚏⁣³⁹, ⁴⁰

💡 **Tip**

| More templates |
| --- |
| By now, you have seen various templates. Just take your time and have a look at all the available templates. What about gift coupons, certificates or business cards? Be sure to check out some of the additional categories in the template section on the *Office* website. There you will find lots of additional folders and more templates. |

# 4.11 A Book Template

Among the templates in the *Available Templates* folder you will find a few book templates as well. Just take a look at these templates:

☞ **Open the *Books* folder within the *Other books* folder** 🔗**55, 56**

You will find a number of book templates:

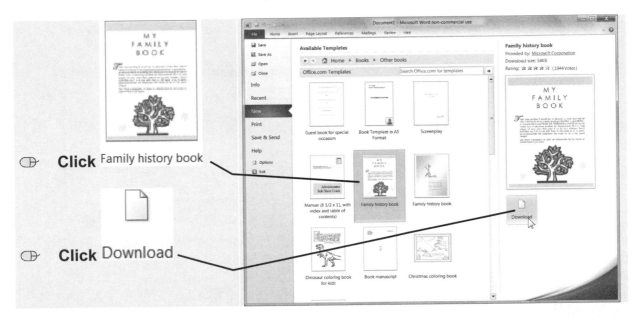

☞ **Click** Family history book

☞ **Click** Download

You will see the first page of the family history book:

This is one of the most extensive templates, the book consists of 23 pages to which you can add text and photos:

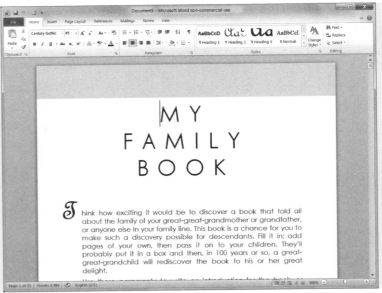

☞ **Take your time and browse through the book**

**Tip**

**Insert photos**

You can fill in the *Family History Book* template in the same way as the other templates you have used in this chapter. If you want to add photos, you will need to do it in the way we have discussed in *Chapter 3 Pictures in a Document*. For instance, the photo box on page 5:

🖱️ **Click the box**

👉 **Insert a photo** ✂️³³

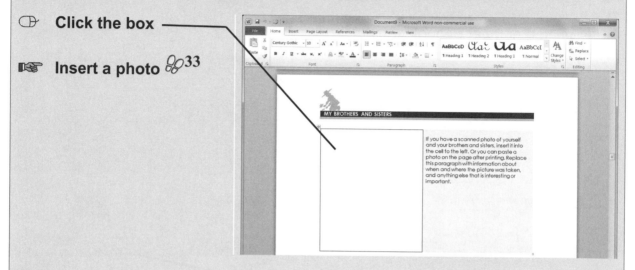

When the photo is inserted, the size of the image may not be automatically adjusted to fit the photo box:

The photo stretches the box out somewhat:

You have learned how to solve this problem:

👉 **Shrink or enlarge the image by using the sizing handles** ✂️⁴⁴

You can also crop the photo, if you need to.

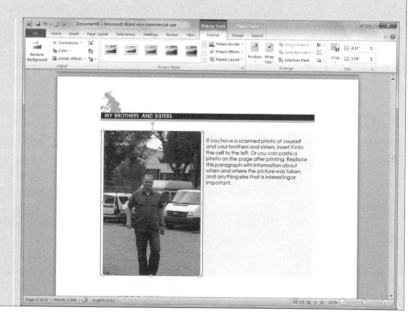

## 4.12 Add a Page To a Book

If the book does not have enough pages for your entire family history, you can easily add new pages. You can do this by copying and pasting an existing page. Just try to do this with the last page of the book:

☞ **Zoom out to 50% of the page size** ✇57

Now you will see two pages next to each other:

☞ **Drag the scroll bar all the way down** ——

Now you will see the book's last page:

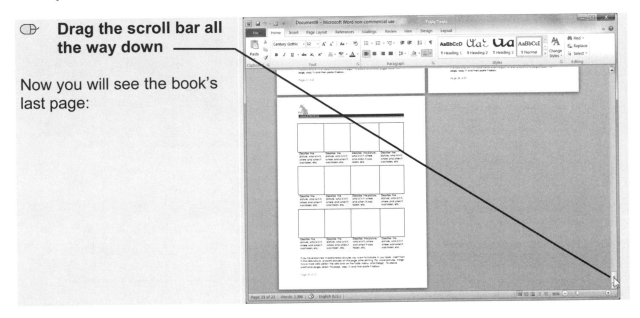

Copy the last page:

☞ **Position the mouse pointer in the margin next to the image** ——

The pointer will turn into ⤢:

☞ **Press the mouse button and keep it pressed in**

☞ **Drag the mouse downwards** ——

☞ **Release the mouse button**

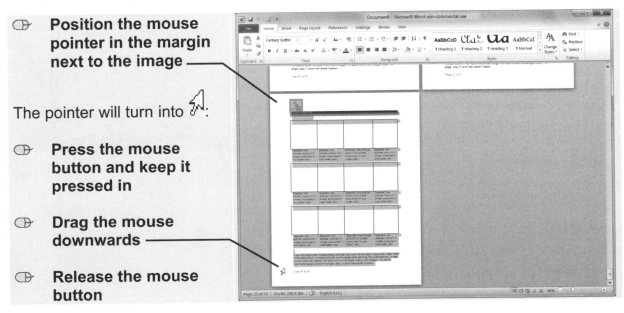

You have selected the text and the images on the page. Now you can copy the page:

☞ **If necessary, click the** Home **tab**

☞ **Click** 

Now the page has been copied to the clipboard.

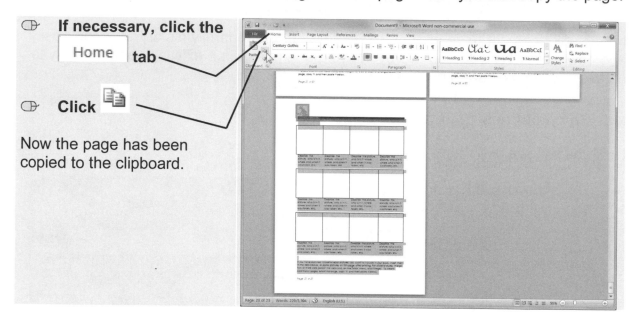

Place the copied page in back of the last page:

☞ **Click a spot next to the last sentence**

⌨ **Press** Enter ←

A new, blank page will be added:

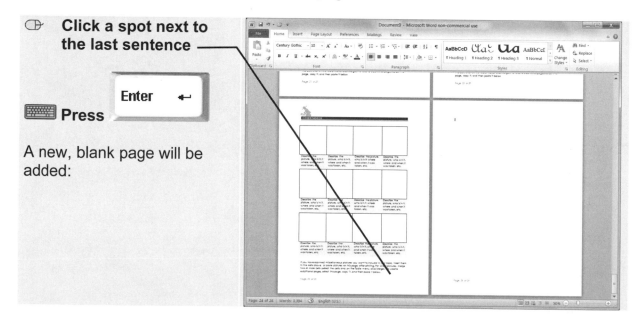

Now you can paste the copied page:

 **Click** 

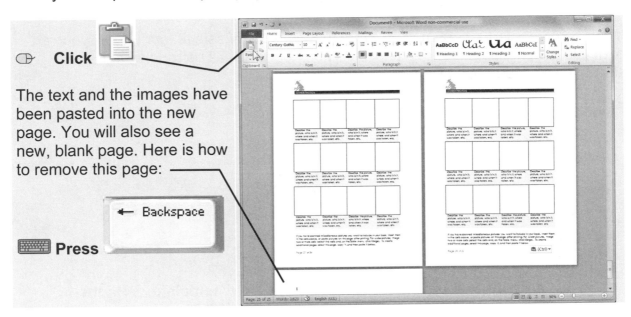

The text and the images have been pasted into the new page. You will also see a new, blank page. Here is how to remove this page: ——

← Backspace

**Press**

Now the book consists of 24 pages.

☞ **Close the document and do not save the changes** 🐾39, 40

💡 **Tip**

> **Use photos and text to tell your story**
> Does this family tree book give you some ideas? Do you want to write your own personal history as well, but you're not sure how to begin? In that case, Visual Steps has just the right book for you!
>
> In the book **Creating a Photo Book for Seniors** (ISBN 978 90 5905 247 5, available fall 2011) you will find a number of ideas to inspire you. For example, on how to write a travel narrative, a personal history, a baby diary, a wedding album, an anniversary book or a family cookbook.
>
>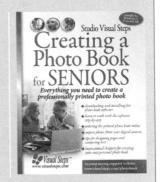
>
> Use the free album software to record your personal stories, including photos and illustrations. An online print service will provide you with a professionally printed and nicely bound book!
>
> In this book you will learn step by step how to use the free album software, how to transfer photos from your digital camera to your computer and how to scan photos. We also provide numerous writing tips and lay out examples. Never before has it been so easy to record your own unique (illustrated) story in a beautiful edition!

# 4.13 Set Up Your Document as a Booklet

If you have created a document in *Word* that consists of sets of four pages, you can print this document as a folded booklet. The paper size will be roughly half of the standard US paper size of 8.5" x 11".

Start by opening a new template:

☞ **Open a document based on the** Report (Equity theme) **template, from the Reports, Project and status reports category** 🔗**58, 59**

You will see the first page of the report:

In *Word 2010* the report consists of three pages. In *Word 2007* the report will consist of two pages.

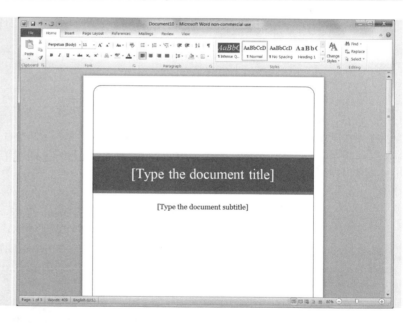

☞ **View all of the report's pages**

First, you are going to adapt the page size to the folded booklet size:

- **Click the** Page Layout **tab**

- **By** Page Setup **click**

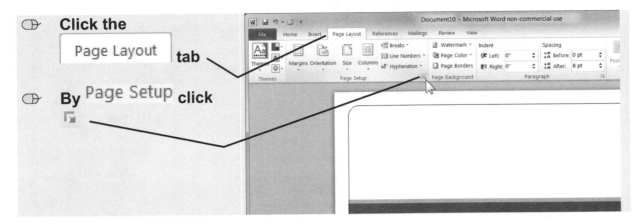

The *Page Setup* window will be opened:

- **By** Multiple pages: **click** ▼

- **Click** Book fold

- **Click** OK

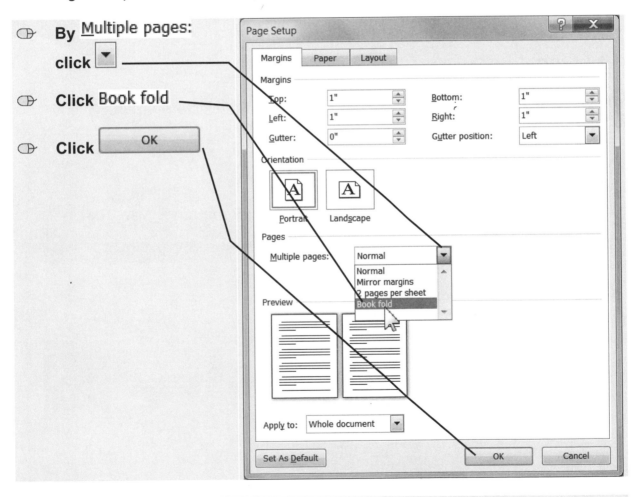

☞ **Zoom out to 50% of the page size** 🕮57

Now you will see the report in the folded booklet format:

Since the pages have become smaller, but the font size has remained the same, you will not be able to fit as much text onto a single page.

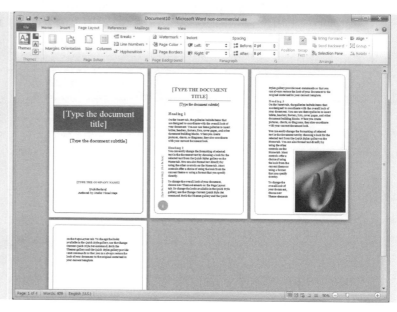

# 4.14 Copy Text From the Internet

You can see what happens when you add text to this booklet by copying some text from the Internet. This will save you some time typing.

☞ **Open *Internet Explorer*** ✇60

☞ **Open the website http://en.wikipedia.org/wiki/Rembrandt_Van_Rijn** ✇61

Here you will see the *Wikipedia* website, the online encyclopedia:

The text contains many blue hyperlinks. When you click one of these links, a page concerning that topic will be opened.

## Please note:

Some websites contain copyrighted texts.

First you are going to select the text you want to copy:

- **Position the mouse pointer at the beginning of the first sentence**

- **Press the mouse button and keep it pressed in**

- **Drag downwards until you reach the**
  **Name and signature**
  **paragraph**

- **Release the mouse button**

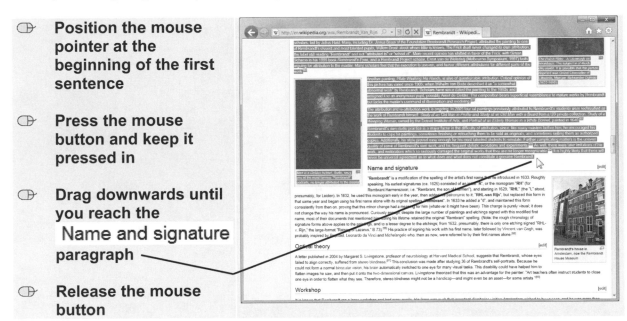

Now you can copy the text:

**Alt**

- **Press**

- **Click** Edit

- **Click** Copy

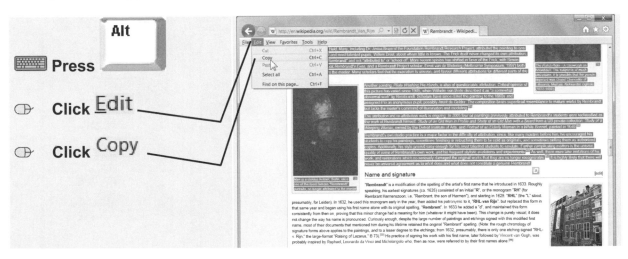

The text has been copied. Now you are going to return to *Word*:

- **On the task bar, click** [W] **(*Word 2010*) or** [W] **(*Word 2007*)**

Indicate the spot where you want to paste the copied text:

⊕⊦  **Click the main text of the report**

You will see that right away the entire text is selected:

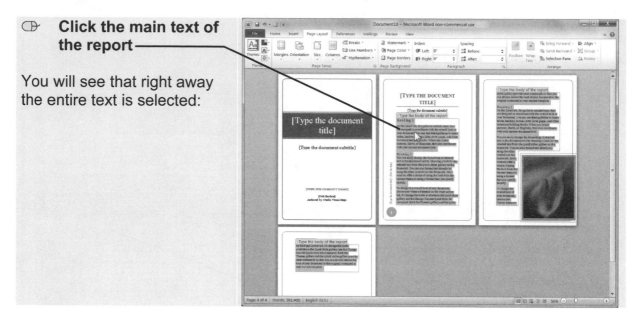

Now you are going to copy the text:

⊕⊦  **Click the** Home **tab**

⊕⊦  **Click**

The text will be pasted:

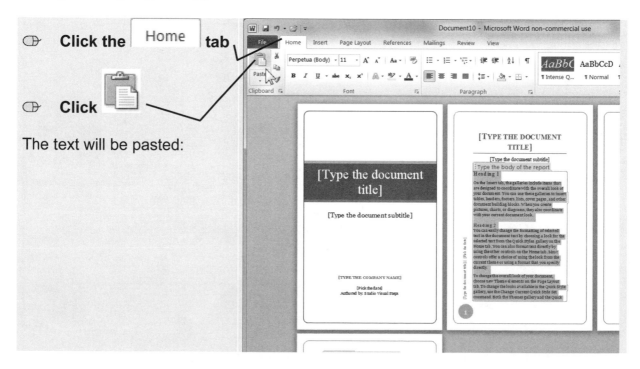

You will see that all the blue hyperlinks have also been copied:

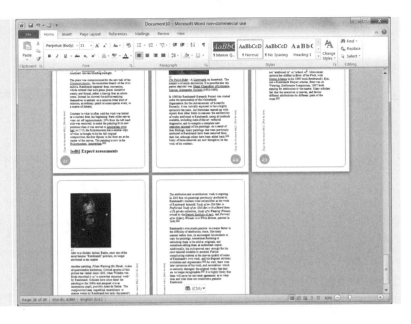

You can delete the hyperlinks one by one, as you have learned previously, but that is a lot of work! There is an easier solution:

☞ **Undo the last operation** 🦶**23**

It is much more convenient to copy text from a document or a website with the *Paste Special* command. This way, you can make sure that the text will take on the formatting of the document where the text is pasted. Here is how to do that:

👆 **By** 📋 **click Paste** ▾

👆 **Click**
**Paste Special...**

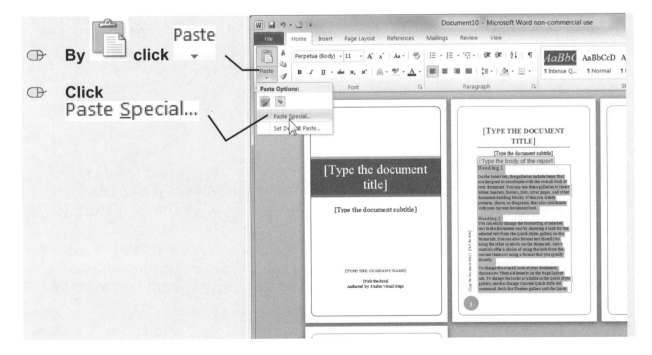

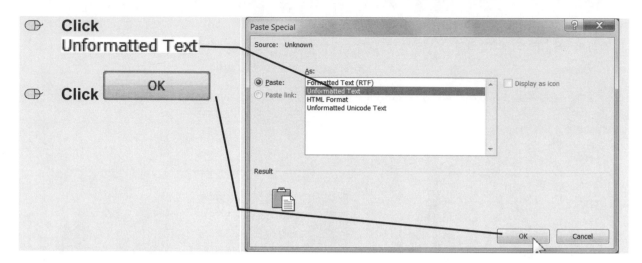

**Click** **Unformatted Text**

**Click** OK

Now the text will be pasted once more, but without the website's formatting:

You will see this result:

Now the text has been pasted into the report, without any hyperlinks or other graphics.

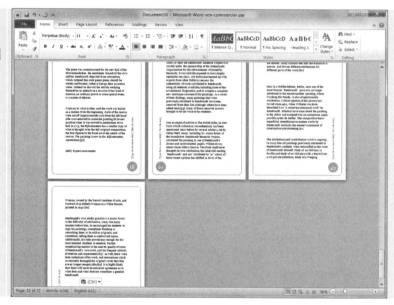

## Please note:

If you copy text from another document, or from the Internet, you will need to read this text very carefully. For example, a *Wikipedia* page may contain many footnotes. These notes will be inserted into the text as a number, such as Dutch history.[2].

For the purpose of this exercise, the content of the report is not important. You have created a nineteen of twenty-page document, which you are going to print as a booklet with text on both sides. In the following section you will learn how to do this.

☞ **Close *Internet Explorer*** 🦶14

# 4.15 Print Your Document as a Booklet

In case of a folded booklet, four pages will be printed on both sides of a single sheet. The first sheet will contain page 1 and page 8 on one side and page 2 and page 7 on the other side. If you would have to print a 36 page book, you would need to make a lot of calculations. Fortunately, *Word* can do this for you.

Previously, you have changed the page setup to *Book fold*. If you tell *Word* to print the pages manually, on both sides, they will automatically be put in the right order.

☞ **Click the** **File** **tab**

☞ **Click Print**

In *Word 2007*:

☞ **Click**

☞ **Click**

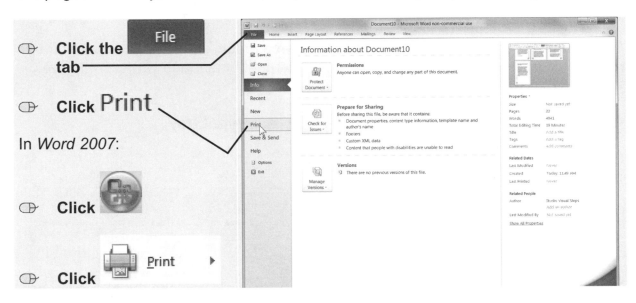

Change the setting to *Manually Print on Both Sides*:

☞ **Click** Print One Sided — Only print on one sid

☞ **Click** **Manually Print on Both** — Reload paper when pror

In *Word 2007*:

☞ **Check the box** ✔ **next to** ☐ Manual duple**x**

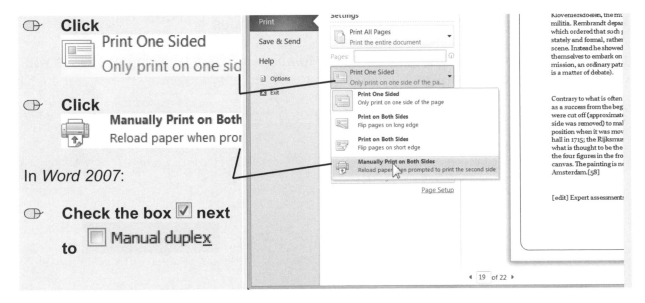

You do not need to print this document if you do not want to. If you decide to print the document, you can do that as you learned in *Chapter 2 Writing and Printing a Letter*. With a booklet you will probably see the following windows:

When the first four pages have been printed, you will see this message:

 **Please note:**

Make sure to place the pages in the tray in reverse order. The page that was printed first should now be put on top of the stack. Underneath that page you should have the page that was printed second and so forth.

☞ **Put the printed pages in your printer's paper input tray**

Continue printing:

👉 **Click** OK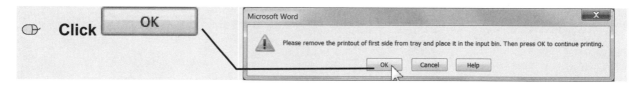

Now the back side of the pages will be printed. Afterwards you can put all the pages in the right order and staple them together.

☞ **Close the document and do not save the changes** ℘℘ 39, 40

In this chapter you have learned how to use templates. In the following exercises you can practice the operations you have just learned.

# 4.16 Exercises

Have you forgotten how to do something? Then you can use the number next to the footsteps to find the information in the appendix *How Do I Do That Again?*

## Exercises: Using and Printing a Template

In this exercise you can practice filling in a template and printing the document on both sides.

☞ Open a document based on the Family newsletter template, from the *Newsletters* category. 🐾**58, 59**

☞ Select the text OUR FAMILY NEWSLETTER. 🐾**62**

☞ Type the text Family news.

☞ Insert the *Sisters* photo in the first photo box. 🐾**33**

☞ Insert the *Beach* photo in the photo box on the second page. 🐾**33**

☞ Shrink the images by using the sizing handles. 🐾**44**

☞ Select the text in this box:

Family Name
Street Address, Address 2, City, ST ZIP code
Phone - (555) 235-0125
Fax - (555) 235-0125
E-mail address

🐾**62**

☞ Type your own name and address and other data.

If you want to print the newsletter:

☞ Print the newsletter on both sides. 🐾**63, 64**

☞ Close the document and do not save the changes. 🐾**39, 40**

☞ Close *Word*. 🐾**14**

## 4.17 Background Information

| **Dictionary** | |
|---|---|
| **Book fold** | A page layout that is used to convert your document into a booklet. This layout ensures the correct printing order for the booklet. |
| **Content box** | A box with a predefined format, in which you can enter your own data. |
| **Half letter** | You can use the half letter size for the production of booklets. The paper dimensions are half the size of the standard letter size. |
| **Hyperlink** | A navigational tool on a website that will connect the user to information in a different location. When a hyperlink is clicked, you will jump to another section of the same webpage or a new webpage will be opened. |
| **Letter** | The letter size is one of the most commonly used paper sizes in the US. The dimensions are 8.5" x 11". |
| **Template** | A sample document which contains predefined elements such as text boxes and image boxes. |
| **Theme** | A theme is a combination of colors, fonts and graphical effects. You can apply a theme to a file as a single unit. |
| **Wikipedia** | Online encyclopedia that is edited and maintained by users. |

*Source: Word and Windows Help and Support*

## 4.18 Tips

 **Tip**

**Templates**
*PowerPoint* and *Excel* also contain a variety of templates.

# 5. Bookkeeping

The strength of *Microsoft Excel* lies in its ability to perform calculations. *Excel* is also known as a 'spreadsheet program'. *Spread* means that the text is spread out over multiple columns, in a *sheet*. In fact, a spreadsheet looks like a big sheet of graph paper. In each of the boxes or *cells* you enter data. This could be in the form of numbers, values, text, or underlying formulas that calculate information from other cells. A spreadsheet is an ideal tool for creating a summary or a report for further analysis.

In this chapter you will learn how to create a simple household budget. When you enter the correct formulas, the totals are rapidly and accurately calculated. *Excel* also provides simple tools to present data pictorially (as charts or graphs). This helps you see more easily how well your earnings and expenses are developing.

In this chapter you will learn how to:

- distinguish columns, rows, and cells;
- move the cursor and select cells;
- enter numbers and text;
- change the column width and insert columns;
- create ranges;
- add, subtract, divide and enter formulas;
- round off figures;
- adapt and copy formulas;
- use *Sum* for automatic additions;
- copy, rename and save workbooks;
- use data from a different workbook in your calculations;
- format cells and use borders and padding;
- use conditional formatting;
- create, move and modify a chart;
- print a workbook.

 **Please note:**

If you want to do the exercises in this chapter, you will need to download the corresponding practice files from the website that goes with this book. Download the files to your computer and store them in the (*My*) *Documents* folder. In *Appendix A Downloading the Practice Files* at the back of this book you can read how to do this.

## 5.1 Opening Excel

Here is how to open *Excel*:

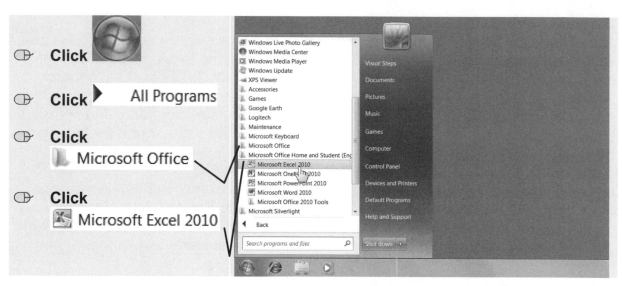

Click

Click ▶ **All Programs**

Click
**Microsoft Office**

Click
**Microsoft Excel 2010**

You will see the *Excel* window:

The top part of the window contains the *Ribbon*:

In *Chapter 1 The Office Programs* you have already learned how to customize the ribbon and the *Quick Access* toolbar.

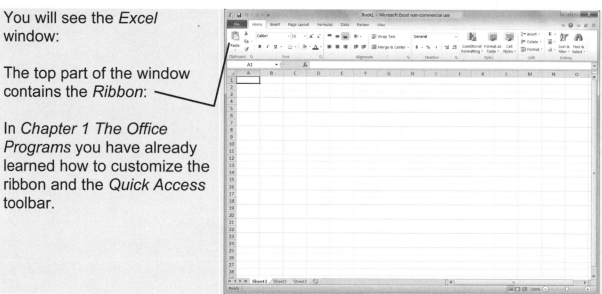

# 5.2 Select Cells

Below the ribbon you will see the *Excel* worksheet:

The worksheet looks like a sheet of graph paper or grid. Each worksheet is divided into columns, rows and cells.

The first cell has a bold outline: ——

This means the cell is currently selected.

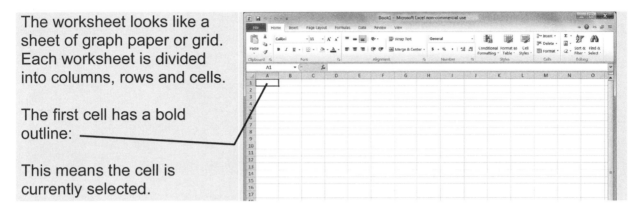

A worksheet consists of columns (vertical) and rows (horizontal). The columns are indicated by letters, the rows are indicated by numbers:

Above the selected cell you will see ⬚ A ⬚. This cell is in column A: ——

To the left of the cell you will see ⬚ 1 ⬚. This will tell you that the selected cell is in row 1: ——

So, the selected cell is called cell A1. In the top of the toolbar, you will also see this name in the *Name Box*: ——

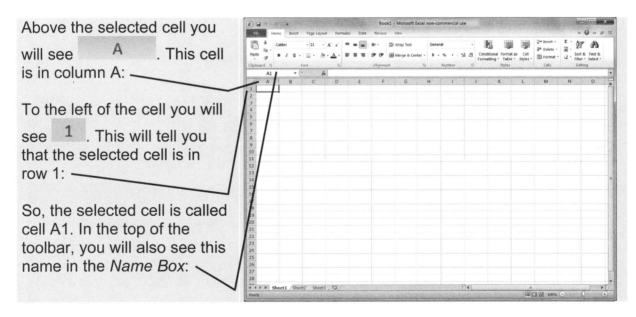

You can select a different cell with the arrow keys:

Arrow keys ——

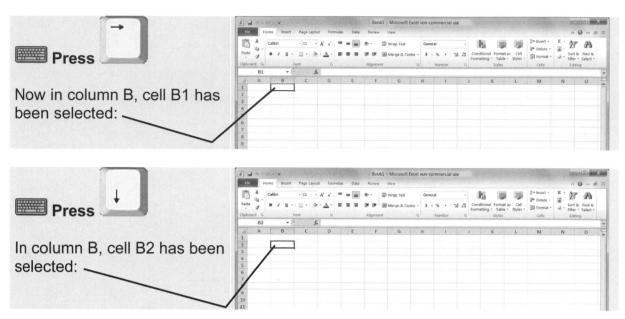

**Press**

Now in column B, cell B1 has been selected:

**Press**

In column B, cell B2 has been selected:

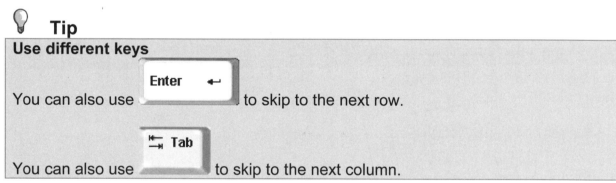

## Tip

**Use different keys**

You can also use **Enter** to skip to the next row.

You can also use **Tab** to skip to the next column.

Or you can simply select a cell by clicking it with the mouse pointer:

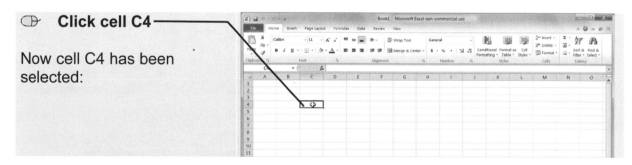

**Click cell C4**

Now cell C4 has been selected:

## Please note:

Do not forget to click the cell. If you merely hover the mouse over the cell, you will not select the cell. Once you have clicked the cell, its outline will become bold and the cell will be selected.

There are other ways of quickly selecting a specific cell. Use this key to jump to the first cell in the same row:

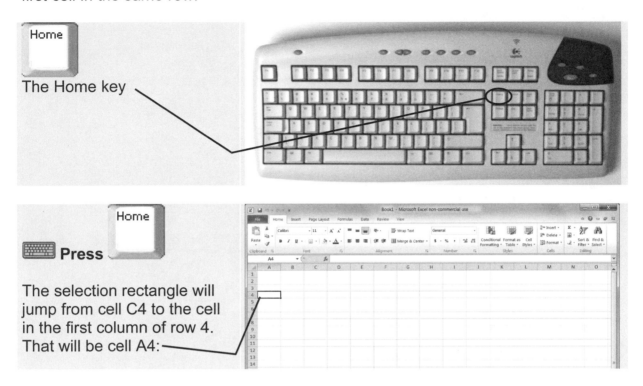

The Home key

Press

The selection rectangle will jump from cell C4 to the cell in the first column of row 4. That will be cell A4:

You can also select cell A1 at once. Use the following key combination:

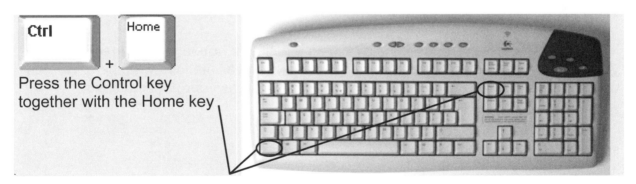

Press the Control key together with the Home key

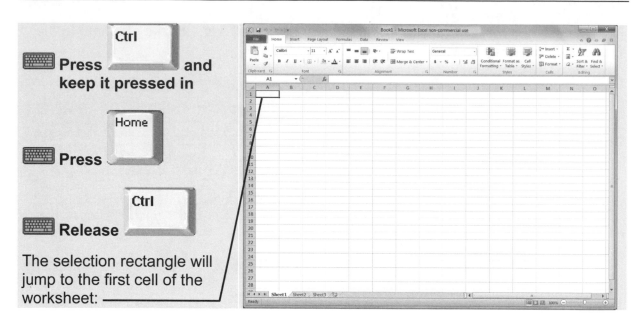

## 5.3 Enter Text

You can enter various data types in a cell, for instance:

- numerical values with which you can make calculations;
- text for names, comments or descriptions;
- dates.

You can practice these operations by creating a simple household budget. This way, you will learn how to enter data in *Excel* and perform calculations with the data. You will start by entering the title for the column that contains your housing costs:

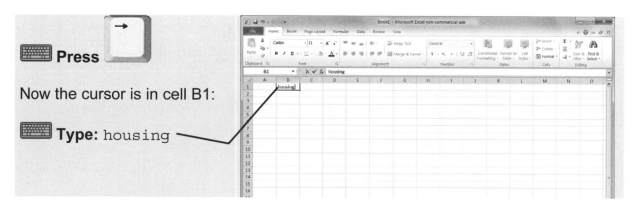

## HELP! I have made a typing error.

You can easily correct typing errors with the **← Backspace** key.

**Please note:** do not press **←** or **Enter ←**. This will move the cursor to a different cell.

Has the cursor already moved to another cell?

☞ **Click the cell once again**

⌨ **Type the correct text**

Now you can select the cell next to cell B1 and enter text in this cell as well. This will be the column where you enter the expenses for your car or public transportation:

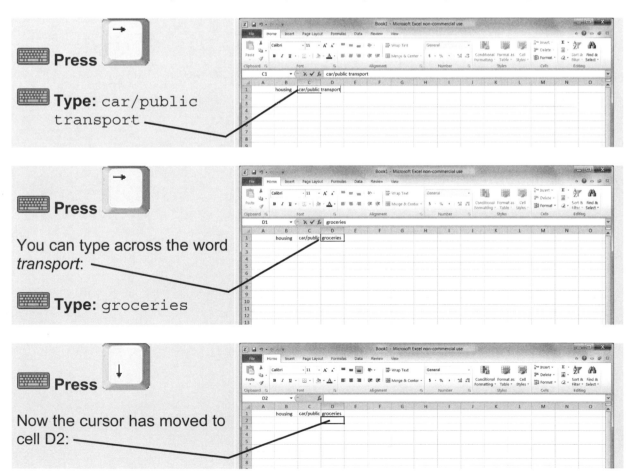

⌨ **Press →**

⌨ **Type:** car/public transport

⌨ **Press →**

You can type across the word *transport*:

⌨ **Type:** groceries

⌨ **Press ↓**

Now the cursor has moved to cell D2:

## 5.4 Change the Column Width

The space in a cell is restricted. If you type a word that is too long, part of that word will not be displayed:

The words 'car/public transport' are too wide for the cell:

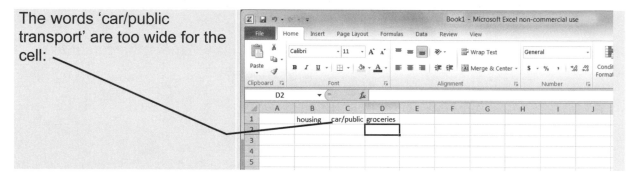

You can change the column width by dragging the mouse:

👆 **Position the mouse pointer ✛ between the column headers**

C ✛ D

The pointer will turn into ✛:

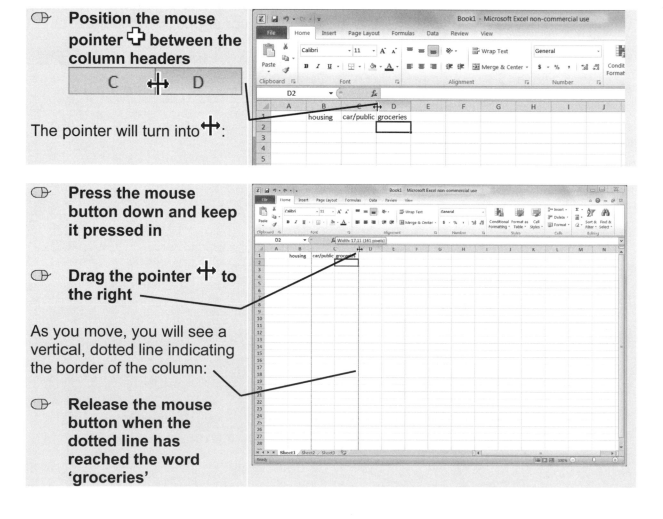

👆 **Press the mouse button down and keep it pressed in**

👆 **Drag the pointer ✛ to the right**

As you move, you will see a vertical, dotted line indicating the border of the column:

👆 **Release the mouse button when the dotted line has reached the word 'groceries'**

Now the width of the entire column has increased. In this way you do not change the width of a single cell, but of the whole column. The width of the other columns will not change, but they will reposition themselves accordingly, a little further to the right. Now you can type the next column title:

☞   **Click cell E1**

Cell E1 is selected:

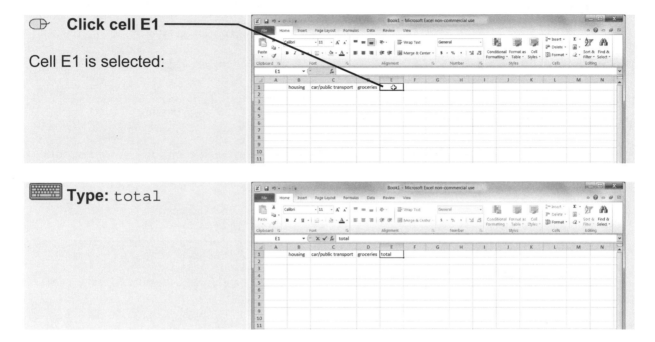

⌨   **Type:** total

You have finished setting up the columns.


## 5.5 Create Sequences

You can save a lot of time by using the automatic, built-in sequences (or ranges) in *Excel*. For example, you can make a list of all the months in a year. First, you need to type the first month of the range:

☞   **Click cell A2**

⌨   **Type:** January

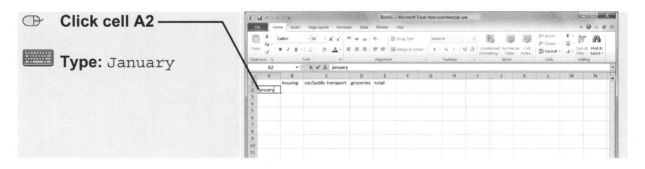

Next, you can complete the range:

**Position the mouse pointer on the lower right-hand corner of cell A2**

The pointer will turn into ✚:

The lower right-hand corner is also called the *handle* of the cell.

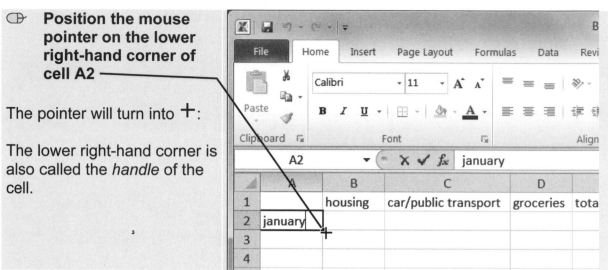

**Press the mouse button down and keep it pressed in**

**Drag the pointer ✚ to cell A13**

While you are dragging, you will see the other months appear next to the mouse pointer:

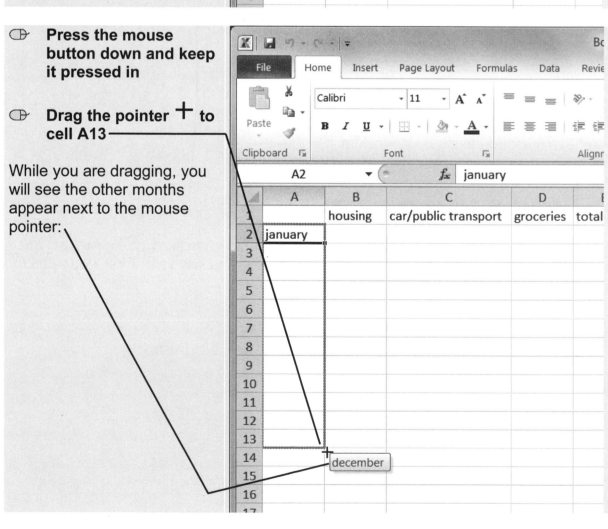

**Release the mouse button**

All the months of the year are neatly listed one below the other:

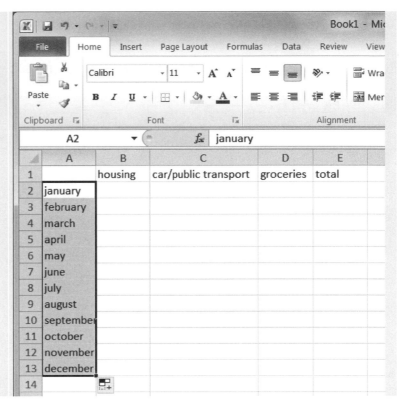

 **HELP! I have made a mistake while dragging the mouse.**

The easiest way to correct mistakes in *Excel*, is to simply undo the last operation:

☞ **Undo the last operation** 𝒜𝒞**23**
☞ **Try again**

💡 **Tip**

**Additional ranges**
In *Excel* you can use the same method to create the following sequences:

Monday-Tuesday-Wednesday-Thursday etc.
mon-tue-wed-thu etc.
jan-feb-mar-apr etc.

You can also drag the ranges horizontally:

# 5.6 Enter Numbers

Entering numbers works the same way as entering text.

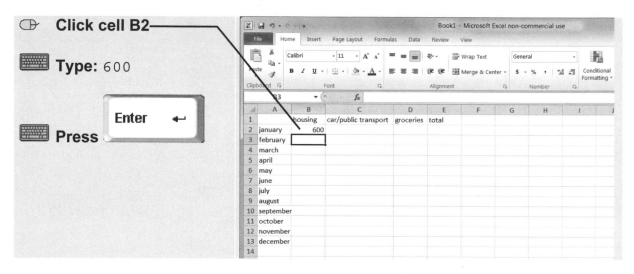

⊕ **Click cell B2**

⌨ **Type:** 600

**Press** Enter ↵

---

💡 **Tip**

**To the next cell**

You will see that you can press Enter ↵ to skip to the next cell.

---

When it comes to the position of the data in a cell, *Excel* makes a distinction between text and numbers:

A number will be aligned to the right of the cell:

Text will be aligned to the left of the cell:

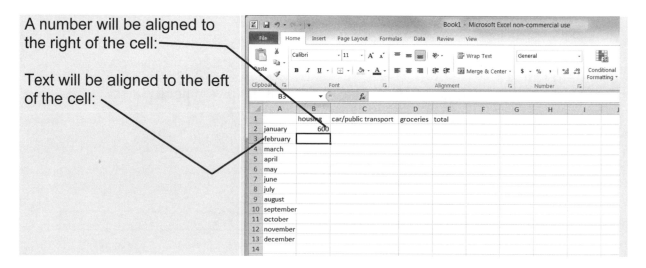

Now you can enter the remaining figures for this sample worksheet:

⌨ **Type the data from the example you see here**

|  | A | B | C | D | E |
|---|---|---|---|---|---|
| 1 |  | housing | car/public transport | groceries | total |
| 2 | january | 600 | 125 | 250 |  |
| 3 | february | 600 | 200 | 300 |  |
| 4 | march | 600 | 150 | 270 |  |
| 5 | april | 750 | 160 | 320 |  |
| 6 | may | 600 | 200 | 200 |  |
| 7 | june | 600 | 220 | 250 |  |
| 8 | july | 600 | 100 | 330 |  |
| 9 | august | 690 | 150 | 300 |  |
| 10 | september | 600 | 200 | 200 |  |
| 11 | october | 600 | 320 | 350 |  |
| 12 | november | 600 | 100 | 250 |  |
| 13 | december | 600 | 150 | 200 |  |
| 14 |  |  |  |  |  |

The data has been entered. Now you can use these values to perform various calculations. For example, you can add up all the numbers in a row or column.

# 5.7 Addition

You can let *Excel* calculate the total amount of all your expenses in January: housing, the car, public transportation and groceries. To do this, you will need to enter a formula. You enter the formula in the cell that is going to display the results.

To calculate the total amount for January, you need to select cell E2:

☞ **Click cell E2**

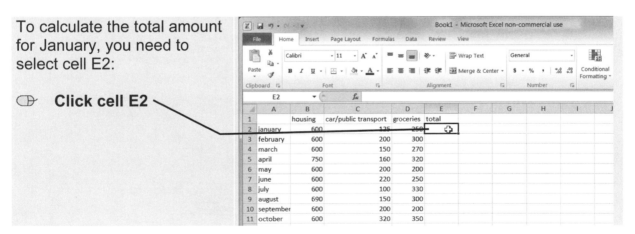

In cell E2 you want to see the total amount of expenses for January. In *Excel*, a formula always starts with =.

**Type:** =

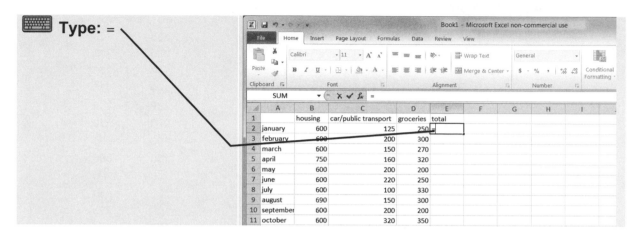

Now, *Excel* is ready to compose a formula. By clicking another cell, you can indicate that you want to compute the number in that cell. In cell B2 you will find the expenses for housing in the month of January. You want to include that cell in the formula:

**Click cell B2**

You will see that B2 will be entered in the formula in cell D2:

You want to add the numbers:

**Type:** +

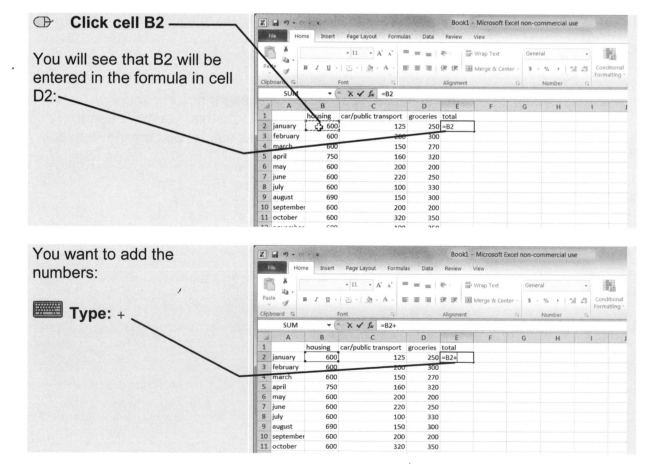

Afterwards, you can select another cell. In this case that will be cell C2. This cell contains the expenses for the car and public transportation in January:

☞ **Click cell C2**

Now cell C2 will be entered in the formula:

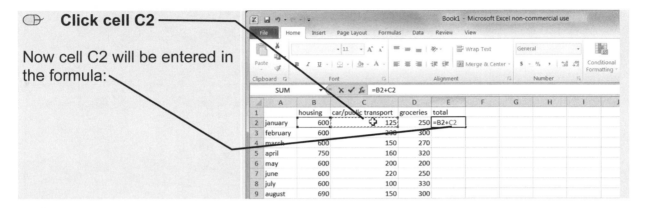

The formula is not yet finished. You are also going to add the costs of the groceries in January:

⌨ **Type:** +

☞ **Click cell D2**

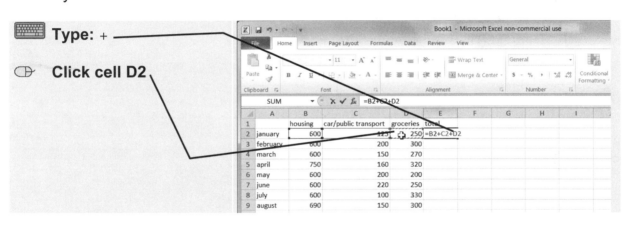

You can conclude the formula by pressing ⏎ **Enter**:

⌨ **Press** ⏎ **Enter**

In cell E2 you will find the sum of all these amounts:

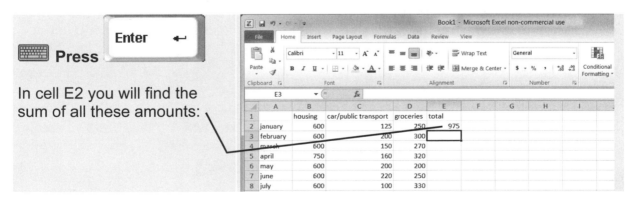

Since cell E2 now contains a formula, if you make a change to one of the numbers that make up the formula, the total (sum) will adjust immediately. Just give it a try:

 **Click cell B2**

**Type:** 650

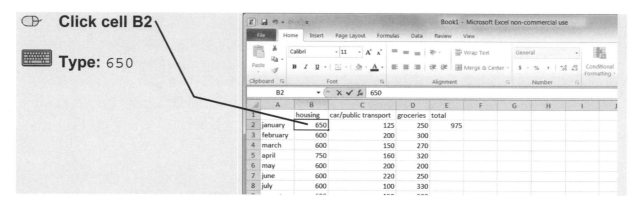

---

 **Tip**

**Change the content of a cell**
To change the content of a cell, you do not need to delete the old content first. You can type over the old data with the new value right away.

---

**Press** Enter ←

In cell E2 you will immediately see the new amount:

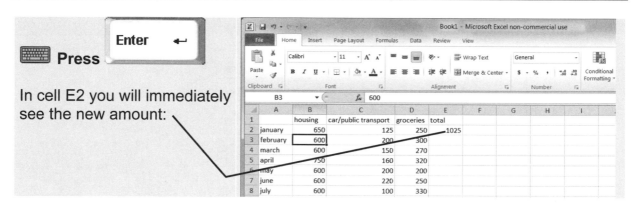

---

 **Tip**

**Which formula does the cell contain?**
Do you want to know what the formula is within a specific cell? Here is how to find it:

 **Click the cell**

☞ **Look at the formula bar**

There you will see the formula =B2+C2+D2 :

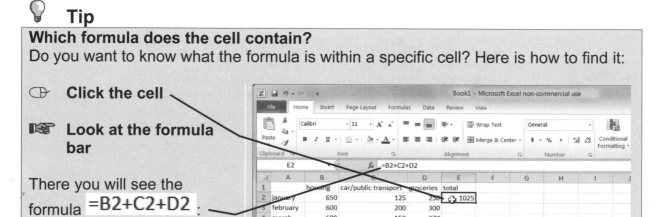

# 5.8 Insert Columns

If you decide to add another category for your costs and expenses, you can always insert a blank column later on. By default, columns are inserted to the left of the currently selected column. So you will need to select the column that is to the right of where you want the new column to appear:

The | Home | tab is still open:

☞ **Click cell E1**

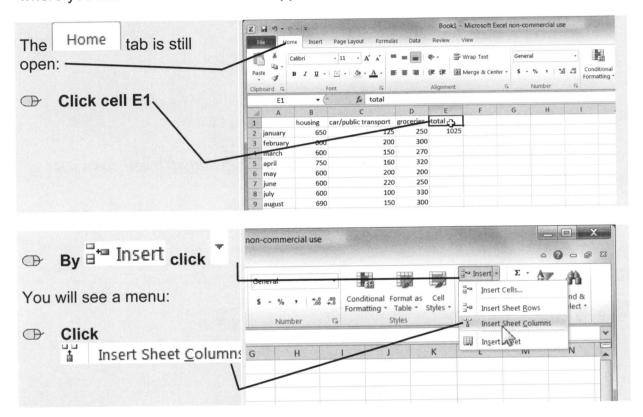

☞ **By** Insert **click**

You will see a menu:

☞ **Click** Insert Sheet Columns

The new column will be inserted. You can add a new column title right away:

⌨ **Type:** insurance

⌨ **Press** Enter ←

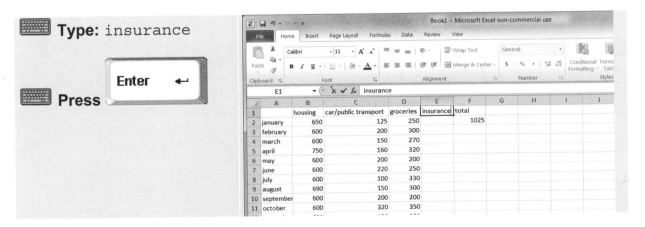

## Tip

**Insert rows**
By default, new rows are inserted above the row where the cursor is. This is how you insert a row:

👉 **Click the row above which you want to insert a new row**

👉 **By** ⊟⁺ **Insert** **click** ▾

👉 **Click** ⊟⁺ Insert Sheet Rows

# 5.9 Division

If you pay your insurance premiums once a year, you can spread these costs over twelve months. *Excel* can divide the amount for you:

👉 **If necessary, click cell E2**

Enter a new formula:

⌨ **Type:** =

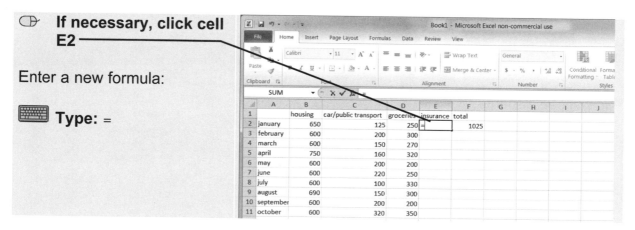

A formula does not have to have references to other cells. You can also enter a calculation which contains only numbers:

⌨ **Type:** 2000

*Excel* uses the / sign for division:

⌨ **Type:** /12

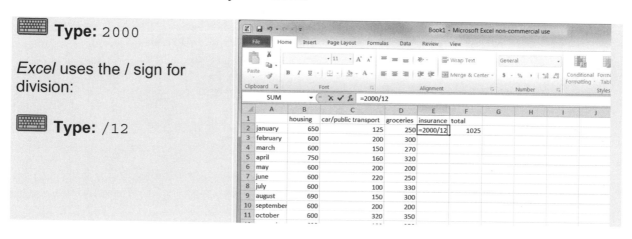

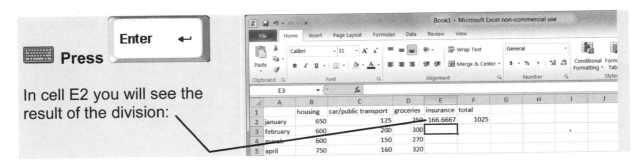

 **Press**

In cell E2 you will see the
result of the division:

---

💡 **Tip**

**Multiplying**

In *Excel*, you do not use the x sign to multiply numbers. Instead, you use the asterisk
(star) *.

A multiplication will look like this: =6*2 .
You can also use the cell names: =A2*G5 .

---

# 5.10 Rounding Numbers

The result of the division is a number with seven digits following the decimal point.
This makes your budget a bit less easy to understand. It is better to make the
numbers more manageable by rounding them off to a number without decimal

points. *Excel* has a special command to do this: .

👉 **Click cell E2**

Here is the number you want
to round off.

The [ Home ] tab is still
open:

👉 **Click**

One of the digits will
disappear:

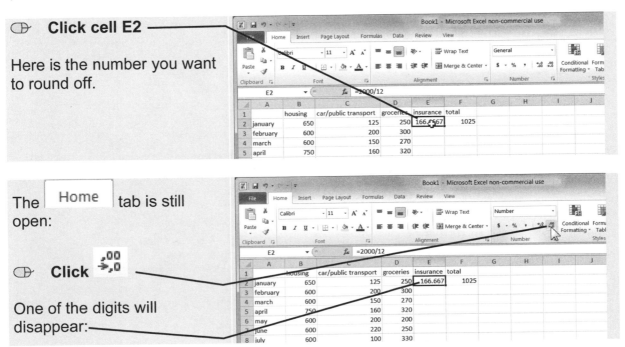

Each time you click this button, one of the digits after the decimal point will disappear:

 **Click** 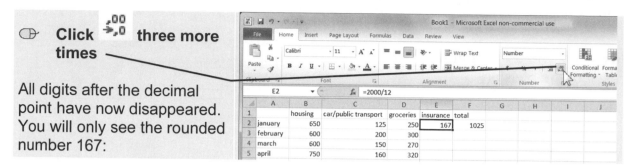 **three more times**

All digits after the decimal point have now disappeared. You will only see the rounded number 167:

### Please note:

The digits that follow the decimal point no longer appear on your screen, but *Excel* still uses them for its calculations. Therefore you may sometimes see irregular outcomes when you use the rounded number for other calculations.

## 5.11 Edit a Formula

You have added a new column, but the formula that calculates the total expenses in January has not changed. The insurance costs are not yet included. You can clearly see this:

☞ **Click cell F2**

☞ **Click the right side of formula in the formula bar**

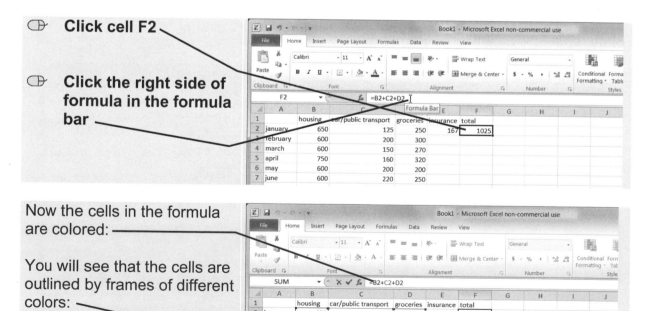

Now the cells in the formula are colored:

You will see that the cells are outlined by frames of different colors:

This way, you can see at a glance which cells are included in the formula. This is a very useful function, especially with extensive calculations in a large worksheet. You are going to add the insurance expenses to the formula:

**Type:** +

**Click cell E2**

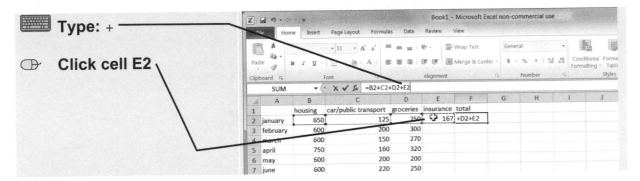

Conclude the formula:

**Press** Enter

In cell F2 you will see the correct result:

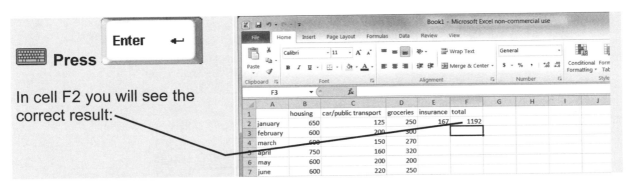

# 5.12 Copy a Formula

Now you have entered two formulas in your worksheet. That is, the calculation of the insurance expenses per month, and the sum of all expenses per month. But you want to apply these formulas to the other months of the year as well. You can do this by copying the formulas. It is very quick and you will prevent typing errors. Here is how to do it:

**Click cell F2**

**Position the pointer on the handle of cell F2**

The pointer will turn into +:

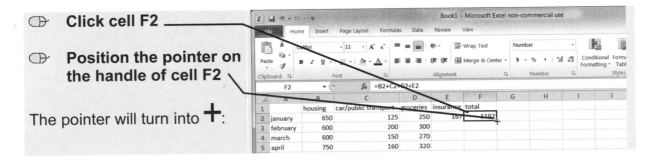

Now you can drag the mouse:

👆 **Press the mouse button down and keep it pressed in**

👆 **Drag the pointer to cell F13**

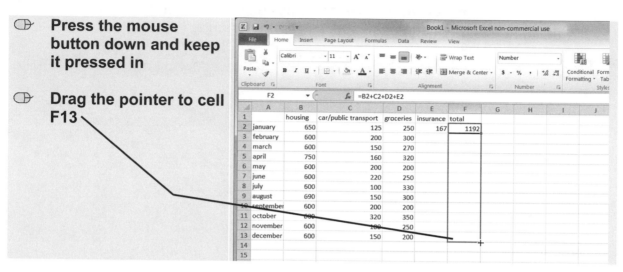

👆 **Release the mouse button**

Now the formula has automatically been copied from cell F3 to cell F13:

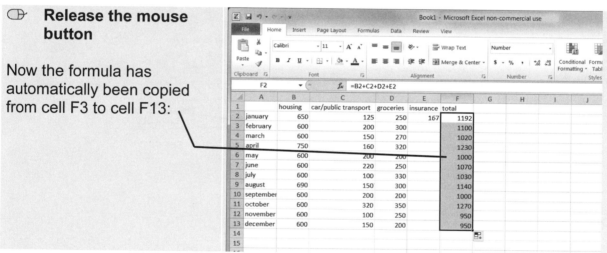

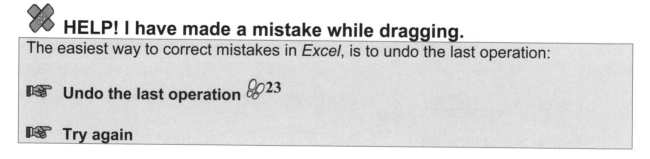

## HELP! I have made a mistake while dragging.

The easiest way to correct mistakes in *Excel*, is to undo the last operation:

☞ **Undo the last operation** ✂23

☞ **Try again**

*Excel* has automatically adapted the formulas to the line where the cursor is:

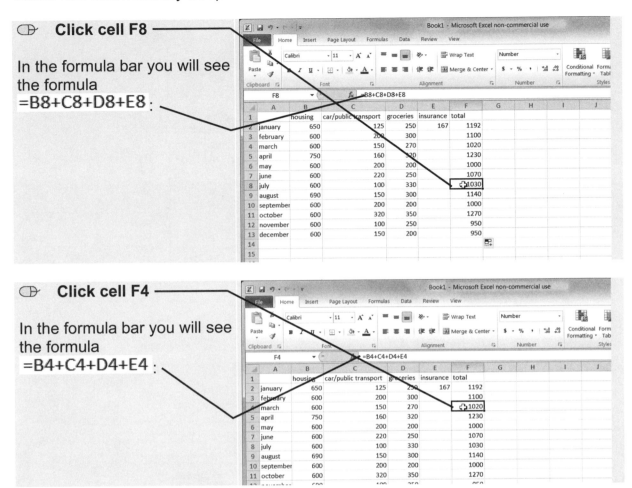

☞ **Click cell F8**

In the formula bar you will see the formula
=B8+C8+D8+E8 :

☞ **Click cell F4**

In the formula bar you will see the formula
=B4+C4+D4+E4 :

The calculation of the monthly insurance costs contains only numbers. You can copy this formula in the same way:

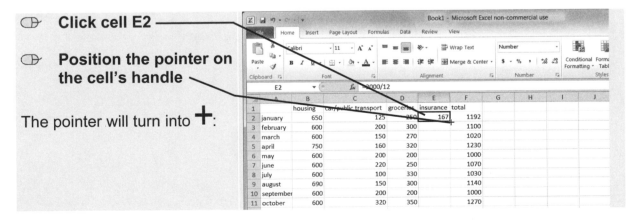

☞ **Click cell E2**

☞ **Position the pointer on the cell's handle**

The pointer will turn into ✚:

Now you can drag the mouse:

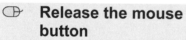 **Press the mouse button down and keep it pressed in**

 **Drag the mouse pointer to cell E13**

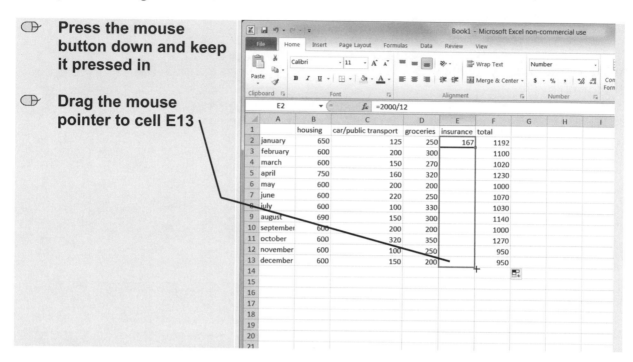

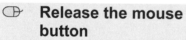 **Release the mouse button**

Now you will see the same amount in cells E3 to E13:

The amounts in the *Total* column have been re-calculated as well:

# 5.13 Totals

If you need to add the numbers in an entire column or row, you can use a formula for this calculation. If you have many numbers to add, entering the formula can be time consuming. The formula may also become difficult to read and you run the risk of making mistakes. Fortunately, *Excel* has a function that allows you to add up all the numbers in a column or a row automatically. It is called *AutoSum*.

☞ **Click cell F2**

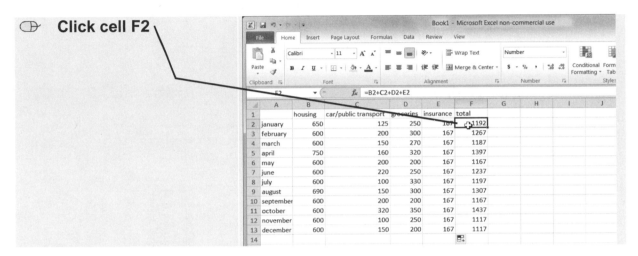

First, select the cells you want to add up:

☞ **Press the mouse button down and keep it pressed in**

☞ **Drag the pointer to cell F13**

☞ **Release the mouse button**

Now all the totals have been selected:

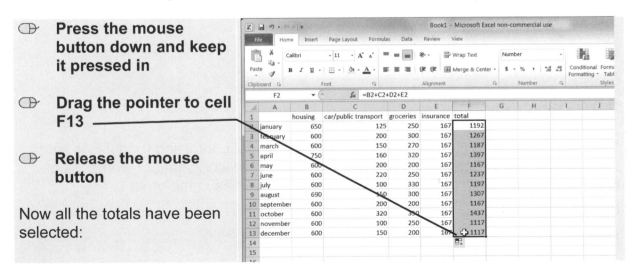

 **Please note:**

You will need to drag when the mouse pointer turns into ✚. You will see that the mouse pointer can adopt different shapes in *Excel*. These shapes all have a different meaning and function.

Now you can use the *AutoSum* command to add up the selected cells:

The [ Home ] is already opened:

☞  **Click** **Σ**

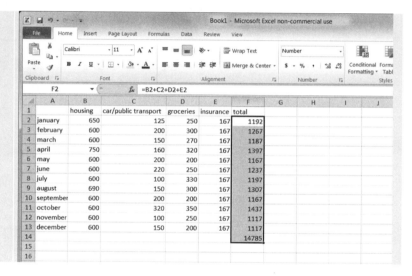

Below the selected column you will see the total amount (14785) for this column:

| | A | B | C | D | E | F | G | H | I | J |
|---|---|---|---|---|---|---|---|---|---|---|
| 1 | | housing | car/public transport | groceries | insurance | total | | | | |
| 2 | january | 650 | 125 | 250 | 167 | 1192 | | | | |
| 3 | february | 600 | 200 | 300 | 167 | 1267 | | | | |
| 4 | march | 600 | 150 | 270 | 167 | 1187 | | | | |
| 5 | april | 750 | 160 | 320 | 167 | 1397 | | | | |
| 6 | may | 600 | 200 | 200 | 167 | 1167 | | | | |
| 7 | june | 600 | 220 | 250 | 167 | 1237 | | | | |
| 8 | july | 600 | 100 | 330 | 167 | 1197 | | | | |
| 9 | august | 690 | 150 | 300 | 167 | 1307 | | | | |
| 10 | september | 600 | 200 | 200 | 167 | 1167 | | | | |
| 11 | october | 600 | 320 | 350 | 167 | 1437 | | | | |
| 12 | november | 600 | 100 | 250 | 167 | 1117 | | | | |
| 13 | december | 600 | 150 | 200 | 167 | 1117 | | | | |
| 14 | | | | | | 14785 | | | | |

## 5.14 Save

You have completed your first *worksheet*. A worksheet containing formulas is also called a *(calculation)model*. It is important to save your worksheet or workbook at regular intervals. You do this in *Excel* in the same way as in the other *Office* programs:

In the top left of the window:

☞  **Click** 💾

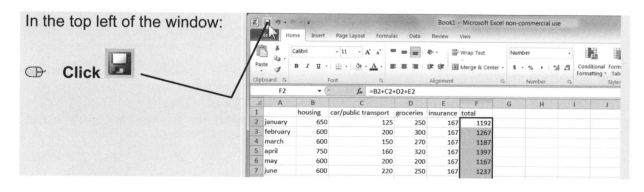

If this is the first time you save the workbook, the *Save As* window will be opened:

By default, *Excel* will store the file in the (*My*) *Documents* folder:

Enter the file name:

**By File name: type:**
exercise budget

**Click** **Save**

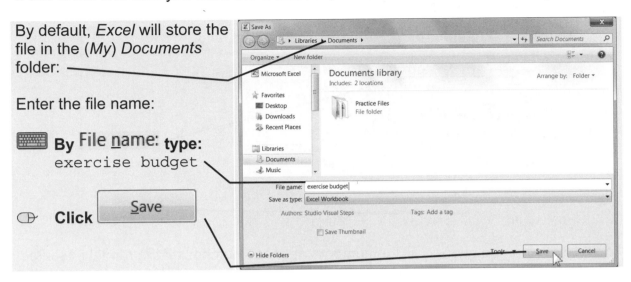

Now the budget is stored on your computer, in the (*My*) *Documents* folder.

## 5.15 Test

It is very important to test a calculation model, because you will need to completely rely on its outcomes later on. You can test the model by changing random amounts. This is the only way to check if all the formulas have been entered correctly. Carefully check the results of your model, after you have finished testing. If they appear to be illogical or irregular, then check the model once more.

**Click cell C7**

**Type:** 100

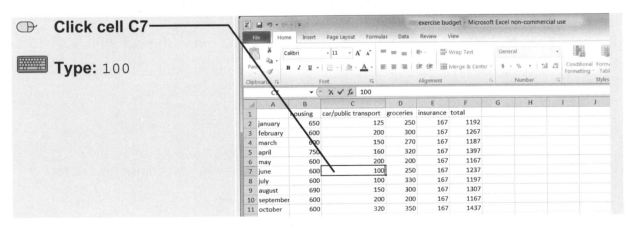

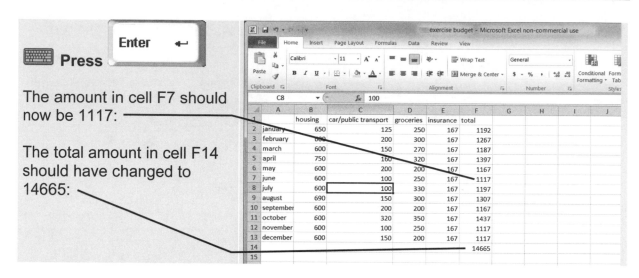

 **Press** [Enter ←]

The amount in cell F7 should now be 1117: ───

The total amount in cell F14 should have changed to 14665: ─

In this way you can change all the numbers at once and check if the model executes the calculations correctly.

 **Undo the last operation** ✇²³

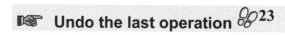 **Please note:**

Be careful not to alter the cells that contain formulas. Since *Excel* automatically overwrites cells, you will lose your formula and the changes will no longer be calculated correctly.

 **HELP! I have entered a number in the wrong cell.**

It may happen that you type something in the wrong cell. This is easily corrected.

If you notice you have done something wrong while typing and the cursor is still positioned in the cell:

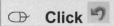 **Press** [Esc]

If you have already moved the cursor to a different cell, you can undo the operation with the *Undo* button on the *Quick Access* toolbar:

⊕ **Click** 🔄

# 5.16 Copy the Worksheet

Up till now, you have only used a single worksheet for the *exercise budget* workbook. This workbook consists of three worksheets. At the bottom of the window you will see the tabs for these worksheets.

Click  Sheet2

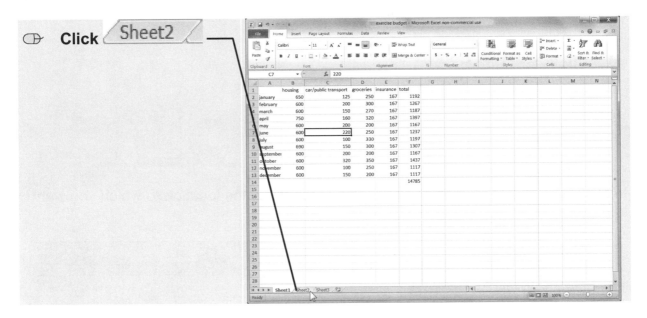

Now *Sheet2* will be opened:

You will see an empty worksheet:

Click  Sheet1

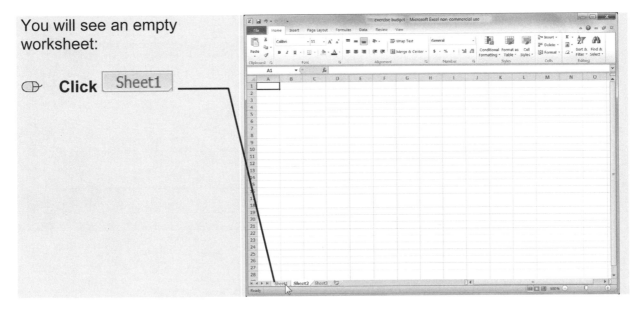

You will see the model on the first worksheet once again. You can copy this worksheet:

☞ **Right-click Sheet1**

You will see a menu:

☞ **Click Move or Copy...**

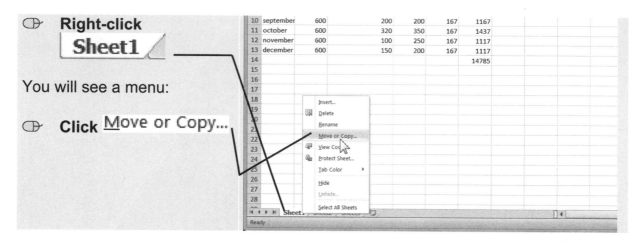

In the *Move or Copy* window you will need to indicate the location to which you want to move or copy this worksheet:

☞ **Click Sheet2**

The new sheet will be inserted above *Sheet2*.

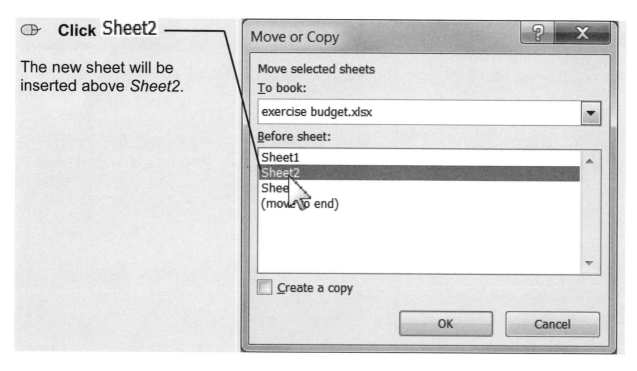

But you want to copy the selected worksheet, not move it:

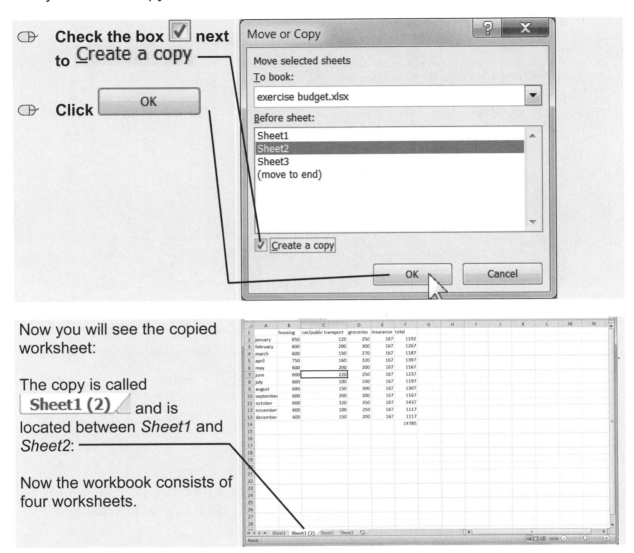

- ☞ **Check the box ☑ next to** <u>C</u>reate a copy
- ☞ **Click** OK

Now you will see the copied worksheet:

The copy is called **Sheet1 (2)** and is located between *Sheet1* and *Sheet2*:

Now the workbook consists of four worksheets.

💡 **Tip**

**Add new worksheets**
You can also add a new worksheet by pressing a tab. Here is how to do that:

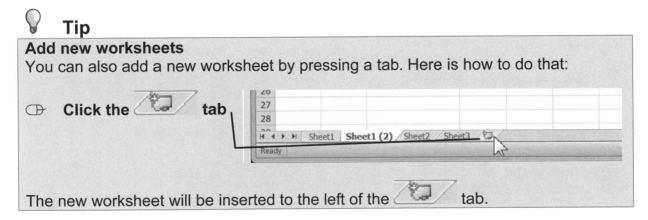

- ☞ **Click the** tab

The new worksheet will be inserted to the left of the tab.

### Tip
**Delete a worksheet**
If you no longer need a worksheet, you can delete it. Here is how to do that:

- **Right-click the tab of the worksheet you want to delete**

- **Click** **Delete**

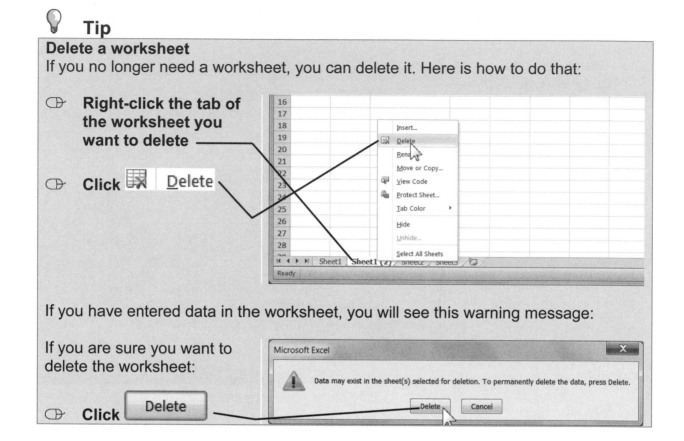

If you have entered data in the worksheet, you will see this warning message:

If you are sure you want to delete the worksheet:

- **Click** **Delete**

# 5.17 Delete Cells

You are going to use the copied worksheet to record your monthly income and to calculate how much money you have left per month. To do this, you are going to delete all the unnecessary data:

- **Click cell B1 and keep the mouse button pressed in**

- **Drag to cell F14**

- **Release the mouse button**

The names of the months have not been selected:

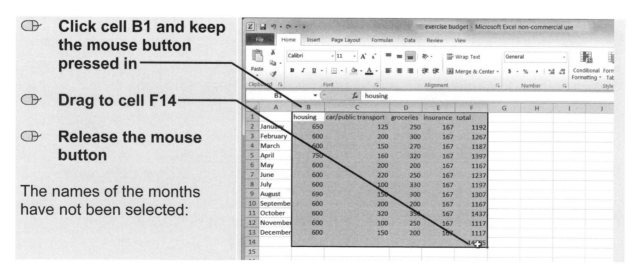

Delete all content from the cells:

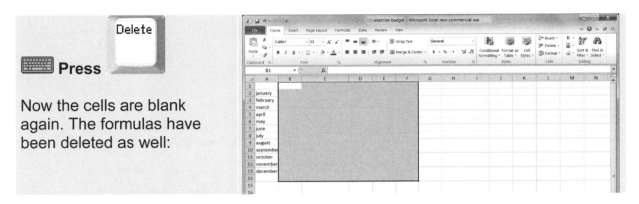

**Press**

Now the cells are blank again. The formulas have been deleted as well:

Now you can go ahead and enter the new data in this worksheet:

**Type the data from this example**

|  | A | B | C | D | E |
|---|---|---|---|---|---|
| 1 |  | income | expenses |  | reserve |
| 2 | january | 1400 |  |  |  |
| 3 | february | 1400 |  |  |  |
| 4 | march | 1400 |  |  |  |
| 5 | april | 1400 |  |  |  |
| 6 | may | 1400 |  |  |  |
| 7 | june | 2000 |  |  |  |
| 8 | july | 1400 |  |  |  |
| 9 | august | 1400 |  |  |  |
| 10 | september | 1400 |  |  |  |
| 11 | october | 1400 |  |  |  |
| 12 | november | 1400 |  |  |  |
| 13 | december | 1900 |  |  |  |
| 14 |  |  |  |  |  |

# 5.18 Worksheet Names

By giving a name to your worksheet, it will help you organize and keep track of where your data lies within the workbook. Enter a name that is easy to identify. This is also helpful later on when you want to copy data from one worksheet to another. Here is how to change the name of the worksheet that contains the income:

**Right-click**

**Sheet1 (2)**

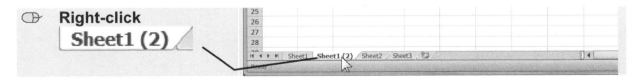

You will see a menu:

☞ **Click** Rename

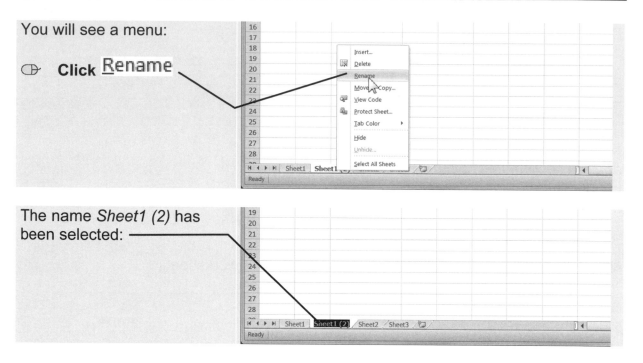

The name *Sheet1 (2)* has been selected:

Now you can enter a name for this worksheet:

⌨ **Type:** Reserve

⌨ **Press** Enter ↵

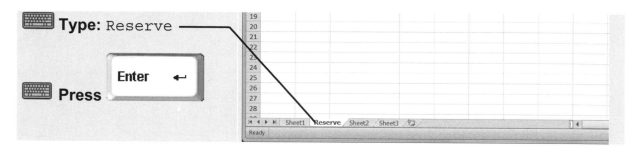

You can rename *Sheet1* in the same way:

☞ **Enter this name for *Sheet1*:** Expenses 👣66

Now both worksheets have been renamed:

☞ **Click** Reserve

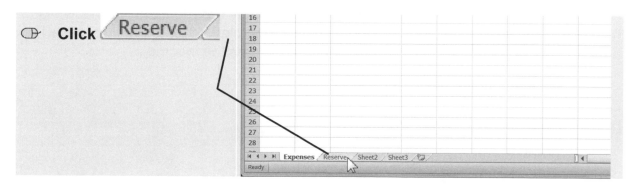

# 5.19 Use Data From a Different Worksheet

In the *Reserve* worksheet you are going to calculate how much money you have left at the end of the month. You will not need to enter the expenses again; you can copy these numbers from the *Expenses* worksheet. First, select the cell where you want to see the results:

**Click cell C2** ————

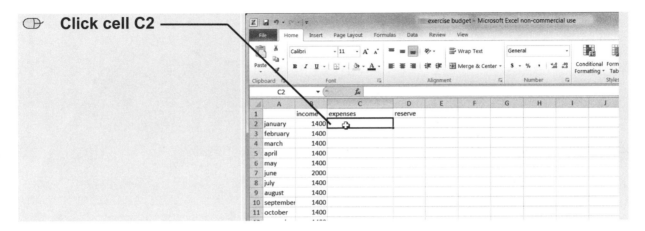

Enter a new formula:

**Type:** = ————

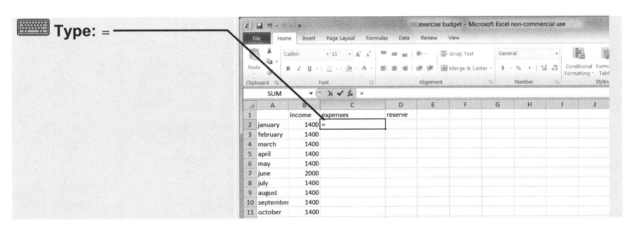

The total amount of your expenses in January is recorded in the *Expenses* worksheet:

**Click** Expenses

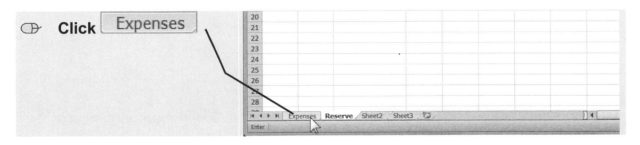

Select the cell that contains the total amount for January:

**Click cell F2**

**Press** Enter

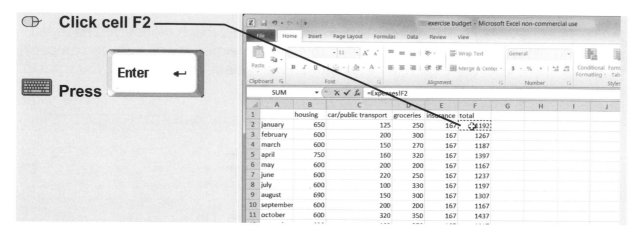

*Excel* will automatically jump back to the *Reserve* worksheet:

Now the total amount of the January expenses has been entered:

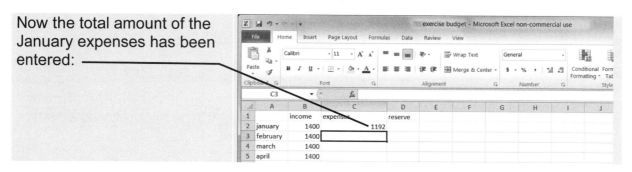

Just check what the formula for this cell is:

**Click cell C2**

In the formula bar you will see **=Expenses!F2**.

This means that this cell contains the content of cell F2 in the *Expenses* worksheet.

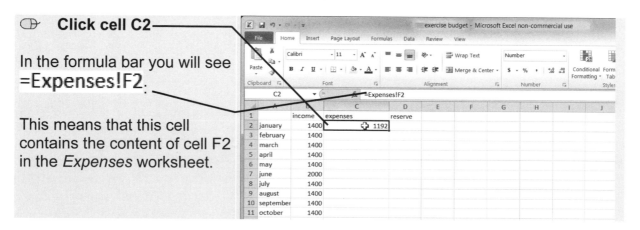

 **Tip**

**Automatic adjustment**
If the amount in cell F2 in the *Expenses* worksheet is altered, the amount in cell C2 in the *Reserve* worksheet is also adjusted automatically.

You can enter the expenses for the remaining months by copying the formula for the month of January:

**Position the pointer on the handle of cell C2**

The pointer will turn into **+**:

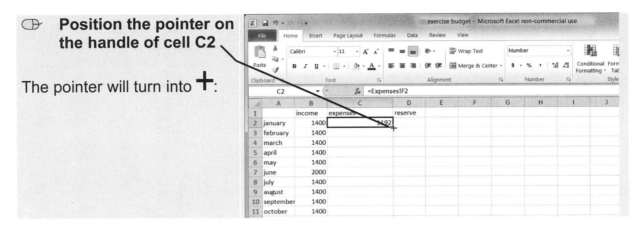

Now you can drag the mouse:

**Press the mouse button down and keep it pressed in**

**Drag the pointer to cell C13**

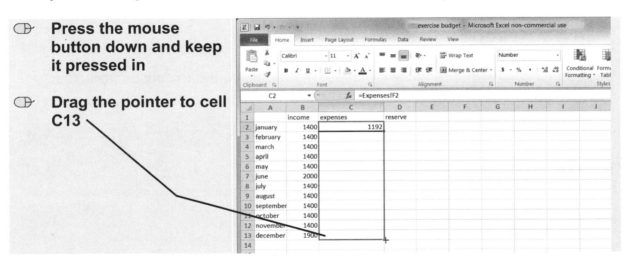

**Release the mouse button**

The expenses for the rest of the year will be entered:

Check one of the cells:

☞  **Click cell C12** ————

The formula bar shows
=Expenses!F12, these are
the expenses for November
in the *Expenses* worksheet:

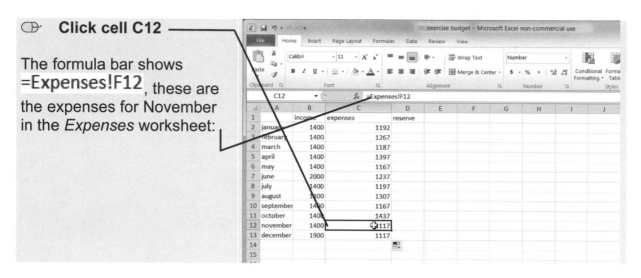

## 5.20 Subtraction

You can calculate your monthly reserves by subtracting the expenses from your
income. Start with January:

☞  **Click cell D2** ————

This cell will contain a
formula:

⌨ **Type:** =

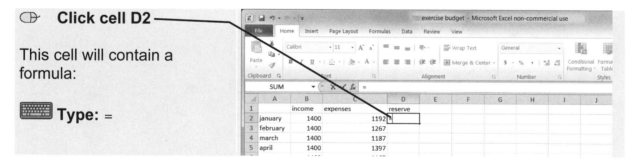

Up till now you have clicked the cells for your calculations with the mouse. But this is
not necessary. Sometimes it is easier to type the formula by hand:

⌨ **Type:** b2-c2 ————

You will see that the cells you
have typed are immediately
outlined in a color:

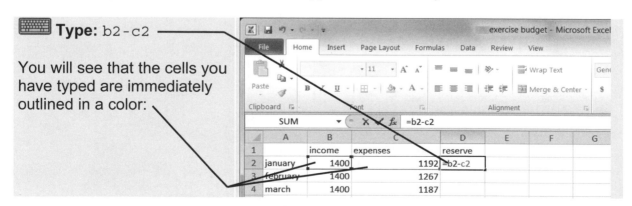

**Tip**

| **Capital letters and lower case letters in formulas** |
| --- |
| You can use capital letters as well as lower case letters to type cell names in a formula. |

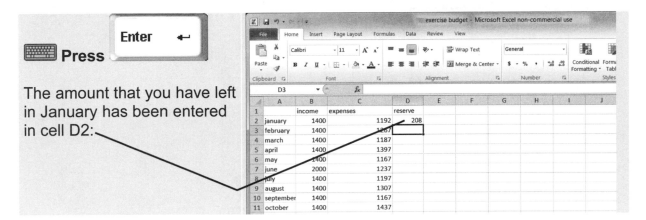

The amount that you have left in January has been entered in cell D2:

You can copy the formula for the January reserve to the other months:

☞ **Copy the formula from cell D2 to cell D13** ⅋⅋⁶⁷

You will see that the amounts in the *Reserve* column have been filled in:

With the *AutoSum* function you can calculate the totals for three columns at once. First you need to select the columns you want to add up:

☞ **Click cell B2 and keep the mouse button pressed in**

☞ **Drag to cell D13**

☞ **Release the mouse button**

All the numbers are selected:

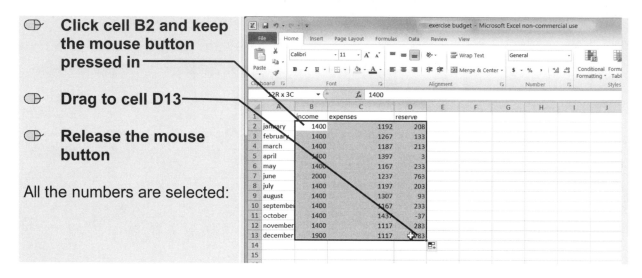

Now you can get the totals for the three separate columns simultaneously:

The **Home** is still opened:

☞ **Click Σ**

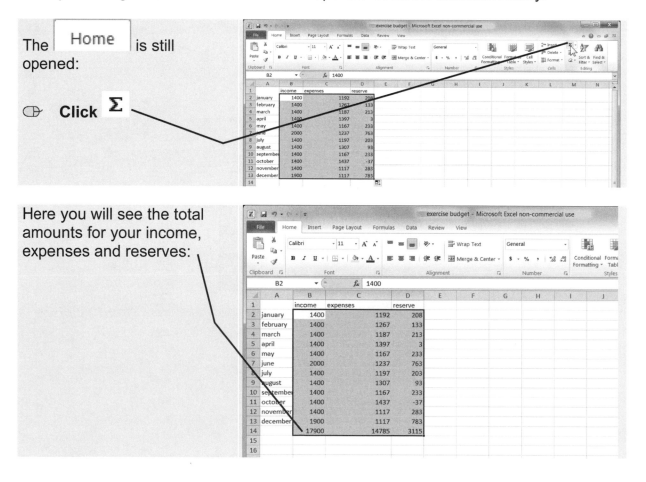

Here you will see the total amounts for your income, expenses and reserves:

# 5.21 Formatting Cells

You can make your *Excel* workbooks easier to read by formatting certain cells in the worksheets. If you want to display some numbers as currency, for example in US dollars, you can do that like this:

The cells B2 up to and including D14 are still selected:

☞ **Click $**

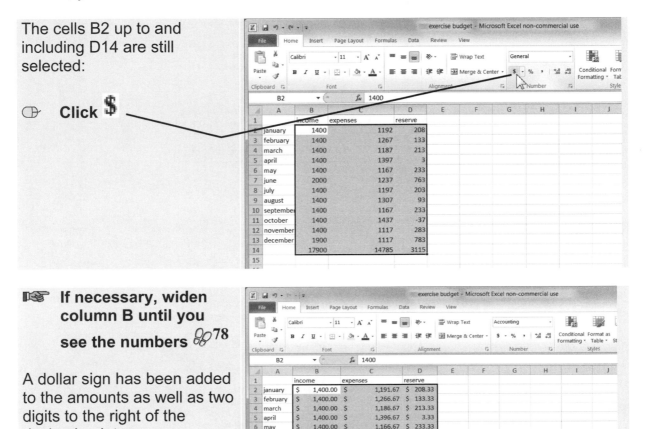

☞ **If necessary, widen column B until you see the numbers** ✂️ **78**

A dollar sign has been added to the amounts as well as two digits to the right of the decimal point:

You can format text and numbers in the same way you do with *Word*. For example, you can accentuate the totals by rendering them in bold letters:

☞ **Select the cells B14 up to and including D14** ✂️ **68**

The ⬚Home tab is still open:

☞ Click **B**

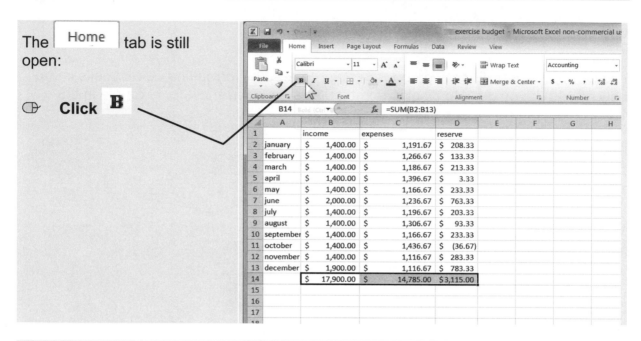

Now the totals will be displayed in bold letters:

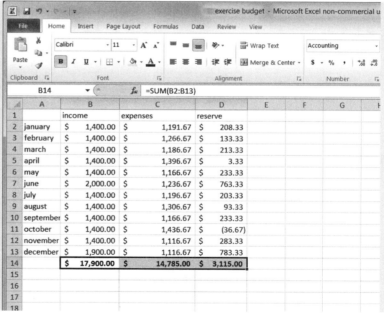

 If necessary, widen column D until you see the numbers ℘℘78

💡 **Tip**

**Change font type, size and color**
You can change the font type, the size and the colors of the text and numbers in the cells in the same way as you would change these items in *Word*.

# 5.22 Use Borders and Padding

If you want to emphasize the total amounts in the worksheet, you can underline the cells above the totals:

☞ **Select the cell B13 up to and including D13** 🐭⁶⁸

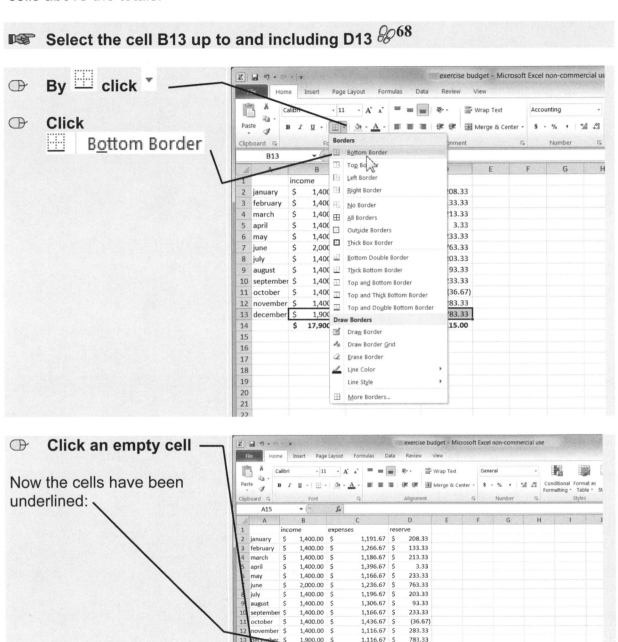

**Now the cells have been underlined:**

You can also insert a border for the column titles:

☞ **Select the cells A1 up to and including D1** 🦶**68**

By ⊞ **click** ▾

**Click**
⊞ **Top and Double Bottom Border**

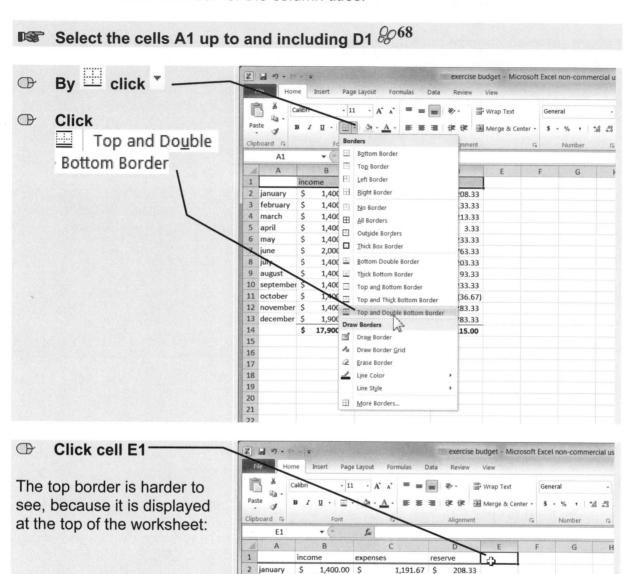

**Click cell E1**

The top border is harder to see, because it is displayed at the top of the worksheet:

You can add a background color to the column titles:

☞ **Select the cells A1 up to and including D1** 🦶**68**

By  click ▾

You will see a menu with all the fill colors:

For example, click

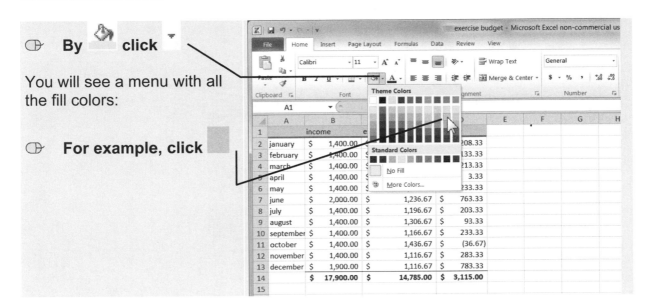

View the result:

Click an empty cell ────

Now the cells have been filled with the selected color:

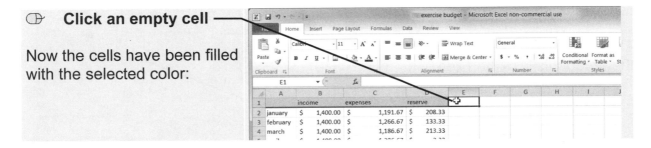

# 5.23 Conditional Formatting

It can be very useful to see at once if you have spent more than you have earned in a given month. This means you will be eating into your savings. *Excel* can help you by displaying a negative reserve in red, so it will stand out. You can set this up with the *Conditional Formatting* button from the *Home* tab:

☞ **Select the cells D2 up to and including D13** 🕮**68**

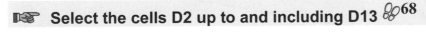

**Please note:**

First, you will need to select the cells for which you want to set the conditional formatting options.

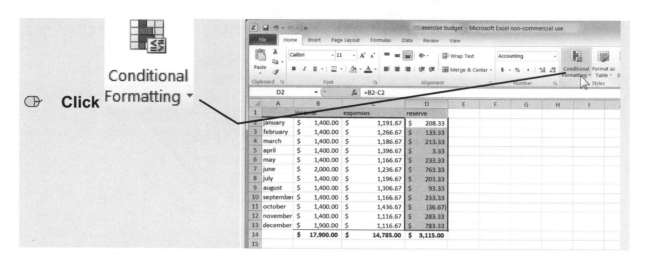

Click *Conditional Formatting*

Select the highlight rules for these cells:

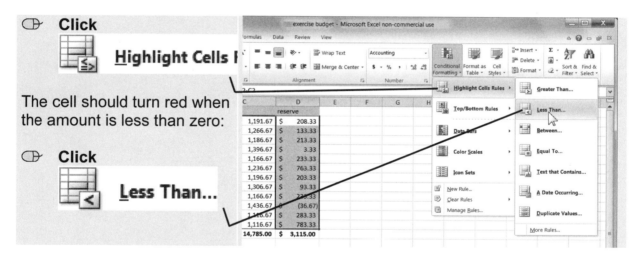

Click *Highlight Cells Rules*

The cell should turn red when the amount is less than zero:

Click *Less Than...*

Now the *Less Than* window will be opened:

Here you can enter the number that will be used for the conditional formatting:

Here you will see the type of formatting that will be applied:

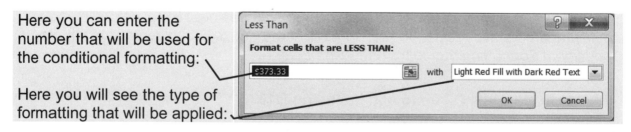

If the value is less than zero, you will have a deficit:

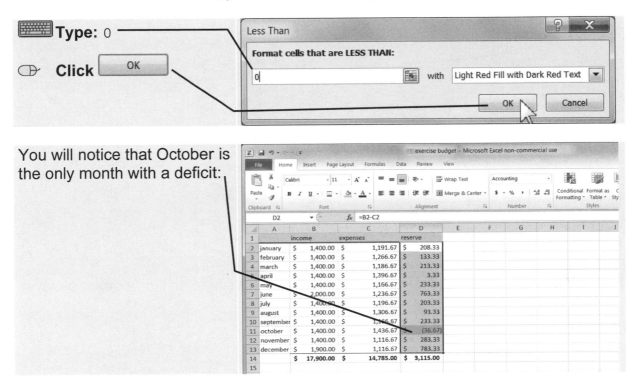

**Type:** 0

**Click** OK

You will notice that October is the only month with a deficit:

You are going to test this setting by reducing the income for a single month, which will result in a negative reserve:

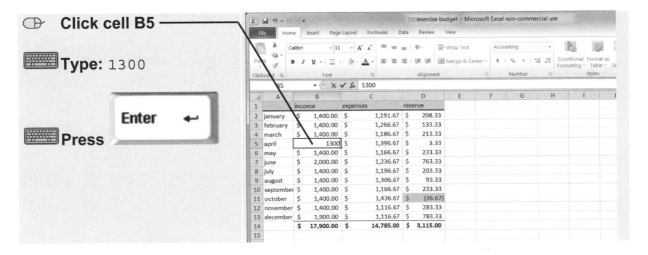

**Click cell B5**

**Type:** 1300

**Press** Enter

Cell D5 will turn red:

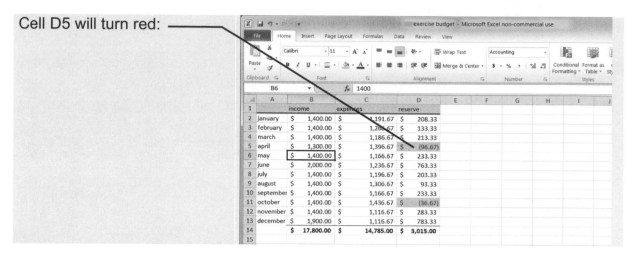

 **Tip**

**Remove conditional formatting**
This is how you remove the conditional formatting for a single cell, or a group of cells:

☞ **Select the cells** 🦶68

✋ **Click** Conditional Formatting ▾

✋ **Click** 🧹 Clear Rules

✋ **Click**
Clear Rules from Selected

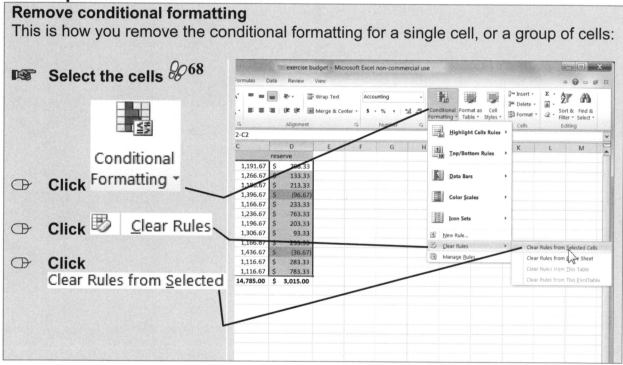

# 5.24 Create a Chart

The well-known proverb 'a picture is worth a thousand words' certainly applies to *Excel*. A spreadsheet can turn into an incomprehensible mess of data. In such a case a chart will be much easier to read. You can see at a glance if a certain item is rising or falling. It just takes a few mouse clicks to create a well-ordered chart in *Excel*.

First, select the data you want to include in the chart:

☞ **Select the cells A1 up to and including D13** 🐾**68**

 **Tip**

**Totals**
Usually it is not very relevant to include the totals in a chart. When you want to include widely varying figures in the chart, it will be difficult to create a clear chart. The lowest value will be barely visible and the highest value will strongly prevail. That is why, in most cases, you will not be including the totals in a chart.

Now you will insert a column chart:

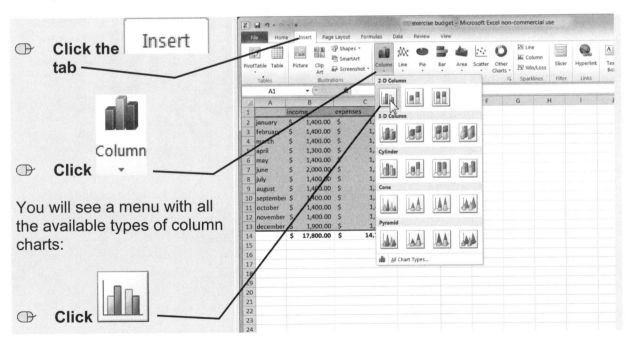

Click the **Insert** tab

Click **Column ▾**

You will see a menu with all the available types of column charts:

Click

The chart will be inserted in the worksheet:

In the ribbon you will see the

**Chart Tools**

section, including the *Design*, *Layout* and *Format* tabs:

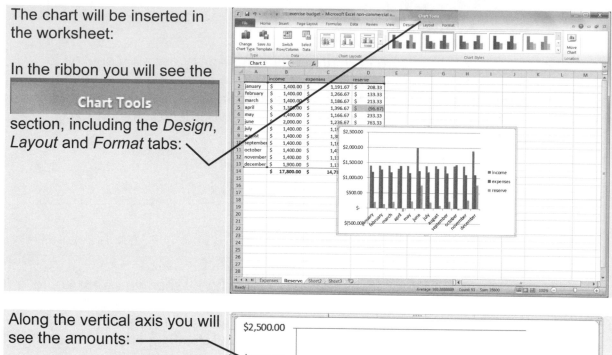

Along the vertical axis you will see the amounts:

Along the horizontal axis you will see the months:

To the right of the chart you will see the *legend*, where the colors of the columns are explained:

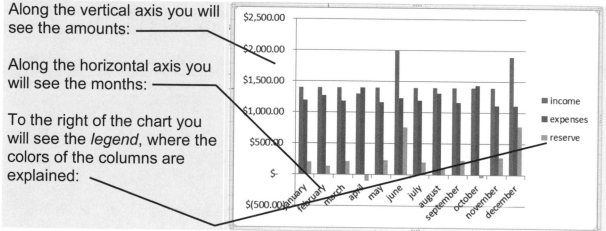

## HELP! My chart looks very different.

Does your chart display the months along the vertical axis, and the amounts along the horizontal axis? Then you just need to switch the rows and columns:

☞ **If necessary, click the** Design **tab**

☞ **Click** Switch Row/Column

Now you will see the same chart as the example in the book.

# 5.25 Move a Chart

The chart has been inserted into the *Reserve* worksheet. But you can drag the chart to any location you want:

**Position the mouse pointer at the edge of the chart** ⎯⎯⎯⎯⎯

The pointer will turn into ⬦ :

**Press the mouse button down and keep it pressed in**

**Drag the chart to the right side of the data**

**Release the mouse button**

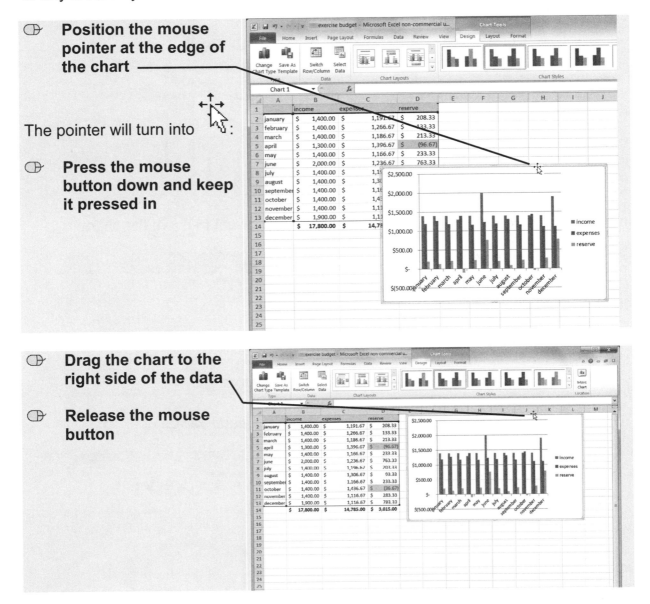

By adding the column chart to your worksheet, it makes it a little crowded. If you move the chart to a separate worksheet, you will have more room for the chart and it will be easier to read:

The | Design | tab is still open:

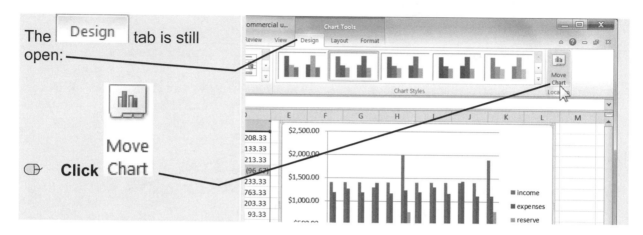

⊕ **Click** Move Chart

In the *Move Chart* window you can choose where you want to move the chart:

⊕ **Click the radio button** ⊙ **next to** New sheet:

⊕ **Click** OK

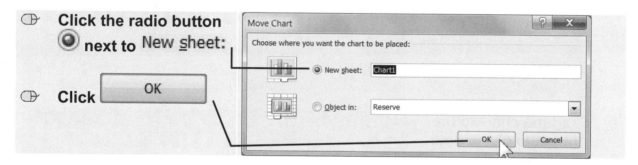

The chart will be moved and a new worksheet called *Chart1* will be opened:

You will see that the chart has become much easier to read:

For the months where the expenses exceed the income, you will see the reserve drop below the zero line:

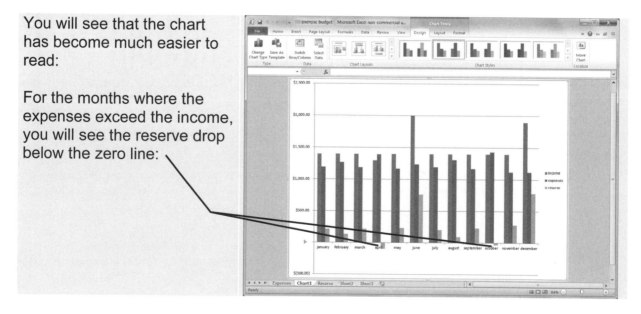

# 5.26 Select a Different Chart Type

The chart you have just created is one of the best-known chart types: a *column chart*. This type of chart is often used to compare different sets of data, or different periods with one another.

Another popular type of chart used for comparisons is the *line chart.* You can convert the column chart into a line chart with just a few mouse clicks:

Make sure the Design tab is open:

☞ **Click** Change Chart Type

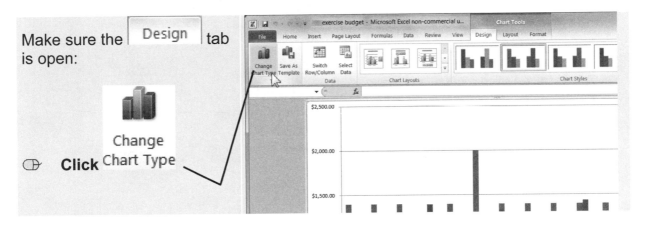

Select the line chart in the *Change Chart Type* window:

☞ **Click**

☞ **Click** OK

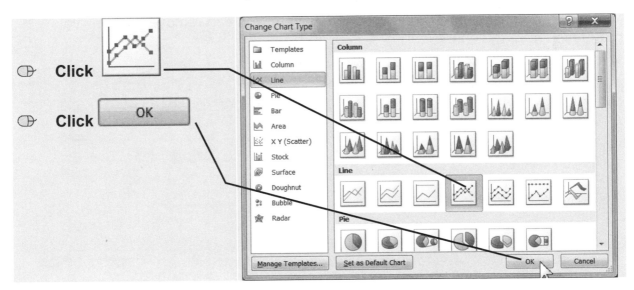

The chart will immediately be converted to the new chart type:

In the line chart you can clearly see where the expenses exceed the income:

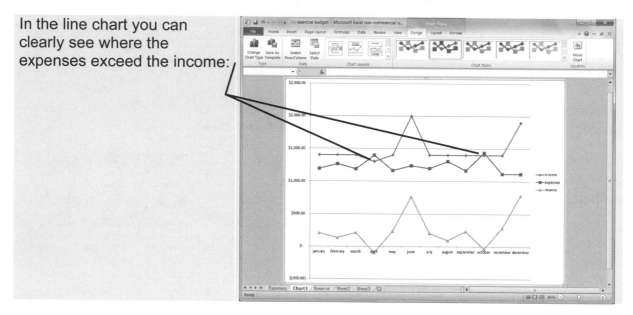

## 5.27 Select Data

In the line chart, the lines for the *income* and *expenses* provide enough information. Actually, the *reserve* line is redundant. If you want, you can remove the reserve information from the chart:

The [ Design ] tab is still open:

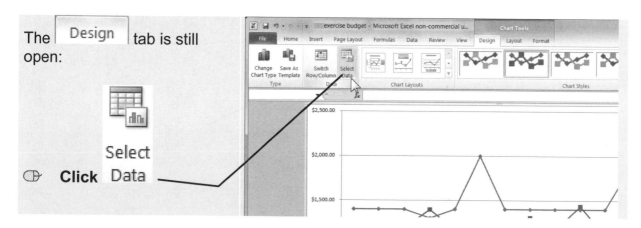

☞ **Click** Select Data

Now you will see the *Reserve* worksheet once again:

On the worksheet the *Select Data Source* window has been opened:

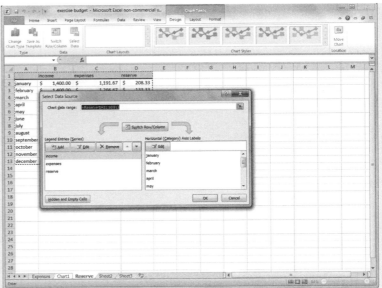

You are going to select a new data range for the chart:

⊕ **Click**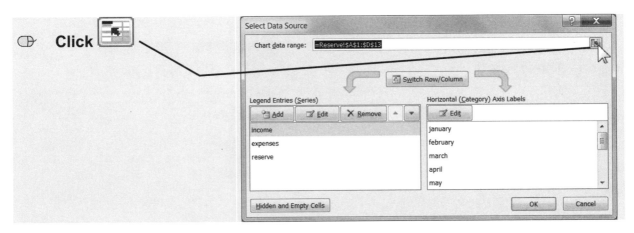

The *Select Data Source* window will be minimized. Now you can select the relevant data in the *Reserve* worksheet and use it in the chart:

☞ **Select the cells A1 up to and including C13** ✂**68**

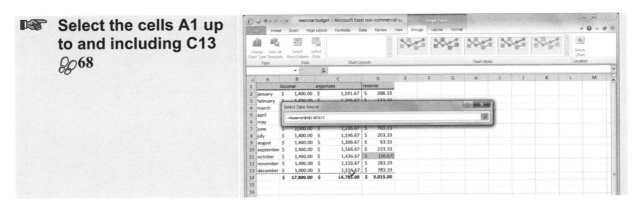

Maximize the *Select Data Source* window once again:

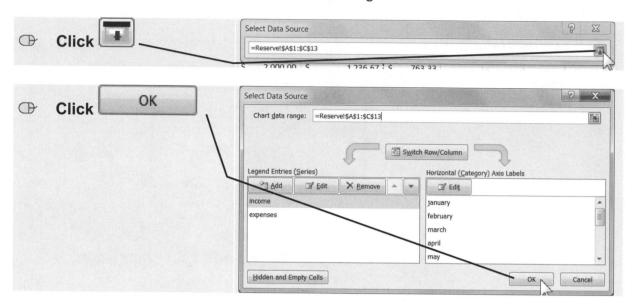

⊕  **Click** [OK]

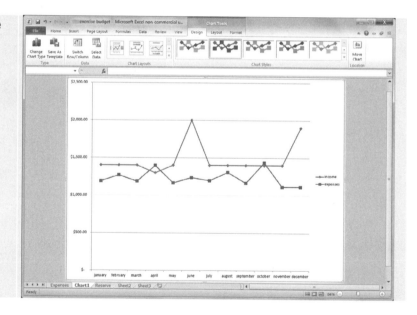

The chart will be adapted right away:

You will see that the reserve line has disappeared:

# 5.28 Change the Chart Layout

You can modify the default chart even further. You can change the chart layout:

**By** Chart Layouts **click**

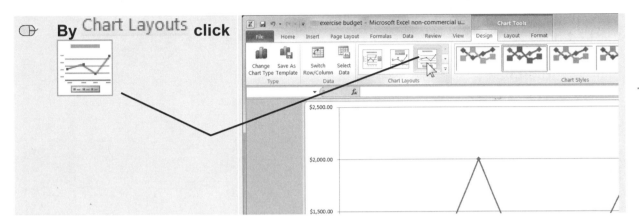

The new layout will be applied to the chart right away:

At the top of the chart you will see a text box for the title:

Now the legend has been placed below the chart:

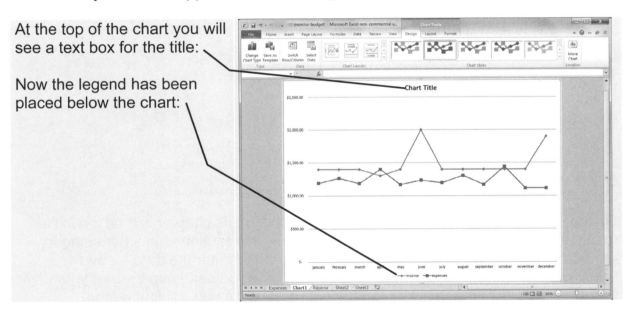

Enter a title for the chart:

☞  **Click Chart Title**

The cursor is positioned in
the text box:

☞  **Double-click
    Chart Title**

The text has been selected:

⌨ **Type:** Annual per
month

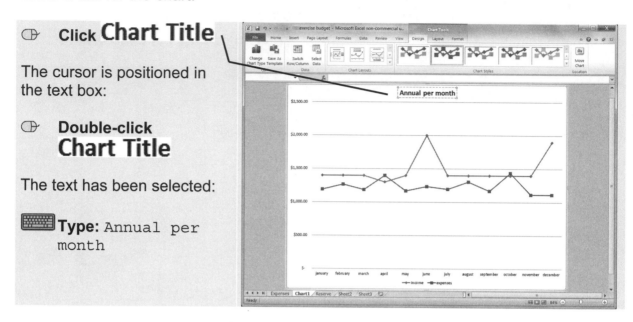

You have finished with this worksheet:

☞  **Save the changes** 🐾⁶⁹

☞  **Close the document** 🐾⁷⁰, ⁷¹

# 5.29 Your Own Budget

Of course, the calculation model you have created in this chapter is a bit too limited
to use for your own personal budget. In the model, the total amounts per category
are added per month, while it would be more useful to enter the data for every
transaction or withdrawal on a daily basis. This way, you can keep track of your day-
to-day expenses or revenues. In the *budget* practice file you will find a more
extensive model, suited for this purpose:

☞  **Open the *budget* practice file from the *Practice Files* folder** 🐾⁷²

The *budget* worksheet will be opened:

At the top of the sheet you will see the categories for your expenses and income:

At the bottom of the sheet you will see the other sheets that are included in this workbook: ———

Each month has its own sheet and a separate sheet is created for the year's totals.

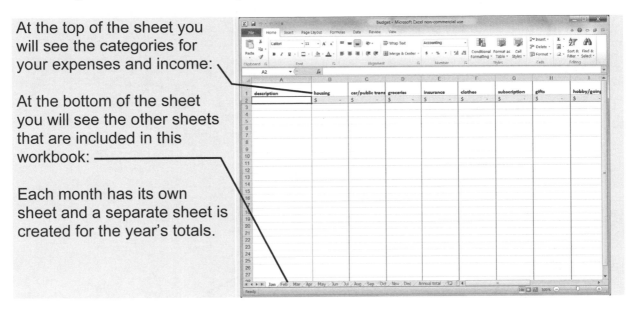

Based on what you have previously learned in this chapter, you can enter your own data into this workbook. You can practice doing that now. Start by entering some expenses for January:

⊕ **Click cell A3** ———

⌨ **Type:** gas

⌨ **Press** | ⇆ Tab | **twice**

Now the cursor has moved to the **car/public trans** column:

⌨ **Type:** 44.26

⌨ **Press** | Enter ↵ |

On line 2 the totals for each column will automatically be computed. Now the cursor has moved to the next line in the **description** column: ———

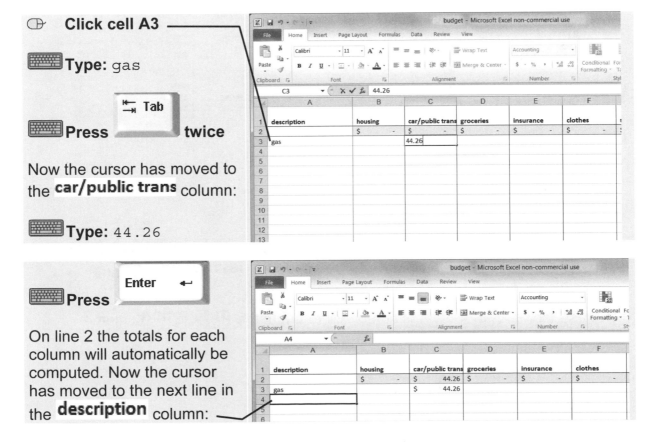

In the worksheet you have a single column for your income. That could be your salary, or a social security payment, or other income. It may also include the money you get for your birthday or even your lottery winnings:

**Type:** salary

The **income** column is not visible:

**Drag the scroll bar to the right**

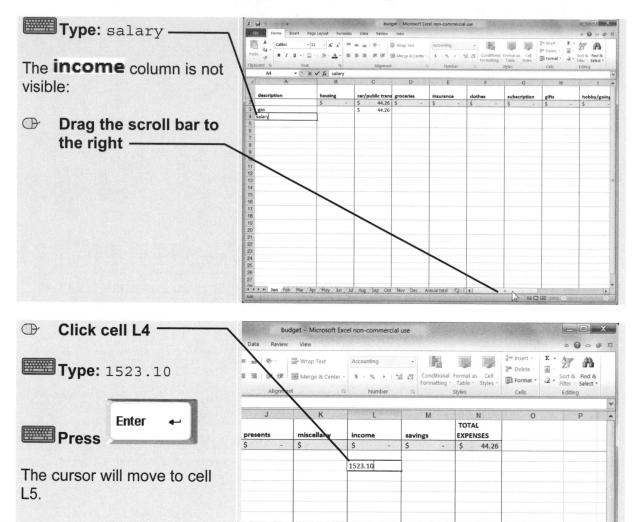

**Click cell L4**

**Type:** 1523.10

**Press** Enter ↵

The cursor will move to cell L5.

**Please note:**

Since you clicked the cell where you have entered the amount, the cursor will move downwards to the next cell, instead of skipping to the **description** column.

If you use the  Tab key, the cursor will return to the **description** column.

**Tip**

**Which category should I use?**

The budget contains ten expense categories. You can use them for the following expenses, for example:

| | |
|---|---|
| **housing** | All housing costs, such as rent, mortgage payment, maintenance, repairs, gas, electricity, water, local taxes. |
| **car/public trans** | All car and transportation costs, such as gas, repairs and taxes. Costs for public transportation, such as train tickets, bus fares, taxi cabs, etcetera. |
| **groceries** | All groceries, such as food, cleaning products, toiletry items, etcetera. |
| **insurance** | All insurance costs, such as your health insurance, house insurance, car and travel insurance, etcetera. |
| **clothes** | All clothing expenses. |
| **subscription** | Expenses for magazine and newspaper subscriptions. |
| **gifts** | Expenses for charities and donations. |
| **hobby/going** | Costs for your hobby, such as membership fees or dues for your baseball club or golf club. All expenses for eating out, visiting a bar, or spending a weekend out of town. |
| **presents** | Expenses for birthday presents and Christmas presents. |
| **miscellany** | Here you can enter all the expenses that do not belong to one of the other categories. For instance, income tax payments, or for buying a lottery ticket. |

Apart from the expenses, you can also record your income:

| | |
|---|---|
| **income** | These are all the amounts you receive, such as salary, a holiday bonus, a pension or annuities. You can also enter all sorts of extra allowances here, like child support or tax returns. And keep in mind birthday gifts and the money you win in a lottery or by gambling. |

Many people put regular sums of money into their savings account:

| | |
|---|---|
| **savings** | All the money you save for expensive purchases or for an upcoming vacation or an unexpected disaster. |

In the budget, the amounts you save are not calculated as expenses, because you are not spending that money.

Go ahead and fill in a few entries for the month of January:

| Description: | Category: | Amount: |
|---|---|---|
| health insurance | insurance | 98.00 |
| groceries Walmart | groceries | 53.80 |
| groceries pharmacist | groceries | 8.75 |
| donation WWF | gifts | 3.00 |
| contribution First Aid Club | hobby/going | 32.00 |
| mortgage | housing | 425.00 |
| electricity | housing | 124.00 |
| birthday present Emma | presents | 15.00 |
| groceries Walmart | groceries | 56.97 |
| jeans and t-shirt | clothes | 79.80 |
| subscription Chicago Times | subscription | 26.90 |
| to savings account | savings | 100.00 |

Of course you will have many more entries to enter in a regular month. But, for this exercise you do not need to enter them. Now you can enter some expenses and revenues for the month of February:

**Click** `Feb`

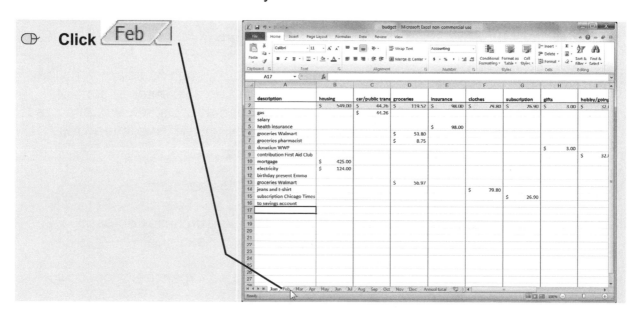

Fill in these entries for February:

| Description: | Category: | Amount: |
|---|---|---|
| salary | income | 1523.10 |
| health insurance | insurance | 98.00 |
| gas | car/public trans | 43.12 |
| groceries Walmart | groceries | 44.50 |
| birthday present Peter | presents | 19.00 |
| dinner with John | hobby/going | 62.00 |
| mortgage | housing | 425.00 |
| electricity | housing | 124.00 |
| groceries pharmacist | groceries | 13.00 |
| groceries Walmart | groceries | 66.23 |
| boots | clothes | 99.00 |
| subscription Chicago Times | subscription | 26.90 |
| to savings account | savings | 125.00 |

In this way you can record all your monthly income and expenses. In the last worksheet, all the totals are assembled:

⊕ **Click**

/ Annual total /

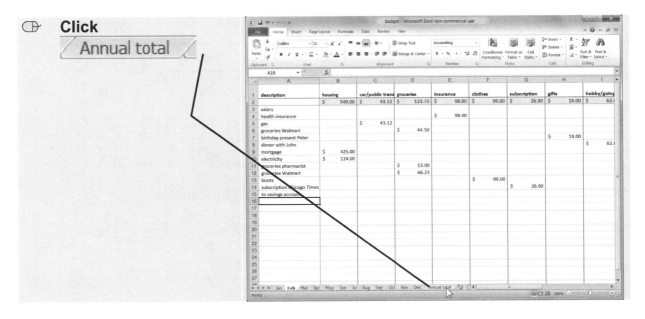

You will see the *Annual Total* worksheet:

Here you see the total
expenses, income and
savings per month:

These totals are used in the
chart at the right-hand side:

Here you will see the total
monthly expenses per
category:

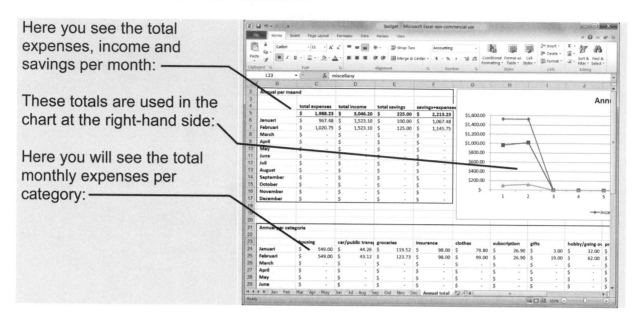

The data in this last worksheet is extracted from the 12 monthly worksheets where
you recorded your income and expenses. In this chapter you have learned how to do
this.

☞ **Click cell C24**

You will see this message

**Automatic calculation**
Data cannot be modified.
A value is calculated
automatically.

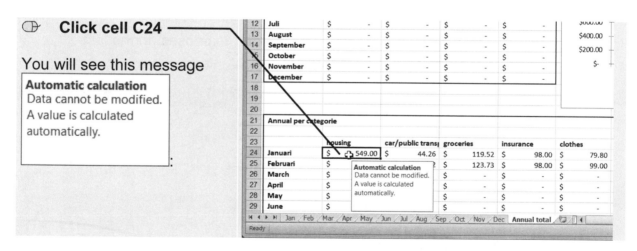

In the formula bar you can check the original location of this data:

You will see the formula
**=Jan!B2**:

In this cell you will see the
number form cell B2 in the
*Jan* worksheet.

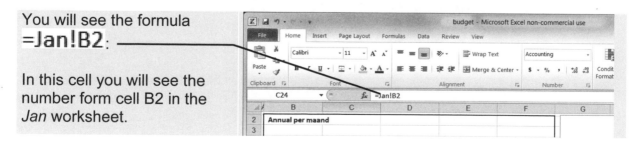

On the *Annual Total* tab you will see another chart:

**Drag the scroll bar to the right**

**Click next to the chart's title**

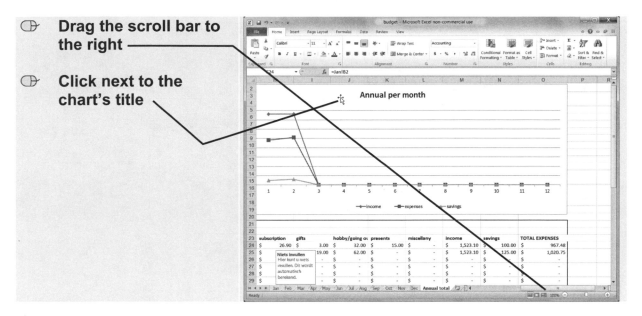

In this chapter you have learned how to create such a chart. The green line in the chart is the savings line, that is, the money you save every month.

# 5.30 Print Preview

In the previous section you have selected the chart. When you take a look at the print preview, *Excel* automatically assumes you want to print the chart:

**Click the** File **tab**

**Click** Print

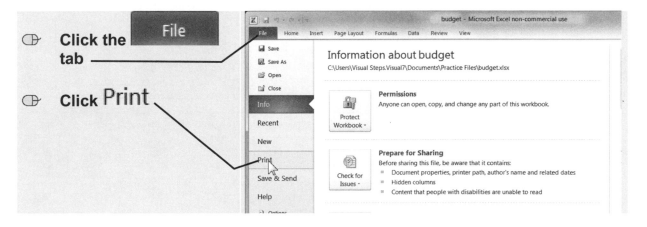

In *Excel 2007* you will do it like this:

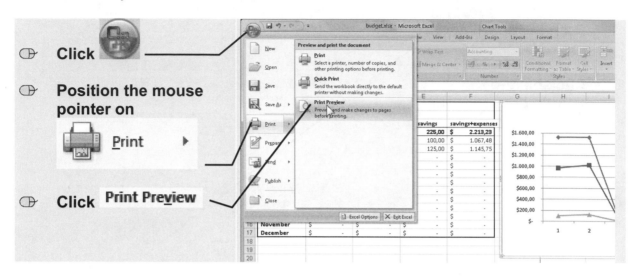

Click

Position the mouse
pointer on

Print ▶

Click **Print Preview**

The print preview looks the same as in *Word*:

You will only see the chart in
the print preview:

By the print settings you will
see
Print Selected Chart
Only print the selected chart:

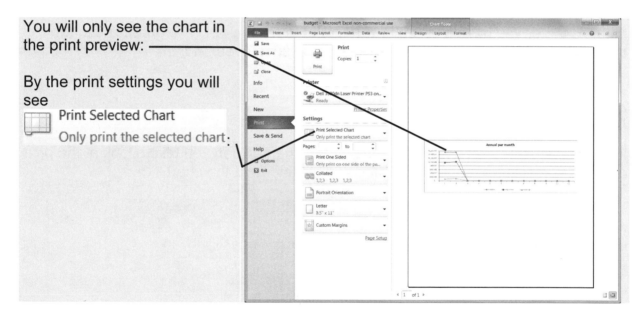

On a portrait oriented page the chart will be printed as a very small image. To make the chart appear larger, you can change the page orientation to landscape:

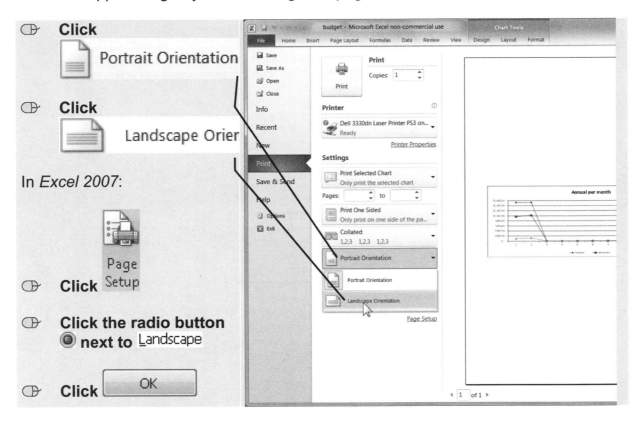

☞ **Click**     Portrait Orientation

☞ **Click**     Landscape Orier

In *Excel 2007*:

☞ **Click** Page Setup

☞ **Click the radio button** next to Landscape

☞ **Click** OK

The print preview will be adapted right away:

You will see that the chart becomes larger when the paper orientation is set to landscape:

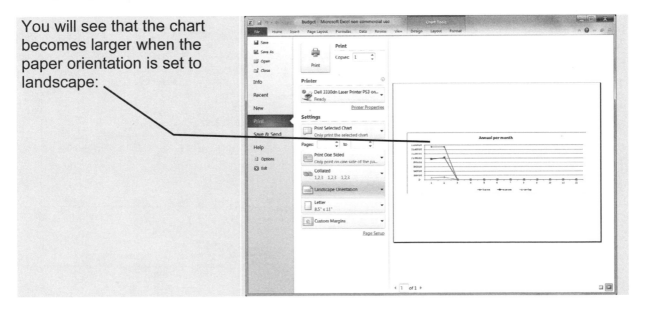

For the moment, you do not need to print the chart. Go back now to the *Annual Total* worksheet:

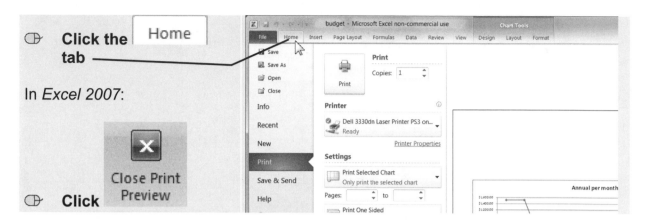

**Click the** `Home` **tab**

In *Excel 2007*:

**Click** `Close Print Preview`

# 5.31 Print a Selection

In *Excel* you can define precisely which cells you want to print:

☞ **Select the cells B2 up to and including B17** ✎**68**

☞ **Open the print preview** ✎**73, 74**

You will see the entire worksheet in the print preview:

By the print settings you will see

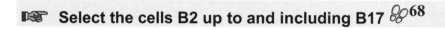
`Print Active Sheets`
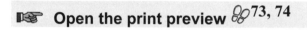
`Only print the active sh`

The worksheet does not fit on a single page. You will need four pages to print the worksheet ◄ `1` of 4 ►:

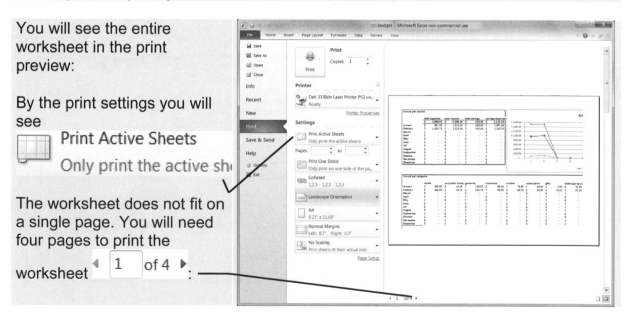

## HELP! I can only see three printable pages.

If you see three pages, the page orientation may be set to portrait. If you want to see four pages:

☞ **Select** [icon] Landscape Orientation

This is how to print only the selected cells in *Excel 2010*:

**Click**
Print Active Sheets
Only print the acti...

**Click**
**Print Selection**
Only print the cu...

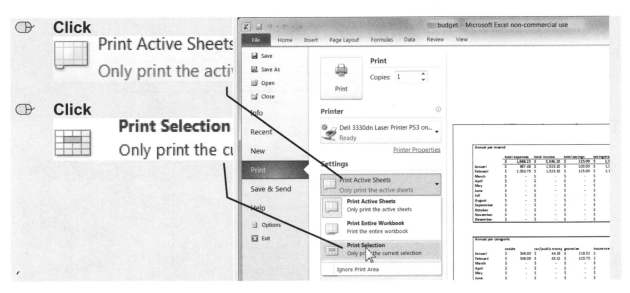

Now you will see only the cells that were selected in the print preview:

You can print the page:

**Click** Print

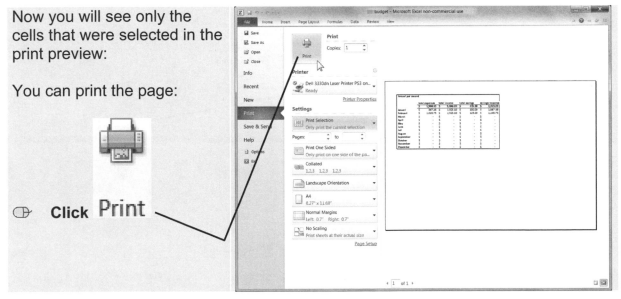

In *Excel 2007* you cannot display the selected cells in the print preview. But you are still able to print the selected cells exclusively:

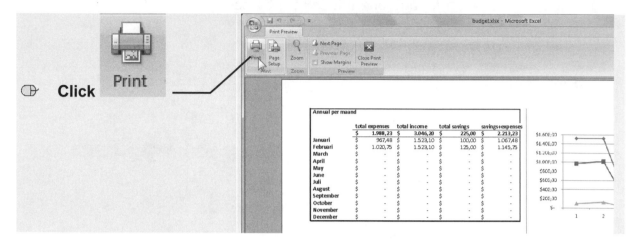

⊕  **Click**  Print

In the *Print* window you can choose which part of the worksheet you want to print:

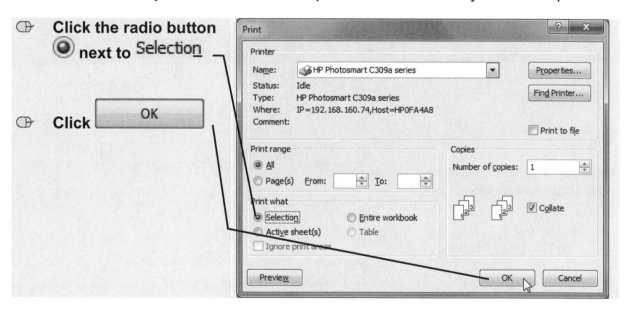

⊕  **Click the radio button**
   ⊙ **next to** Selection

⊕  **Click**  OK

The selection will be printed.

# 5.32 Print the Worksheet On a Single Page

Previously, you have seen that it will take four pages to print the entire worksheet. These are not full pages, however. Just take a look:

**Click** Print Selection
Only print the curr

**Click** **Print Active Sheets**
Only print the active

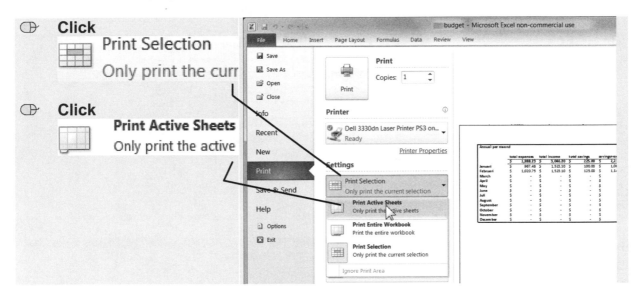

You will see the print preview for the entire worksheet:

**Click**

You will see that the second page contains only a few lines:

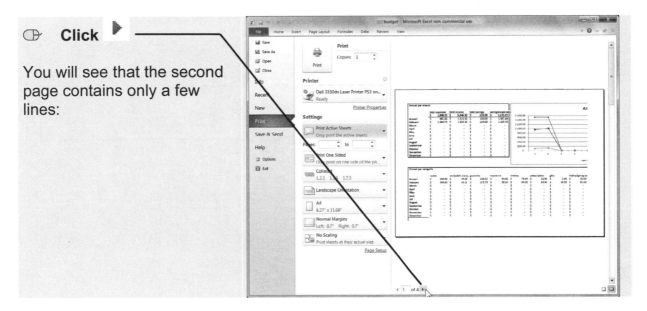

Here is how to print the entire worksheet on a single page, in *Excel 2010*:

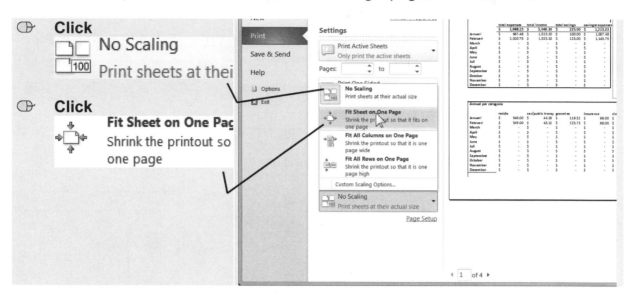

Now the worksheet has become smaller, so it will fit on one page:

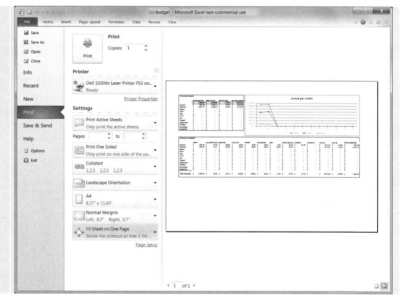

In *Excel 2007* you can do it like this:

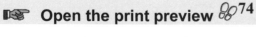
**Open the print preview** ✂74

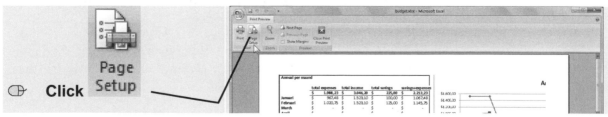

⊕ **Click the radio button ⊙ next to** <u>F</u>it to:

The settings

1 ⬍ page(s) wide

by 1 ⬍ tall have

already been entered:

⊕ **Click** OK

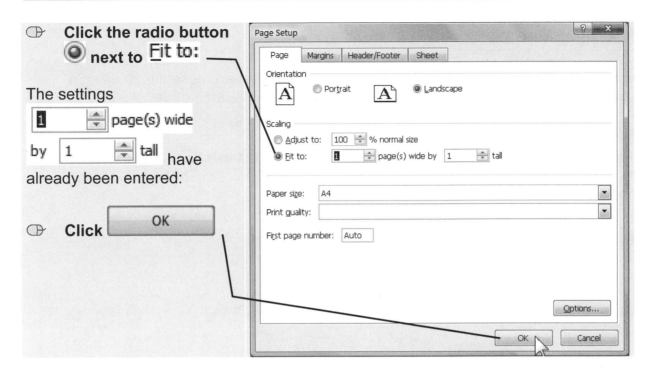

The print preview will be adjusted:

Now the worksheet will fit on one page:

You do not need to print this page:

⊕ **Click** Close Print Preview

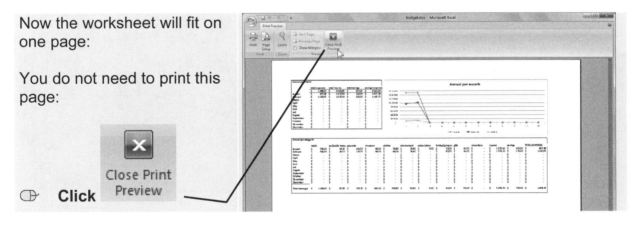

Now you have finished with this worksheet:

☞ **Close the document and do not save the changes** ✂75, 76

Now you will see a blank window.

In this chapter you have learned how to work with *Excel*. Now you have your own calculation model and the skills to record your own income and expenses in your budget. In the following exercises you can practice the operations you have learned in this chapter.

# 5.33 Exercises

In this chapter you have executed many commands that are essential to using a spreadsheet. It is a good idea to repeat these operations once more.

Have you forgotten how to do something? Then you can use the number next to the footsteps to find the information in the appendix *How Do I Do That Again?* at the back of this book.

## Exercise: Calculate Totals

For this exercise you will need a blank worksheet:

At the top left of the window:

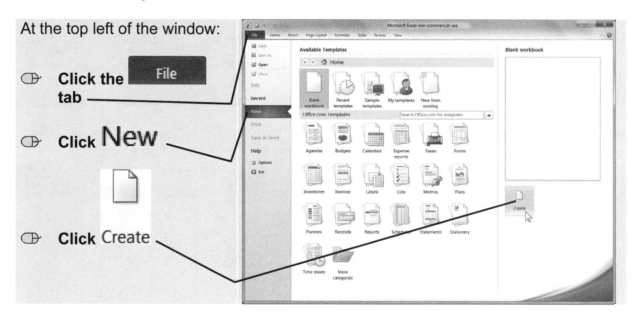

☞ **Click the** File **tab**

☞ **Click** New

☞ **Click** Create

In *Excel 2007*:

☞ **Click** , New , Create

A new, blank workbook will be opened:

☞ Type Monday in cell A2. $\frac{QQ}{}$77

☞ Drag a range containing the other days of the week to the cells A3 up to and including A8. $\frac{QQ}{}$67

☞ Type the following data: 🐾77

| 1 | | car | clothes | groceries | |
|---|---|---|---|---|---|
| 2 | Monday | | | | |
| 3 | Tuesday | | | | |
| 4 | Wednesday | | | | |
| 5 | Thursday | | | | |
| 6 | Friday | | | | |
| 7 | Saturday | | | | |
| 8 | Sunday | | | | |
| 9 | | | | | |

☞ Widen column A to fit the text. 🐾78

☞ Enter the following data: 🐾77

| | A | B | C | D | E |
|---|---|---|---|---|---|
| 1 | | car | clothes | groceries | |
| 2 | Monday | 46.95 | 3.5 | 14 | |
| 3 | Tuesday | | | 23.12 | |
| 4 | Wednesday | | 54.99 | | |
| 5 | Thursday | | | 13.1 | |
| 6 | Friday | | | | |
| 7 | Saturday | | 46 | 63.94 | |
| 8 | Sunday | 45.88 | | | |
| 9 | | | | | |

☞ Type total in cell E1. 🐾77

☞ Type the formula for calculating the total Monday expenses in cell E2. 🐾79

☞ Copy the formula from van cell E2 to cells E3 up to and including E8, by dragging a range. 🐾67

☞ Select cells B2 up to and including B8. 🐾68

☞ Use *AutoSum* to calculate the total car expenses in cell B9. 🐾80

☞ Copy the formula from cell B9 to cells C9, D9 and E9 by dragging a range. 🐾67

☞ Check the model.

| ◢ | A | B | C | D | E | F |
|---|---|---|---|---|---|---|
| 1 | | car | clothes | groceries | total | |
| 2 | Monday | 46.95 | 3.5 | 14 | 64.45 | |
| 3 | Tuesday | | | 23.12 | 23.12 | |
| 4 | Wednesday | | 54.99 | | 54.99 | |
| 5 | Thursday | | | 13.1 | 13.1 | |
| 6 | Friday | | | | 0 | |
| 7 | Saturday | | 46 | 63.94 | 109.94 | |
| 8 | Sunday | 45.88 | | | 45.88 | |
| 9 | | 92.83 | 104.49 | 114.16 | 311.48 | |
| 10 | | | | | | |

☞ Insert a dollar sign in cells B2 up to and including E9.
🐾**81**

☞ Make cell B9 up to and including E9 bold. 🐾**82**

☞ Add a border to the bottom of cells B8 up to and including E8. 🐾**83**

☞ Save the workbook as `weekly expenses` in the (*My*) *Documents* folder.
🐾**84**

Now you can record a few expenses:

☞ Modify the numbers according to the example below:

| ◢ | A | B | C | D | E | F |
|---|---|---|---|---|---|---|
| 1 | | car | clothes | groceries | total | |
| 2 | Monday | $ 46.95 | $ 3.50 | $ 14.00 | $ 64.45 | |
| 3 | Tuesday | | | $ 23.12 | $ 23.12 | |
| 4 | Wednesday | | $ 54.99 | $ 5.25 | $ 60.24 | |
| 5 | Thursday | $ 10.00 | | $ 13.10 | $ 23.10 | |
| 6 | Friday | | | | $ - | |
| 7 | Saturday | | $ 46.00 | $ 63.94 | $ 109.94 | |
| 8 | Sunday | $ 45.88 | | | $ 45.88 | |
| 9 | | **$102.83** | **$104.49** | **$119.41** | **$326.73** | |

If the formulas have been entered correctly, the total expenses in cell E9 will be:
$ 326.73.

☞ Save the modified data. 🐾**69**

# Exercises: Create a Chart

In this exercise you will practice creating and modifying a chart.

☞    Select cells A1 up to and including D8. 🐾**68**

☞    Insert a column chart ▥ in the worksheet. 🐾**85**

☞    Position the chart next to the table that contains the data. 🐾**86**

☞    Move the chart to a new worksheet. 🐾**87**

☞    Change the chart's layout to ▦. 🐾**88**

☞    Enter this title for the chart: `weekly expenses`. 🐾**89**

☞    Close *Excel* without saving the changes. 🐾**75, 76**

# 5.34 Background Information

| Dictionary | |
|---|---|
| **Alphanumeric data** | Text or numbers that cannot be used for calculations in *Excel*. |
| **AutoSum** | Function that calculates all numbers in a range of cells. |
| **Calculation model** | Specific overview in *Excel* which can be used for calculations. |
| **Cell** | The smallest unit in a table. |
| **Column** | Vertical range of cells. |
| **Formula** | Formulas are equations that perform calculations on values in your worksheet. A formula always starts with an equal sign (=). |
| **Formula bar** | A bar at the top of the *Excel* window where you can enter or modify values or formulas for cells or charts. |
| **Numeric data** | Numbers that can be used for calculations. |
| **Ribbon** | The ribbon is the toolbar containing commands at the top of the *Excel* window. The commands are arranged in tabs. Each tab has its own set of buttons, arranged in logical groups. |
| **Row** | Horizontal range of cells. |
| **Spreadsheet** | A software program that is used for calculating numbers, for instance, *Excel*. |
| **Worksheet** | A worksheet consists of cells, arranged in columns and rows. The worksheet is used to modify and save data. |
| **Zoom percentage** | Percentage which indicates how much the image of the worksheet on the screen has been enlarged or diminished. |

*Source: Microsoft Excel Help*

## Numeric and alphanumeric data

You have already noticed that *Excel* distinguishes between text and numbers. Text will be displayed to the left side of a cell, numbers to the right.

This resembles the way in which we use text or numbers in everyday life. Just take a look:

| text | numbers |
|------|---------|
| car | 25 |
| bus | 1215 |
| plane | 3 |
| train | 197 |

If it would be the other way round, it would seem very strange and is harder to read:

| text | numbers |
|------|---------|
| car | 25 |
| bus | 1215 |
| plane | 3 |
| train | 197 |

*Numbers* that can be used for calculations are also called *numeric* data. Numeric data can only consist of the numbers 0 up to and including 9, with a comma or a full stop as a decimal marker, where necessary (or with a minus sign, for negative numbers).

Text or numbers that cannot be used for calculations, are called *alphanumeric* data. Alphanumeric data can consist of every possible character, letters as well as numbers. An example of a number which cannot be used for calculations, is the hardware ID of your computer. This usually consists of digits (and sometimes letters), but you cannot use it for calculations.

A *telephone number* is an alphanumeric number as well. You do not perform calculations on such a number. Telephone numbers are often typed with the area code and the home number separated by a dash, or the area code is set inside brackets or parentheses.

## More Excel

Would you like to know about savings, loans and investments? Please take a look at *Bonus online chapter 10 Savings, Loans and Investments*. In *Appendix C Opening the Bonus Chapters* you can read how to open this chapter.

# 5.35 Tips

 **Tip**

**Enlarge or shrink the view**

With large spreadsheets, you will not be able to view all the columns and rows on your screen. If a worksheet is just a little too large, you can adjust the zoom percentage. Usually, this percentage is set to 100%. If you decrease the percentage, every item will be displayed a bit smaller, and more data will fit on the screen. Make sure that the contents in the spreadsheet are still clearly visible. This is how you change the zoom percentage:

In the lower right side of the window:

☞ **Click** 100%

You will see this window:

☞ **Click the radio button ⦿ next to the desired percentage**

☞ **Click** OK

If you do not like this view, return to the old percentage, that is, 100%.

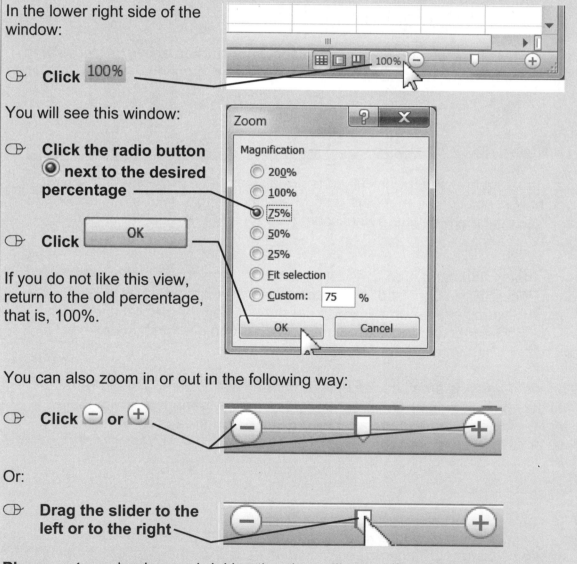

You can also zoom in or out in the following way:

☞ **Click ⊖ or ⊕**

Or:

☞ **Drag the slider to the left or to the right**

**Please note:** enlarging or shrinking the view will only affect the display on your screen. It will not affect the print size of the worksheet.

**Tip**

**Save in a different file format**
If you are familiar with earlier *Excel* editions, you will know that the *Excel* files could be identified by the .xls extension, for instance, *Myfile.xls*. In *Excel 2010* and *2007* the extension has changed to .XLSX, instead of .XLS.

In *Excel 2010* and *2007* the default file format is Excel Workbook (*.xlsx) . The file will get the extension .XLSX. If you have opened an existing *Excel* file and you want others to view this file without having *Excel 2010* or *2007* installed, you can save this file in a different file format. This is how you do it.

In *Excel 2010*:

☞ **Click the** File **tab,** 🖫 Save As

☞ **By** Save as type: **click**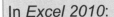

☞ **Click** Excel 97-2003 Workbook

In the bottom right of the window:

☞ **Click** Save

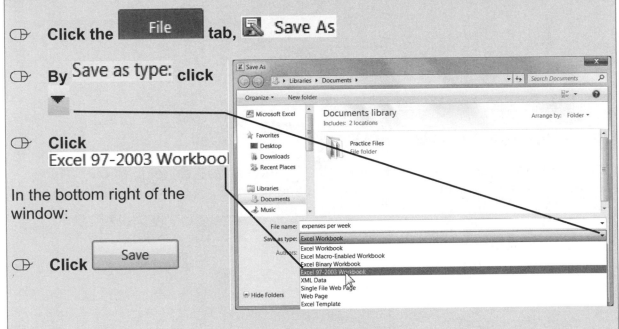

In *Excel 2007*:

☞ **Click** , Save As ▶

*- Continue reading on the next page -*

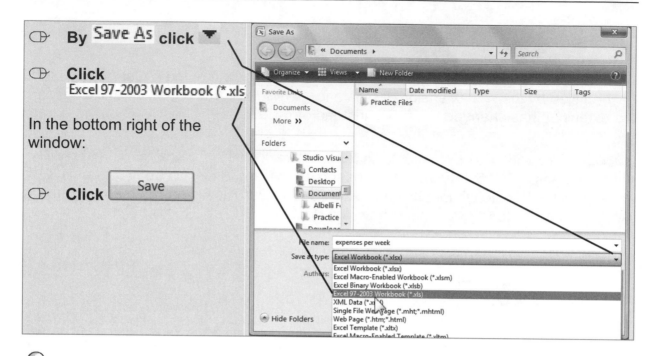

- By Save As click ▼

- Click
Excel 97-2003 Workbook (*.xls

In the bottom right of the window:

- Click  Save

## 💡 Tip

**What can you do if you see these signs ####  in a cell**

If the contents of your cell look like this ####, the entered value does not fit into the cell. You can solve this problem by widening the columns. This is how you do it:

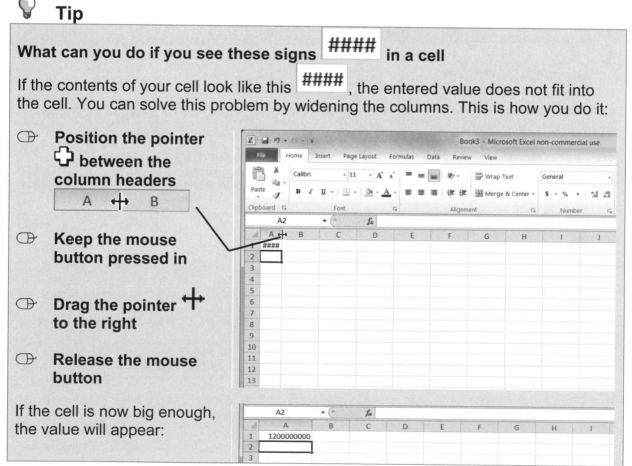

- **Position the pointer ✛ between the column headers**
  A ↔ B

- **Keep the mouse button pressed in**

- **Drag the pointer ↔ to the right**

- **Release the mouse button**

If the cell is now big enough, the value will appear:

**Tip**

**Create ranges of numbers and dates**
In *Excel* you can also create the following ranges:

If you enter a date in a cell and drag the handle ✛, the range will be completed with subsequent dates:

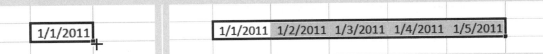

If you have entered a single number, the content of the cell will be copied:

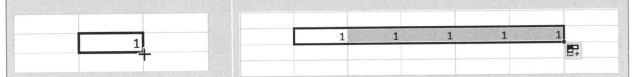

If you want to create a range of numbers, you will need to tell *Excel* what the next number in the sequence should be. To do this, you need to select two cells:

- **Place the mouse pointer in the first cell**
- **Press the mouse button and keep it depressed**
- **Drag to the cell with the subsequent number**
- **Release the mouse button**

Now you can create a range of numbers by dragging the handle of the second cell:

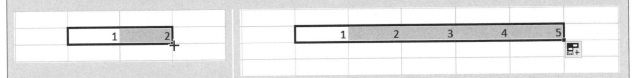

They do not need to be subsequent numbers, *Excel* can also complete these types of ranges:

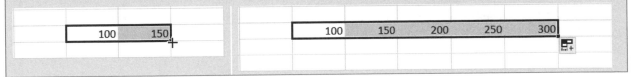

**Tip**

**Regularly test your worksheet**
Always maintain a critical eye while viewing the results of your calculations, even if you are using the model for quite a while. Regularly check the model for errors. It often happens that one of the formulas is accidentally replaced by a value you have entered. Initially, you will not notice this. Test the model by replacing all the values one by one. This way you can check if the calculations are executed correctly. And you will be alerted to possible errors.

 **Tip**

**Set the print area**
If you just want to print part(s) of a worksheet, you will need to select the printable area first. This is called the *print area*.

☞ **Open the *exercise budget* file form the (*My*) *Documents* folder** 𝄞139

☞ **Select the cells A1 up to and including E14** 𝄞68

☞ **Click the**

Page Layout **tab**

**Click** Print Area ▾

**Click** 🗐 Set Print Area

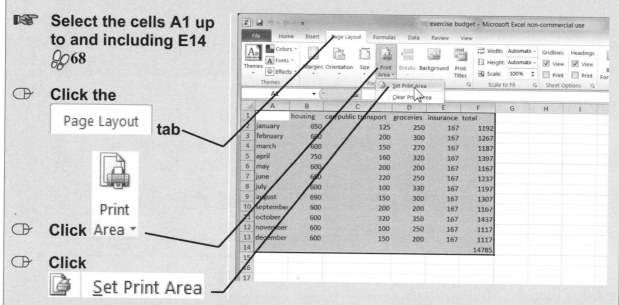

Now the selected area is surrounded by a dotted line:

Only this specific area will be printed.

**Tip**

## Relative and absolute cells

When you copy a formula, the formula will automatically be adapted. If you copy a formula to a line below the current line, *Excel* will automatically increase the line number by one. If you copy the formula =A1+B1 from line 1 to the line below, the formula in line 2 will be: =A2+B2, in line 3: =A3+B3, etcetera.

Usually this is the right way to go, but not always. If you are using a constant value in a cell (for example, the sales tax percentage), you do not want to change this constant when the cell is copied.

A cell reference that does not change when you copy or move a formula, is called an absolute. An absolute reference always refers to the same cell, even if you copy or move the formula. You can indicate this in the formula by inserting a $ in front of the column and row number.
If you want to insert an absolute reference to cell A1 in the formula, it will look like this: '=$A$1*B5'. When you copy this formula to the cell below, the formula will be: '=$A$1*B6'. B5 will turn into B6 because that is a relative cell reference, but '$A$1' will not change.

 **Tip**

## Calculate Name cells

Formulas that contain cell references are difficult to read. This can be a nuisance if you want to look for mistakes in a formula or if you want to change a formula. Instead of cell references, you can also use cell names in your formulas. You can enter these cell names for a single cell, or for a group of cells:

 **Type the data from this example**

|  | A | B | C | D | E |
|---|---|---|---|---|---|
| 1 |  | housing | car/public transport | groceries |  |
| 2 | january | 650 | 125 | 250 |  |
| 3 | february | 600 | 200 | 300 |  |
| 4 | march | 600 | 150 | 270 |  |
| 5 | april | 750 | 160 | 320 |  |
| 6 | may | 600 | 200 | 200 |  |
| 7 | june | 600 | 220 | 250 |  |
| 8 | july | 600 | 100 | 330 |  |
| 9 | august | 690 | 150 | 300 |  |
| 10 | september | 600 | 200 | 200 |  |
| 11 | october | 600 | 320 | 350 |  |
| 12 | november | 600 | 100 | 250 |  |
| 13 | december | 600 | 150 | 200 |  |
| 14 |  |  |  |  |  |

*- Continue reading on the next page -*

☞ **Select cells B2 up to and including B13** 👣68

🖱 **Click the *Name box***

⌨ **Type:** housing

⌨ **Press** Enter ↵

☞ **Change the name of cells C2 up to and including C13 to *car*** 👣65

☞ **Change the name of cells C2 up to and including C13 to *groceries*** 👣65

⌨ **Type this in cell E2:**
=housing+car+groceries

In the formula bar you will see the formula
=housing+car+groceries.

⌨ **Press** Enter ↵

You will see the results in cell E2:

☞ **Copy the formula from E2 to cell E3 up to and including E13** 👣67

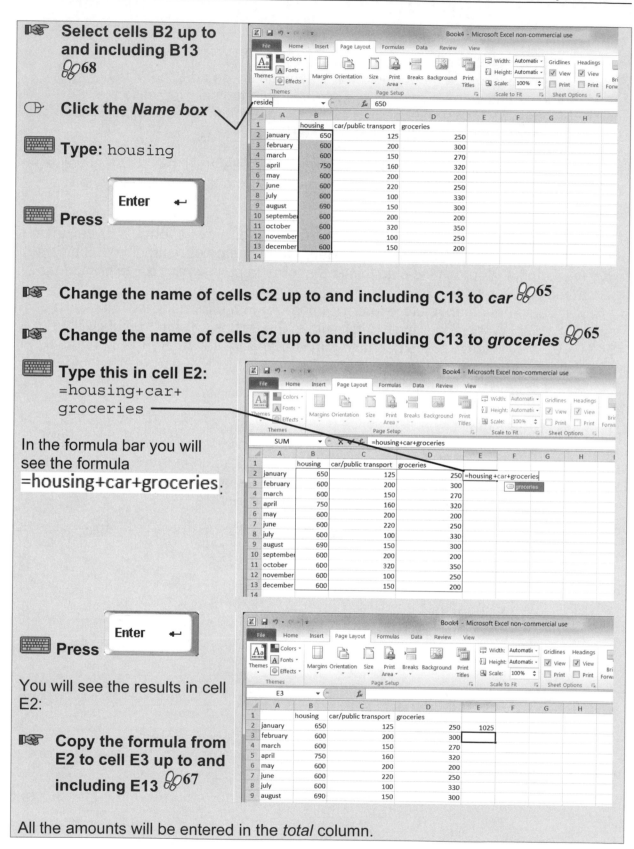

All the amounts will be entered in the *total* column.

# 6. Using Excel as a Database

You can use an *Excel* worksheet to keep track of various types of information. For instance, a list of your favorite movies, a membership list, or a list of all your staff. You can also use *Excel* to maintain lists of your CD collection, your books, or your stamp collection.

A technical term for such a list is a *database*. An *Excel* worksheet is well ordered, neat and tidy, and can contain hundreds of columns and thousands of rows. You do not need to perform calculations, but will instead use the simple, yet powerful, sorting tool in *Excel*. This is a great help in creating and maintaining such lists.

Furthermore, there are many options available that will allow you to select specific records from large lists (in *Excel* this is called *filtering*). This option lets you easily find people or objects in a specific list, sorted or unsorted.

In this chapter you will learn how to:

- create a book list;
- sort data in ascending or descending order;
- sort data in a list by multiple levels;
- filter data from a list;
- use customized filters.

# 6.1 Creating a Book List

To get a clear picture of the way *Excel* can be used as a database you will need to create a list yourself. In the following examples, we will be working with a list of books. But it could just as well be a membership list, a list of customers, employees, CDs, DVDs or stamps.

☞ **Open** *Excel* 👣⁹⁰

 **Please note:**

In this chapter you will practice working with *Excel* as a database by creating a booklist. If you do not want to enter the data yourself, you can get started right away by downloading the *books* workbook from the website that accompanies this book. In *Appendix A Downloading the Practice Files* at the back of this book, you can read how to do this.

 **Enter the data from the example below** 👣⁷⁷

| | A | B | C | D | E | F |
|---|---|---|---|---|---|---|
| 1 | | author | author | | | |
| 2 | title | first name | surname | publisher | year | genre |
| 3 | Faithful Place | Tara | French | Viking Adult | 2010 | thriller |
| 4 | The Passage | Justin | Cronin | Ballatine Books | 2010 | thriller |
| 5 | Broken | Karin | Slaughter | Delacorte Press | 2010 | thriller |
| 6 | Hangman | Fay | Kellerman | William Morrow | 2010 | thriller |
| 7 | Windows 7 for Seniors | Studio | Visual Steps | Visual Steps Publishing | 2009 | computer books |
| 8 | Bones | Jonathan | Kellerman | Ballatine Books | 2009 | thriller |
| 9 | Sarah's Key | Tatiana | de Rosnay | St. Martin's Griffin | 2008 | fiction |
| 10 | The Confession | John | Grisham | Doubleday | 2010 | thriller |
| 11 | Jamie at Home | Jamie | Oliver | Hyperion | 2008 | cooking |
| 12 | Picasa for Seniors | Studio | Visual Steps | Visual Steps Publishing | 2010 | computer books |
| 13 | The Essential New York Times Cookbook | Amanda | Heser | W.W. Norton & Company | 2010 | cooking |
| 14 | Life In Miniature | Linda | Schlossberg | Kensington | 2010 | fiction |
| 15 | | | | | | |

Most likely, you have already noticed that *Excel* recognizes certain names when you begin typing. Once you enter certain data for the first time, such as the publisher's name, the year and the genre, they will automatically be entered the next time.

☞ **Widen the columns so that all the text fits** 👣⁷⁸

☞ **Make rows 1 and 2 bold** 👣⁸²

After you have entered the information about these books, it is a good idea to save your worksheet before you continue further.

☞ **Save the worksheet as** *books* **in the (***My***) *Documents* folder** 👣⁸⁴

# 6.2 Sorting

You have entered the books in random order. But if you want to look up a book, it would be easier to sort the books by their title, in alphabetical order. This is how you sort items in alphabetical order:

**Click a title**

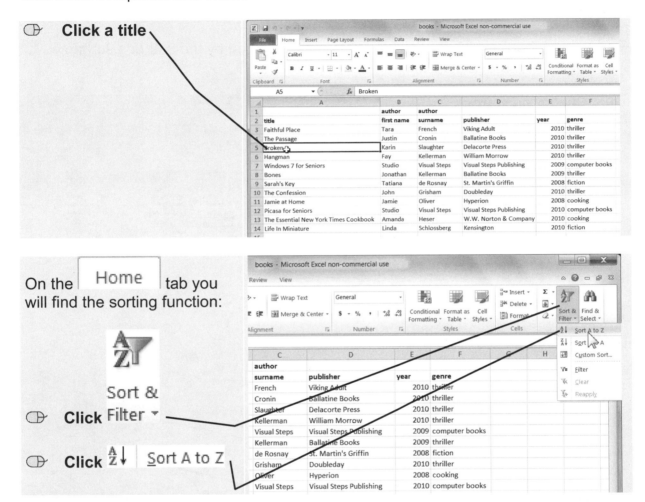

**On the** Home **tab you will find the sorting function:**

**Click** Sort & Filter ▾

**Click** A↓ Sort A to Z

Now all the books have been sorted alphabetically, by their title:

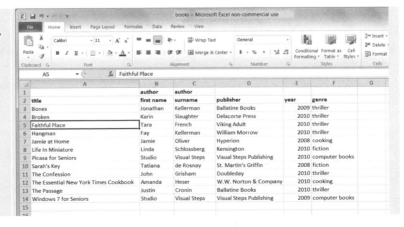

**Please note:**

Not only have the titles been sorted, but all the data in the rows that go with the title have been sorted as well. Each surname still matches the correct author, publisher, etcetera.

**Please note:** this will not work if there are any blank columns in between the data.

Perhaps the books in your bookcase at home are sorted by the author's surname. You can do the same thing with this list:

**Click a surname**

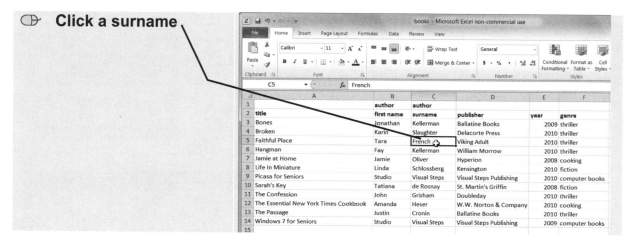

Now you are going to sort the list:

**Click Filter ▾**

**Click Sort A to Z**

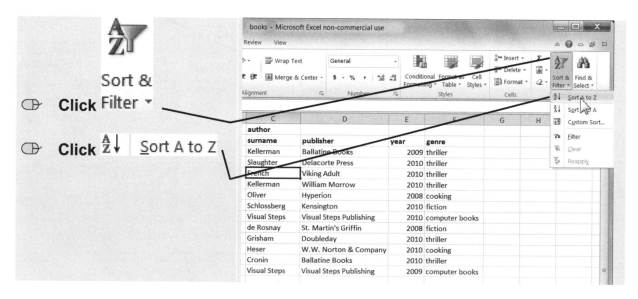

Now all the books have been sorted alpabetically, by the author's surname:

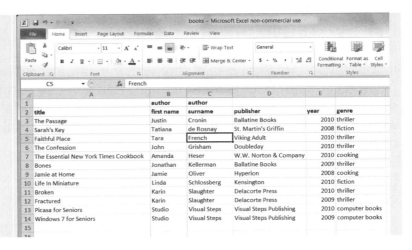

You see how easy it is to quickly sort your list in any way that you want.

 **Please note:**

Be careful when you do your sorting. Select a single cell in one column. If you have selected multiple cells, only those selected cells will be sorted. The corresponding data, such as first names, addresses and years will not be included. This means the list will no longer be accurate.

 **HELP! The sorting action has gone wrong.**

If a problem occurs while sorting, just click the Undo button  on the *Quick Access* toolbar.

 **Tip**

**Sorting in reverse order**
So far you have sorted the data in ascending order only. That is to say, from lowest (top of the column) to highest (bottom of the column). This method of sorting is the most commonly used method. But there are several other ways of sorting:

By clicking Sort & Filter ▼ and then Z A↓ Sort Z to A on the Home tab, you can sort the data in descending order. That is, from highest (top of the column) to lowest (bottom of the column). This type of sorting method is great for score lists (who has scored the most points, for example), or sales volume lists (the employee with the most sales will be at the top of the list).

# 6.3 Sorting Multiple Levels

If you have more than one author with the same surname, it is a good idea to do an initial sort on the author's first name. Then you can sort the list a second time on the surname. The name 'Faye Kellerman' will then precede 'Jonathan Kellerman'. Start with the column that has the least important order, in this case, the author's first name:

☞ **Sort the list by first name** 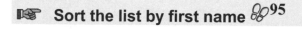⁹⁵

Now you will see 'Amanda' at the top of the list:

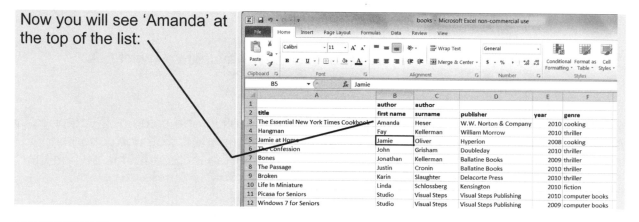

☞ **Sort the list by surname** 🐾⁹⁵

Now the list has been sorted by surname:

People that have the same surname will then be sorted by their first name:

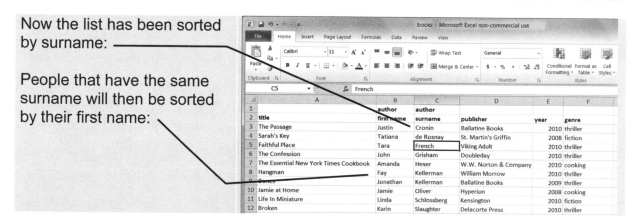

In the meantime, you are going to save the most recent changes in the workbook:

☞ **Save the workbook** 🐾⁶⁹

It is recommended that you save your work regularly, no matter if you are simply practicing with *Excel* or using it for real work. When you have finished saving, you can resume your work where you left off.

# 6.4 Filtering

If you do not want to view all the data in your worksheet, but just a specific category, you can *filter* (select) the data. This is especially useful if you have very long lists, with many columns because superfluous data will not be displayed.

☞ **Click a random cell in the booklist**

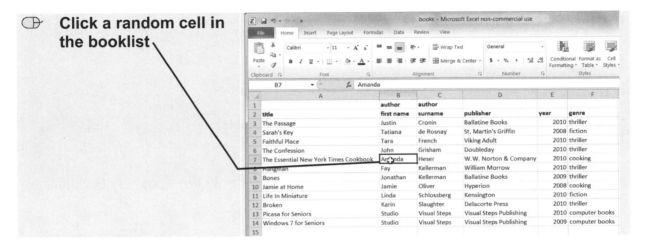

This is how you use the *Filter* function:

☞ **Click** Sort & Filter ▾

☞ **Click** ▼= **Filter**

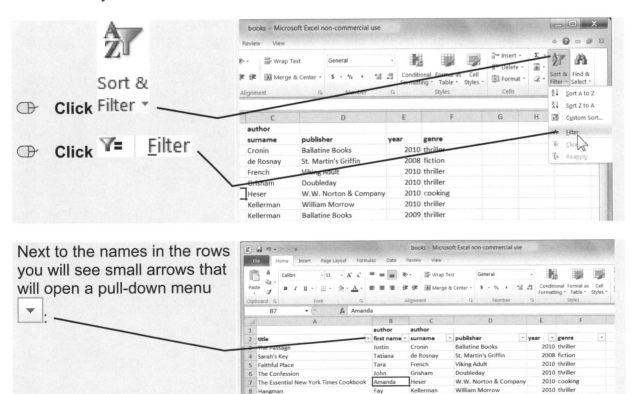

Next to the names in the rows you will see small arrows that will open a pull-down menu ▼:

**Position the mouse pointer in the publisher column next to** [▼]

The pointer will turn into a ⇩:

**By publisher click** [▼]

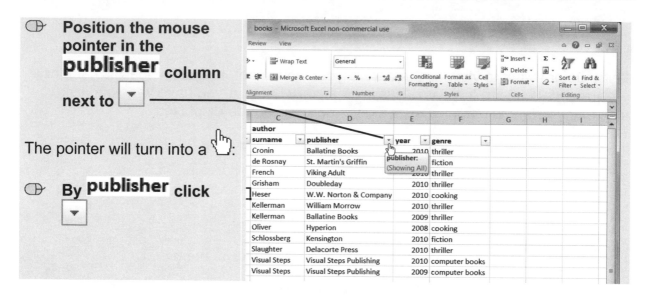

In this example, you will use the *Filter* function to show only the books by Ballatine Books:

**Uncheck the box** ☑ **next to (Select All)**

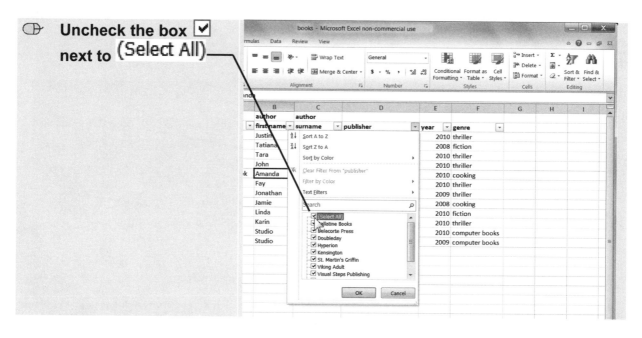

**Check the box ☑ next to Ballatine Books**

**Click OK**

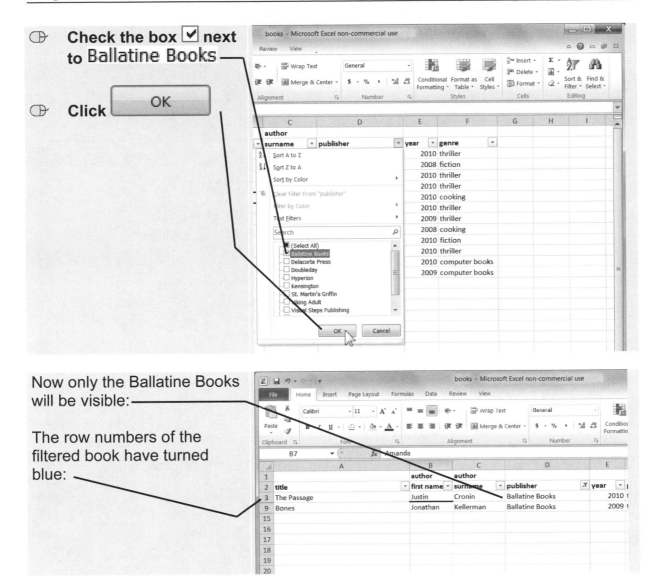

Now only the Ballatine Books will be visible:

The row numbers of the filtered book have turned blue:

The blue row numbers indicate that you are not looking at the complete list, but just a part of it. Also note, that the small icon on the button in the

**publisher** ▼ field has changed. This indicates that you have filtered the data by this field and by this name.

You can easily return to the full booklist:

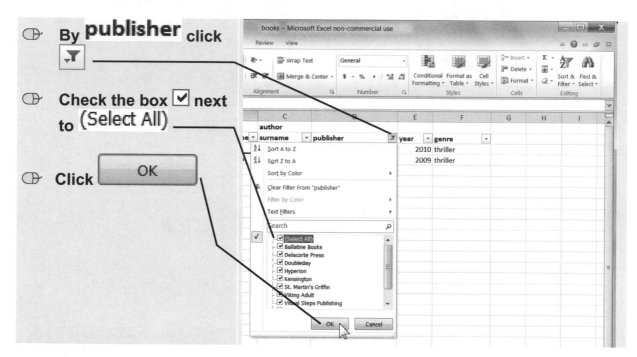

By **publisher** click

Check the box ☑ next to **(Select All)**

Click **OK**

## 💡 Tip

**Find data**
You can also filter the data by using the find option. Here is how you do that:

In the search box:

⌨ **Type:** Visual

Click **OK**

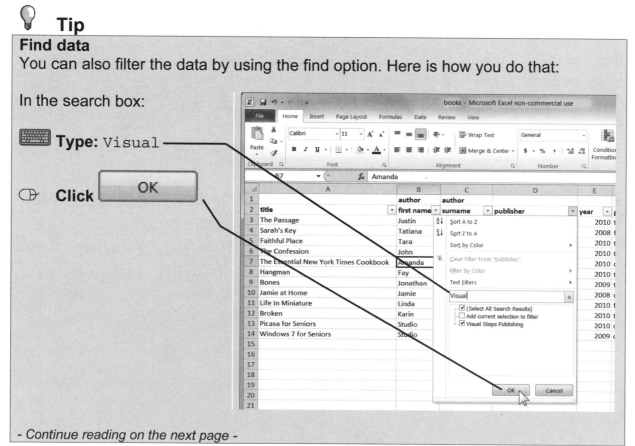

*- Continue reading on the next page -*

Now, only the books by Visual Steps Publishing will be displayed in the list.

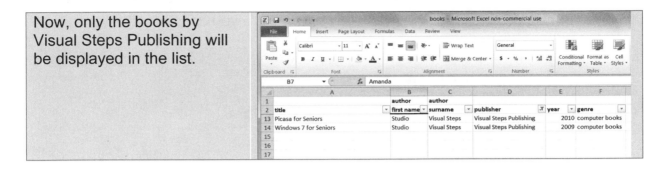

# 6.5 Custom Filters

You can also enter various other search arguments. For instance, you can filter all the books that have been published before the year 2010:

⊕ By **year** click ▼

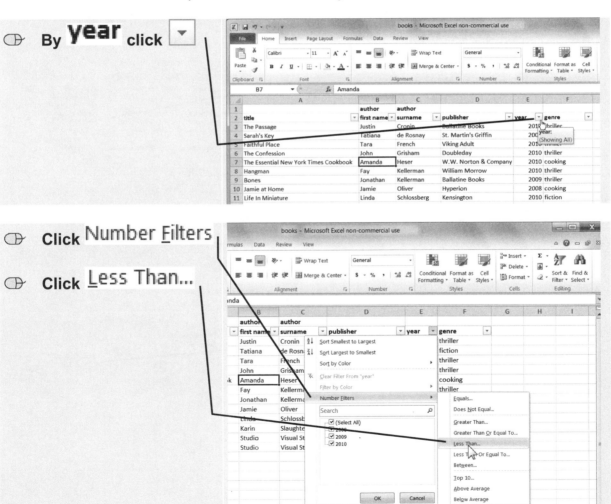

⊕ Click Number Filters

⊕ Click Less Than...

The *Custom AutoFilter* window will now be shown. Here you can enter the year:

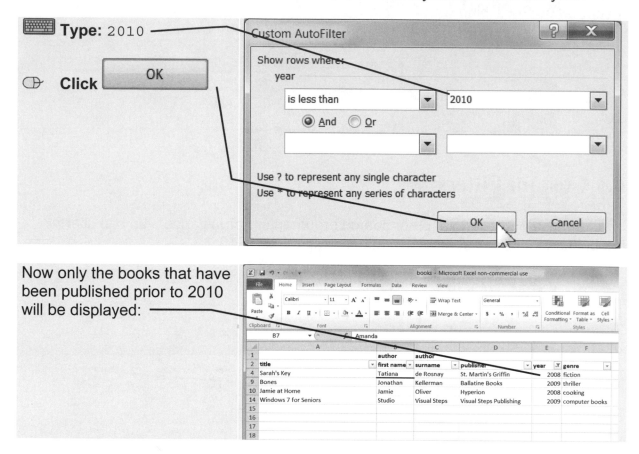

⌨ **Type:** 2010

☞ **Click** OK

Now only the books that have been published prior to 2010 will be displayed:

Of course you can sort these books by year as well:

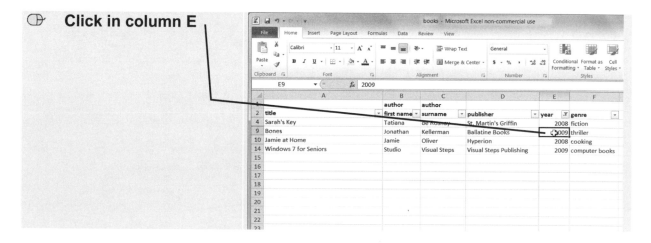

☞ **Click in column E**

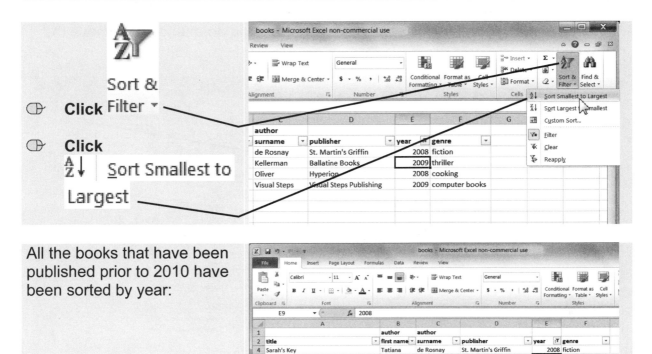

⊙ **Click** Sort & Filter ▾

⊙ **Click** A/Z ↓ Sort Smallest to Largest

All the books that have been published prior to 2010 have been sorted by year:

You can remove the filter:

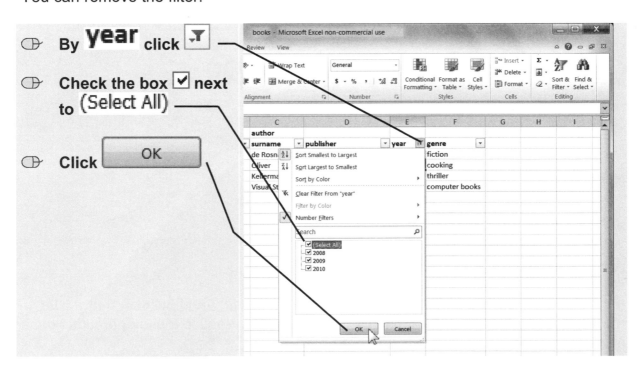

⊙ **By** **year** **click** ▼

⊙ **Check the box** ☑ **next to** (Select All)

⊙ **Click** OK

Now once again you will see the entire booklist. You can go ahead and remove the filter buttons:

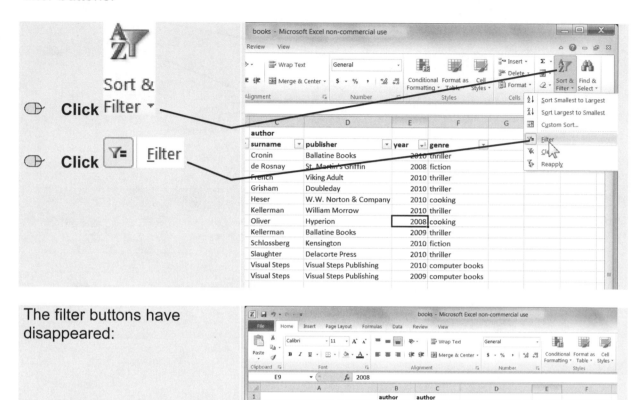

The filter buttons have disappeared:

Now you can close the workbook:

👉 **Save the changes** 🦶🦶⁶⁹

👉 **Close the workbook** 🦶🦶⁷⁰, ⁷¹

In this chapter you have learned how to create a booklist, and how to sort and filter the items in the list. In the following exercises you can practice these operations once more.

# 6.6 Exercises

Have you forgotten how to do something? Then you can use the number next to the footsteps to find the information in the appendix *How Do I Do That Again?* at the back of this book.

 **Please note!**

> In these exercises you are going to use a worksheet containing information about cars. If you do not want to enter the data yourself, you can open the workbook *cars* from the *Practice Files* folder. In *Appendix A Downloading the Practice Files* at the back of this book, you can read how to download these files to your computer.

## Exercise: Sorting

☞ Open a new workbook. ℘**91, 92**

☞ Enter the following data:

| | A | B | C | D | E | F | G |
|---|---|---|---|---|---|---|---|
| 1 | license number | make | model | year built | driver | miles | |
| 2 | 5AOJ230 | Chevrolet | Camaro | 2002 | Frank | 75000 | |
| 3 | 5BBM299 | Chrysler | Town and Country | 2004 | Peter | 92000 | |
| 4 | 4nQE750 | Toyota | Prius | 2008 | Joyce | 56000 | |
| 5 | 4PKC592 | Mitsubishi | Outlander | 2003 | Ida | 104000 | |
| 6 | 5EKR790 | Jeep | Cherokee | 2009 | Michael | 11000 | |
| 7 | 4YCH428 | Ford | Mustang | 1997 | Alex | 143000 | |
| 8 | 2CMK720 | Nissan | Altima | 2010 | Roy | 6400 | |
| 9 | | | | | | | |

☞ Save the list as *cars* in the (*My*) *Documents* folder. ℘**84**

☞ Sort the list alphabetically, by the driver's names. ℘**95**

☞ Sort the list by license number. ℘**95**

☞ Undo the last operation. ℘**23**

☞ Sort the list by year built, in descending order (the newest car will appear at the top of the list). ℘**96**

# Exercise: Filtering

☞   Activate the *Filter* function. 👣**97**

☞   Set the filter to display only the car made by Ford. 👣**98**

☞   Display the full list again. 👣**99**

☞   Use a custom filter to display all cars that are built before 2003. 👣**100**

☞   Display the full list again. 👣**99**

# Exercise: Top 10

In the menu under the filter buttons you will also find the *Top 10* option. You can use this option to filter the highest or lowest values from the list. You can choose to display ten values, but you can also choose any other number as well, for instance, three or fifteen.

☞   Make sure that the *Filter* function is activated. 👣**97**

☞   Click the filter button ▼ next to *miles*.

☞   Click Number Filters, Top 10... .

Now you will see the *AutoFilter top 10* window:

☞   Click ▼ until you reach 3.

☞   Click  OK .

This way, you will see the top three cars with the highest mileage.

☞   Display the full list again. 👣**99**

☞   Close *Excel* without saving the workbook. 👣**75, 76**

# 6.7 Background Information

| | |
|---|---|
| **Dictionary** | |
| **Database** | A database is a digital archive; the information is stored in such a way that retrieval of the data is optimized. This is the most important feature of a database. |
| **Filter** | A function in *Excel* which lets you display specific data. As soon as you de-activate the filter, the data will be displayed in its entirety once more. |
| **Sort** | Ordering data. Sorting in ascending order displays the items from the lowest to the highest; sorting in descending order displays the items from the highest to the lowest. |

*Source: Microsoft Excel Help*

## 6.8 Tips

 **Tip**

**Select cells for sorting**
Make sure that you have not selected multiple cells, rows, or columns if you want to sort the data. If you have selected multiple items, the sorting action will only be applied to the selected area, and only the selected items will change place. As a result you may see that in a booklist, the title no longer matches the author. Or in an address list, the name no longer matches the address.

 **Tip**

**Applying multiple filters**
You can apply an additional filter, even after having activated another filter (this will result in displaying part of the list). For instance, first you can filter all thrillers in your booklist, and then all books which have been published by Ballantine Books.

The filter button of the genre column will turn into a different symbol,

as well as the filter button of the publisher column. It can be very useful to filter on multiple levels, especially with large databases.

 **Tip**

**Sort by date**
*Excel* sorts by numerical or alphanumerical order and checks the cell where the item is stored to determine whether the item is (alpha) numerical. This would cause problems when you would want to sort items by date. If you would only look at the numbers, this ascending order would be correct:
01/12/2005
21/06/2006
30/01/2005

But if it concerns dates, very likely you would prefer the following order:
30/01/2005
01/12/2005
21/06/2006

*Excel* will display a list of dates in the same way as the second example above, but only if you have entered the data as dates. If you do not type slashes between the year, month, and day, *Excel* will not recognize the 'number' as a date, and the sorting order will be wrong.

# 7. Printing Labels

If you are planning to send a large number of letters or greeting cards, it can be very useful to set up the address labels so that they can be printed automatically. You can buy labels in assorted sizes from your local office supply store.

For example, you can use mailing labels to send a newsletter to members of your club, or use them for your own Christmas card or other type of card such as a Thank You card. This saves you a lot of time writing and typing the addresses by hand.

In *Word* you can use the *Mail Merge* function to easily and quickly print label sheets. The *Mail Merge* function works as a *wizard*. A wizard is a small program that guides you through a number of steps in creating a specific type of document.

You can use the data from an existing address list to populate your labels. You can use lists that are created in *Excel* or *Word*. In the previous chapter you learned how to make an address list in *Excel*. In this chapter you will learn how to create an address list in *Word* by using a table.

In this chapter you will learn how to:

- create a table in *Word*;
- make labels with an address list from *Word*;
- make labels with an address list from *Excel*;
- format labels;
- add an illustration;
- print labels.

 **Please note:**

If you want to do the exercises in this chapter, you will need to download the corresponding practice files from the website that goes with this book. Download the files to your computer and store them in the (*My*) *Documents* folder. In *Appendix A Downloading the Practice Files* at the back of this book you can read how to do this.

# 7.1 Create a Table in Word

If you enter your addresses in a table in *Word*, you can use the data to print labels. Creating a table in *Word* is easy, just give it a try:

☞ **Open** *Word* ℰ¹

A blank document will be opened. In order to have enough space for the table, you will need to change the page orientation from portrait to landscape:

⊕ **Click the** [ Page Layout ] **tab**

⊕ **Click** [ Orientation ▾ ]

⊕ **Click** [ Landscape ]

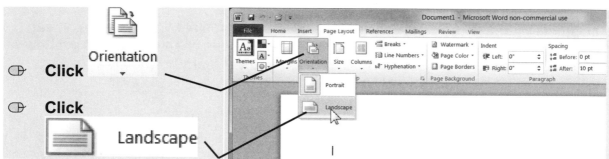

Now you will see the page in the landscape format:

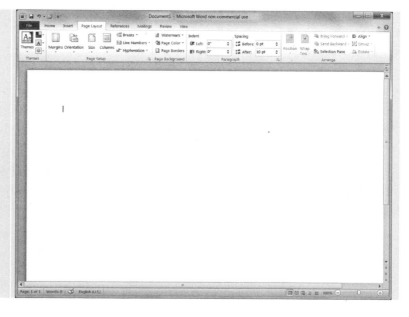

On the *Insert* tab you will find the command for inserting a table:

**Click the tab**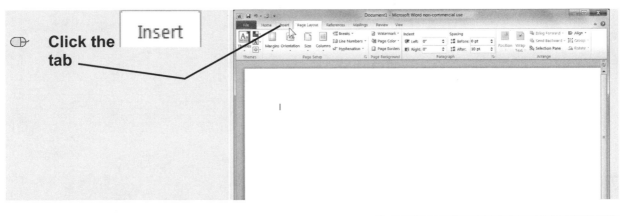

**Click**

Now you will see a menu where you can indicate how many rows and columns the table must contain:

You are going to select seven columns and eight rows:

**Move the mouse pointer over the menu**

Right away, you will see a preview of the table in your document:

When you see **7x8 Table**:

**Click**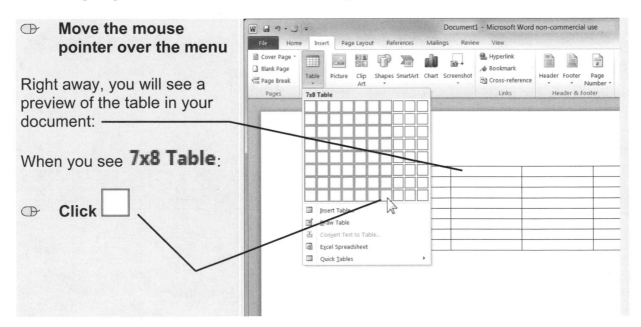

You will see the table in *Word*:

In the ribbon you will see the

**Table Tools** , including the *Design* and *Layout* tabs:

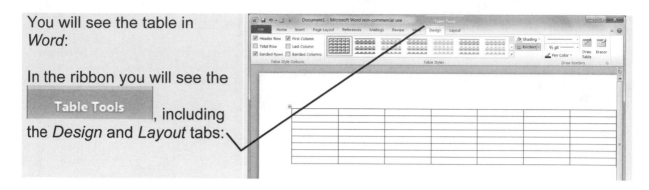

# 7.2 Fill in a Table

Just like a worksheet in *Excel*, a *Word* table also consists of rows, columns and cells. You can create the titles for your columns in the cells of the first row:

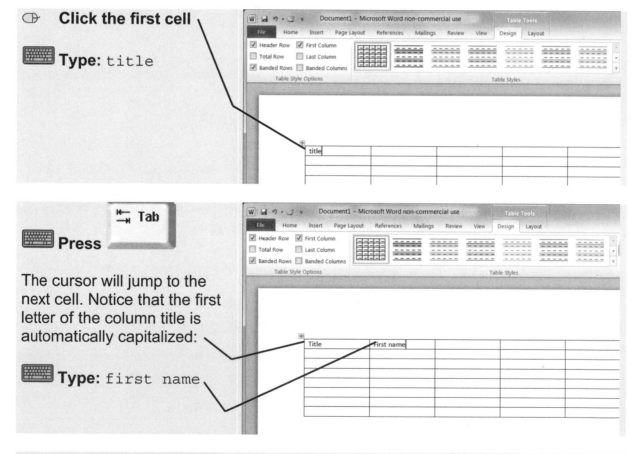

☞ **Click the first cell**

⌨ **Type:** title

⌨ **Press** Tab

The cursor will jump to the next cell. Notice that the first letter of the column title is automatically capitalized:

⌨ **Type:** first name

🖙 **Type the column titles in row 1 from the example below:**

| Title | First name | Letter | Surname | Address | Residence | State |
|-------|-----------|--------|---------|---------|-----------|-------|
|       |           |        |         |         |           |       |

# 7.3 Add a Column

It is better to enter the zip code in a separate column. Here is how to add an extra column to the table:

**Click the** Layout **tab**

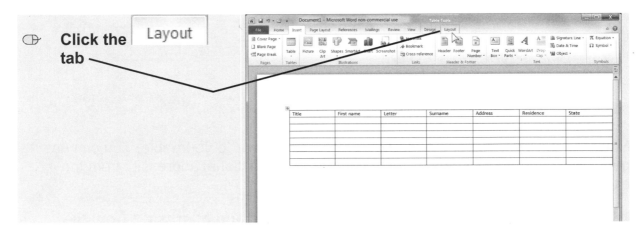

You are going to insert a column to the right of the *Address* cell:

**Click the cell called**
*Address*

**Click** Insert Right

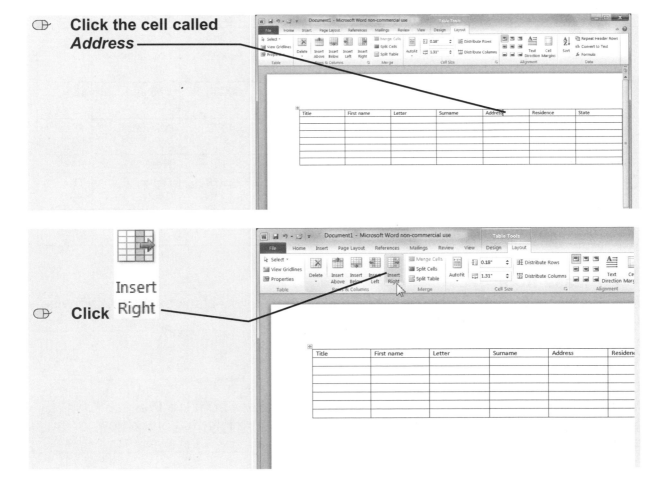

You will see that a new column has been added:

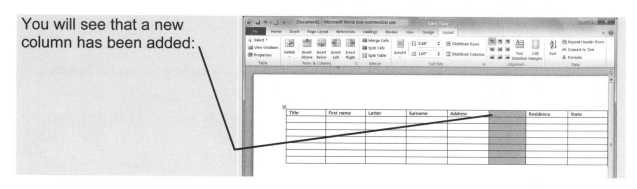

☞ **Enter this title for the new column:** *Zip code* 📎77

Now you can start entering a few names and addresses to your table. You can use genuine people and addresses, or you can copy the fictional addresses from the example below:

☞ **Fill in all the rows in the table with the names and addresses from the example below** 📎101

| Title | First name | Letter | Surname | Address | Zip code | Residence | State |
|-------|-----------|--------|---------|---------|----------|-----------|-------|
| Mrs. | Maria | M. | Borne | 130 Bridge Road | 60086 | Chicago | IL |
| Mrs. | Rita | R. | Grayson | 641 Sunset Avenue | 90291 | Los Angeles | CA |
| Mrs. | Joyce | J. | Leigh | 3564 Green Street | 60086 | Chicago | IL |
| Mrs. | May | M. | Cuttler | 1432 Newton Avenue | 64972 | Miami | FL |
| Mr. | Hank | H. | Mayhue | 16 Broad Street | 89134 | New Orleans | LA |
| Mrs. | Yvonne | Y. | Harrington | 151 Clinton Place | 25678 | Dallas | TX |
| Mr. | Alex | A. | White | 1308 Columbia Road | 68945 | Las Vegas | NV |

 **Please note:**

Make sure that the table does not contain any unnecessary blank spaces. Otherwise the labels will not print correctly.

 **Tip**

**Use the practice file**
You can save time typing by using the *directoryword.docx* from the *Practice Files*. See *Appendix A Downloading the Practice Files* for more information on how to download these files.

# 7.4 Change the Column Width

In this example the address *641 Sunset Avenue* is too long to fit the cell. This forces an extra line in the cell. If you narrow the zip code column a bit, the address will fit in the cell:

**⌖ Position the pointer on the line between the column headers**

The pointer will turn into ⁺‖⁺:

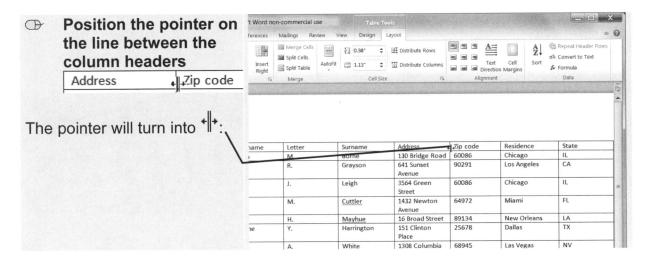

Now you can drag the border of the column:

**⌖ Press the mouse button down and keep it pressed in**

**⌖ Drag to the right**

The dotted line indicates the width of the *Address* column:

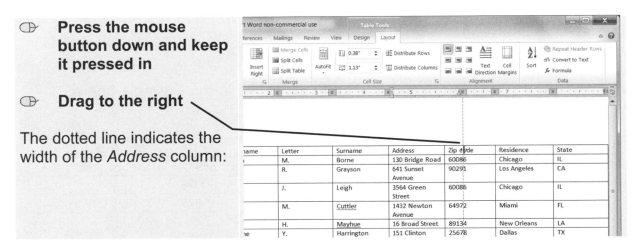

**⌖ Release the mouse button**

You will see that the *Zip code* column has become smaller and the *Address* column has become wider:

# 7.5 Add a Row

You can practice adding a couple of rows to the table. This is the easiest way to do it:

**Click the last cell**

**Press** Tab

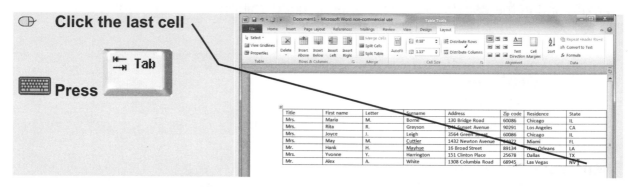

**A new row has been added to the table:**

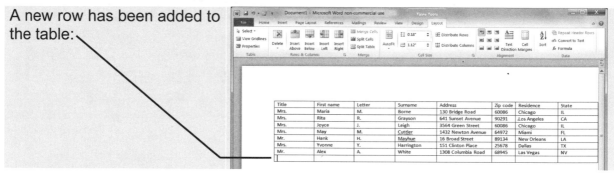

Add four more address rows to the table:

☞ **Add four rows with names and addresses, like in the example below**
&101

| Mr. | Peter | P. | Johnson | 169 Buchanan Place | 37924 | New York | NY |
| Mrs. | Chris | C. | Hollingsworth | 6 Grove Street | 64972 | Minneapolis | MN |
| Mr. | Michael | M. | Bones | 10 Chambers Street | 60086 | Chicago | IL |
| Mr. | Ed | E. | Smith | 1100 Pipeline Road | 15679 | Kansas City | KS |

💡 **Tip**

**Add a row below or above another row**
If you want to insert a row above or below another row, you can do it like this:

☞ **Click the row above or below which you want to insert a new row**

☞ **Click the** Layout **tab**

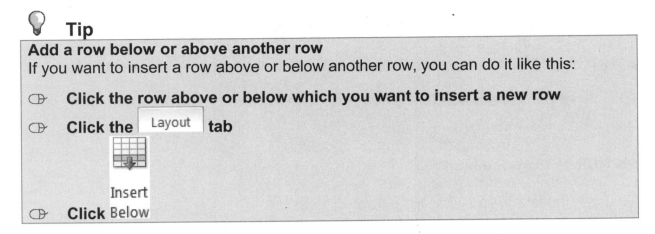

☞ **Click** Below

Before you start creating the labels for this address list, you are going to make the titles in the top row bold. This way, *Word* will know that the top row contains the column titles:

☞ **Position the mouse pointer outside the table at the start of the first row** ──────

The pointer will turn into 🔄:

☞ **Click once**

The top row is now selected:

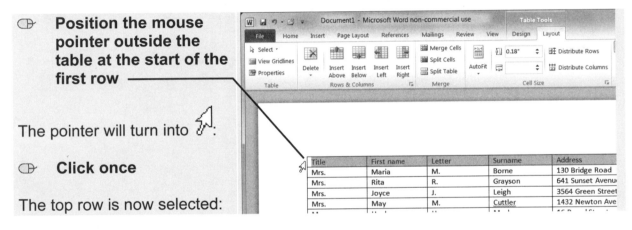

💡 **Tip**

**Drag**
You can also select the cells in the same way as you did in *Excel*: press the mouse button down, keep it pressed in and drag over the cells you want to select.

Now you can make the letters in the top row bold:

The Home tab is still open:

☞ **Click** **B** ──────

Now the titles are rendered in bold:

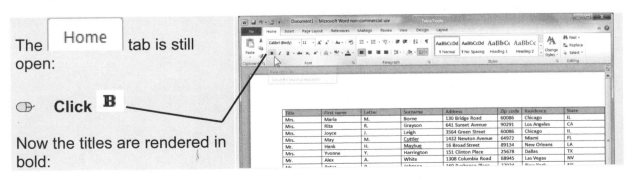

## 7.6 Create Labels With Mail Merge

Before you start creating your labels, you are going to save your document:

☞ **Save the table document as *directoryword* in the (*My*) *Documents* folder** ✏️**32**

☞ **Close the document** ✏️**12, 13**

To make the labels you will need a new document:

☞ **Open a new, blank document** ✏️**41, 42**

You will find the *Mail Merge* function on the *Mailings* tab:

👉 **Click the** | Mailings | **tab**

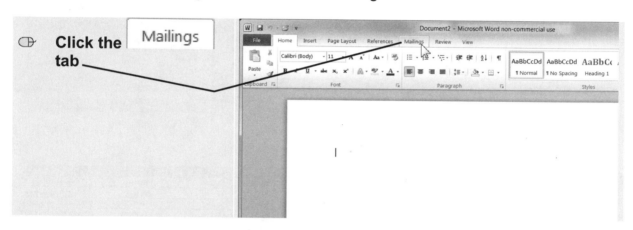

👉 **Click** Start Mail Merge ▾

👉 **Click** 📇 Step by Step Mail Merge Wizard...

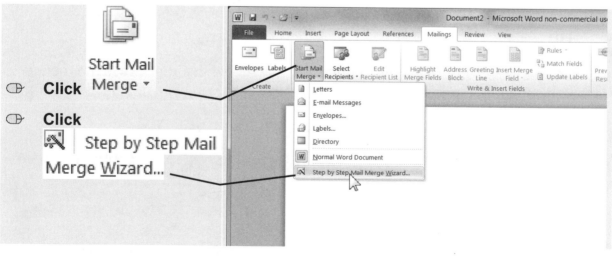

To the right of your window you will see the *Mail Merge* wizard:

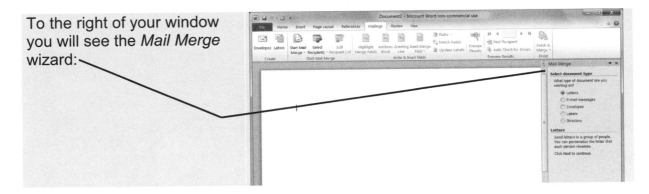

First you are going to choose the type of document you want to create:

☞ **Click the radio button ⊙ next to** Labels

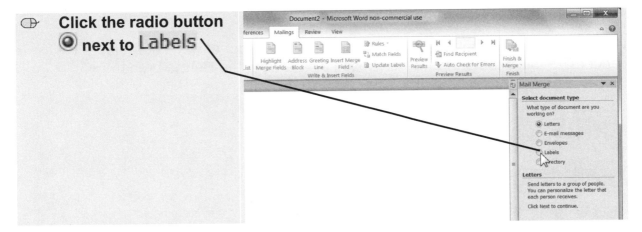

Continue with the next step of the wizard:

☞ **Click**
➡ Next: Starting docur

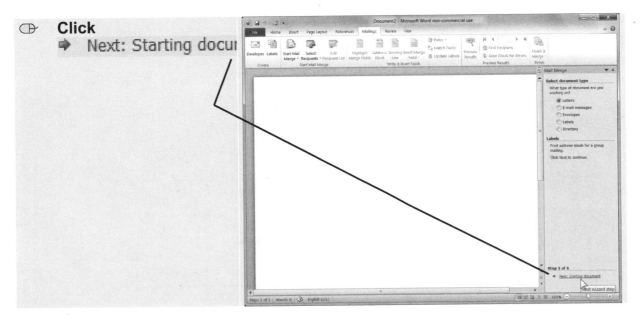

The next step is selecting the type of label you want to use:

☞ **Click** 🏛 Label options...

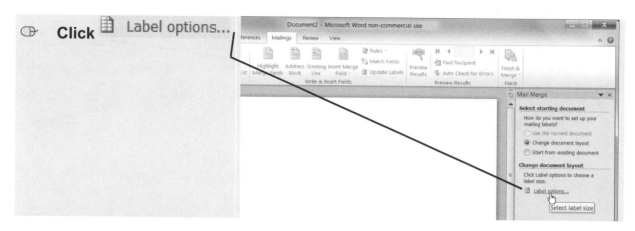

*Word* contains the label specifications for a large number of well-known label vendors. In this example we have chosen a label from the Herma brand:

☞ **By** Label vendors:

**click** ▼

You will see a list of vendors:

☞ **Drag the scroll bar down**

☞ **Click** HERMA

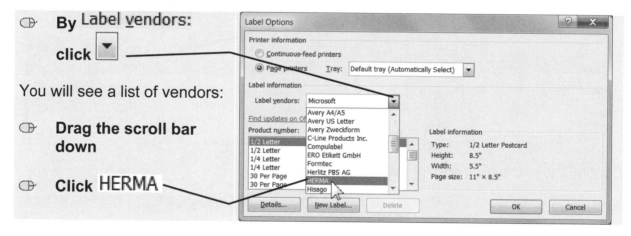

Select the product number for the labels you want to use:

☞ **Drag the scroll bar down**

☞ **Click** HERMA 4615 - SuperPrint

☞ **Click** OK

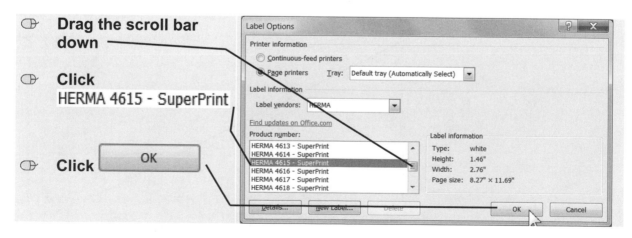

**Tip**

**Your own labels**
Naturally you can use the labels that you may have already purchased, even if they are of a different brand. You can find the product number on the wrapping. It is usually found on the back of the label as well.

If you cannot find your type of label in the list, you can create your own label format. See the *Tips* at the back of this chapter to learn how to do this.

Now you will see the sample labels:

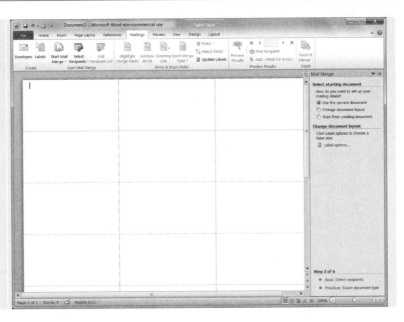

**HELP! I do not see the sample labels in my window.**

If you cannot see the sample labels, the *View Gridlines* option has not been activated. You can easily change this:

☞ **Click the** Layout **tab**

☞ **Click**  View Gridlines

If you want to use an *Excel* address list for your labels, you can skip the next section and continue with section *8.8 Use Excel Address List*.

# 7.7 Use Word Address List

The next step in the wizard is the selection of the addresses. In this section you can read how to use the address list you created in *Word*. In the following section you can read how to use an address list made in *Excel*.

In the lower right corner of the window:

☞ **Click**
➡ Next: Select recipien

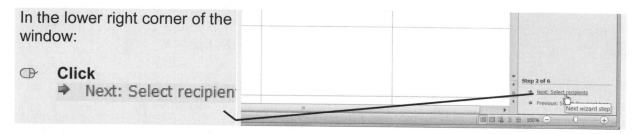

In this case, you are going to use an existing address list:

☞ **If necessary, click the radio button ⦿ next to** Use an existing list

☞ **Click** ▦ Browse...

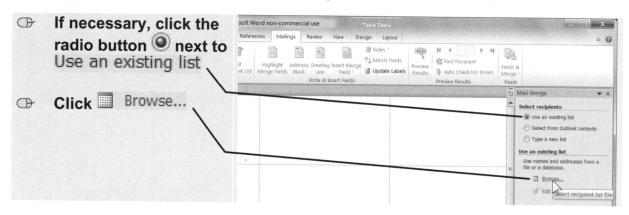

The *Select Data Source* window will be opened. You have stored the address list in the (*My*) *Documents* folder:

☞ **Click** 🗄 Documents

You will see the contents of the (*My*) *Documents* folder:

Your own documents folder will contain other files as well. Look for the *directoryword* file somewhere in there.

☞ **Click**
🖺 directoryword

☞ **Click** Open

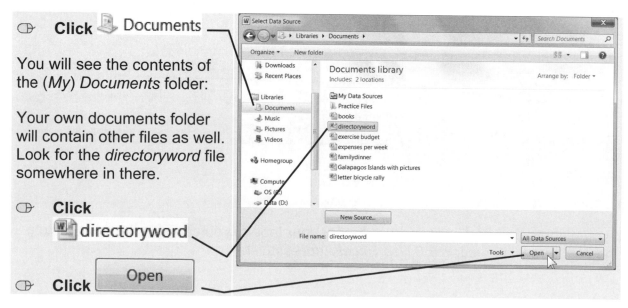

**Please note:**

If you have used the file from the practice files, the file will be stored in the *Practice Files* folder.

☞ **Open the file in the *Practice Files* folder** ✂43

In this window you will see the data you previously entered in the *directoryword* file:

The checked ☑ lines will be used for the labels.
If you want to leave out certain lines, then uncheck the box next to the line.

⊂◉ **Click** OK

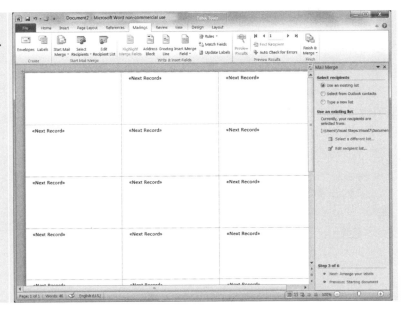

You will see the window with the sample labels once again. Each label now contains the text **«Next Record»**:

In the lower right corner of the window:

☞ **Click**
➡ Next: Arrange your

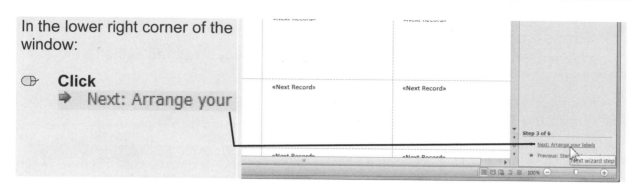

In the next section we will show you how to use an address list created in *Excel*. If you do not want to use an *Excel* address list, you can skip this section. You can continue with section *7.9 Arrange Labels*.

# 7.8 Use Excel Address List

The next step in the wizard is the selection of the addresses. In this section you can read how to use an address list you created in *Excel*.

In the lower right corner of the window:

☞ **Click**
➡ Next: Select recipien

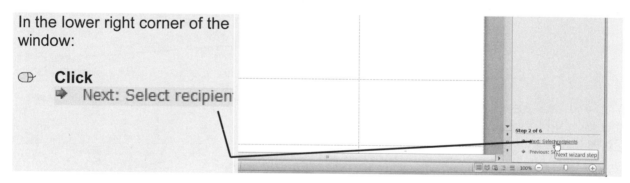

In this case, you are going to use an existing address list:

☞ **If necessary, click the radio button** ⦿ **next to** Use an existing list

☞ **Click** ▦ Browse...

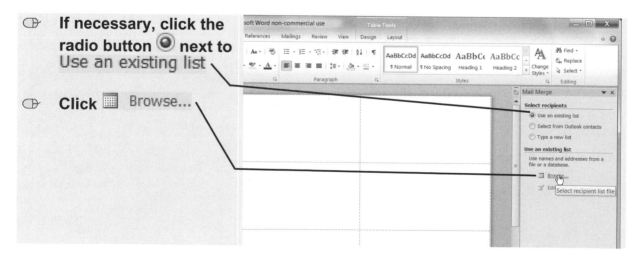

Now the *Select Data Source* window will be opened. The practice file called *directory* has been stored in the *Practice Files* folder:

Click 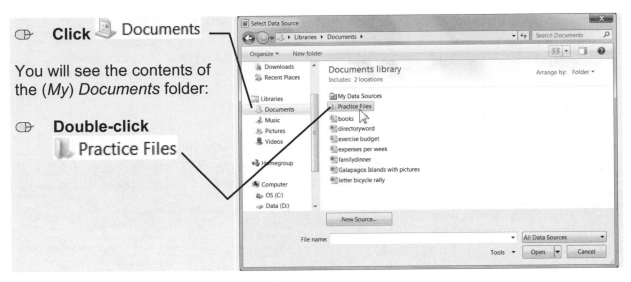 Documents

You will see the contents of the (*My*) *Documents* folder:

Double-click
    Practice Files

Click 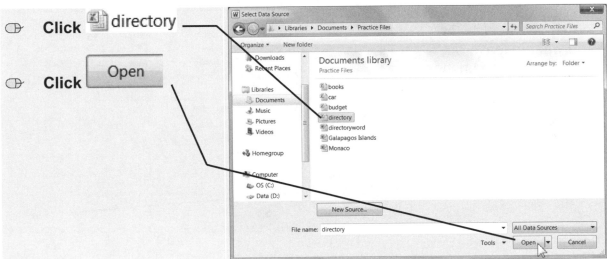 directory

Click Open

Now the *Select Table* window will be opened:

You do not need to change anything in this window. The address list has been entered in sheet1 of the workbook:

☞  **Click**  OK

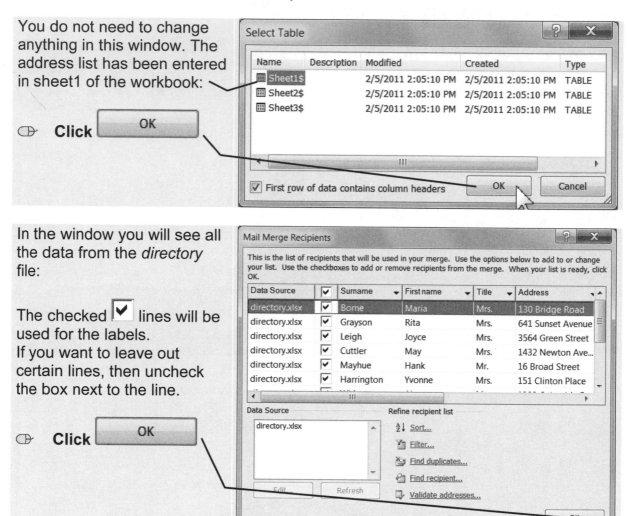

In the window you will see all the data from the *directory* file:

The checked ✔ lines will be used for the labels.
If you want to leave out certain lines, then uncheck the box next to the line.

☞  **Click**  OK

Now you will see the window
with the sample labels once
again. Each label contains
the text
**«Next Record»**:

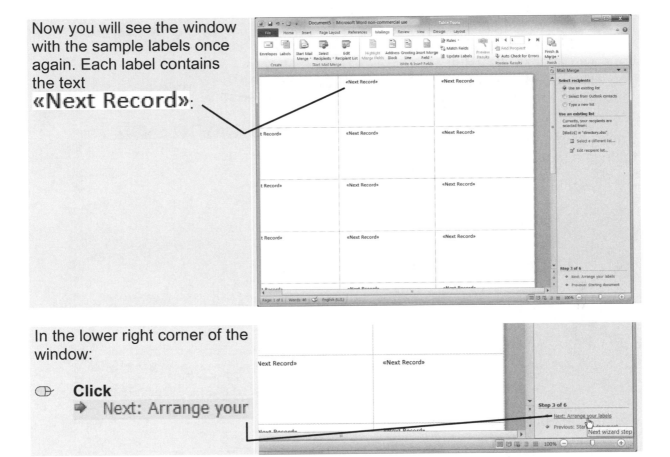

In the lower right corner of the
window:

☞   **Click**
    ➡  Next: Arrange your

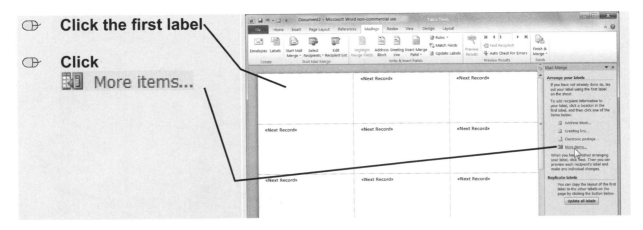

# 7.9 Arrange Labels

The next step is to indicate which items you want to print on the labels. For example,
you can print just the name and address, or a salutation such as Mrs. or Mr. Here is
how to do that:

☞   **Click the first label**

☞   **Click**
    More items...

In this window you can see which fields are present in your own address list. But you will need to select the **Database Fields** option first:

Each column title in your table is a separate field:

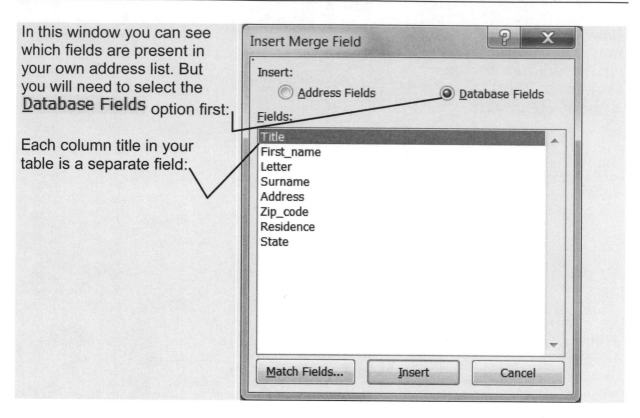

You can insert a selected field:

Start with the **Title** field:

☞ **If necessary, click Title**

☞ **Click** Insert

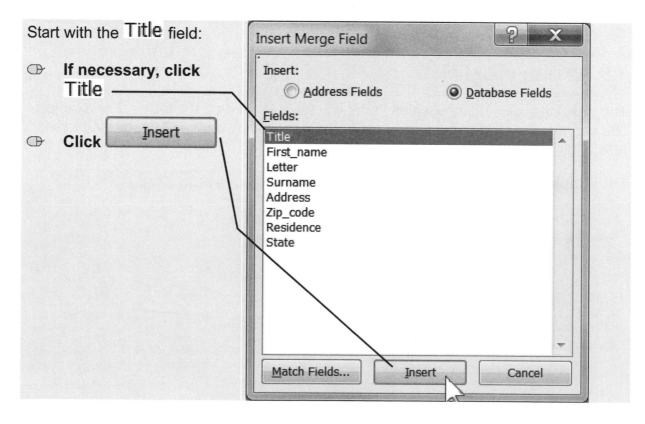

On the first label you will see
«Title» :

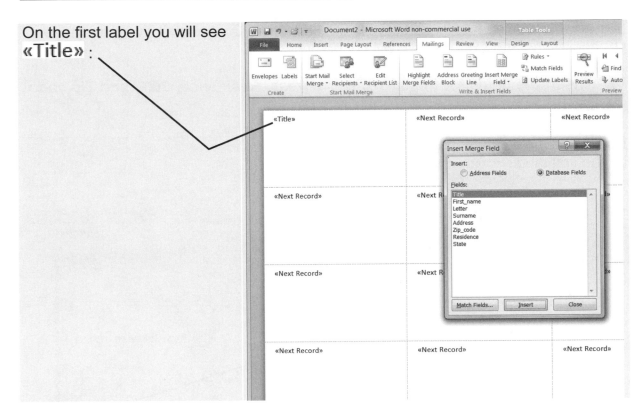

You will need to decide for yourself if you want to print the initials of the first name only or the name in full. In this example we have used only the initials:

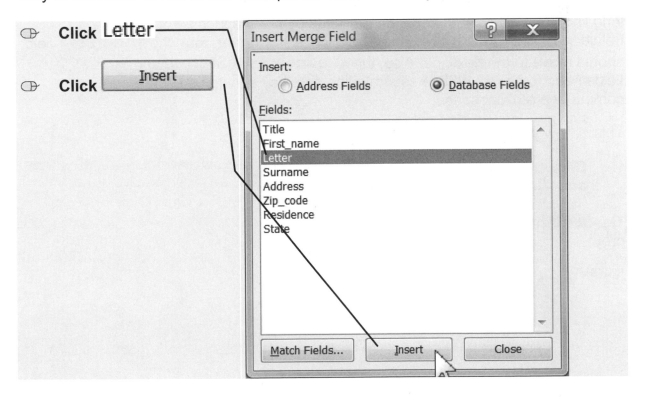

Click Letter

Click Insert

In the same way you can insert the other fields, one after the other. If you only use US addresses, the *Country* field will not be necessary.

☞ **Insert the fields for the *Surname*, *Address*, *Residence*, *State* and *Zip code***
✂102

Now all the fields are lined up on the first label: ——————

☞ **Click** [ Close ]

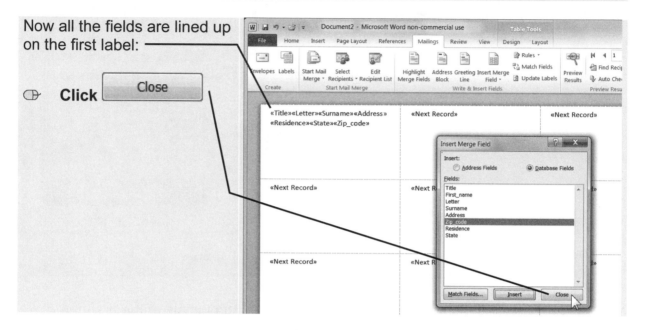

The fields you have inserted are printed on the first label one after the other, in a long line. You will want to separate the fields by blank spaces. For instance, between «Title», «Letter» and «Surname». Furthermore, the «Address» field should move to the next line. Also, the «Residence», «State», and «Zip_code» fields need to be moved to a separate line and they should be separated by a comma and a blank space.

This is how you type a space between the fields:

☞ **Click between «Title» and «Letter»** ——————

The «Letter» field will turn grey:

⌨ **Type a space**

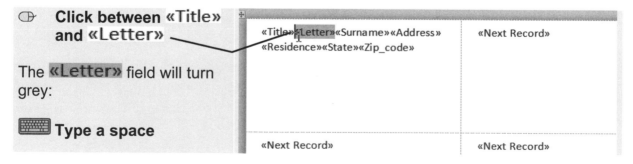

In this example it looks like the «Letter» field has jumped to the next line:

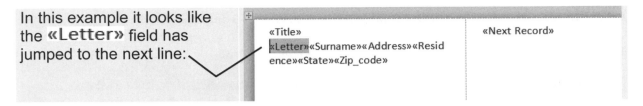

At this stage, you cannot clearly distinguish what each line will look like or how the printed label will turn out. This is especially true for smaller types of labels. Eventually, you will see that all problems will be solved if you enter the spaces and new lines in all the right places.

**Click between «Letter» and «Surname»**

The **«Surname»** field will turn grey:

**Type a space**

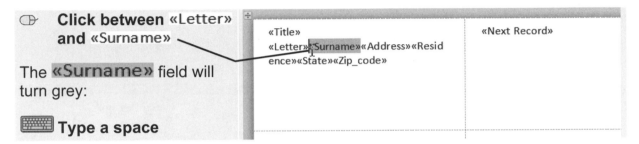

You are going to move the «Address» field to the next line:

**Click between «Surname» and «Address»**

**Press** Enter ↵

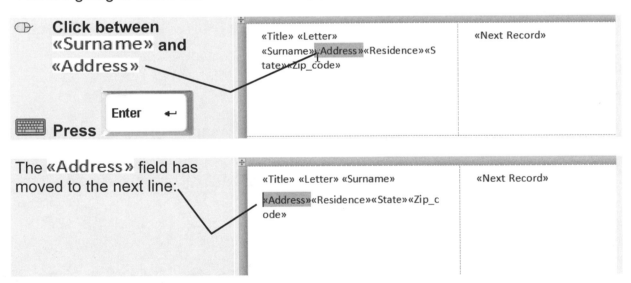

The «Address» field has moved to the next line:

You can edit the last two fields in the same way:

**Click between «Address» and «Residence»**

**Press** Enter ↵

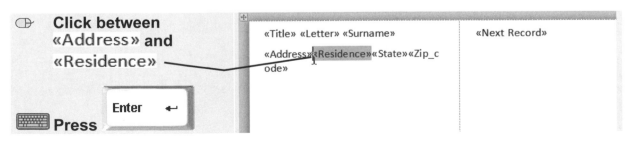

Now the residence, state and zip code have moved to a separate line.

You are going to add another comma and space:

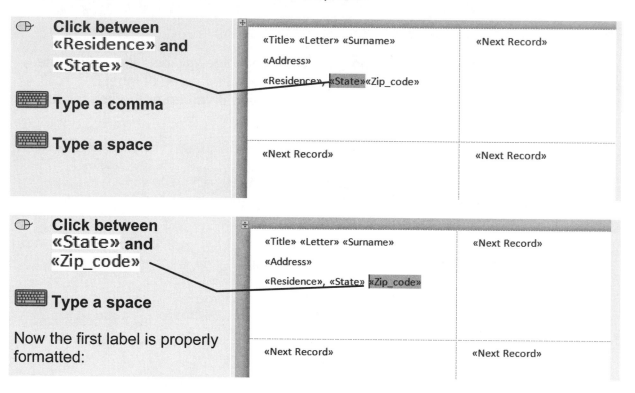

**Click between «Residence» and «State»**

**Type a comma**

**Type a space**

**Click between «State» and «Zip_code»**

**Type a space**

Now the first label is properly formatted:

You can apply this layout to all the other labels:

**Click**

**Update all labels**

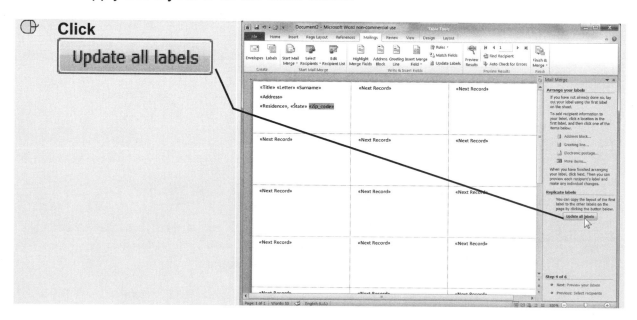

All the labels have the same layout:

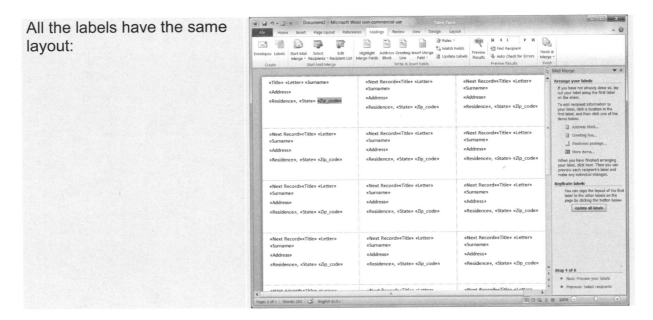

# 7.10 Add an Illustration

If you are going to print labels to use for a special occasion, you may want to add an illustration to them. For example, you can give a Christmas touch to your labels.

If you do not want to add an illustration, you can skip to the next section.

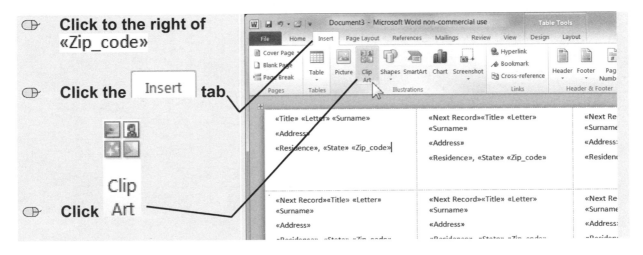

Click to the right of «Zip_code»

Click the Insert tab

Click Clip Art

The *Clip Art* task pane will be opened:

⌨ **Type:** christmas wreath

👆 **Click** Go

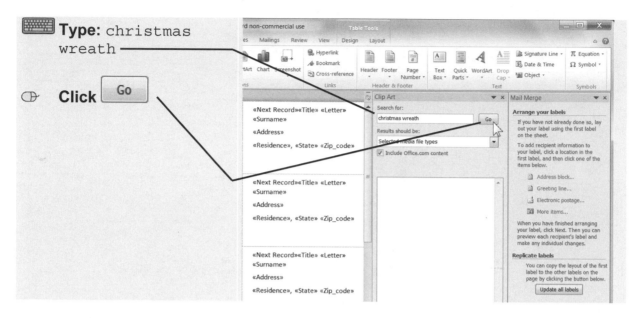

Select one of the illustrations:

👆 **Drag the scroll bar down**

👆 **For example, click**

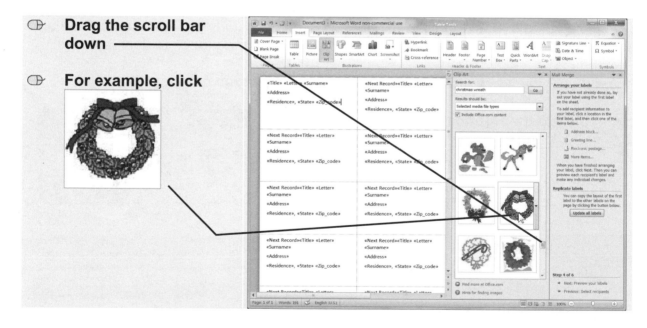

The illustration will be added to the first label: ───────

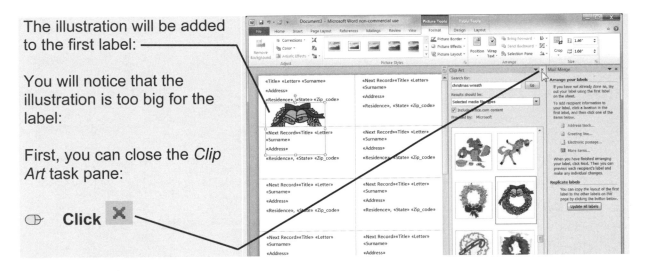

You will notice that the illustration is too big for the label:

First, you can close the *Clip Art* task pane:

☞   **Click** ✖

Shrink the illustration:

☞   **Position the mouse pointer on the handle in the lower right corner** ───────

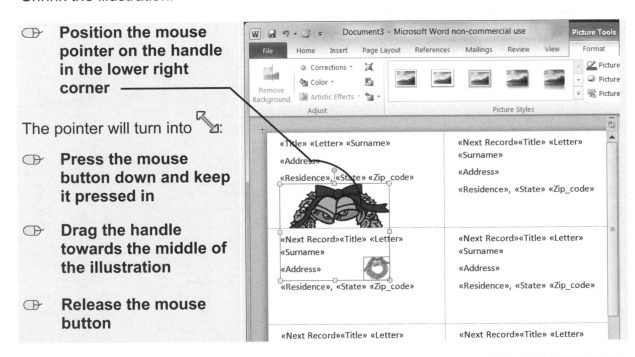

The pointer will turn into ⬉:

☞   **Press the mouse button down and keep it pressed in**

☞   **Drag the handle towards the middle of the illustration**

☞   **Release the mouse button**

The illustration has become smaller:

After you insert the illustration into the text, you may notice that the distance between the address and the residence/zip code has become too wide:

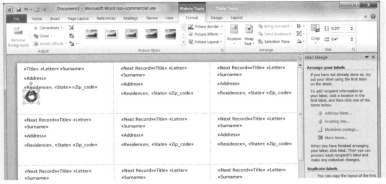

You can alter this by adjusting the text wrapping for the illustration:

The [ Format ] tab is already open:

⊕ **Click** Wrap Text ▾

⊕ **Click** 🖾 Square

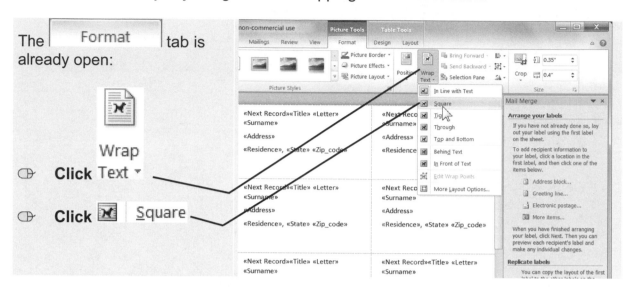

Now you can move the illustration by dragging it:

⊕ **Position the pointer**
   **on the illustration**

⊕ **Press the mouse button**

⊕ **Drag the illustration to the right**

⊕ **Release the mouse button**

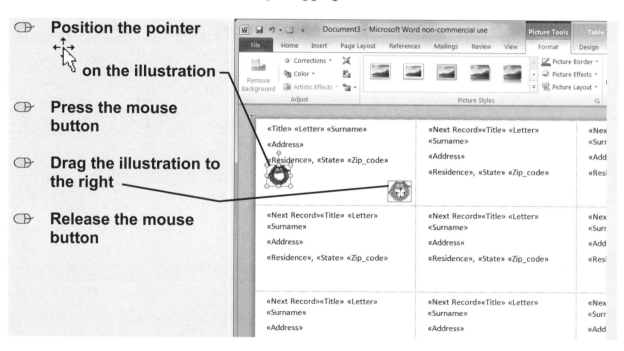

You can also add the illustration to the other labels. Here is how to do that:

👉 **Click**

Update all labels

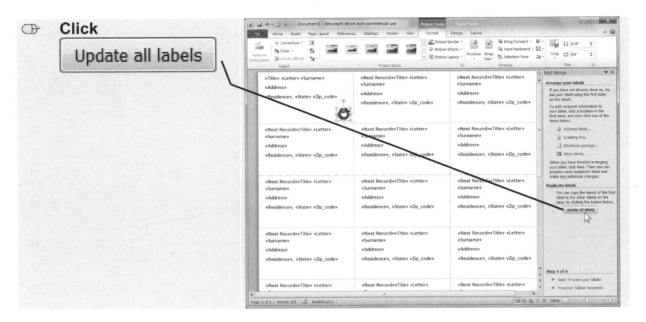

Now the illustration has been copied to all the other labels:

You may notice that the illustration is not positioned correctly on some of the labels. For the moment, this does not matter. This will be corrected in the following steps.

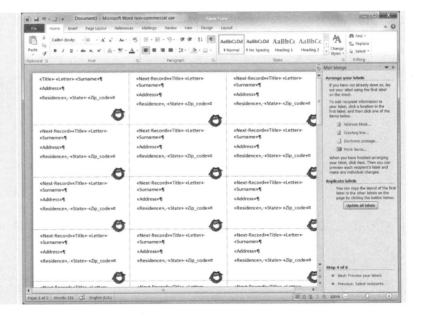

# 7.11 Continue Creating the Labels

Now you can continue with the next step:

In the lower right corner of the window:

☞ **Click**
➡ Next: Preview your lab

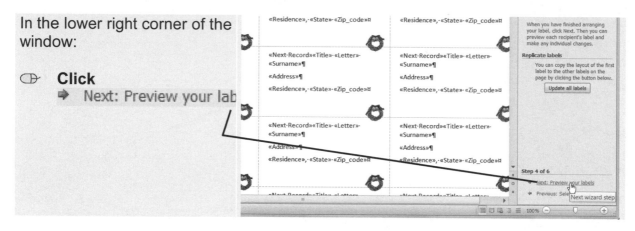

You will see a preview of your labels:

If you discover any errors, you can return to the wizard's previous step(s), by clicking
⬅ Previous: Arrange your labels

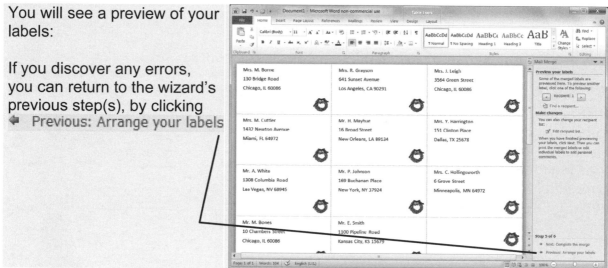

If you are satisfied with the result, you can complete the merge operation:

☞ **Click**
➡ Next: Complete the

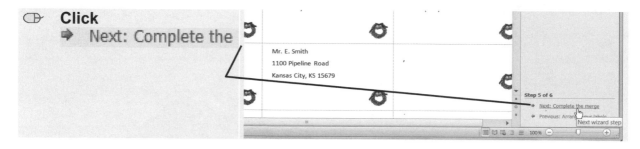

Now the merge has been completed. If you want, you can print the labels from this window. But you can also copy everything to a new document, which you can easily edit and save for use later on:

**Click**

    Edit individual labels...

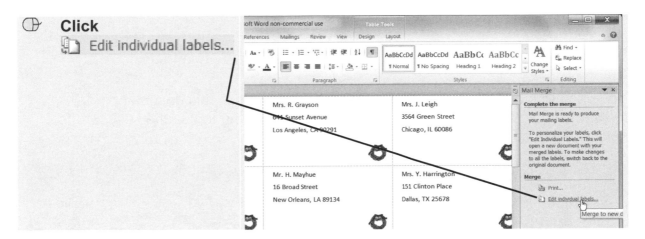

The *Merge to New Document* window will be opened:

**All** has already been selected:

**Click**  OK

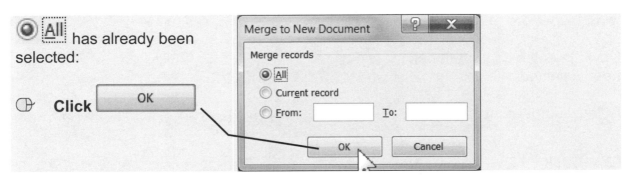

A new window will be opened:

Now you will see the labels in a new *Word* document:

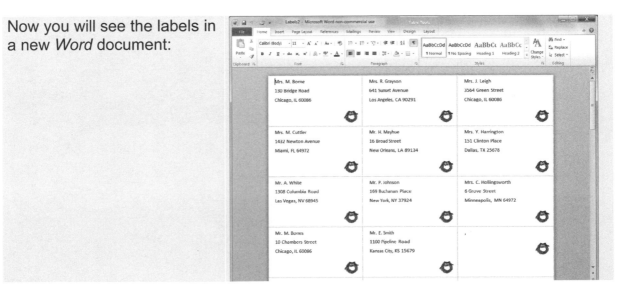

**Please note:**

The blank labels at the bottom of the page still contain images. You will remove this images in the next section.

# 7.12 Format Labels

You can still modify the text and formatting of the labels in this document. For instance, you can select a larger font. First, you are going to use the keyboard to select all the labels:

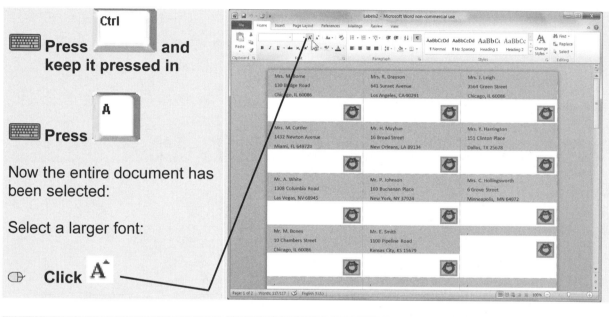

**Press** Ctrl **and keep it pressed in**

**Press** A

Now the entire document has been selected:

Select a larger font:

⊕ **Click** A⁺

The font has been increased by one point:

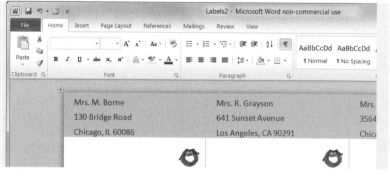

You can also select a different font:

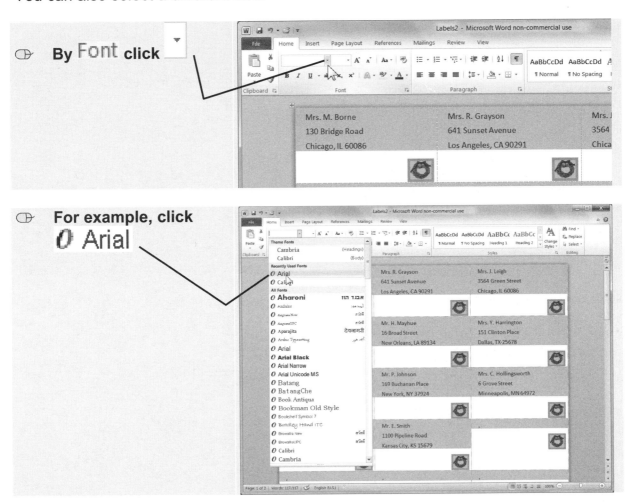

The new font will be applied right away. Now you can see what happens if you italicize all the letters:

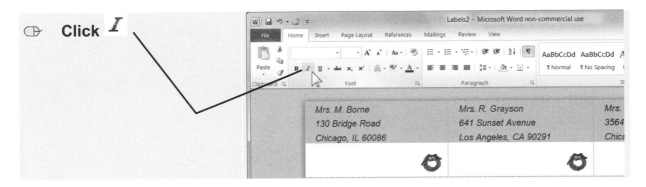

You can delete the illustrations on the blank labels:

You will see the modified labels:

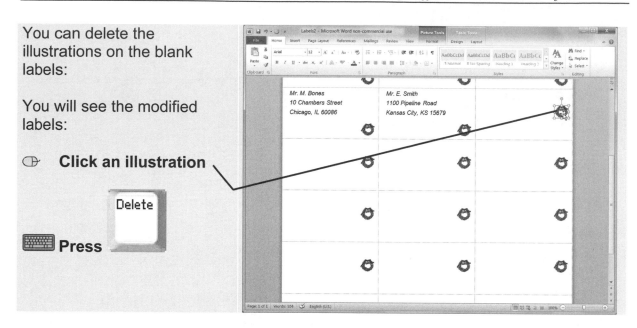

⊖ **Click an illustration**

**Delete**

⌨ **Press**

---

☞ **Delete the illustrations on the other blank labels**

---

 **HELP! I see commas on the blank labels.**

If you see commas on the blank labels as well, you can delete them too:

☞ **Select the comma** ✂️62

**Delete**

⌨ **Press**

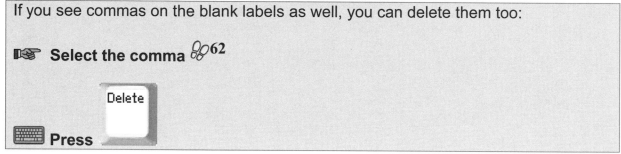

# 7.13 Print Labels

Before you start printing your labels on label paper, it is a good idea to test the print first on a regular piece of print paper. You can print the first page of the document and check to see if the text will fit the label paper. Also, by doing this test beforehand you will discover which way your sheets need to be loaded in the printer's paper tray.

This is how you print a test page:

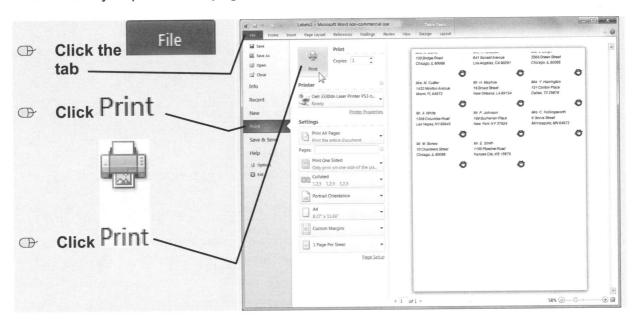

⊕  **Click the** *File* **tab** ——

⊕  **Click** Print ——

⊕  **Click** Print ——

In *Word 2007*:

⊕  **Click** ___, ___ Print ▶ , ___ OK ___

The labels will be printed on regular paper.

Now you can compare this printed page to the label paper. If you place the pages on top of each other and hold them against the light, you can check the position of the text on the labels. You may feel that the labels are printed too close to the top border.

 **Please note:**

If the labels do not fit the page exactly, it is best not to solve this problem by adding extra lines to the page. This will cause the labels to shift too much. It is better to modify the margins.

This is how to edit the margins:

☞ **Click the** | Page Layout | **tab**

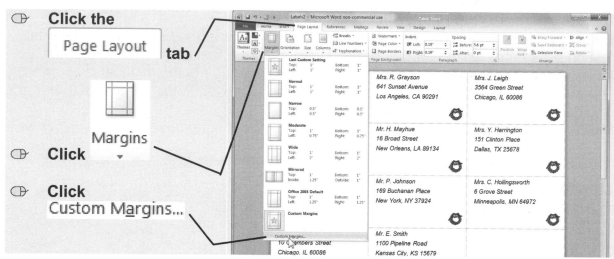

☞ **Click** Margins ▾

☞ **Click** Custom Margins...

 **HELP! I cannot click the Margins option.**

If you cannot click the *Margins* option, it is possible that you have accidentally selected an illustration. To activate the option:

☞ **Click a random spot in the text**

Now the *Page Setup* window will be opened. Here you can set the top margin to 0.1", for example. You can also use the other settings to solve problems with the left, right or bottom portions of your labels.

All margins for the selected label type are set to 0:

⌨ **Type:** 0,1"

In the bottom of the window:

☞ **Click** OK

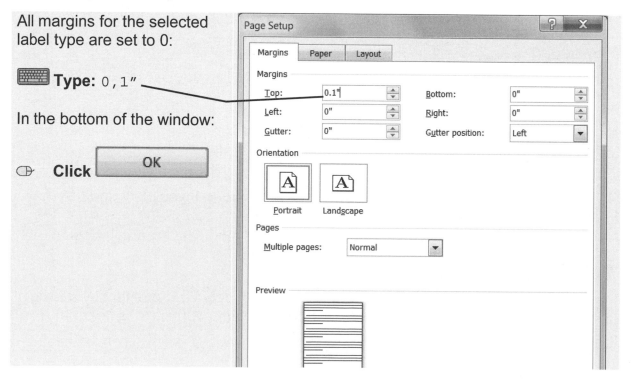

You will see an error message which tells you the margins may be outside the printable area of the page. Ignore this message, otherwise the labels will shift too much:

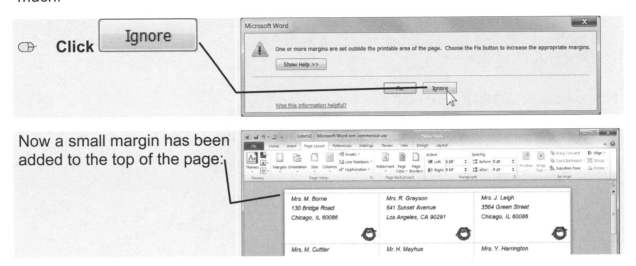

☞ **Click** Ignore

Now a small margin has been added to the top of the page:

Check the new settings by doing another test print. You may need to experiment a few more times before you finally have the right settings for your specific labels.

 **Tip**

**Insert enter above «Title»**
If you think the recipients' names at the top are too close to the border, you can insert an Enter above the «Title». You can do this while formatting the labels.

You can save this document and use it again later on:

☞ **Save the document as *Labels* in the (*My*) *Documents* folder** *ᏠᏠ*³²

 **Tip**

**Product number**
If you insert the label's product number into the file name, it will be easier to retrieve the matching label paper at a later stage.

☞ **Close the document** *ᏠᏠ*¹²,¹³

Afterwards, you will see the merge document once more. Close this document as well:

☞ **Close the merge document and do not save the changes** *ᏠᏠ*³⁹,⁴⁰

In the following exercises you can repeat the operations you have learned in this chapter.

# 7.14 Exercises

Have you forgotten how to do something? Then you can use the number next to the footsteps to find the information in the appendix *How Do I Do That Again?* at the back of this book.

## Exercise : Mail Merge

In the exercise you will repeat the operations with the *Mail Merge wizard*.

☞  Open a new document. ❧**41, 42**

☞  Open the *Mail Merge wizard*. ❧**103**

☞  Select the labels document type. ❧**104**

☞  Select a label type, for example *Herma 4615*. ❧**105**

☞  Select the addresses, use the addresses from the ▣directoryword file. ❧**106**

☞  Insert the following fields: *First name*, *Surname*, *Address*, *Residence*, *State* and *Zip code*. ❧**107**

☞  Type blank spaces between the fields and a comma after *Residence*.

☞  Arrange the fields in this way: *Title*, *First name* and *Surname* are printed on a separate line, *Address* on the next line and *Zip code* and *Residence* on the last line. ❧**108**

☞  Apply this formatting to all labels. ❧**109**

☞  View the print preview and check if the names and addresses are rendered correctly. ❧**110**

☞  Complete the merge operation. ❧**111**

☞  Open the labels in a new *Word* document. ❧**112**

☞  Close *Word* and do not save the document. ❧**39, 40**

# 7.15 Background Information

**Dictionary**

| | |
|---|---|
| **Field** | An element on a label, for example, the name or the address. |
| **Mail merge** | Merging the data from a data list with a document, in order to print a series of separate documents with specific data. Use this function to automatically add addresses and print series of labels, envelopes, greeting cards, booklets, newsletters, and other types of publications. |
| **Preview labels** | Preview of the size of the selected labels. |
| **Wizard** | A small program that helps you create a document step by step. |

*Source: Microsoft Word Help*

# 7.16 Tips

💡 **Tip**

**Create a label with a single address**

In this chapter you have learned how to create labels by using an address list. But there is another method of creating a label for a single name or address:

👆 **Click the** Mailings **tab,** Labels

Enter the address:

One single label or a full page?

It is important to match the label size to the *Word* settings.

👆 **Click** Options...

You will see the *Label Options* window:

Select your label vendor:

Here you can select your label type:

Have you finished?

👆 **Click** OK

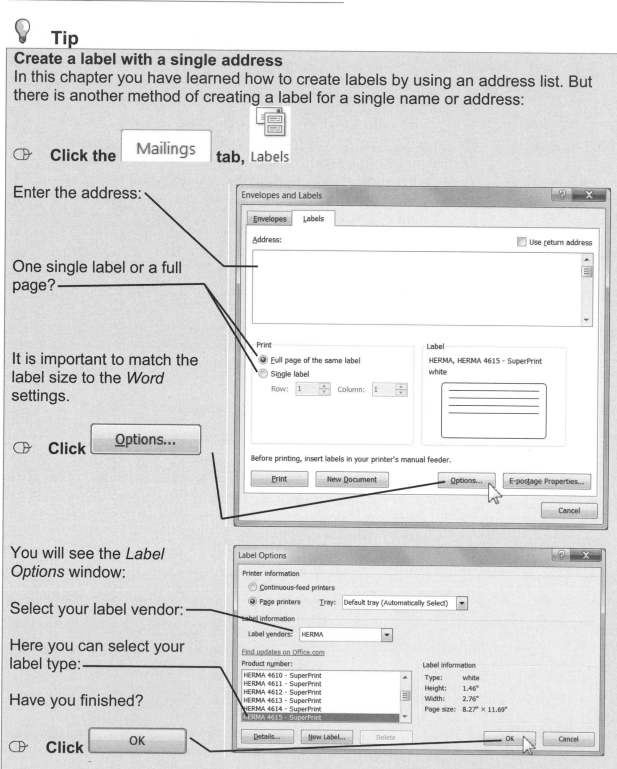

- *Continue reading on the next page* -

Now you can print the labels:

 **Click** Print

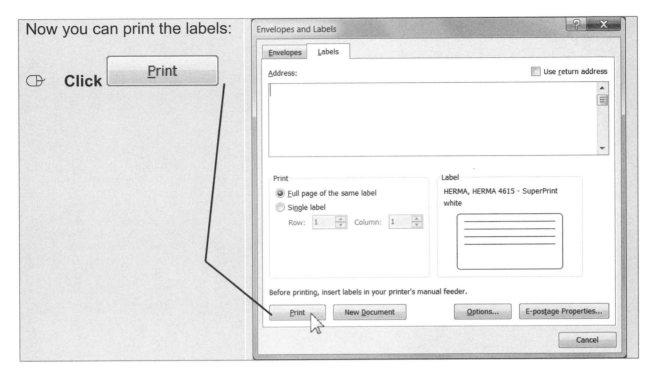

 **Tip**

**Suitable data sources to use with the Mail Merge Wizard**
The following data sources can also be used with the *Mail Merge Wizard*:
- an address list made in *Word* (as a table);
- an address list made in *Excel*;
- the *Outlook Contacts* list;
- an *Access* database file;
- text file with specific formatting (CSV files).

**The Outlook Express address book or the Windows (Live) Mail Contacts folder**
You cannot directly use the *Outlook Express* address book or the *Contacts* folder from *Windows (Live) Mail* in the *Word* program.

 **Tip**

**Inserting addresses from Outlook**
If you use *Outlook* and want to use the addresses from your Contacts list, in step 3 of the *Mail Merge Wizard* you can select the option
⊙ Select from Outlook contacts. This data source will then be used for the mail merge operation.

**Tip**

**Edit data during the merge operation**
While you are executing the merge operation, you can still change the data or remove specific people from your address list. You can do this when you see the following window:

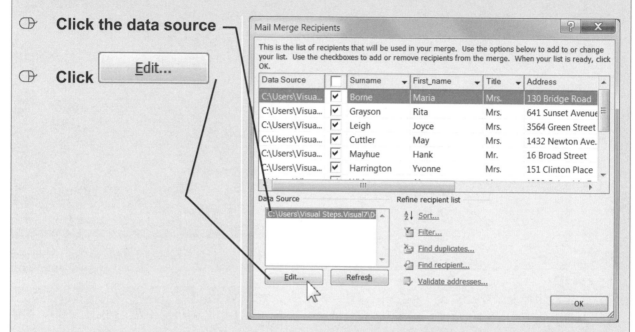

☞ **Click the data source**

☞ **Click** Edit...

Now you will see the *Data Form* window, where you can edit or add data. Also, you can delete a person from the list or add a new person:

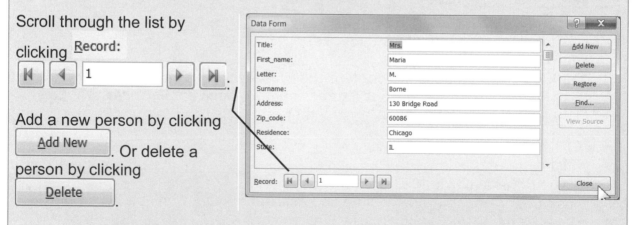

Scroll through the list by clicking Record:

Add a new person by clicking Add New . Or delete a person by clicking Delete .

When you have finished editing the list:

☞ **Click** Close

If you have made any changes, *Word* will eventually ask you to save the changes.

## 💡 Tip

**Set your own label size**

If you cannot find your vendor or label type in the list, you can create your own labels with the correct size:

☞ **Click** New Label...

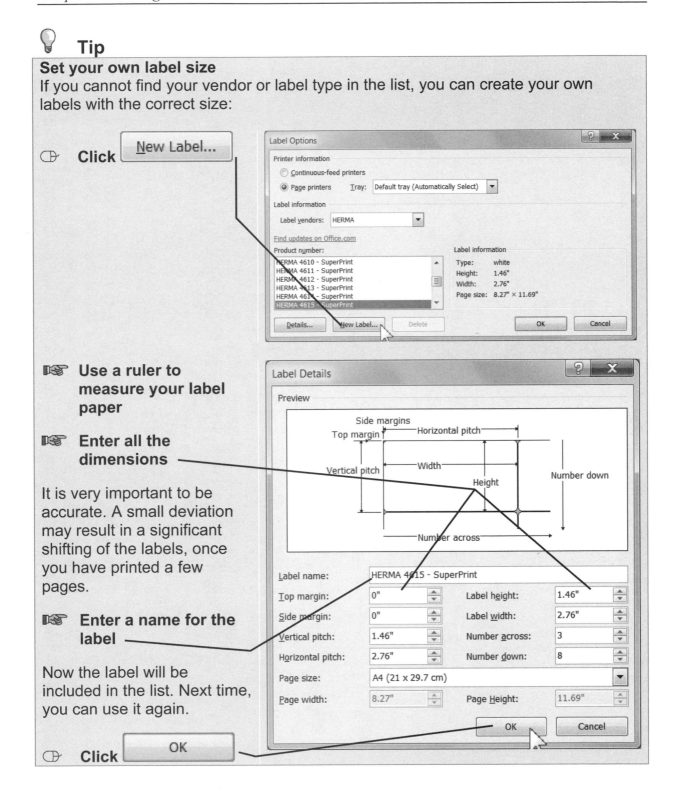

☞ **Use a ruler to measure your label paper**

☞ **Enter all the dimensions**

It is very important to be accurate. A small deviation may result in a significant shifting of the labels, once you have printed a few pages.

☞ **Enter a name for the label**

Now the label will be included in the list. Next time, you can use it again.

☞ **Click** OK

# Notes

Here you can take notes.

# 8. Creating a Photo Album

*PowerPoint* is a program you can use to create presentations. A presentation consists of a number of slides. You can view these slides on a computer or project them on a screen with a beamer. You can create a presentation, for example, to support a speech you are going to deliver at your company or club.

In this chapter you will learn how to create a presentation in the form of a photo album containing vacation pictures. While you are creating this photo album you will become acquainted with the most important *PowerPoint* functions. For instance, you will learn how to add text, illustrations, audio clips, video clips and voice messages to your slides. You can make your album even livelier by altering the styles or by adding different transitions and animations.

If you want to share your presentation with others, you can send your presentation by e-mail, burn it on a CD, or copy it to a USB stick. The *PowerPoint Viewer* program enables people to view presentations on computers even when the *PowerPoint* program is not installed.

In this chapter you will learn how to:

- create a photo album;
- select a theme;
- modify the title slide and enter a page title;
- move, duplicate, replace, enlarge, shrink and remove photos;
- add a new slide;
- render a photo full screen;
- add a caption;
- change the style of the pictures and add illustrations;
- edit photos and illustrations;
- add sound clips, voice messages and video clips;
- crop a video file;
- move, duplicate and remove slides;
- add slide transitions and animations;
- compress the presentation and send it by e-mail;
- package the presentation and use it elsewhere;
- download and install the *PowerPoint Viewer*;
- view the presentation with the *PowerPoint Viewer*.

# 8.1 Opening PowerPoint

This is how you open *PowerPoint*:

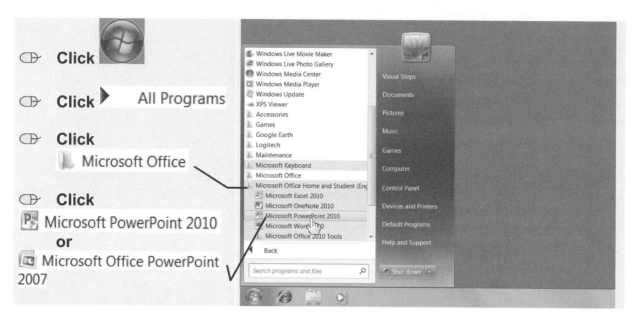

Now you will see the *PowerPoint* startup window:

At the top of the window you will see the ribbon:

In *Chapter 1 The Office Programs* you learned how to customize the ribbon and the *Quick Access* toolbar. You can easily add additional commands to the *Quick Access* toolbar as well as the ribbon as needed.

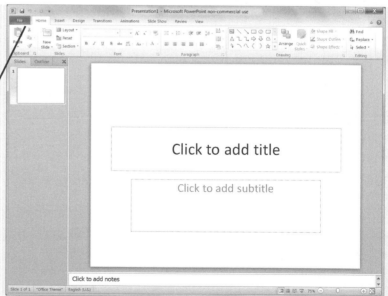

## 8.2 Create a Photo Album

In *PowerPoint* you can quickly and easily create a photo album with your favorite pictures.

 **Please note:**

If you want to do the exercises in this chapter, you will need to download the corresponding practice files from the website that goes with this book. Download the files to your computer and store them in the (*My*) *Documents* folder. In *Appendix A Download the Practice Files* at the back of this book you can read how to do this.

Click the  Insert  tab

By [photo album icon] click
Photo Album ▾

Click
New Photo Album...

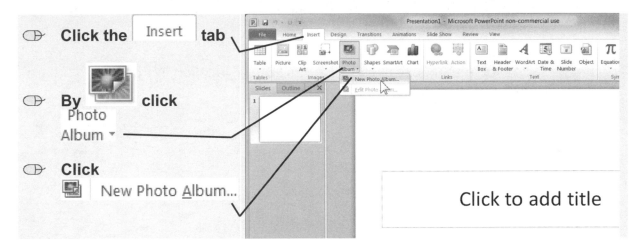

Now the *Photo Album* window will be opened. In this window you can select the pictures you want to include in your photo album:

Click  File/Disk...

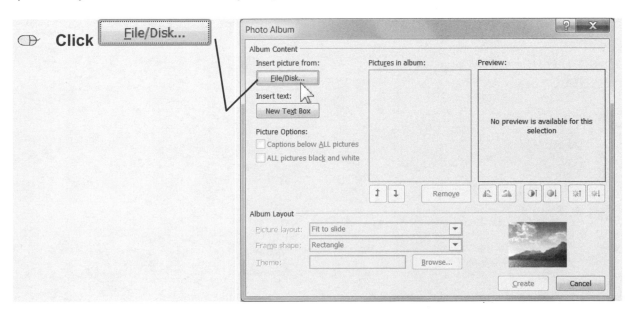

By default, the *Insert New Pictures* window will display the contents of the *Pictures* folder. You will need to browse to a different folder which contains the practice files:

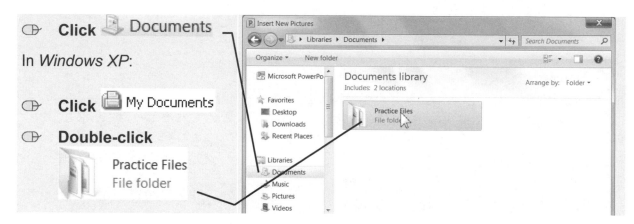

Click  Documents

In *Windows XP*:

Click My Documents

Double-click

Practice Files
File folder

The practice files folder contains twelve pictures from a vacation in Portugal. You are going to add these pictures to the album:

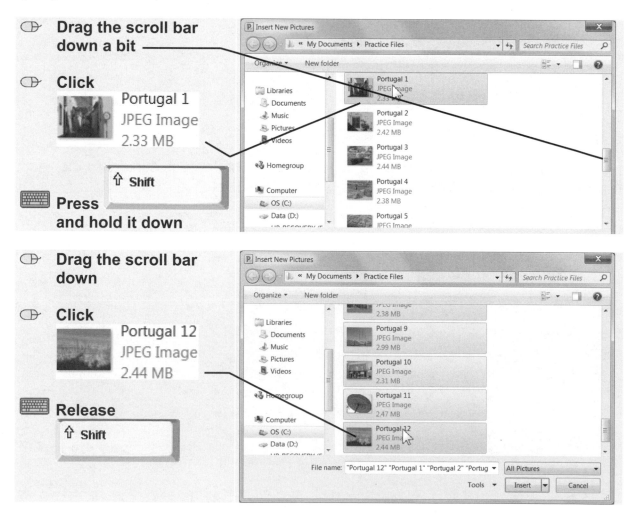

Drag the scroll bar down a bit

Click

Portugal 1
JPEG Image
2.33 MB

⇧ Shift

Press and hold it down

Drag the scroll bar down

Click

Portugal 12
JPEG Image
2.44 MB

Release

⇧ Shift

Now you have selected all of the photos from the Portugal vacation:

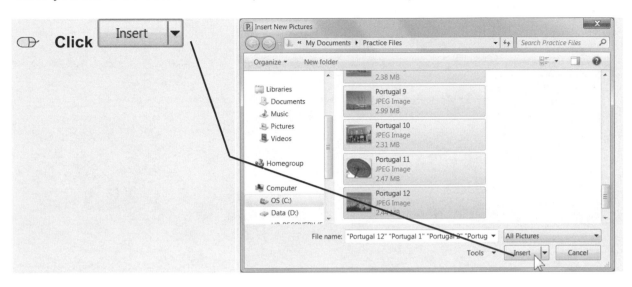

☞ **Click** Insert ▼

💡 **Tip**

**Insert individual pictures**

If you do not want to add all the photos, you can keep the **Ctrl** button pressed as you select the photos you want. This allows you to skip a photo from the list.

Now you will see the *Photo Album* window once again:

Here you can use the ⬆ ⬇ buttons to change the order of the photos:

With these buttons, you can rotate the selected photo ◁ ▷ ,

adjust the brightness ◑ ◐ or change the contrast ◑ ◐ :

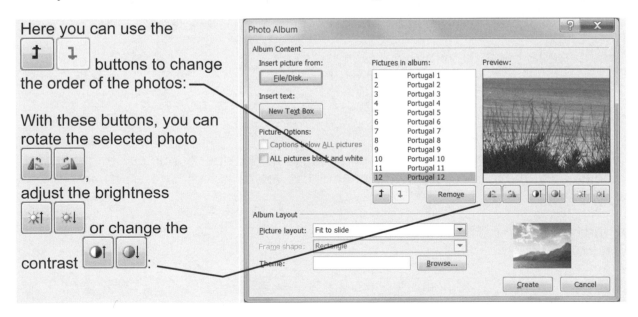

If you do not change anything in this window, the pictures will be fit to the slide and displayed full screen, on separate pages. In this example we will select the option for 2 pictures on one slide:

By Picture layout:

click ▼

Click
2 pictures with title

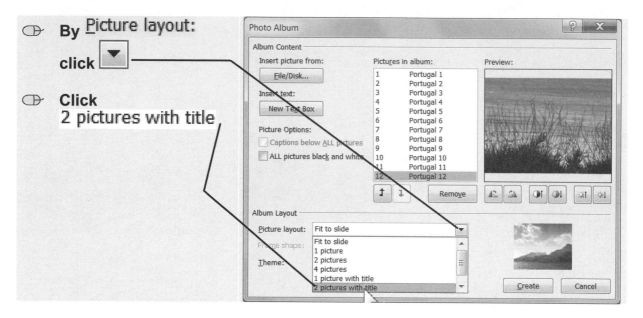

You can also select a *frame* for the photos:

By Frame shape:

click ▼

Click
Simple Frame, White

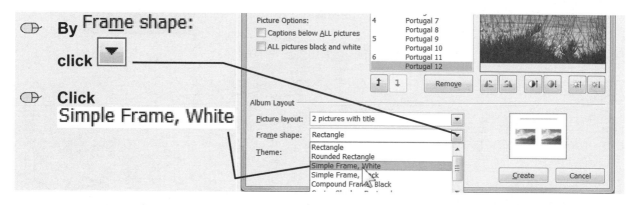

In a little while, you will see that you can change the number of photos per page and modify the frame for each individual photo. Now you can create the actual photo album:

In the bottom right of the window:

Click Create

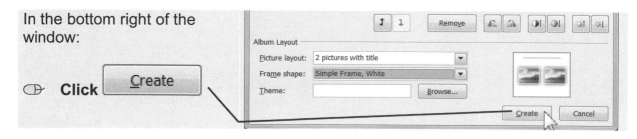

The photos will now be added to the album. Your newly created album will then open in a new window:

*PowerPoint* automatically adds a title slide to the album:

Here you see the slides in the album:

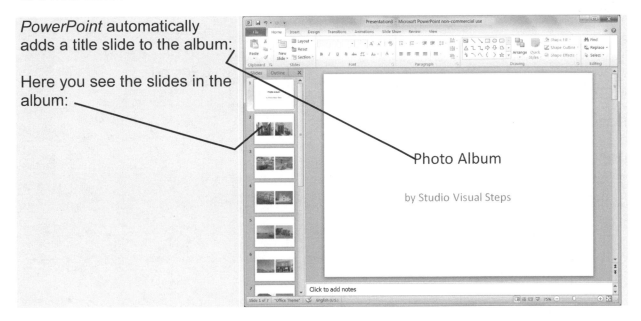

The photo album appears in the basic default state with a white background. All the slides look the same. In the next section you will learn how to customize your photo album and make it a little more attractive.

## 8.3 Select a Theme

First, you are going to select a theme for your photo album. By using a theme, you will automatically add exactly the same background and style to each slide. A theme contains colors, pictures, and fonts.

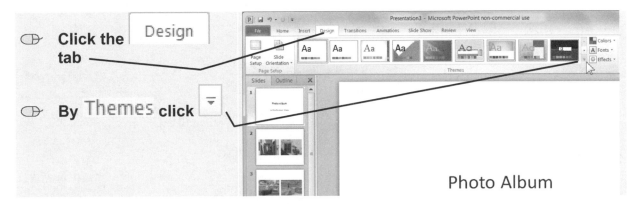

☞ **Click the** Design **tab**

☞ **By** Themes **click** ▼

Now you will see the available themes in *PowerPoint*:

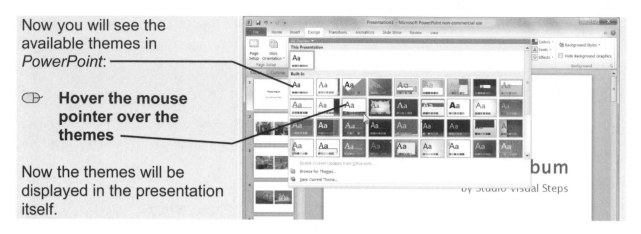

☞ **Hover the mouse pointer over the themes**

Now the themes will be displayed in the presentation itself.

In this example you are going to select the *Paper* theme:

☞ **Click [Aa] (paper)**

The selected theme will automatically be applied to all the slides in the album.

Here you see the title slide with the new theme:

The other slides have been modified as well:

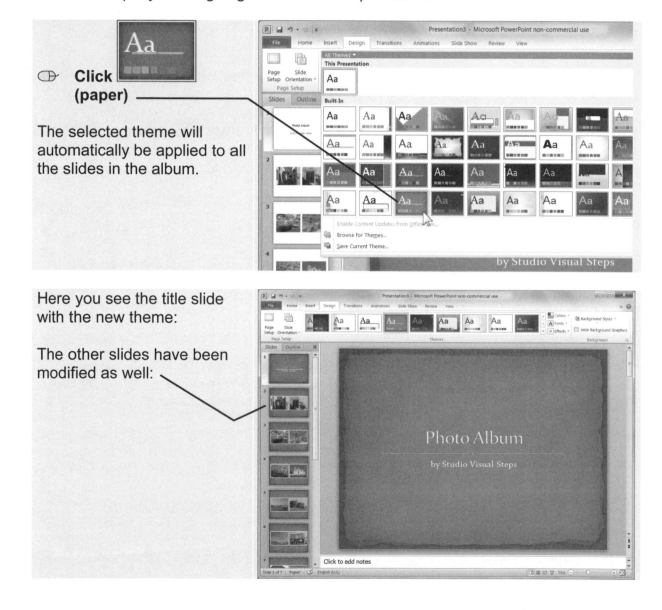

## 8.4 Edit the Title Slide

At the beginning of the photo album, *PowerPoint* has inserted a title slide. You can use this slide to state the subject of the photo album:

**Click**

**Photo Album**
**three times**

Now you have selected the text:

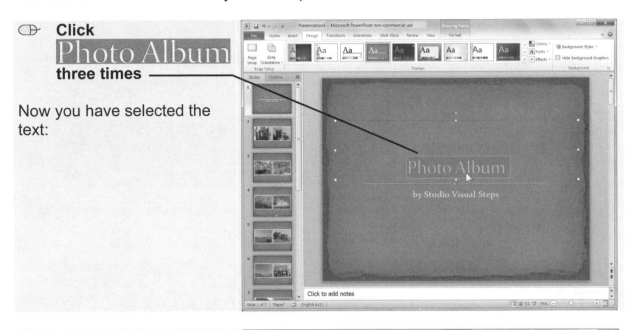

**Type:** Our holiday in Portugal

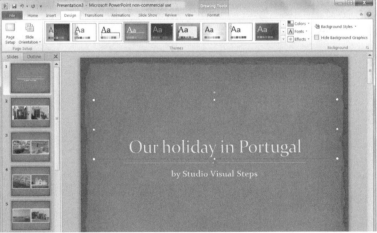

 **Tip**

**Name**
In the title slide in this example you can see the text
by Studio Visual Steps. This is where you will see your own name. In *Chapter 4 Using Templates* you have learned how to change the name that is automatically displayed in your documents. But if you prefer a different name for this album, just change it in the same way as you have done for the title of this slide.

# 8.5 Enter a Page Title

By default, each page in the photo album is formatted in the same way. Just take a look at the second slide:

**Click**

This is the first page with photos:

The photos are positioned next to each other and both photos have a white frame:

Above the photos you will see a title box:

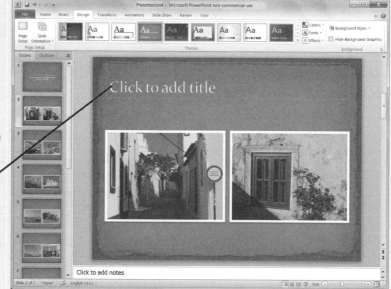

**Click the title box**

**Type:** The village

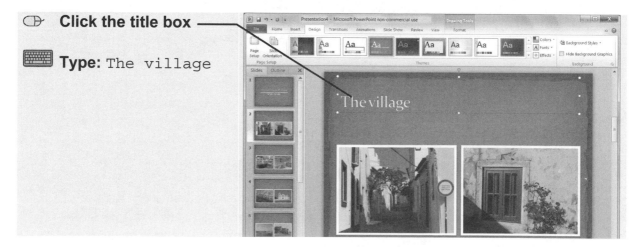

# 8.6 Move Photos

The photos do not have a fixed position. You can position them on the page yourself, anywhere you want to.

☞ **Go to the third slide** &#8477;113

☞ **Add this title to the slide:** Fishing &#8477;114

You can move photos by dragging them around:

⊖ **Position the mouse pointer on the photo on the right side of the page**

The pointer will turn into a ✥:

⊖ **Hold the mouse button down and drag the photo up a bit**

⊖ **Release the mouse button**

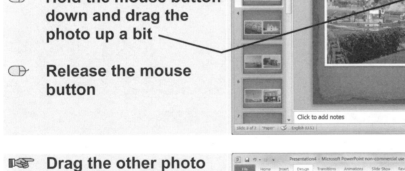

☞ **Drag the other photo to a position below the first photo** &#8477;46

You can see that it is easy to position the photos anyway you like.

# 8.7 Add Photos by Duplicating

If you want to add a photo with exactly the same size and frame, you can just duplicate one of the other photos on the page:

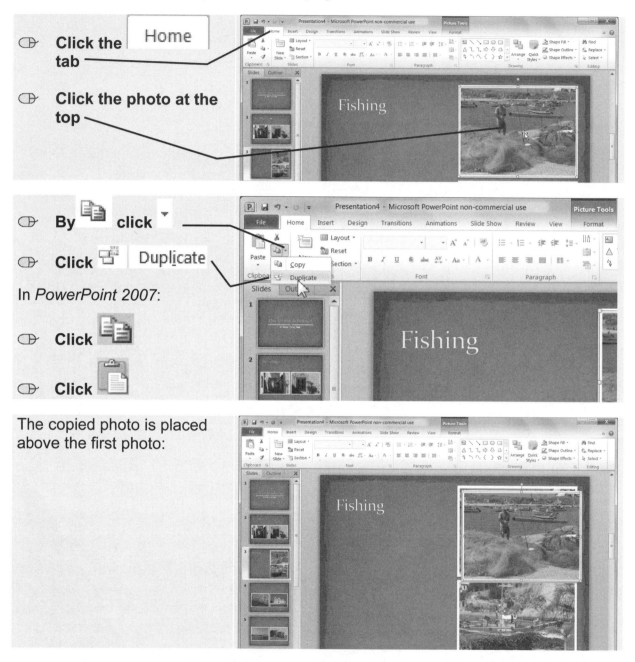

☞ **Click the** Home **tab**

☞ **Click the photo at the top**

☞ **By** 📋 **click** ▾

☞ **Click** 📋 Duplicate

In *PowerPoint 2007*:

☞ **Click** 📋

☞ **Click** 📋

The copied photo is placed above the first photo:

☞ **Drag the copy down to the left side of the lowest photo** 🔖46

Of course you will probably not want to display two identical pictures on the same page. In the next section we will explain how to change the photo you just copied.

## 8.8 Select a Different Photo

The final collection of photos and their order in the album has not been established yet. This is how to select a different photo:

☞  **Right-click the photo**

You will see a menu:

☞  **Click**

      Change Picture...

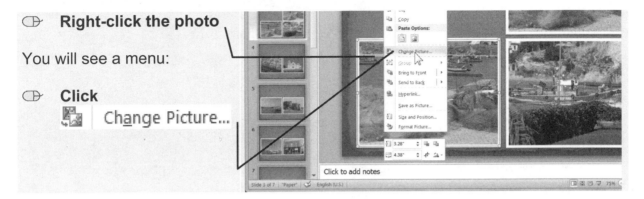

Now the *Insert Picture* window will be opened. Select one of the practice files:

☞  **Drag the scroll bar down**

☞  **Click**

      Portugal 5
      JPEG Image
      2.56 MB

☞  **Click**  Insert

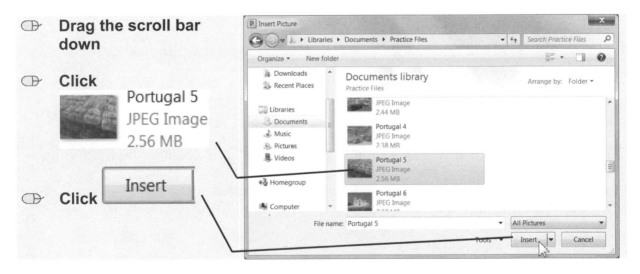

You will see the new photo:

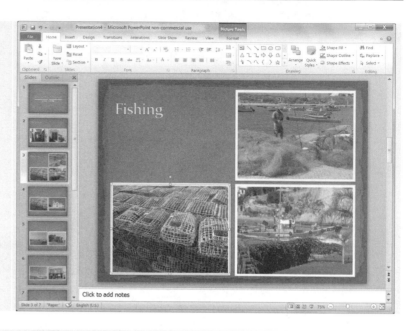

☞ **Go to the fourth slide** 𝒪𝒪¹¹³

☞ **Type this title for the slide:** The church of Ferragudo 𝒪𝒪¹¹⁴

## 8.9 Delete a Photo

The fourth slide contains the same photo you have just inserted into the third slide. This is how you remove a photo from the album:

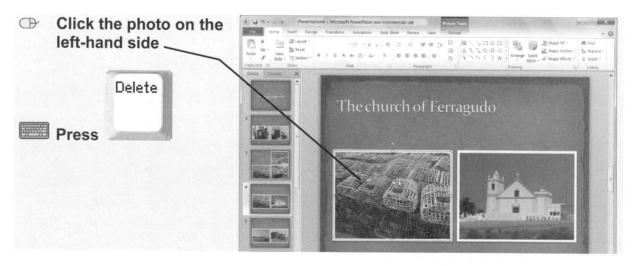

Now the photo will be removed.

# 8.10 Enlarge a Photo

While you were creating the album, all the photos are inserted with the same size. But you can enlarge or shrink these photos:

- 👉 **Click the photo**

- 👉 **Position the mouse pointer on the handle in the upper left corner**

The pointer turns into a:

- 👉 **Hold the mouse button down and keep it pressed in**

- 👉 **Drag the handle outwards and to the left**

- 👉 **Release the mouse button**

☞ **Now drag the photo until it is positioned below the title** 🐾⁴⁶

# 8.11 Insert a New Slide

The number of slides in the photo album has not yet been defined. This is how you insert a new, blank slide:

- 👉 **By** [ ] **click** New Slide ▾

Here you see the different types of slides you can use:

- 👉 **Click** Blank

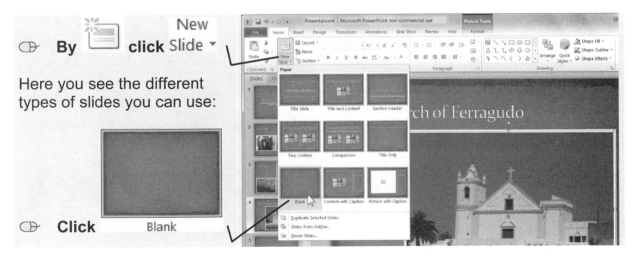

The new slide will be inserted underneath the current slide:

Here you see the new, blank slide:

# 8.12 Render a Photo Full Screen

Your album will look more attractive if you vary the format of the photos now and then. You can render some of the photos in full screen mode. This is how to do that:

**Click the** Insert **tab**

**Click** Picture

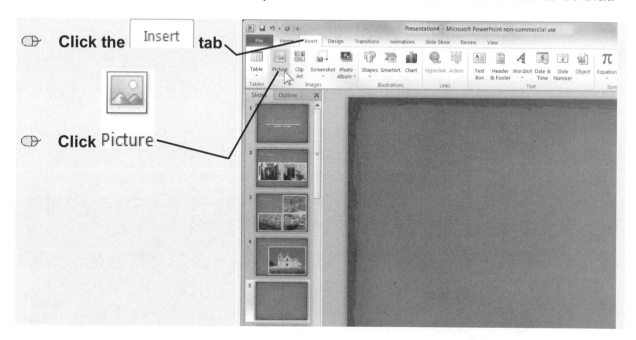

Now the *Insert Picture* window will be opened. The folder containing the practice files has already been selected:

**Drag the scroll bar down**

**Click**

Portugal 8
JPEG Image
2.38 MB

**Click** Insert

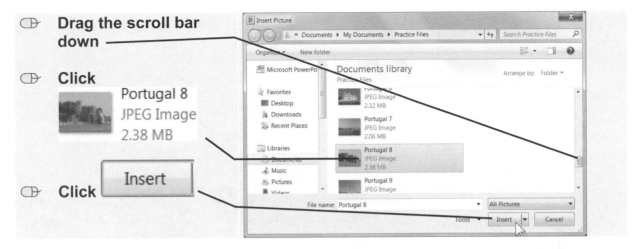

You will see that the photo is displayed the same size as the slide:

# 8.13 Add a Caption

When you were creating this album, you have added a title to two of the photos. That does not mean that you have to leave it at that: you can add extra text to any photo. This is how you add a caption to a photo that is displayed full screen:

**Click the** Insert **tab**

A

Text Box

**Click** Box

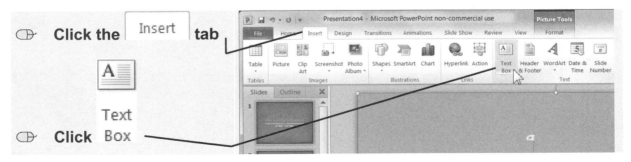

You will not see any effect yet. You will need to position the text box on top of the photo by dragging it:

The mouse pointer turns into
⊥:

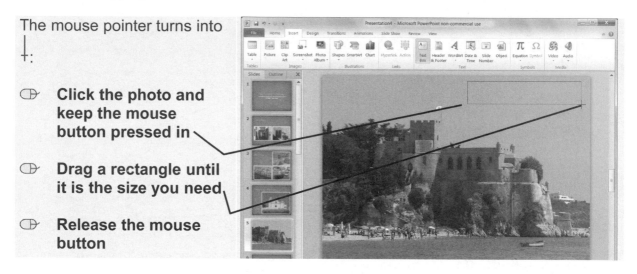

⊕  **Click the photo and keep the mouse button pressed in**

⊕  **Drag a rectangle until it is the size you need**

⊕  **Release the mouse button**

Now you are ready to enter the text:

⌨  **Type:** The fort of São João do Arade

### 🩹 HELP! How do I type an ã?

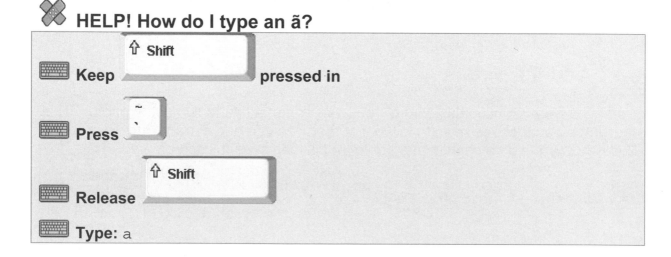

⌨  **Keep**  ⇧ **Shift**  **pressed in**

⌨  **Press**  ~`

⌨  **Release**  ⇧ **Shift**

⌨  **Type:** a

You can format the text in the same way you did with the *Word* and *Excel* programs:

☞ **Select the text in the text box** $\mathscr{G}^{37}$

☞ **Change the font size to 24 pts** $\mathscr{G}^{24}$

☞ **Make the text bold** $\mathscr{G}^{115}$

If the text does not fit on a single line anymore, you can widen the text box:

☞ **Position the mouse pointer on the handle on the left**

☞ **Keep the mouse button pressed down and drag the border to the left**

☞ **Release the mouse button**

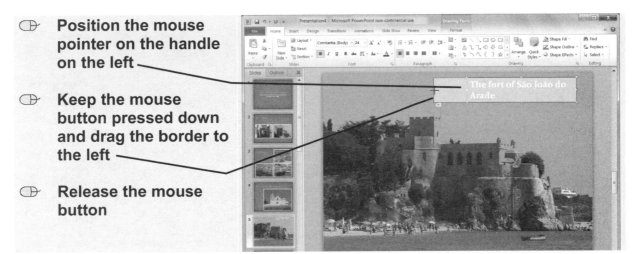

This is how the current slide looks:

## 8.14 Change the Picture Style

Up to this point, the photos in the album have the same layout, rectangular. You can change the style for each individual photo:

☞ **Go to the sixth slide** ✀113

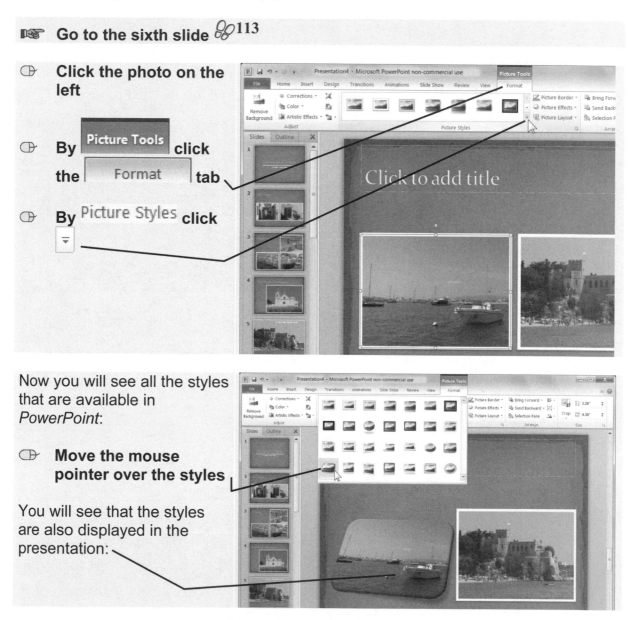

Now you will see all the styles that are available in *PowerPoint*:

☞ **Move the mouse pointer over the styles**

You will see that the styles are also displayed in the presentation:

In this example you are going to select the *Metal Oval* style:

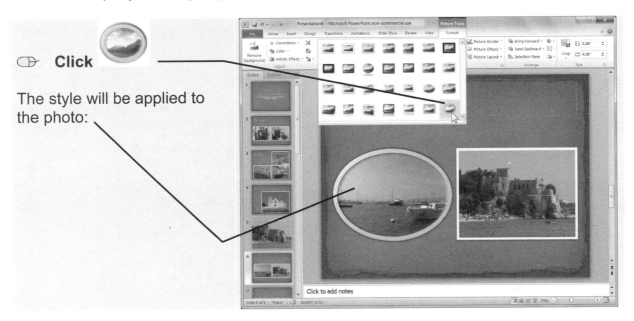

**Click**

The style will be applied to the photo:

With the picture styles you can make each picture in the album look different.

☞ **Delete the photo on the right** 🐾**51**

# 8.15 Insert an Illustration

You can use the illustrations you already know from *Word* in *PowerPoint* as well:

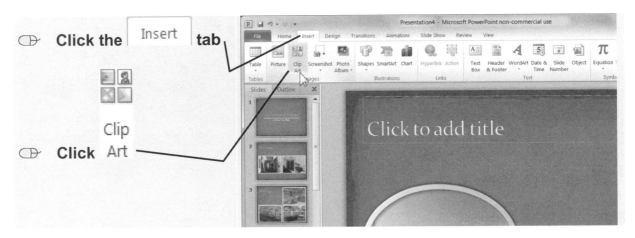

**Click the** Insert **tab**

Clip

**Click** Art

Now the *Clip Art* task pane will be opened:

⊕ **Double-click the search box**

⌨ **Type:** beach

⊕ **Click** Go

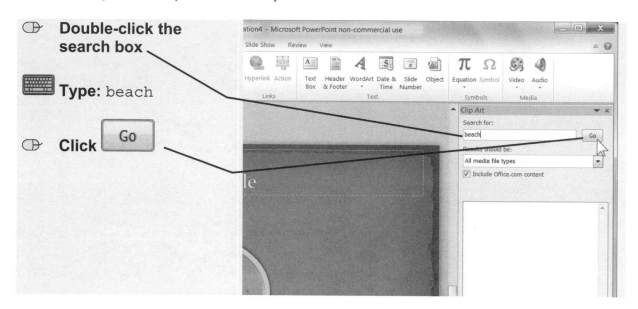

Select an illustration:

⊕ **Drag the scroll bar down a bit**

⊕ **For example, click**

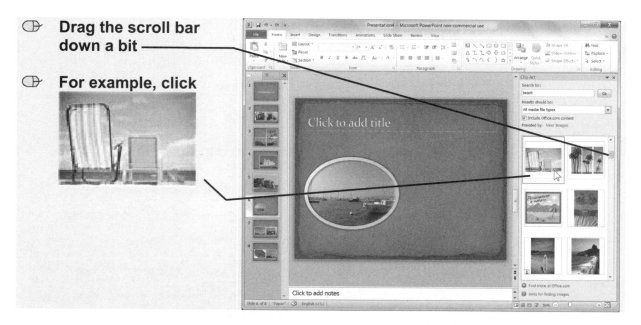

The illustration will be inserted in the slide:

☞ **Shrink the illustration** 👣116

☞ **Drag the illustration next to the photo** 👣46

Now the slide looks like this:

You can close the *Clip Art* task pane:

⊕ **Click** ✖

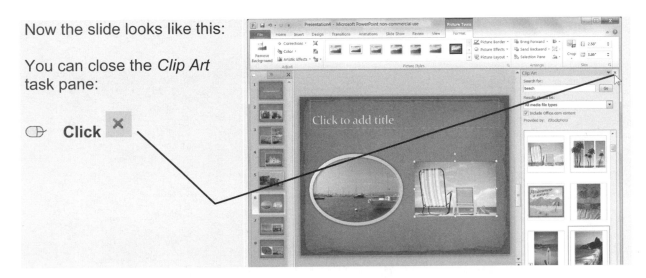

Before you continue, it is a good idea to save your photo album presentation:

☞ **Save the presentation as** *photo album* **in the** (*My*) *Documents* **folder** 👣117

## 8.16 Edit Photos and Illustrations

You can use the commands in the *Format* tab to modify a picture and adapt it to your taste.

☞ **Go to the fourth slide** 👣113

This is how you can adjust the brightness and contrast within a picture:

⊕ **Click the photo**

⊕ **If necessary, click the** Format **tab**

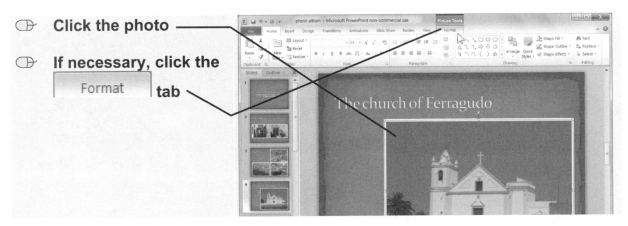

☞ **Click**
   ☼ **Corrections** ▾

☞ **Move the mouse
   pointer over the
   options**

The brightness and contrast
within the picture changes as
you move through the
options:

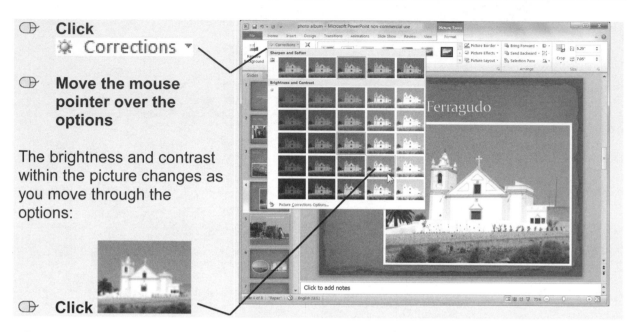

☞ **Click**

💡 **Tip**

**Brightness and contrast in Word 2007**
In *Word 2007* you can correct the picture in the same way, but you will need to use
two buttons: ☼ Brightness ▾ and ◐ Contrast ▾ . This is how you adjust the
brightness:

☞ **Double-click the photo**

The  ▢ Format  tab will be opened:

☞ **Click** ☼ Brightness ▾ , [☼ +20 %]

Now the photo has become
much brighter:

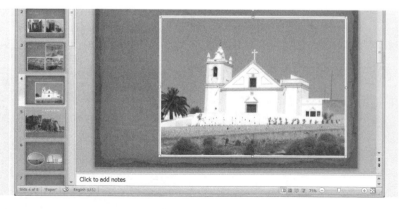

You can also edit the illustration you have inserted in the sixth slide:

☞ **Go to the sixth slide** 👣¹¹³

If you are not satisfied with the colors in this illustration, you can adjust them like this.

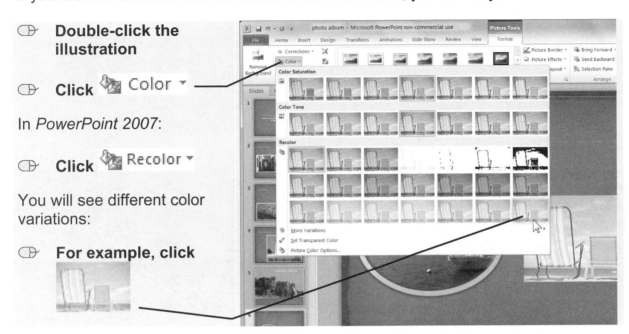

🖰 **Double-click the illustration**

🖰 **Click** Color ▾

In *PowerPoint 2007*:

🖰 **Click** Recolor ▾

You will see different color variations:

🖰 **For example, click**

Now the illustration in the slide will have changed color:

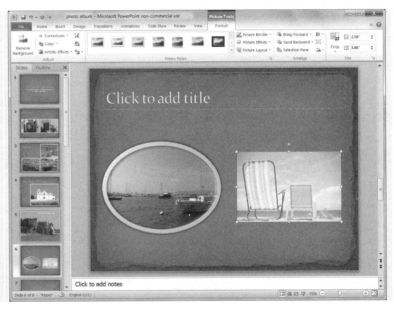

💡 **Tip**

**Reset the original illustration**

You can use the  button to discard all changes and reset it to its original format.

# 8.17 Add a Sound Clip

In *PowerPoint* you can easily add a sound clip from the *Media Gallery* to a slide with just a few mouse-clicks. Go ahead and try this for the title slide:

☞ **Go to the title slide** 🐾113

The first slide has been opened:

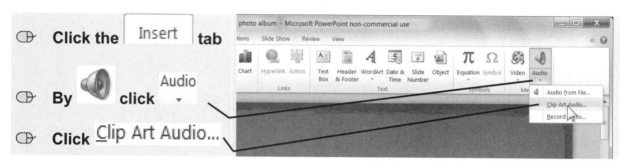

⊕ **Click the [ Insert ] tab**

⊕ **By 🔊 click Audio ▾**

⊕ **Click Clip Art Audio...**

💡 **Tip**

**Adding audio clips in PowerPoint 2007**

To add an audio clip in *PowerPoint 2007*, you need to use the 🔊 Sound ▾ button. The Clip Art Audio... option is called Sound from Clip Organizer... in *PowerPoint 2007*.

Now the *Clip Art* task pane will be opened. You will see all the available sound clips:

⊕ **Click Claps Cheers**

 **Please note:**

In *PowerPoint 2007* you will now see a window where you can choose if you want to start the sound in the slide show automatically, or when the icon is clicked.

In the center of the slide you will see an icon and in *PowerPoint 2010* a toolbar: —

At the same time, **Audio Tools** will appear, displaying the Format and Playback tabs in version 2010 and Options in 2007:

These tabs are displayed any time a sound clip has been selected.

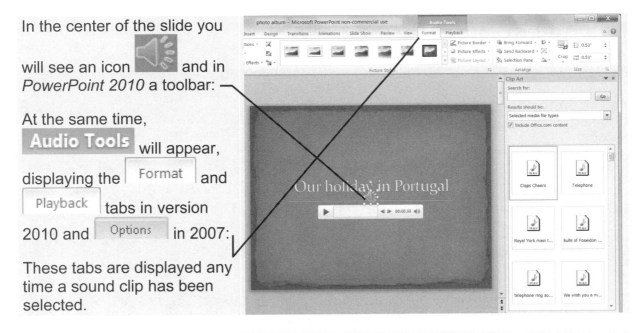

☞ **Close the *Clip Art* task pane** ✍**118**

You will see that the icon representing the sound clip is covering the title of the slide.

☞ **Move the icon to the bottom right side of the slide** ✍**46**

Now the toolbar has covered the icon. You can use the toolbar to test the sound clip:

👆 **Click** ▶

The sound clip will be played:

In *PowerPoint 2007*:

👆 **Double-click** 🔊

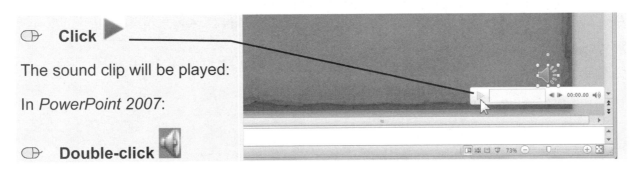

💡 **Tip**

**Audio file**
Instead of a sound clip, you can also add an audio file (audio clip) to a slide. For example, you can add an MP3 audio file containing a favorite song.

To insert this kind of file, you will need to select the 🔊 Audio from File... option, instead of the Clip Art Audio... option. Select the music file from your computer's

hard drive and click Insert.

## 8.18 Add Recorded Message to a Slide

*PowerPoint* also contains an option for adding a recorded voice message to a slide.

☞ **Connect a microphone to your computer**

 **Please note!**

If you do not have a microphone, you can just read through this section.

☞ **Go to the fifth slide** ♻113

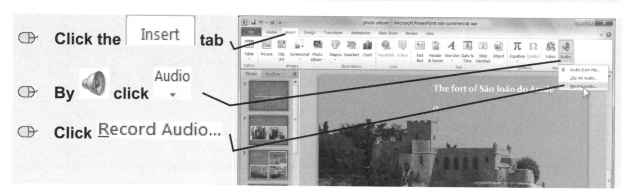

⊕ **Click the** `Insert` **tab**

⊕ **By** 🔊 **click** `Audio ▾`

⊕ **Click** `Record Audio...`

**Help! The** `Record Audio...` **option is disabled.**

The `Record Audio...` will only be active if you have a microphone connected to your computer. If a microphone is connected but the option is still disabled, then *PowerPoint* has not yet recognized this microphone. This is what you can do next:

☞ **Save the presentation** ♻69

☞ **Close *PowerPoint*** ♻14

☞ **Open *PowerPoint*** ♻119

☞ **Open the presentation** ♻120

☞ **Try again**

Now the *Record Sound* window will appear. This is how you start the recording:

⊕ **Click** ⬤

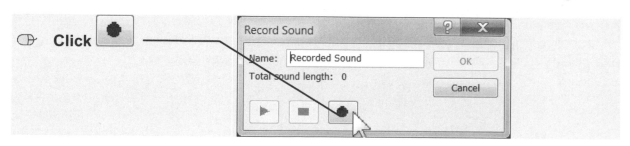

☞ **Record this voice message:**
While we were having our breakfast, we enjoyed a view of the fortress on the other side of the river.
Unfortunately, the fortress is not open to the public.

⊕ **Click**

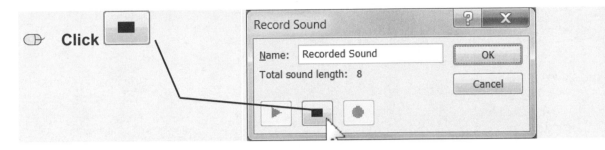

Before adding the recording to the slide, you can play it back:

⊕ **Click**

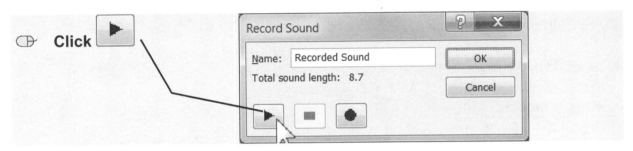

If you are satisfied with the recording:

⊕ **Click** OK

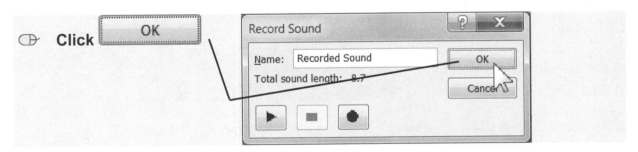

Now you will once again see

the 🔊 icon in the center of the slide:

☞ **Move the icon to the bottom right of the slide** 👣⁴⁶

A sound clip or an audio file that is included in a presentation can be played by clicking the play button ▶. If you prefer, you can set the clip to start automatically, when the slide appears on the screen:

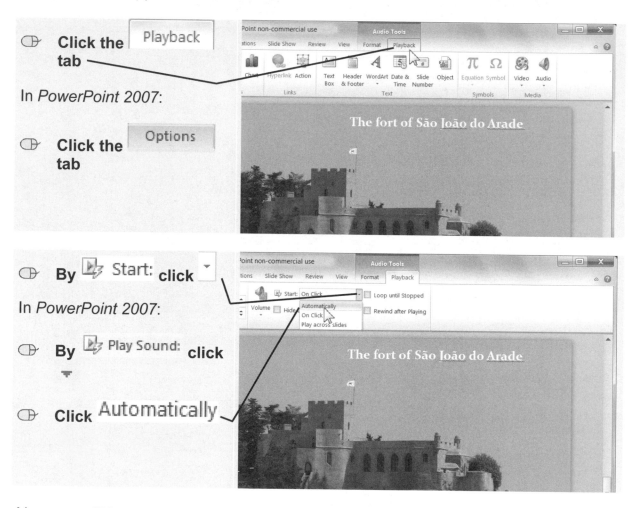

☞ **Click the** Playback **tab**

In *PowerPoint 2007*:

☞ **Click the** Options **tab**

☞ **By** Start: **click** ▾

In *PowerPoint 2007*:

☞ **By** Play Sound: **click** ▾

☞ **Click** Automatically

Now you will hear the sound as soon as the slide appears on the screen. You can also hide the icon while the sound clip is being played:

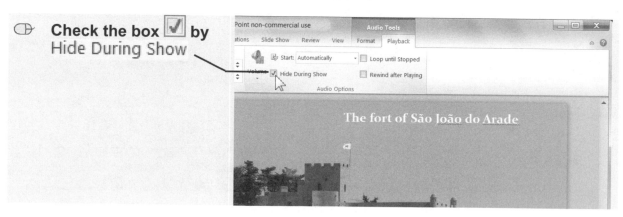

☞ **Check the box ☑ by** Hide During Show

# 8.19 Add a Slide with a Video Clip

Adding a video clip to a slide is just as easy as adding a sound clip. Just give it a try:

☞ **Go to the last slide** 🦶**113**

Now you will add a new slide that contains only a title:

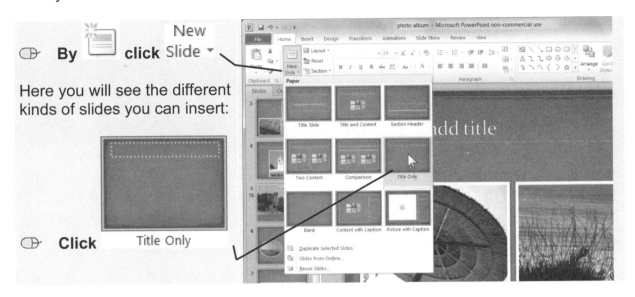

⊕ **By** [icon] **click Slide ▾**

Here you will see the different kinds of slides you can insert:

⊕ **Click** Title Only

The new slide will be inserted after the current slide.

☞ **Enter the following title for the new slide:** Video 🦶**114**

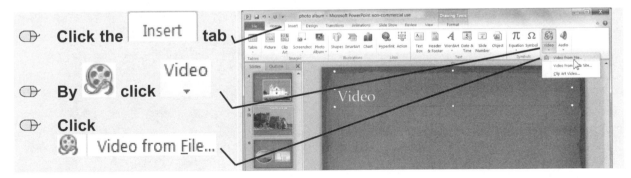

⊕ **Click the** Insert **tab**

⊕ **By** [icon] **click** Video **▾**

⊕ **Click**
[icon] Video from File...

👉 **Please note:**

In *PowerPoint 2007* this option is not called Video ▾ , but Movie ▾ .

You are going to use one of the sample files included in *Windows*:

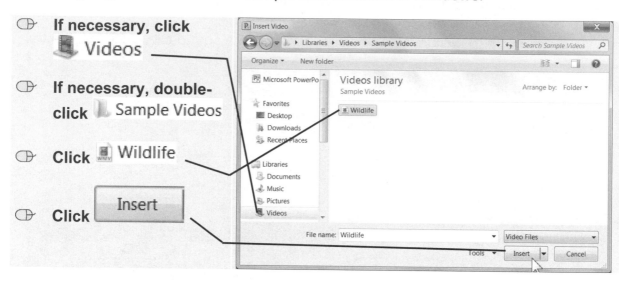

- ☞  **If necessary, click**
  🖥 **Videos**

- ☞  **If necessary, double-click** 📁 **Sample Videos**

- ☞  **Click**  **Wildlife**

- ☞  **Click** [ Insert ]

### ✕ HELP! I do not have that file.

You can also find this video file in the *Practice Files* folder. You have copied this folder to the (*My*) *Documents* folder.

### ➥ Please note:

In *PowerPoint 2007* you will see a window where you can indicate how you want the movie to start. You can have it start automatically or by clicking the play button.

Now a black area with a toolbar below is inserted into the slide. This black area is the first *frame* (image) of the video:

At the same time, you will see

the [ **Video Tools** ]

button with its [ Format ] and

[ Playback ] tabs. These tabs will be displayed when a video file has been selected:

In *PowerPoint 2007* you will

see the [ Options ] tab.

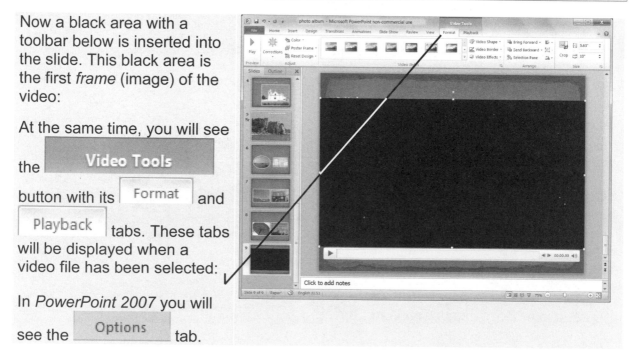

In *PowerPoint 2010*:

☞ **Shrink the video file, so you can see the title** ᴇᴇ**116**

☞ **Position the toolbar to the center of the bottom of the slide** ᴇᴇ**46**

Now you can take a look at the video clip:

In the toolbar:

☞ **Click ▶**

In *PowerPoint 2007*:

☞ **Double-click the video clip**

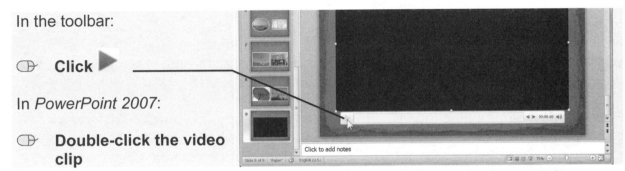

Now you will see the clip and hear the accompanying music:

💡 **Tip**

**Edit a video file**
In *PowerPoint*, you can edit a video file the same way you edit a picture. Earlier on in this chapter you learned how to do this. You will find all the editing options by the

 tab.

For example, you can use the ☀️ Corrections button to adjust the brightness and contrast of the video clip. You can use the 🎨 Color ▾ button to change the color shade of the video. Video Styles will allow you to adjust the border and shape of the video image.

**Tip**

**Insert or link**

In this chapter you have learned how to *insert* a sound clip and a video clip into your presentation. This means that the file has been copied from its original location and stored in your presentation. When you copy your presentation to another computer, or send the presentation to someone else by e-mail, the sound and video clips will be included automatically. They have become a part of your presentation.

If you insert a lot of video or sound clips into your presentation, the presentation file will become very large. To solve this problem, you can decide to *link* these clips to your presentation, instead of inserting them. The slide will then contain a shortcut to the original file, which is stored on your computer's hard drive.

**Please note:** when you choose to link clips and you copy your presentation to a different computer, the audio and video files which were linked will not be included in the presentation. If you want to be able to play the sound and video clips on the other computer, you will need to copy the folder containing the audio and video files to the other computer as well. The folder containing the copied clips must have the same name and be stored in the same location as on the original computer (where you have created the presentation). Otherwise, *PowerPoint* will not be able to find the files while the presentation is viewed. This is how you link an audio file to your presentation:

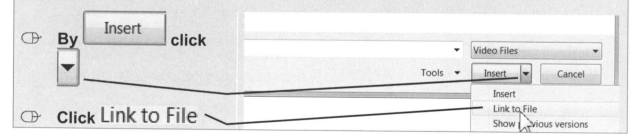

## 8.20 Crop a Video File

*PowerPoint 2010* allows you to crop a video file. If you think the video file you have added to your presentation is too long, you can remove part of it from the beginning or the end of the file. You cannot do this in *PowerPoint 2007*.

- **Click the** Playback **tab**
- **Click** Trim Video

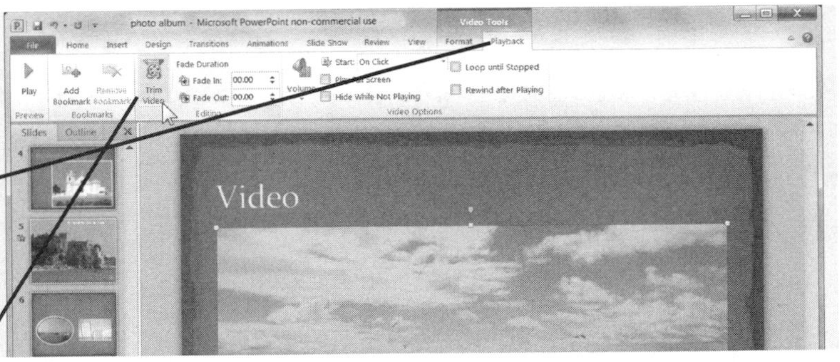


Now the *Trim Video* window will be opened. You are going to shorten the video clip by cutting away the images of the horses (at the beginning) and birds (at the end of the clip):

Change the start time of the video by moving the green marker:

- **Position the mouse pointer on**

The pointer will turn into:

- **Drag to the right, until the start time reaches** 00:04.192

## Tip

**View a video frame by frame**

You can use the and buttons to skip through the video one frame at a time. This way you can exactly determine the spot to crop the video.

Afterwards, you do the same thing with the red end marker 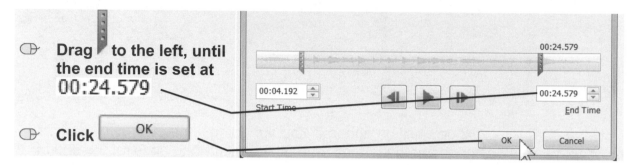 at the end of the video:

🖰 **Drag ▌to the left, until the end time is set at 00:24.579**

🖰 **Click** [ OK ]

Now you will see the first frame of the video you have cropped:

💡 **Tip**

**Crop an audio file**
You can crop an audio file in exactly the same way:

🖰 **Click the** 🔊 **icon of the audio file**

🖰 **Click the** Playback **tab**

🖰 **Click** Trim Audio

*- Continue reading on the next page -*

In the *Trim Audio* window you can drag the begin and end markers to trim the audio file:

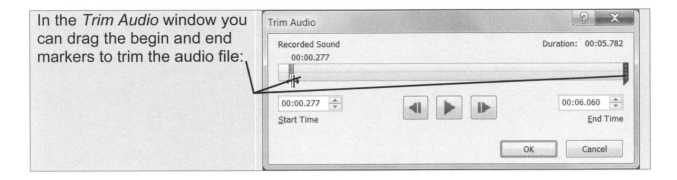

## 8.21 Select a Poster Frame

By default, a video file will start by displaying the first frame on the slide. But you have seen earlier that the first frame may also be a black area. In *PowerPoint* you can select a different frame or image as a sample image for the video file. This is called a *poster frame*. This option is not available in *PowerPoint 2007*.

**Click the tab** `Format`

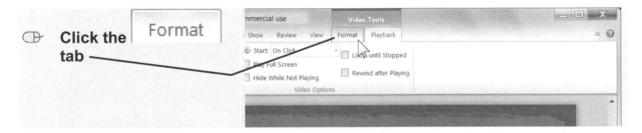

You can select any random frame as your first sample frame. Play the video by using the toolbar below the video frame:

**Click** ▶

As soon as you see the koala bear:

**Click** ❙❙

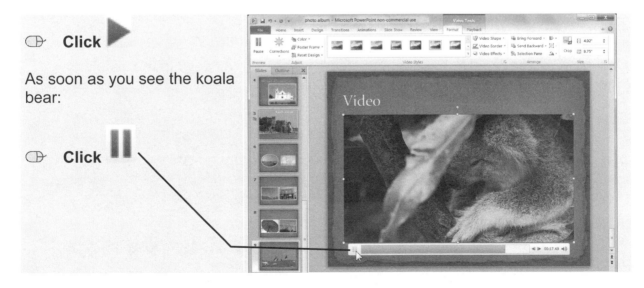

👆 **Click**
   📠 Poster Frame ▾

👆 **Click**
   📠    Current Frame

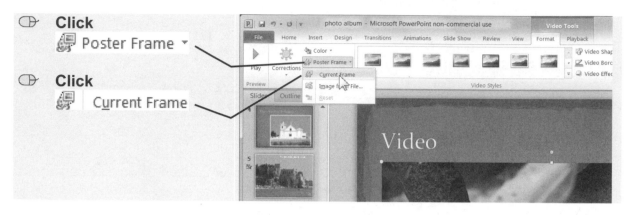

You will see the message
**Poster Frame Set:**

You will also see the new
sample frame in the
thumbnail view of the slide:

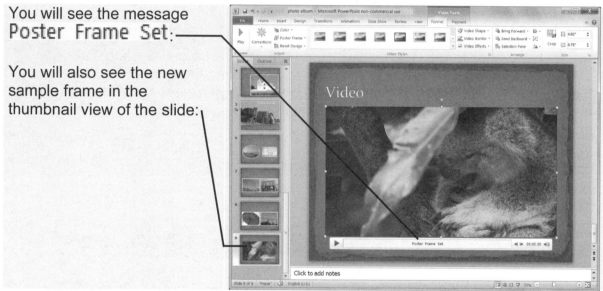

# 8.22 View the Presentation

Until now you have edited your photo album in the normal view. In the slide show
view you can see what your presentation will look like on a full screen.

☞ **Go to the first slide** 𝄢113

In the bottom right of the
window:

👆 **Click** 🖳

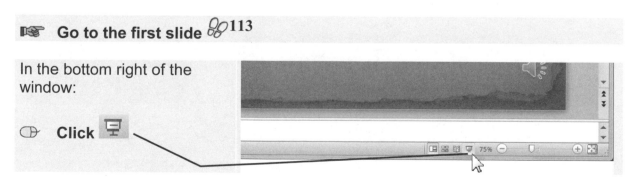

The first slide will be displayed full screen. This is how you play the sound clip of the applause during the slide show:

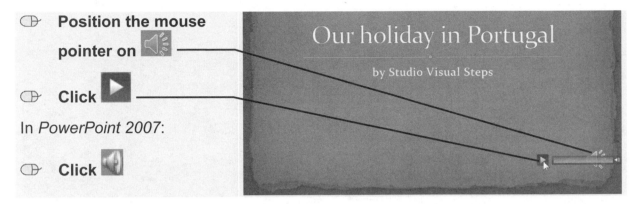

☞ **Position the mouse**

  **pointer on** 🔊

☞ **Click** ▶

In *PowerPoint 2007*:

☞ **Click** 🔊

Skip to the following slide by clicking the mouse once:

☞ **Click the slide in a random spot**

You will see the next slide

☞ **Click this slide and the next two slides, in any spot**

Now you will see the fifth slide, which contains the full screen photo of the fortress. You have also added recorded audio to this slide. This will be played automatically when the slide is displayed.

☞ **View the next couple of slides, until you see the *Video* slide** 🐾 **121**

The video clip will be played when you click the slide show window:

☞ **Click the slide show window**

You can just click ▶, but the video will also be played when you click a random spot in the window. This can be very useful during a presentation, because you do not have to be very accurate while clicking the window.

Now you will see the video:

**HELP! I see the next slide instead of the video.**

Most likely you have clicked somewhere above or beside the slide show window, instead of directly in the window.

When the video has finished, you can go to the next slide:

In the top of the slide show window:

 **Click the slide**

 **HELP! The video has started playing once more.**

Most likely you have clicked inside of the slide show window instead of above the window.

After the last slide you will see a black screen. This means the slide show has ended.

 **Click the black screen**

The slide show stops and you will return to the normal view.

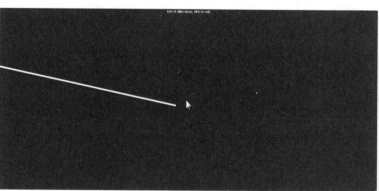

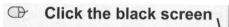 **Tip**

**Quickly stop a slide show**
This is how you can quit the slide show view and return to the normal view:

 **Press** Esc

If a video is being played:

 **Press** Esc **twice**

# 8.23 Move and Duplicate Slides

The slide sorter is the view that arranges the slides in the most ordered way and gives you a good idea of all your slides in the *PowerPoint* presentation. In this view you will see thumbnails of all your slides. Here you can quickly change the order of the slides in your presentation. Give it a try:

☞ **Click** ▦

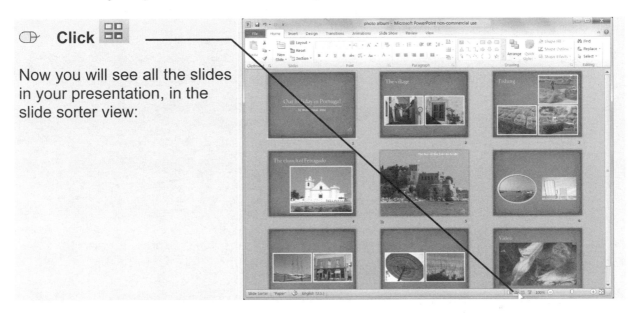

Now you will see all the slides in your presentation, in the slide sorter view:

By dragging the slides you can change their order. For instance, this is how you place the slide with the fortress before the slide displaying the church:

☞ **Position the mouse**

**pointer on**

☞ **Keep the mouse button pressed and drag the slide to the left of slide 4**

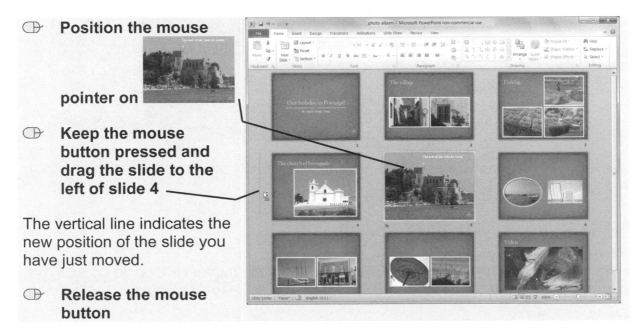

The vertical line indicates the new position of the slide you have just moved.

☞ **Release the mouse button**

If you want to include the same slide twice in your presentation, you can duplicate the slide.

You can do this by using the *Copy*  and *Paste* buttons on the Home tab:

Now the slide has been copied to the *Windows* clipboard. Next, you will need to indicate where you want to paste the copy of the *Phishing* slide:

**Click between slides 5 and 6**

You will see a blinking vertical line between slides 5 and 6:

**Click**

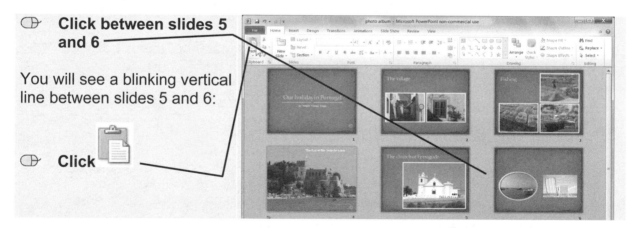

The copy of the slide will be pasted between the church slide and the slide containing the illustration.

💡 **Tip**

**Replacing photos**
Earlier in this chapter you learned how to replace the photos in the photo boxes. You can do the same thing with the photos on the slide you have just copied.

## 8.24 Delete Slides

If you decide you no longer want to use a particular slide, you can always delete it. This is how you delete the copied *Phishing* slide:

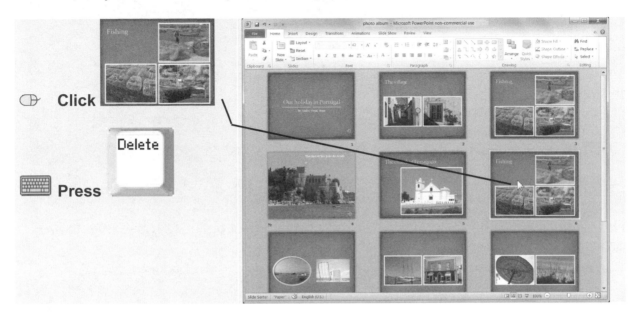

**Click**

**Press**

The copied slide has been deleted.

☞ **Save the changes in your presentation** ✂ᵍ⁶⁹

## 8.25 Add Transitions

Your presentation will become even more attractive if you add some of the special effects that are available in *PowerPoint*. For example, you can add *transitions*. A transition is an animated effect that appears when you go from one slide to another, during the slide show presentation. The new slide can glide into view from the side, above or from the middle of the screen, for example.

You can practice by adding a transition between the first and second slide of the presentation. Then you will select the *Transition to this slide* option on the *Transitions* tab.

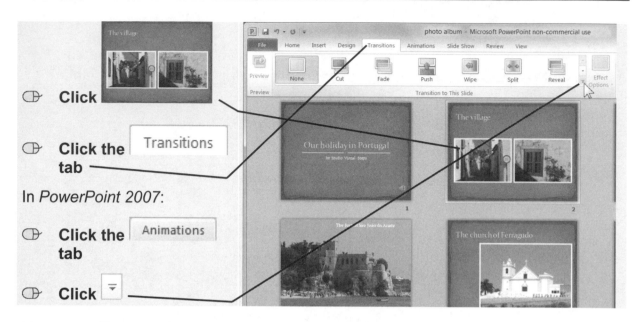

☞ **Click** 

☞ **Click the** Transitions **tab**

In *PowerPoint 2007*:

☞ **Click the** Animations **tab**

☞ **Click** ▼

Now you will see a window with dozens of special effect options. These effects are grouped in different categories, to help you choose easier.

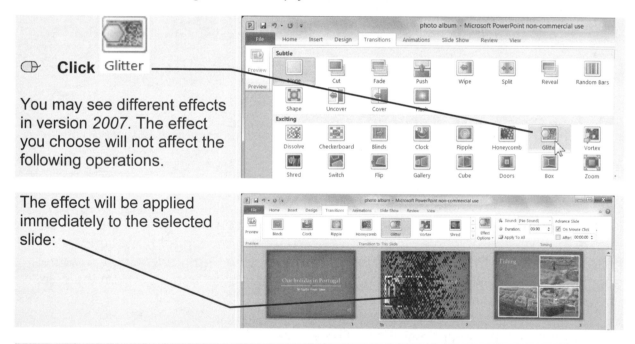

☞ **Click** Glitter

You may see different effects in version *2007*. The effect you choose will not affect the following operations.

The effect will be applied immediately to the selected slide:

☞ **Try out some of the other transition effects** ᨖ**122**

For example, in the end you are going to select the *Ferris Wheel* transition effect:

☞ **Select the** Ferris Wheel **transition** ᨖ**122**

You can also set the speed for the transition.

Currently, the transition takes two seconds. You can tell this by the

🕐 Duration: 02.00 ⇕

icon:

You are going to change this into three seconds:

👉 **Click 🔼 four times**

In *PowerPoint 2007* you can set the duration of the transition by

Transition Speed: Fast ▾ .

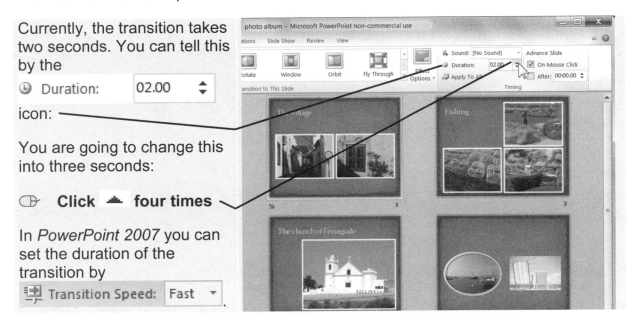

Now you can view the results:

👉 **Click** Preview

You are also going to add a sound effect to the transition, for instance, the *Wind* sound:

👉 **By 🔊 Sound: click** ▾

In *PowerPoint 2007*:

👉 **By 🔊 Transition Sound: click** ▾

👉 **Click** Wind

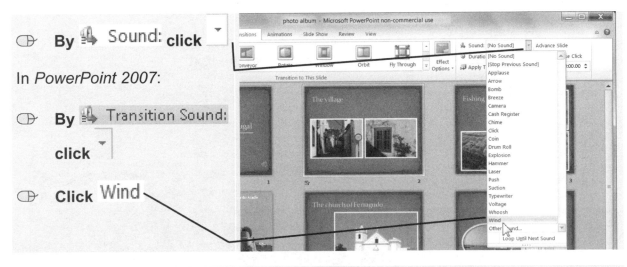

☞ **View the preview of the transition** 🔗**123**

The transition will be displayed. During the transition you will hear the sound effect.

 **Tip**

**Transition icon**

In the slide sorter view you will see the  icon below the second slide. This icon indicates that you have set a transition for this slide. You can also view the transition in the following way:

☞ **Click** 📊

**Please note:** the same icon also appears below any slide that contains a media clip that is played when the slide is displayed.

## 8.26 Use Animations

Up to this point in normal view, you will see all the text and objects on a slide at the same time. By using *animations*, you can allow the components on a slide to display in a special way. Just try it for yourself:

☞ **Click the** [ Animations ] **tab**

☞ **Double-click**

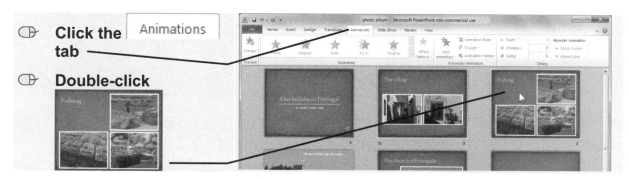

Now you will see the slide in the normal view. You can add an animation to any element on the page. Start by adding an animation to the text:

☞ **Click the text box**

☞ **Click** [Fly In]

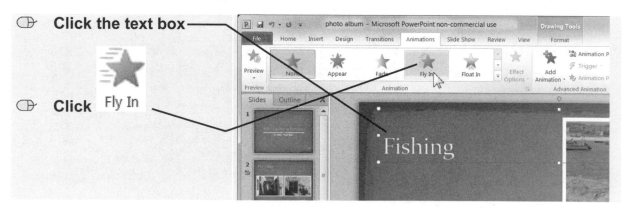

##  Please note:

The effect will be applied instantly to the slide:

Next to the text box, you will see the number ⓵:

You can also add animations to the photos as well:

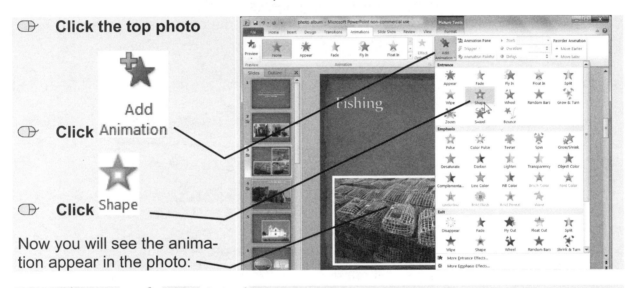

- 👆 **Click the top photo**

- 👆 **Click** Add Animation

- 👆 **Click** Shape

Now you will see the animation appear in the photo:

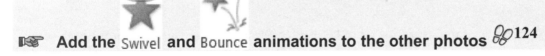

☞ **Add the** Swivel **and** Bounce **animations to the other photos** 🐾**124**

##  Please note:

Now you are going to view a preview of the animation effects:

- 👆 **Click** Preview

All animations will be displayed, one after the other. During the slide show, the animations will start one by one, as soon as you click the mouse. This way, you can tell a story about the first photo, and display the second photo when you have finished your story.

☞ **View the slide show in the slide show view** 🐾125

The slide show will start with the selected slide.

💡 **Tip**

**Play animations one after the other, during a presentation**
You can also set the animations to be played one after the other, as soon as the slide is displayed. Start with the text:

⊕ **Click** 1

⊕ **By** ▶ Start: **click** ▾

⊕ **Click** With Previous

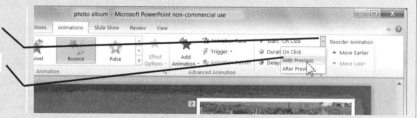

Now the text will be displayed as soon as the slide appears. The number 1 has turned into 0. This means you will not need to click the mouse to display this element.

Now the top photo has the number 1. To make this photo appear automatically, after the text has been displayed:

⊕ **Click** 1

⊕ **By** ▶ Start: **click** ▾

⊕ **Click** After Previous

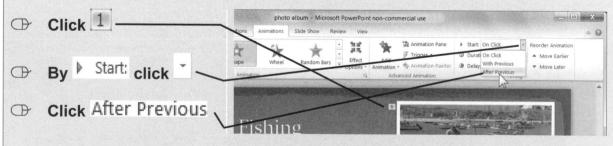

Now the photo also shows the number 0.

☞ **Do the same thing for the other two photos**

*- Continue reading on the next page -*

Now all the photos and the text should show the number ⬛0⬛. As soon as the appears, the text and the photos will be displayed one after the other, includin animation you have selected.

**Please note:** in *PowerPoint 2007* you will not automatically see the numbers. To display the numbers:

 **Click** ⟦≡ Custom Animation⟧

In the right-hand side of the window you will see the *Custom Animation* task bar. In this task bar you can change the order of the animations as well as other things.

# 8.27 Compress the Presentation

In this chapter you have added several media clips to your presentation. In *PowerPoint 2010* you can check the *Backstage* view for *PowerPoint* tips to optimize the view or the file size of these files:

## ➥ Please note:
This option is not available in *PowerPoint 2007*.

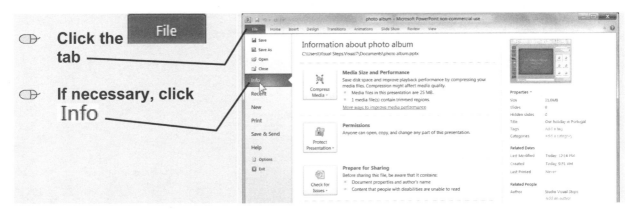

☞ **Click the** ⟦File⟧ **tab** ——

☞ **If necessary, click** Info ——

For this presentation, you can compress the media clips you have inserted to help save disk space. You can do this by compressing the files, or by permanently deleting the parts you have trimmed from a video file. You can select one of three presentation levels: low, internet, and presentation quality.

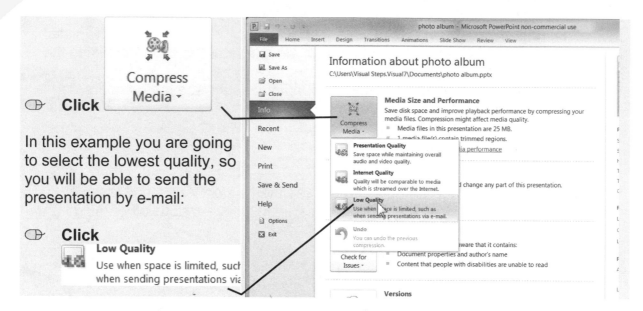

 **Click** Compress Media ▾

In this example you are going to select the lowest quality, so you will be able to send the presentation by e-mail:

 **Click**

**Low Quality**
Use when space is limited, such when sending presentations via

## Please note:

The higher the quality, the more space the presentation will take on your computer. If you want to display the presentation on a big screen, you will need to select **Presentation Quality**.

Here you will see that the compression is in process.

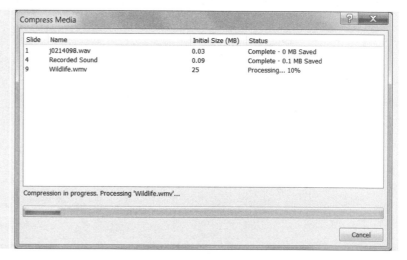

In this example you have saved 23 MB of disk space:

Compression complete. You saved 23 MB.

 **Click** Close

☞ **Save your presentation** ᨊ**69**

Now the presentation file has become much smaller. In the next section you will learn how to send this smaller presentation by e-mail.

## 💡 Tip

**Optimize media compatibility**
If you are going to send your presentation by e-mail, it is recommended to optimize the media compatibility as well. Some media files can be modified to make sure that they will play on other computers.

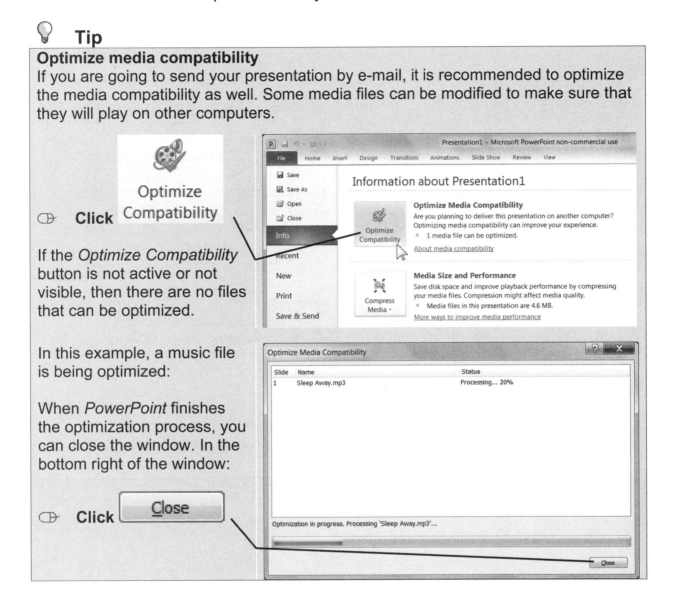

⊕ **Click** Optimize Compatibility

If the *Optimize Compatibility* button is not active or not visible, then there are no files that can be optimized.

In this example, a music file is being optimized:

When *PowerPoint* finishes the optimization process, you can close the window. In the bottom right of the window:

⊕ **Click** Close

# 8.28 Send Presentation By E-mail

Now you are going to send the presentation (including the compressed media files) by e-mail, as an attachment.

 **Please note:**

A media file, such as a sound clip, an audio file, or a video clip, will only be included in the presentation if you have selected to ⟦ Insert ⟧ these files while creating the presentation. The media files have then become a part of the presentation itself.

If you have selected the Link to File option, the presentation will only contain a shortcut to the media files. The original file will not be included in the presentation, and will not be sent in the e-mail package. The presentation will display correctly on your own computer but the person who receives the presentation by e-mail will not be able to view the video files or listen to the audio files.

If your presentation contains a link to a *YouTube* video clip, this clip can only be played on the recipient's computer if there is an active Internet connection.
See the *Tips* in the back of this chapter to read how to add a *YouTube* video clip to your presentation.

 **Please note:**

In *PowerPoint 2007* the media files will not be compressed. This means the attachment to your e-mail message will be much larger than in the example.

This is how you send a presentation as an attachment to an e-mail message in *PowerPoint 2010*:

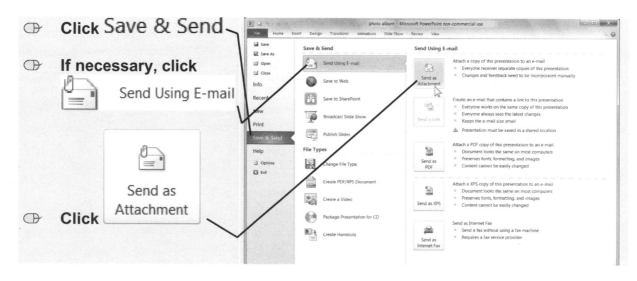

☞ **Click** Save & Send

☞ **If necessary, click**
Send Using E-mail

☞ **Click** Send as Attachment

This is how you do it in *PowerPoint 2007*:

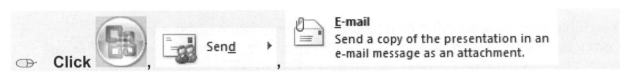

Now your default e-mail program will be opened and a new message will be created:

Here you see the attachment photo album.pptx (6.57 MB):

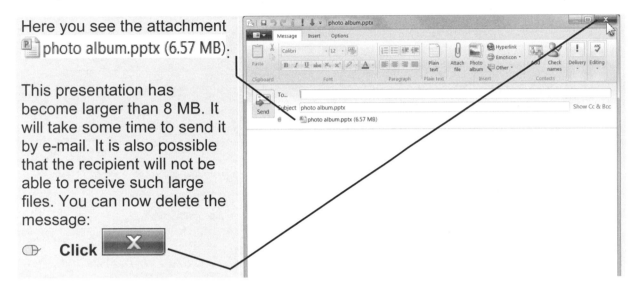

This presentation has become larger than 8 MB. It will take some time to send it by e-mail. It is also possible that the recipient will not be able to receive such large files. You can now delete the message:

Click  **X**

A presentation that does not contain media files, but includes only photos, illustrations or text, will take up a much less space. You will easily be able to send such a presentation by e-mail.

☞ **If necessary, close the window of your e-mail program** ✇14

# 8.29 Undo Presentation Compression

You have compressed the media files in the presentation using low quality compression. In *PowerPoint 2010*, you can undo this compression so the files will regain their original quality settings. In *PowerPoint 2007* you did not have the compression option. So, if you are using *PowerPoint 2007*, you can skip this section.

☞ **Click the** ▐ **File** ▌ **tab** ─────

☞ **If necessary, click** *Info* ─────

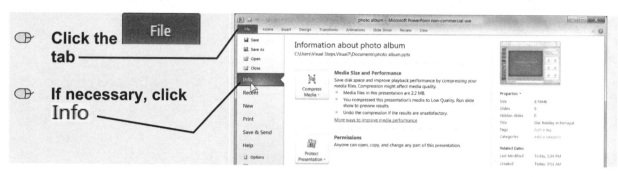

☞ **Click** ⟨Compress Media ▾⟩

☞ **Click** ↶ **Undo** — You can undo the previ... compression.

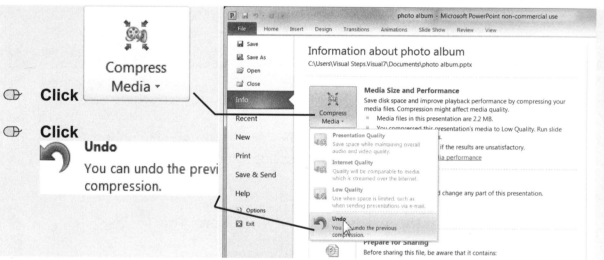

## 🐾 Please note:

You can only undo the compression as long as the presentation is still open in *PowerPoint*. When you close and then reopen the presentation, the  **Undo** — You can undo the previous compression. button will no longer be active.

Now, the media files will be restored to their original size and quality, like they were before the compression operation.

☞ **Save your presentation** 🐾⁶⁹

# 8.30 Package a Presentation for CD

With the *Package for CD* option you can package your presentation. In this context, *Packaging* means that all the necessary files to view your presentation will be copied to a single folder. This includes any media files that have not been inserted, but linked to the presentation. You can burn the packaged presentation to CD or copy it to your computer's hard drive, a USB stick or other external storage device.

 **Tip**

**All files will be packaged**
If you package your presentation, you can be certain that all the necessary files are included. This means the presentation can be viewed on a different computer without any problems.

 **Please note:**

To work through the examples in this section, you will need to have a (re)writable CD-r or CD-rw, and a CD burner. If you do not own these devices, you can just read through this section.

Now you are going to package your presentation and burn it to a CD:

☞ **Click the** File **tab**

☞ **Click** Save & Send

☞ **Click** Package Presentation f...

☞ **Click** Package for CD

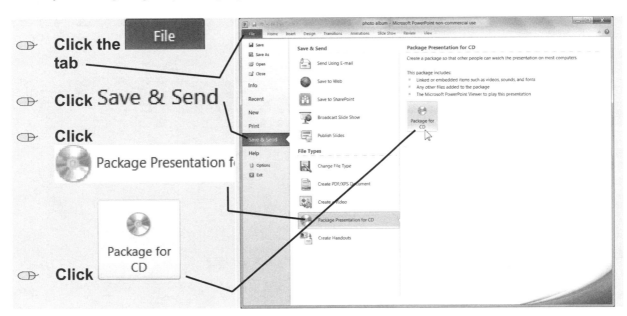

This is how you do it in *PowerPoint 2007*:

☞ **Click** ... , ... Publish ▶ , ... **Package for CD** Copy the presentation and media links to a folder that can be burned to a CD.

Now the *Package for CD* window will be opened:

*PowerPoint* has already entered a name for the CD: ─

You could also add additional presentations to the CD: ─

Just check the packaging options for the CD:

☞ **Click** Options...

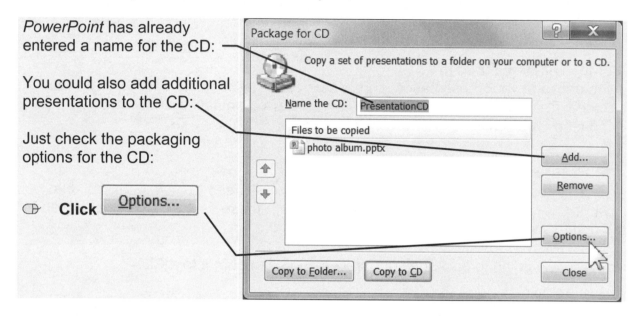

In *PowerPoint 2010*:

You will see that the linked files will be added to the CD: ─

The *TrueType* fonts will be copied as well, to make sure that the text is rendered correctly on different computers: ─

☞ **Make sure that the settings on your screen are identical to this example**

☞ **Click** OK

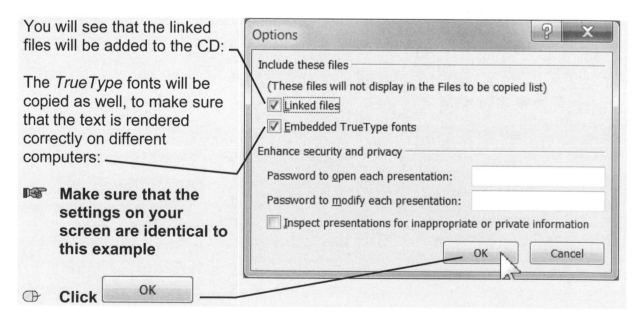

**Please note:**

When you package a presentation for CD, the linked media files will be included. These are the files you have added to the presentation by selecting the Link to File option, instead of the | Insert | option.

A *YouTube* video clip will not be included in the package and cannot be viewed in *PowerPoint Viewer* on a different computer, even when the computer is connected to the Internet. See the *Tips* in the back of this chapter to read how to add a *YouTube* video clip to a slide.

In *PowerPoint 2007* the *Options* window looks a bit different:

The presentation will be packaged as a *Viewer Package*:

You will see that the linked files and the *TrueType* fonts will be included on the CD:

☞ **Make sure that the settings on your screen are identical to this example**

☞ **Click** | OK |

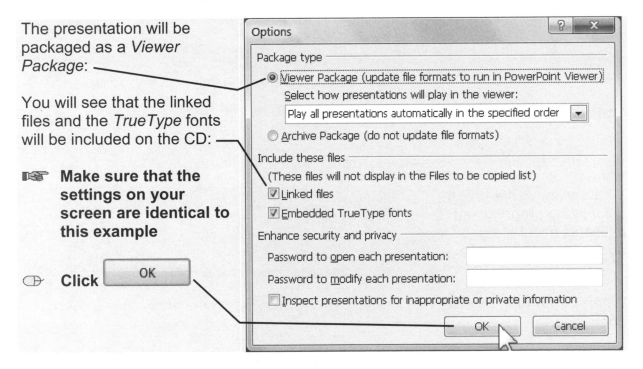

☞ **Insert a blank, writable CD into the CD/DVD burner**

If the *AutoPlay* window opens:

☞ **Click** | X |

Start the packaging process:

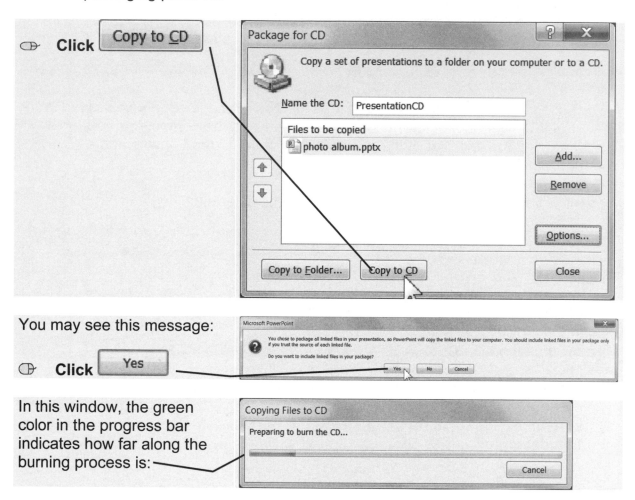

**Click** Copy to CD

You may see this message:

**Click** Yes

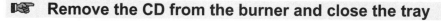

In this window, the green color in the progress bar indicates how far along the burning process is:

When the burning process has finished, your CD/DVD burner's tray will automatically open.

☞ **Remove the CD from the burner and close the tray**

Now you will be asked if you want to copy the same presentation to another CD:

**Click** No

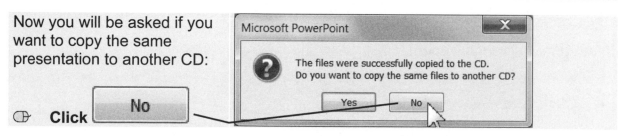

In the next section you can read how to copy the packaged files to a USB stick or another type of external storage device instead of burning them to a CD. In the section after that, you can read how to view the presentation on a computer which does not have *PowerPoint* installed.

# 8.31 Copy the Packaged Presentation to a USB stick or other External Storage Device

Instead of burning the presentation to a CD, you can also copy the package to a USB stick or other external storage device such as an external hard drive.

☞ **Connect a USB stick or external hard drive to the computer's USB port**

 **HELP! I do not own a USB stick or an external hard drive.**
In that case, you can just read through this section.

In the *Package for CD* window:

**Click** [ Copy to Folder... ]

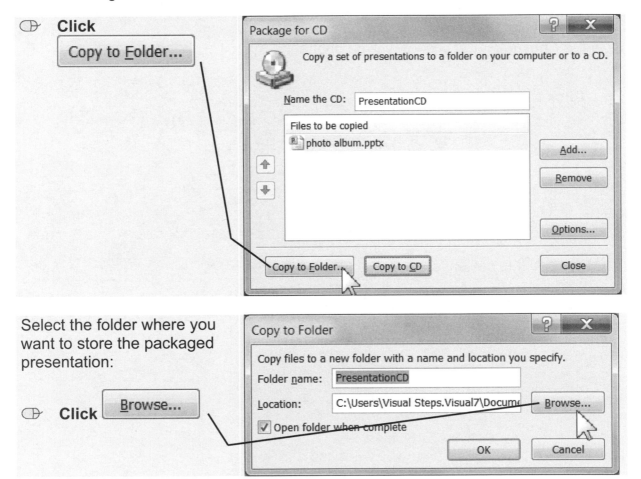

Select the folder where you want to store the packaged presentation:

**Click** [ Browse... ]

You are going to copy the packaged presentation to a USB stick or external hard drive:

☞ **Drag the scroll bar down a bit** ⎯⎯

☞ **Click the USB stick or external hard drive, in this example, it is LaCie (G:)** ⎯⎯

☞ **Click** Select

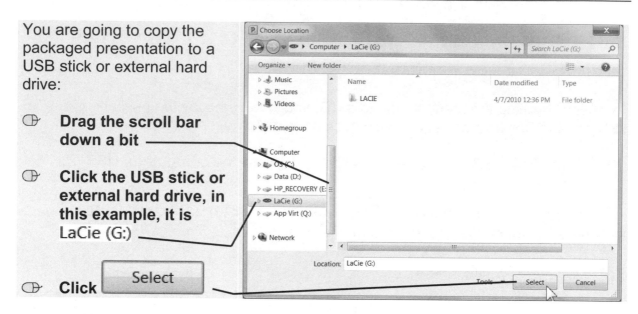

Now the *Copy to Folder* window will be opened:

☞ **Click** OK

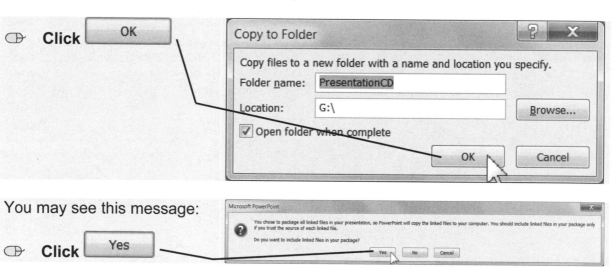

You may see this message:

☞ **Click** Yes

Now the files will be copied. When the copying process has finished, the *PresentationCD* folder window will appear:

In this window you will see the entire presentation, along with some extra files:

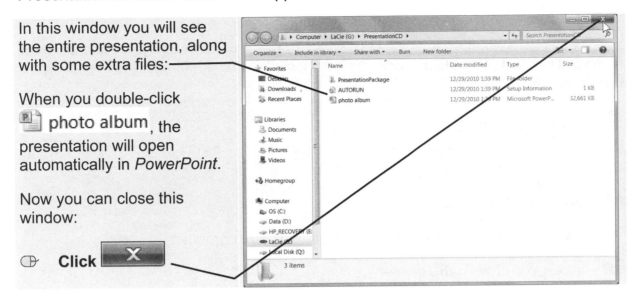

When you double-click  photo album, the presentation will open automatically in *PowerPoint*.

Now you can close this window:

 **Click** ⊞

## 🩹 HELP! The PresentationCD folder does not open automatically.

You can also open the folder manually:

☞ **View the contents of the USB stick** 🦶$^{93}$

## 🢂 Please note:

The *Package for CD* wizard has packaged your presentation in the current form. If you change something in your current presentation, you will need to repackage it.

☞ **Close the *Package for CD* window** 🦶$^{14}$

☞ **Close *PowerPoint* and save the changes** 🦶$^{14}$

## 8.32 View the Packaged Presentation with PowerPoint Viewer

You can view the files on the CD, USB stick or other external storage device even on a computer where *PowerPoint* has not been installed. To do this, you will need to download and install the *PowerPoint Viewer* program.

 **Please note:**

In *PowerPoint 2007* the *PowerPoint Viewer* program is already included. This means you will not need to download and install the program separately.

☞ **Continue at page 397**

You can try out the presentation package on your own computer:

☞ **Insert the disk in the player**

The *AutoPlay* window will be opened:

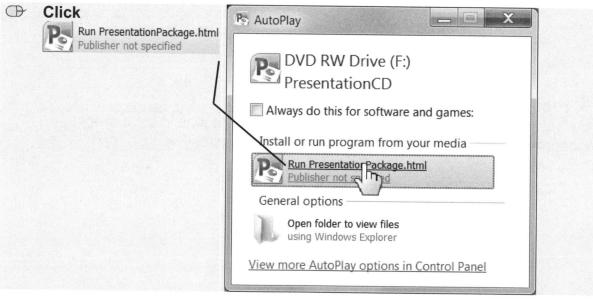

⊕ **Click**

    Run PresentationPackage.html
    Publisher not specified

 **HELP! I do not see this window.**

If the *AutoPlay* window does not open, you can open the file in the following way:

⊕ **Click** 
⊕ **Click** Computer
⊕ **Double-click your disk drive**

You will see a warning message:

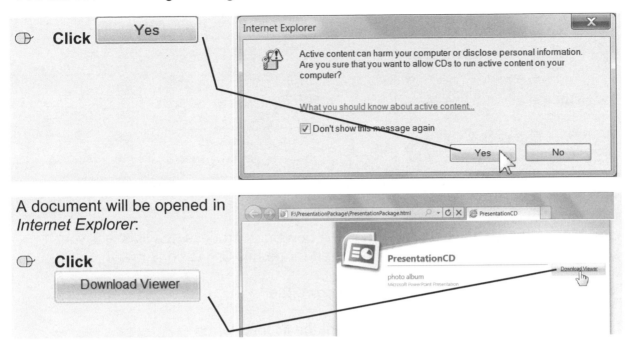

A document will be opened in *Internet Explorer*.

**Click** Download Viewer

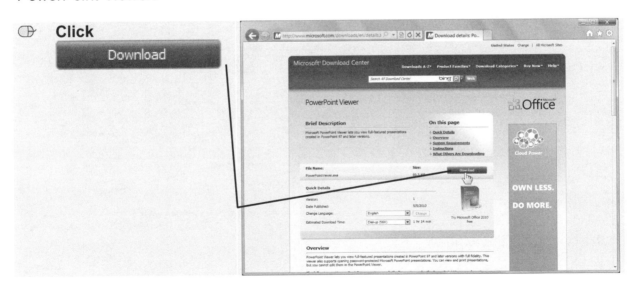

Now you will see the *Microsoft Download Center*. Here you can download for free the *PowerPoint Viewer*.

**Click** Download

You will see a security warning:

In *Internet Explorer 9*, at the bottom of the window:

👉 **Click** Run

In *Internet Explorer 8* you will see a similar window and you can execute the same operations.

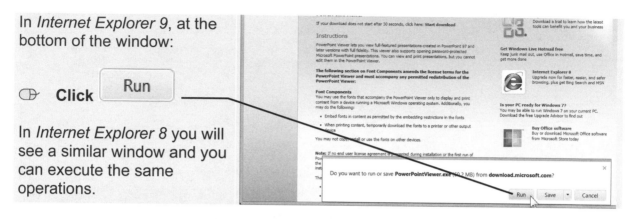

Now the file will be downloaded. When the download process has finished, your screen may turn dark and you will be asked for permission to continue:

☞ **If necessary, give permission to continue**

In the next window you will need to accept the license terms:

👉 **Check the box** ☑ **next to**
Click here to accept the Mic

👉 **Click** Continue

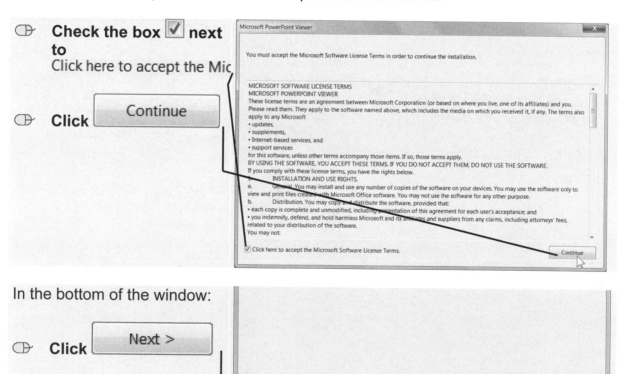

In the bottom of the window:

👉 **Click** Next >

In this window you can choose where to install the program:

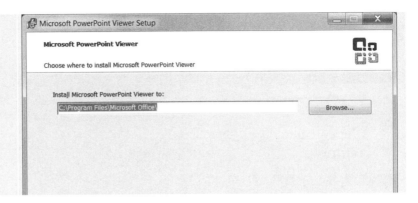

You do not need to change anything here. In the bottom of the window:

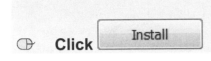

⊕ **Click** | Install |

Now the program will be installed. When the installation process has finished:

⊕ **Click** | OK |

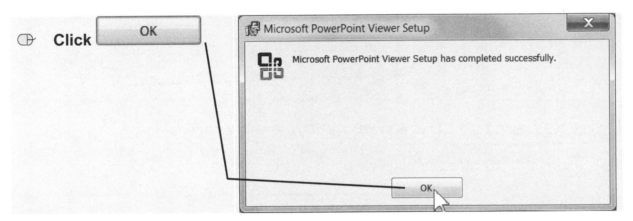

☞ **Close the *Internet Explorer* window** 🐾**14**

Now you can view the presentation in the *PowerPoint Viewer*:

⊕ **Click**

⊕ **Click ▶ All Programs**

⊕ **Click**
   📁 **Microsoft Office**

⊕ **Click**
   P⃝ **Microsoft PowerPoint 2010**
   **or**
   📁 **Microsoft Office PowerPoint 2007**

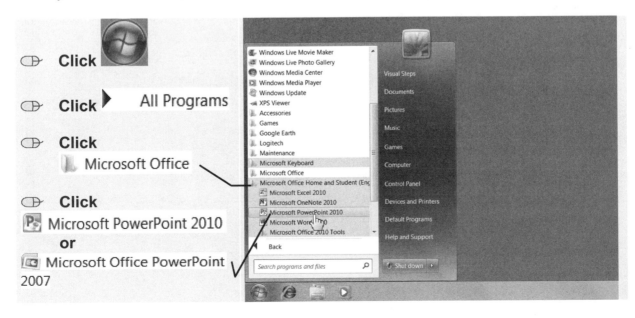

Now the *Microsoft PowerPoint Viewer* window will be opened. You can open the presentation on the CD:

**Drag the scroll bar down**

**Click your drive, for example**
**DVD RW Drive**

**Click photo album**

**Click Open**

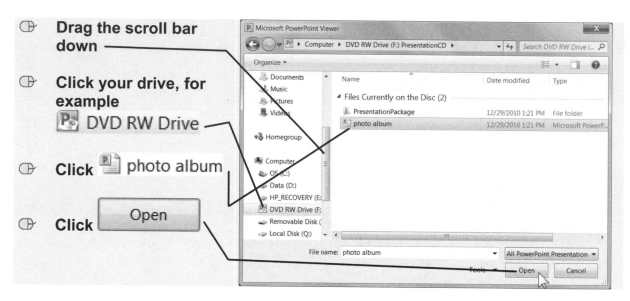

If you have created the CD in *PowerPoint 2007*, this is what you do:

☞ **Insert the CD into the player**

**Click**
Run PPTVIEW.EXE
Published by Microsof

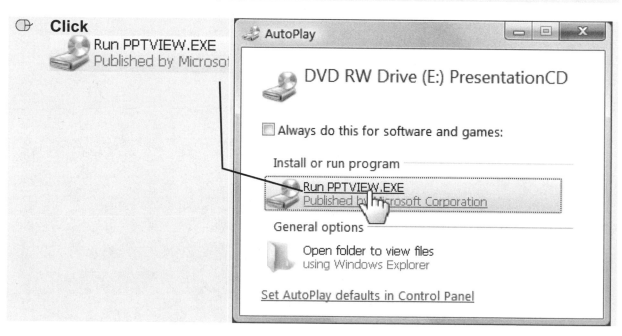

Click [ Accept ]

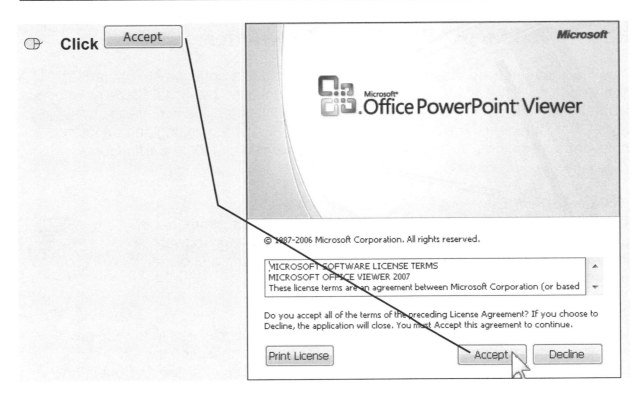

The presentation will be opened in *PowerPoint Viewer.*

Just like in *PowerPoint* itself, you can skip to the next slide or animation with one mouse-click:

Click the slide

View the complete presentation

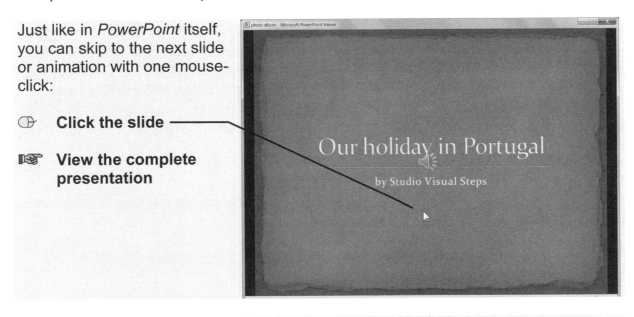

Close all opened windows 🦶🦶¹⁴

In this chapter you have learned how to create a photo album in *PowerPoint.*

# 8.33 Visual Steps Website and Newsletter

You may have noticed that the Visual Steps method is a great way to gather knowledge quickly and efficiently. All the books published by Visual Steps have been written using this same method. There are books available in a wide range of subject areas. For instance, there are books about *Windows*, photo editing and about free software applications, such as *Windows Live Essentials, Google Earth, Google Maps, Picasa* and *Skype*.

### Book + software
One of the Visual Steps books includes a CD with the program that is discussed. The full version of this high quality, easy-to-use software is included. You can recognize this Visual Steps book with an enclosed CD by this logo on the book cover:

### Website
Use the blue *Catalog* button on the **www.visualsteps.com** website to read an extensive description of all available Visual Steps titles, including the full table of contents and a sample chapter (as a PDF file). In this way you can find out if the book is what you expected.

This instructive website also contains:
- free computer booklets and informative guides (PDF files) on a range of subjects;
- free computer tips, that are described using the Visual Steps method;
- a large number of frequently asked questions and their answers;
- information on the free Computer certificate you can obtain on the online test website **www.ccforseniors.com**;
- free 'Notify me' e-mail service: receive an e-mail when a new book is published.

### Visual Steps Newsletter
Do you want to keep yourself informed of all Visual Steps publications? Then you can subscribe (with no strings attached) to the free Visual Steps Newsletter, sent out at regular intervals by e-mail.

This Newsletter provides you with information on:
- the latest titles, as well as older books;
- special offers and discounts;
- new, free computer booklets and guides.

As a subscriber to the Visual Steps Newsletter you have direct access to the free booklets and guides, on the webpage **www.visualsteps.com/info_downloads**

## 8.34 Exercises

In the following exercises will help you master what you have just learned. Have you forgotten how to do something? Use the number beside the footsteps to look it up in the appendix *How Do I Do That Again?*

## Exercise: Creating a Photo Album

☞ Open *PowerPoint*. 🐾119

☞ Insert a photo album. 🐾126

☞ In the *Photo Album* window, select the practice files *Barcelona 1* up to and including *Barcelona 8*. 🐾127

☞ In the *Photo Album* window, select the *2 pictures* layout. 🐾128

☞ Select the *Rounded Rectangle* frame shape and create the album. 🐾129

☞ Select the *Thatch* theme, or any other theme. 🐾130

☞ Enter the following title for the photo album: *A Weekend in Barcelona.* 🐾114

☞ Go to the second slide. 🐾113

☞ Delete the photo on the left. 🐾51

☞ Enlarge the remaining photo. 🐾116

☞ Position the photo in the center of the slide. 🐾46

☞ Add a new slide, with the *Blank* layout. 🐾131

☞ Insert the *Barcelona 1* photo. 🐾132

☞ Go to the fourth slide. 🐾113

☞ Select a new style for the photos. 🐾133

# Exercise: Slide transitions and animations

☞ Select the slide sorter view. 𝒪𝒪**134**

☞ Set the *Newsflash* transition (or any other transition) for slide 2. 𝒪𝒪**122**

☞ Add the *Camera* transition sound to slide 2. 𝒪𝒪**135**

☞ Double-click slide 4.

☞ Set the *Wipe* animation for the photo on the left side. 𝒪𝒪**124**

☞ Set the *Fly In* animation for the photo on the right side. 𝒪𝒪**124**

☞ Watch the slide show in the slide show view. 𝒪𝒪**125**

# Exercise: Video and sound

☞ Go to the title slide. 𝒪𝒪**113**

☞ Add the *Claps Cheers* sound effect. 𝒪𝒪**136**

☞ Close the *Clip Art* task pane. 𝒪𝒪**118**

☞ Position the sound effect icon in the bottom right of the slide. 𝒪𝒪**46**

☞ Set the sound effect to be played automatically. 𝒪𝒪**137**

☞ Add a new slide with the *Title Only* layout. 𝒪𝒪**131**

☞ Enter this title for the slide: *Video*. 𝒪𝒪**114**

☞ Insert the *Wildlife* video. 𝒪𝒪**138**

☞ Watch the slide show in the slide show view. 𝒪𝒪**125**

☞ Save the presentation as *Barcelona* in the (*My*) *Documents* folder. 𝒪𝒪**117**

☞ Close *PowerPoint*. 𝒪𝒪**14**

# 8.35 Background Information

| | |
|---|---|
| **Dictionary** | |
| **Backstage** | In essence, the *Backstage* view (or the *Out* feature set) hides your current document and gives you access to file-related activities. For instance, you can create, save, and print files and modify the settings. The other tabs on the ribbon give you all the necessary commands you need to do things in your document. |
| **Clip Art Gallery** | The *Clip Art Gallery* is an auxiliary program within *Microsoft Office*, which you can use to order and arrange the illustrations and media files on your computer. |
| **Compress** | When a file is compressed or packed, the file will become smaller and take up less space on your computer. |
| **Embed code** | You can use this code to insert a link to a video clip in your presentation, for example, a *YouTube* video clip. The actual video clip will not be inserted into the presentation. You will need an active Internet connection to view the video clip while the presentation is being played. |
| **Frame** | A single image in a video file. In *PowerPoint,* the term *frame* is used to indicate the border of an image. |
| **Insert** | In *PowerPoint* you can insert an audio or video file into your presentation. This means that the audio or video file will automatically be included when you copy your presentation to another computer or send it by e-mail. |
| **Link** | Include a link to an audio or a video file in your presentation. This means that the audio or video file will **not** be included when you copy your presentation to another computer or send it by e-mail. If you want to be able to play the audio files on a different computer, you will need to copy the folder containing the audio or video files to that computer. |
| **Media clip** | A file formatted for a single medium, for instance a file that exclusively contains illustrations, or sounds, animations or films. |

*- Continue reading on the next page -*

| | |
|---|---|
| **Multimedia** | In computer programs, different types of media are used. For instance, sounds (MP3 music files), stills (photos), animated images (videos), or other kinds of information (for instance, text). Multimedia means all these types of media can be used in a program, in combination or separately. |
| **Package** | Wrap the presentation up for use on a different computer. During the packaging process, the inserted and linked media files, the images, and all the fonts will be included in the packaged presentation file. |
| **Poster frame** | The sample image for a video file. |
| **PowerPoint Viewer** | Small software program with which you can view a *PowerPoint* presentation on computers that do not have *PowerPoint* installed. In *PowerPoint Viewer* you cannot edit the presentation. |
| **Rehearsal** | Trial run of the time settings in a presentation. |
| **Slide show view** | The slide show view will take up the full screen, just like a real slide show. This way, you can view the presentation in the same format as your audience later on. You can see what your images, time settings, movies, animated elements and transition effects will look like in the actual presentation. |
| **Slide sorter view** | In the slide sorter view you can view thumbnails of all the slides within the presentation. |
| **Theme** | A combination of theme colors, fonts and effects. A theme combines all these elements and can be applied to a file as a single style element. |
| **YouTube** | *YouTube* is a website where you can upload your video clips and other visitors of the website can view them. |

*Source: Microsoft Office PowerPoint Help*

# 8.36 Tips

 **Tip**

**Set time for slide transitions and animations**

Instead of using a mouse-click to start a slide transition, you can set the transition to occur after a predefined period of time. You can change these time settings with the

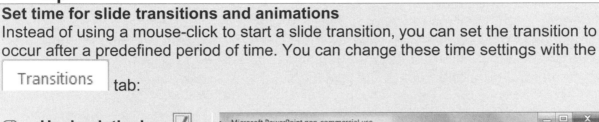

Transitions tab:

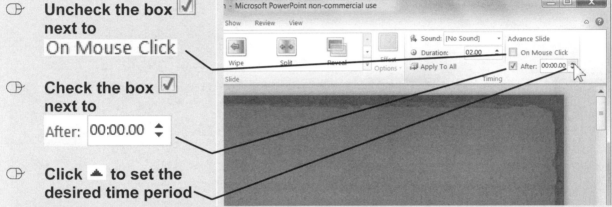

☞ **Uncheck the box** ☑ **next to** On Mouse Click

☞ **Check the box** ☑ **next to** After: 00:00.00 ↕

☞ **Click** ▲ **to set the desired time period**

Now the next slide will automatically appear after the set time interval. This may seem useful, but it is recommended to keep using the On Mouse Click option. If you have finished your story ahead of your time schedule, it is nice to be able to skip to the next slide by clicking. Vice versa, it can be a nuisance if the next slide is automatically displayed and you are still discussing the previous slide.

You can also set the time for animations with the Animations tab. But keep in mind that the time you set is applied to each element of the animation. If you are composing a page image by image, each image is viewed as a separate part of the animation.

By Duration: 02.00 ↕ you can determine the length of the animation:

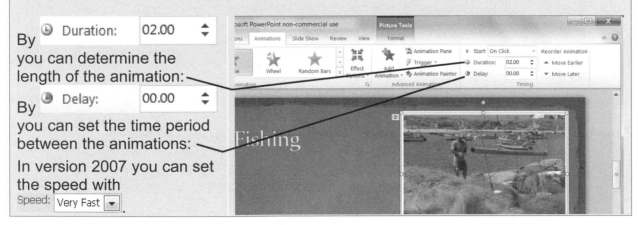

By Delay: 00.00 ↕ you can set the time period between the animations:

In version 2007 you can set the speed with Speed: Very Fast ▼

**Tip**

**Rehearse time settings**

You can include the time settings for the entire presentation in a *rehearsal*. This way, you can try out the timing of your story. *PowerPoint* will record how long it takes you to skip through the slides in your presentation. The time between the various animations is recorded as well. Next, you can save this trial run and use the time settings for the actual presentation. Then you will not need to click the mouse or remote control during the actual presentation.

⊕ **Click** Rehearse Timings **in the** Slide Show **tab**

The slide show will start and you can start talking. At the top left you will see the *Recording* window. To skip to the next slide:

⊕ **Click** ➡

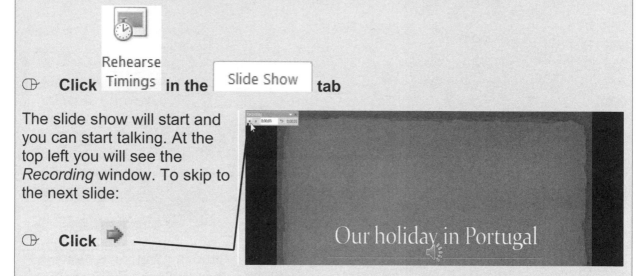

Our holiday in Portugal

At the end of your presentation you will see the following window:

⊕ **Click** Yes

Microsoft PowerPoint

ℹ The total time for the slide show was 0:00:07. Do you want to keep the new slide timings to use when you view the slide show?

Yes    No

Now whenever you start the presentation in slide show view, the recorded time settings will be used. If you do not want to use these time settings anymore:

⊕ **Click** Set Up Slide Show

The *Set Up Slide Show* window will be opened:

⊕ **By** Advance slides **click the radio button** ◉ **next to** Manually

Now the time settings have been disabled but not yet removed. You can enable these time settings again, whenever you want, without having to record the settings a second time.

**Tip**

**Insert a YouTube video clip**
An infinite variety of video clips can be found on the Internet, for example on the *YouTube* website. If you want to use a *YouTube* video clip in your presentation, you can insert a link to the clip in *PowerPoint 2010*.
**Please note:** this option is not available in *PowerPoint 2007*.

☞ **Click the** `Insert` **tab**

☞ **By** [icon] **click** `Video ▾`

☞ **Click** `Video from Web Site...`

You will see this window:

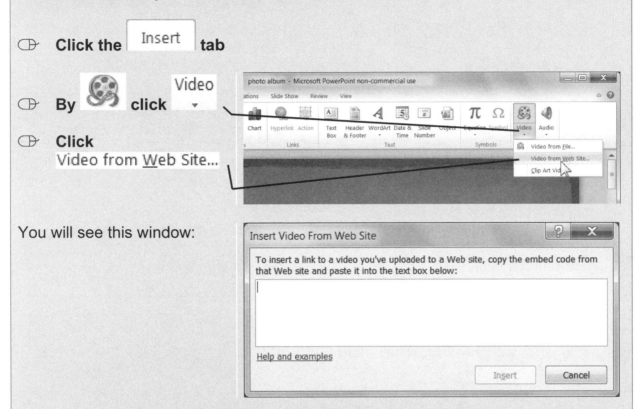

Video websites such as *YouTube* and *Vimeo* have made a special embed code available for each video clip that has been uploaded. You can use code to insert the video clip in a different website or in another program. Here is how to find the embed code for a random video on the www.youtube.com website:

☞ **Click** `Embed`

*- Continue reading on the next page -*

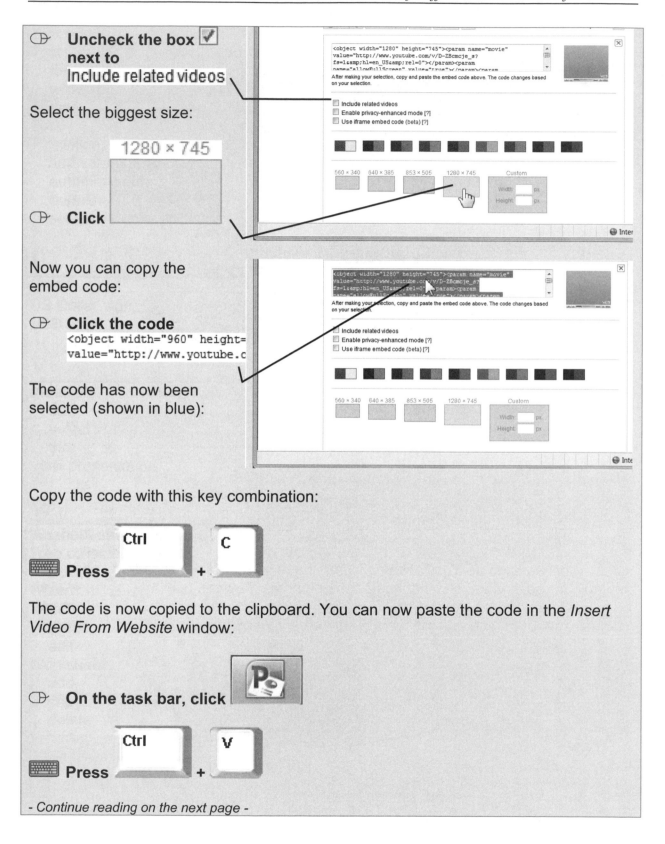

☞ **Uncheck the box** ✔️ **next to** Include related videos

Select the biggest size:

1280 × 745

☞ **Click**

Now you can copy the embed code:

☞ **Click the code**
`<object width="960" height=`
`value="http://www.youtube.c`

The code has now been selected (shown in blue):

Copy the code with this key combination:

⌨️ **Press** Ctrl + C

The code is now copied to the clipboard. You can now paste the code in the *Insert Video From Website* window:

☞ **On the task bar, click**

⌨️ **Press** Ctrl + V

*- Continue reading on the next page -*

The embed code will be displayed in the window:

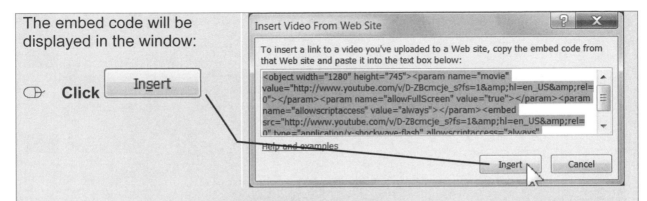

D→ **Click** Insert

**Please note:** do not be fooled by the term 'embed code'. This code simply inserts a link to the video on the website. You will not be copying the actual video clip to your presentation.

In the slide, you will see a black video screen:

You can enlarge and move this video screen in the same way as other videos and photos:

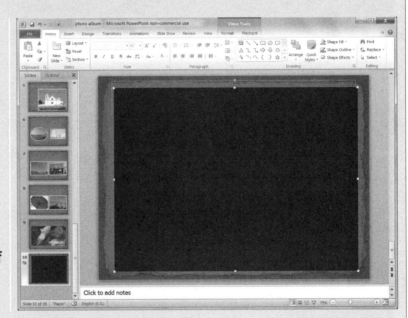

☞ **Enlarge the video screen** &&¹¹⁶

☞ **Position the video screen in the center of the slide** &&⁴⁶

Check if the video is played correctly:

D→ **Double-click the video screen**

*- Continue reading on the next page -*

Now you can see the actual *YouTube* video window in the slide:

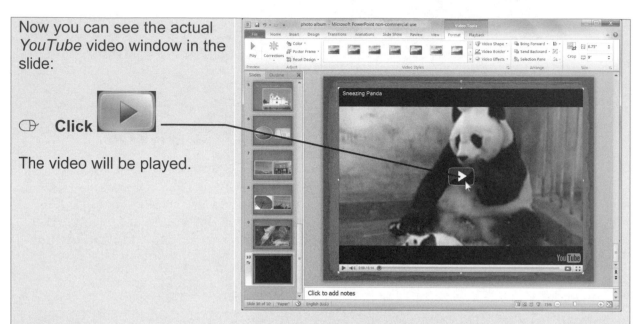

☞  **Click**

The video will be played.

**Please note:** each time you play this video, the clip is downloaded from the *YouTube* website. You will always need to have an active Internet connection to play this video clip. The actual video clip is not stored in your presentation.

**Please note:** if you have added a *YouTube* video clip to your presentation, it will not be displayed in *PowerPoint Viewer*. When you click the black screen, the next slide will be displayed.

## 💡 Tip

**Automatic transitions**

Instead of manually displaying the next slide, you can set the slides to play automatically. This is how to do that:

☞ **Open the slide sorter view** 🐾134

👉 **Click the first slide**

⌨ **Press** ⇧ **Shift**

👉 **Click the last slide**

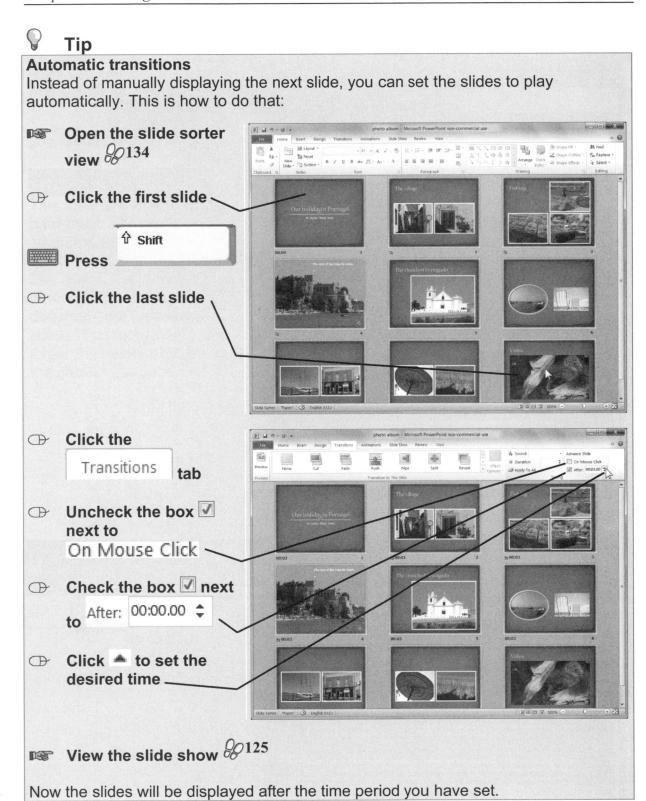

👉 **Click the** Transitions **tab**

👉 **Uncheck the box ☑ next to** On Mouse Click

👉 **Check the box ☑ next to** After: 00:00.00 ⬍

👉 **Click ⬆ to set the desired time**

☞ **View the slide show** 🐾125

Now the slides will be displayed after the time period you have set.

# Notes

Write down your notes here.

# Appendix A. Downloading the Practice Files

As you work through this book, you will need to use the practice files to perform the exercises as described. It is a good idea to download these practice files before you begin. Here is how to do that:

☞ **Open** *Internet Explorer* ⚆⚆60

☞ **Surf to the website www.visualsteps.com/officeseniors** ⚆⚆61

You will see the website that goes with this book.

⊕ **Click**
**Practice files**

You will see the compressed folder which contains the practice files. You need to copy this folder to the (*My*) *Documents* folder:

⊕ **Right-click**
Practice files

⊕ **Click** Save target as...

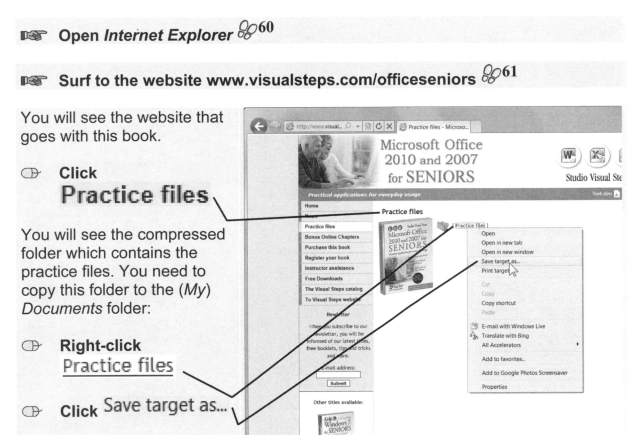

The *Practice files* folder is a compressed folder. You can store this folder in your (*My*) *Documents* folder on your computer.

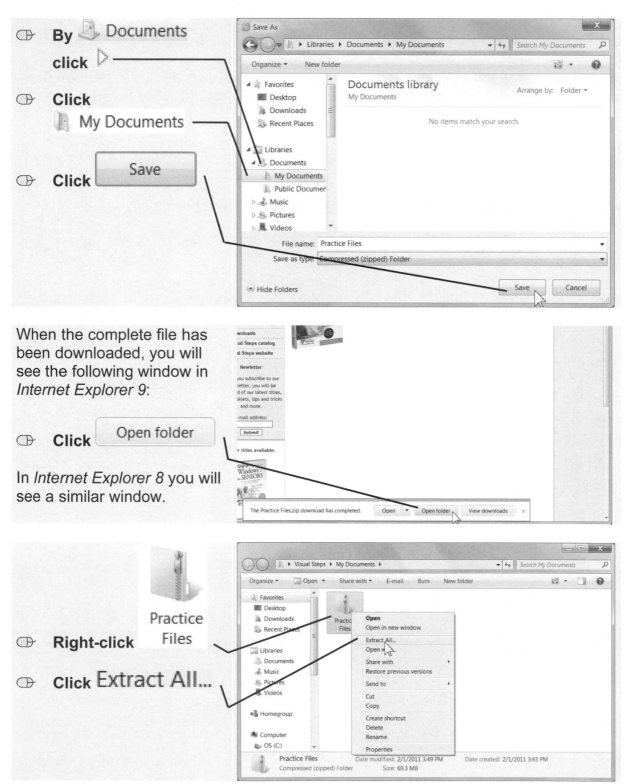

When the complete file has been downloaded, you will see the following window in *Internet Explorer 9*:

👆 **Click** [ Open folder ]

In *Internet Explorer 8* you will see a similar window.

👆 **Right-click** Practice Files

👆 **Click** Extract All...

Now you will extract the files:

☞ **Uncheck the box** ☑
**next to**
Show extracted files wh

☞ **Click** Extract

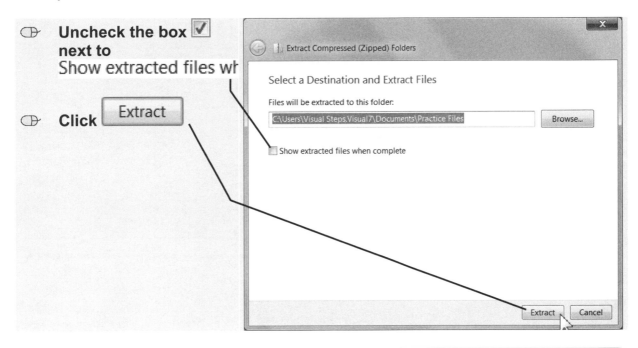

The files will be extracted and
you will see this window:

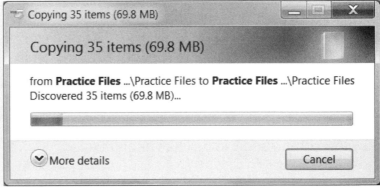

Now the *Practice Files* folder has been stored in the (*My*) *Documents* folder:

You can delete the
compressed folder:

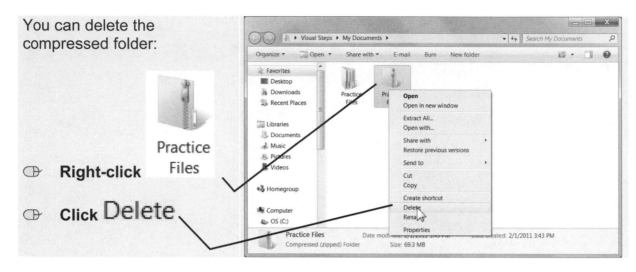

Practice Files

⊕ **Right-click**

⊕ **Click Delete**

You will see the *Delete Folder*
window:

⊕ **Click** Yes

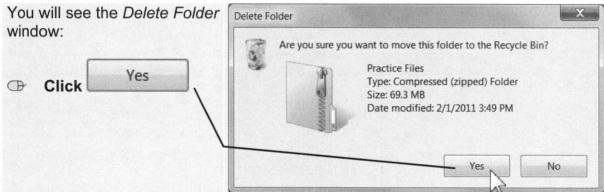

Now the compressed folder has been deleted:

☞ **Close all windows** 🦶14

# Appendix B. How Do I Do That Again?

In this book you will find many instructions and exercises that are marked with footsteps: 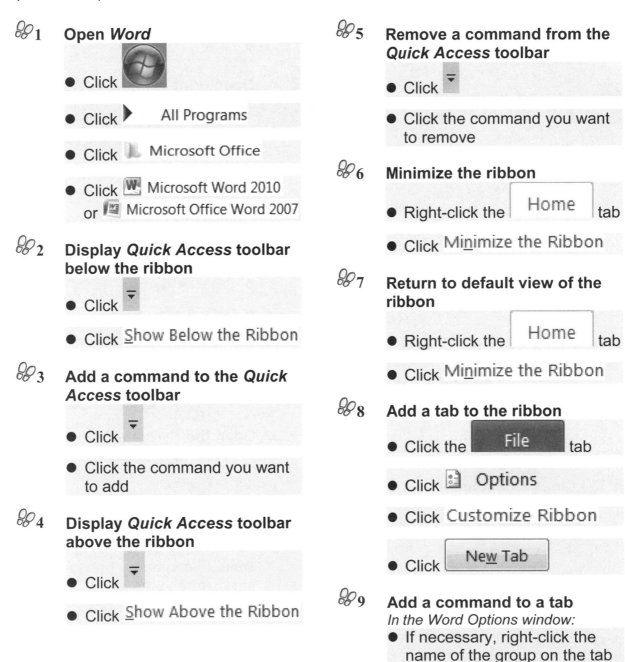1. Find the corresponding number in the appendix below to see how to perform a specific action.

1 **Open *Word***

- Click

- Click ▶ All Programs

- Click Microsoft Office

- Click Microsoft Word 2010 or Microsoft Office Word 2007

2 **Display *Quick Access* toolbar below the ribbon**

- Click ▼

- Click Show Below the Ribbon

3 **Add a command to the *Quick Access* toolbar**

- Click ▼

- Click the command you want to add

4 **Display *Quick Access* toolbar above the ribbon**

- Click ▼

- Click Show Above the Ribbon

5 **Remove a command from the *Quick Access* toolbar**

- Click ▼

- Click the command you want to remove

6 **Minimize the ribbon**

- Right-click the Home tab

- Click Minimize the Ribbon

7 **Return to default view of the ribbon**

- Right-click the Home tab

- Click Minimize the Ribbon

8 **Add a tab to the ribbon**

- Click the File tab

- Click Options

- Click Customize Ribbon

- Click New Tab

9 **Add a command to a tab**
*In the Word Options window:*
- If necessary, right-click the name of the group on the tab where you want to add the

command

- Click the command

- Click **Add >>**

- Click **OK**

🐾10 **View a tab**
- Click the tab

🐾11 **Remove a tab**
- Right-click the tab

- Click **Customize the Ribbon...**

*In the Word Options window:*
- Right-click the name of the tab you want to remove

- Click **Remove**

- Click **OK**

🐾12 **Close a document in *Word 2010***
- Click the **File** tab

- Click **Close**

🐾13 **Close a document in *Word 2007***
- Click

- Click **Close**

🐾14 **Close a window**
- Click **X**

🐾15 **Select all the text in a document**
- If necessary, click the **Home** tab

- Click **Select**

- Click **Select All**

🐾16 **Open print preview in *Word 2010***
- Click the **File** tab

- Click **Print**

🐾17 **Open print preview in *Word 2007***
- Click

- Point the mouse to **Print**

- Click **Print Preview**

🐾18 **Open the *Paragraph* window**
- If necessary, click the **Home** tab

- By ▣ click **Paragraph**

🐾19 **Make line spacing between paragraphs smaller**
- By **After:** click ▼

- Repeat this action until you have reached the desired size

● Click OK

**20 Insert a date**
● Click the spot where you want to insert the date

● Click the Insert tab

● By Text click
Date & Time

● Click the date format

● Click OK

**21 View and use suggested spelling**
● Right-click the word underlined in red

● Click the spelling suggestion you want to use

**22 Change the margins**
● Click the Page Layout tab

● Click Margins ▾

● Click Custom Margins...

● Click ▲ or ▼ for the various margins to set the correct margins

● Click OK

**23 Undo last operation**
● Click ↶

**24 Change the font size**
● By 11 click ▾

● Click the desired font size

**25 Print a document**

● Click Print

*In Word 2007:*
● Click

Print
Select a printer, number other printing options b

● Click OK

**26 Close print preview in *Word 2007***

● Click ✕ Close Print Preview

**27 Open a tab**
● Click the desired tab, for example Mailings

**28 Open the *Envelopes and Labels* window**
● If necessary, click the Mailings tab

● Click Envelopes

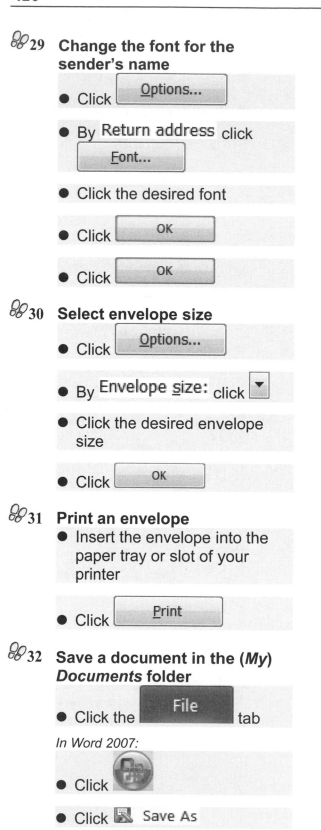

**🐾29   Change the font for the sender's name**

● Click `Options...`

● By `Return address` click `Font...`

● Click the desired font

● Click `OK`

● Click `OK`

**🐾30   Select envelope size**

● Click `Options...`

● By `Envelope size:` click `▼`

● Click the desired envelope size

● Click `OK`

**🐾31   Print an envelope**

● Insert the envelope into the paper tray or slot of your printer

● Click `Print`

**🐾32   Save a document in the (*My*) *Documents* folder**

● Click the `File` tab

*In Word 2007:*

● Click ⊙

● Click 🖫 Save As

● If necessary, click 🖳 Documents

● Type an identifiable name for the document

● Click `Save`

**🐾33   Insert a photo**

● Click the spot where you want to insert the photo

● Click the `Insert` tab

● Click Picture

● Click 🖳 Documents

● Double-click

  📁 Practice Files
     File folder

● Click the photo

● Click `Insert`

**🐾34   Add WordArt text box**

● Click the `Insert` tab

● Click WordArt ▾

● Click the desired style

● Type the text

*In Word 2007:*
- Click [ OK ]

**35 Change the text wrapping**

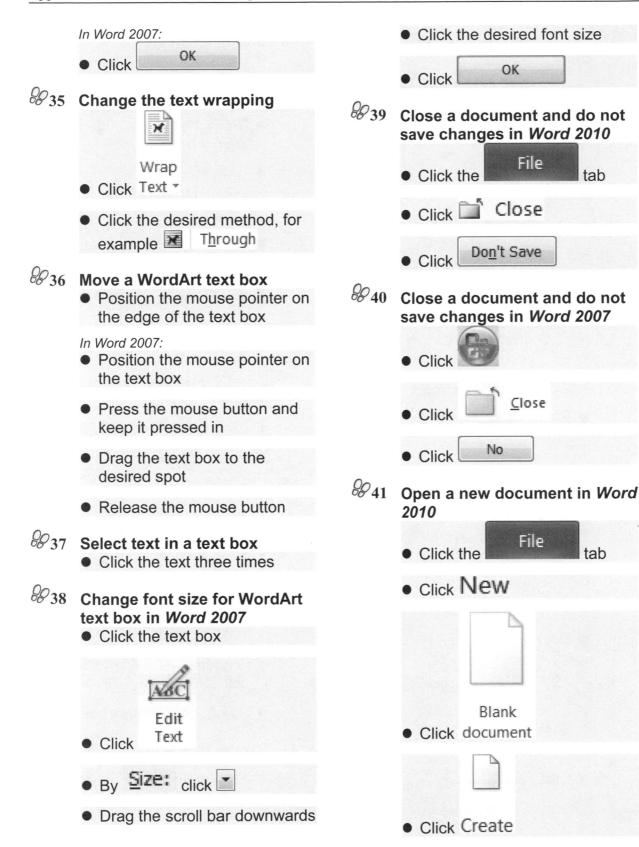

- Click Wrap Text ▾

- Click the desired method, for example ▧ Through

**36 Move a WordArt text box**
- Position the mouse pointer on the edge of the text box

*In Word 2007:*
- Position the mouse pointer on the text box

- Press the mouse button and keep it pressed in

- Drag the text box to the desired spot

- Release the mouse button

**37 Select text in a text box**
- Click the text three times

**38 Change font size for WordArt text box in *Word 2007***
- Click the text box

- Click Edit Text

- By Size: click ▾

- Drag the scroll bar downwards

- Click the desired font size

- Click [ OK ]

**39 Close a document and do not save changes in *Word 2010***
- Click the File tab

- Click ⬓ Close

- Click [ Don't Save ]

**40 Close a document and do not save changes in *Word 2007***
- Click

- Click Close

- Click [ No ]

**41 Open a new document in *Word 2010***
- Click the File tab

- Click New

- Click Blank document

- Click Create

**⚇ 42   Open a new document in *Word 2007***

- Click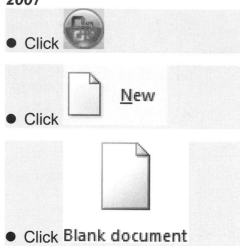

- Click  New

- Click Blank document

- Click  Create

**⚇ 43   Open a practice file**

- Click the  File  tab

*In Excel 2007:*

- Click

- Click  Open

- If necessary, click
  Documents

- Double-click
  Practice Files
  File folder

- Click the desired file

- Click  Open


**⚇ 44   Shrink an image**
- Position the mouse pointer on the handle in the lower right-hand corner

- Press the mouse button and keep it pressed in

- Drag the corner handle inwards to the center of the image

- Release the mouse button

**⚇ 45   Select a position**
- If necessary, click the photo

- Click  Position ▾

- Click the desired position, for
  example

**⚇ 46   Move a photo, illustration or video**
- Position the mouse pointer on the image

- Press the mouse button and keep it pressed in

- Drag the image to the desired position

- Release the mouse button

**⚇ 47   Set the text wrap to right only**

- Click Wrap Text ▾ or

● Click

More Layout Options...

● Click the radio button ⊙ next to Right only

● Click OK

**48 Crop the bottom of a photo**

● Click

● Position the mouse pointer on the sizing handle at the bottom

● Press the left mouse button and drag the handle upwards

● Release the mouse button

*In Word 2010:*

● Click

**49 Adjust the brightness**
● If necessary, click the photo

● Click ☼ Corrections

● Click the desired correction

*In Word 2007:*
● Click ☼ Brightness ▾

● Click the desired correction

**50 Adjust the color**
● If necessary, click the photo

● Click Color ▾

*In Word 2007:*
● Click  Recolor ▾

● Click the desired color

**51 Delete a photo**
● Click the photo

● Press Delete

**52 Enter data in a box**
● Click the box you want to fill in, for example
Delivery address:

● Type the correct data

**53 Open a document based on a template in *Word 2010***

● Click the  File tab

● Click New

● Click 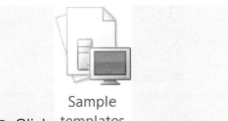 Sample templates

● Click the desired template

● Click the radio button ⊙ by Document

● Click  Create

⌘**54**   **Open a document based on a template in *Word 2007***

● Click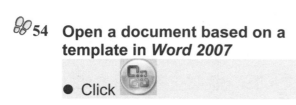

● Click

● Click **Installed Templates**

● Click the desired template

● Click a radio button ◉ by Document

● Click [ Create ]

⌘**55**   **Open the template folder in the *Other Books* folder in *Word 2010***

● Click the  tab

● Click New

● Click   Books

● Click Other books

● Click the desired folder

⌘**56**   **Open the template folder in the *More categories* folder in *Word 2007***

● Click

● Click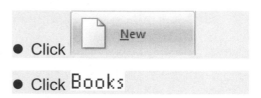

● Click Books

● Click Other books

● Click the desired folder

⌘**57**   **Zoom out**

● Drag the slider ⎁ in the bottom of the window to the left, until it reaches 50%

⌘**58**   **Open a document based on a template from a specific folder in *Word 2010***

● Click the  tab

● Click New

● Click the desired category

● Click the desired template

● Click Download

⌘**59**   **Open a document based on a template from a specific folder in *Word 2007***

● Click

● Click

● Click the desired category

● Click the desired template

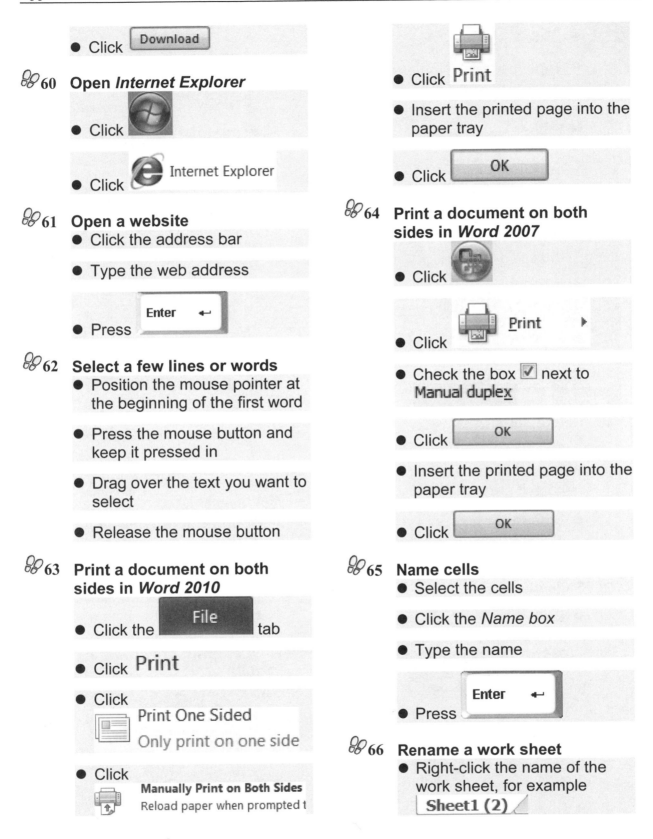

- Click Download

**60  Open *Internet Explorer***

- Click

- Click Internet Explorer

**61  Open a website**
- Click the address bar

- Type the web address

- Press Enter ⏎

**62  Select a few lines or words**
- Position the mouse pointer at the beginning of the first word

- Press the mouse button and keep it pressed in

- Drag over the text you want to select

- Release the mouse button

**63  Print a document on both sides in *Word 2010***

- Click the File tab

- Click Print

- Click Print One Sided — Only print on one side

- Click Manually Print on Both Sides — Reload paper when prompted t

- Click Print

- Insert the printed page into the paper tray

- Click OK

**64  Print a document on both sides in *Word 2007***

- Click

- Click Print ▶

- Check the box ☑ next to Manual duple**x**

- Click OK

- Insert the printed page into the paper tray

- Click OK

**65  Name cells**
- Select the cells

- Click the *Name box*

- Type the name

- Press Enter ⏎

**66  Rename a work sheet**
- Right-click the name of the work sheet, for example Sheet1 (2)

- Click  Rename

- Type the new name

- Press

**⌕ 67   Copy a formula/drag a range**
- Click the cell which contains the formula

- Position the mouse pointer on the cell's handle

- Press the mouse button and keep it pressed in

- Drag over the cells where you want to copy the formula

- Release the mouse button

**⌕ 68   Select cells**
- Click the first cell

- Press the mouse button and keep it pressed in

- Drag to the last cell

- Release the mouse button

**⌕ 69   Save changes**
- Click  Save

**⌕ 70   Close workbook in *Excel 2010***
- Click the  tab

- Click  Close

**⌕ 71   Close workbook in *Excel 2007***
- Click

- Click  Close

**⌕ 72   Open a practice file**
- Click the  File tab

*In Excel 2007:*

- Click

- Click  Open

- If necessary, click 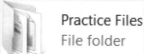 Documents

- Double-click

  Practice Files
  File folder

- Click the desired file

- Click Open

**⌕ 73   Open print preview in *Excel 2010***
- Click the File tab

- Click Print

**⌕ 74   Open print preview in *Excel 2007***
- Click

- Point to Print ▶

- Click **Print Preview**

**75  Close workbook, do not save changes in *Excel 2010***

- Click the  tab

- Click  Close

- Click **Don't Save**

**76  Close workbook, do not save changes in *Excel 2007***

- Click

- Click  Close

- Click **No**

**77  Enter data in a cell**
- Click the cell

- Type the text or a number

**78  Widen a column**
- Position the mouse pointer ✛ between the column headers

  D ╫ E

- Press the mouse button and keep it pressed in

- Drag the pointer ✛ to the right

- Release the mouse button

**79  Entering formulas**
- Click the cell where you want to display the result

- Click the cell which contains the first number

- Press the mathematical symbol you need, for example, +, - etcetera

- Click the cell which contains the second number

- Repeat this until you have completed the formula

- Press

**80  Adding numbers with *Sum***
- Select the cells you want to add

- Click **Σ**

**81  Insert dollar sign and two decimals**
- Select the cells

- Click **$**

**82  Make cells bold**
- Select the cells

- Click **B**

**83  Add a border**
- Select the cells

- By ▦ , click ▾

- Click the desired border

**84  Save the workbook in the (*My*) *Documents* folder**

- Click the **File** tab

In *Excel 2007*:

- Click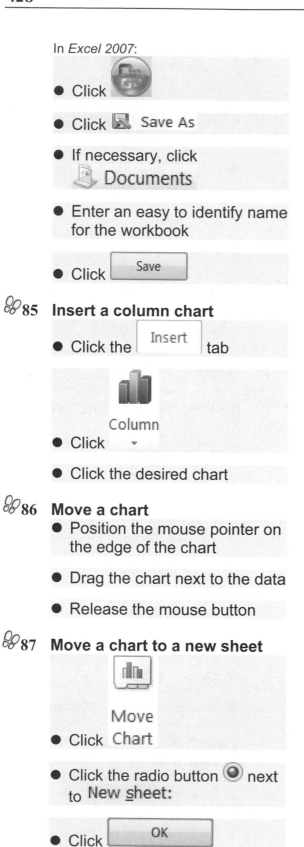

- Click ◫ Save As

- If necessary, click
  📄 Documents

- Enter an easy to identify name
  for the workbook

- Click [ Save ]

### 🦶85   Insert a column chart

- Click the [ Insert ] tab

Column

- Click ▾

- Click the desired chart

### 🦶86   Move a chart

- Position the mouse pointer on
  the edge of the chart

- Drag the chart next to the data

- Release the mouse button

### 🦶87   Move a chart to a new sheet

Move

- Click Chart

- Click the radio button ◉ next
  to New sheet:

- Click [ OK ]

### 🦶88   Change chart style

- By Chart Styles click the
  desired style

### 🦶89   Add a title to the chart

- Click the **Chart Title** box

- Double-click **Chart Title**

- Type the title

### 🦶90   Open *Excel*

- Click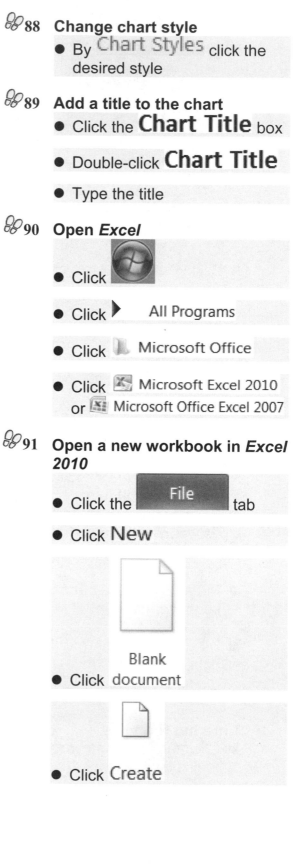

- Click ▶ All Programs

- Click 📒 Microsoft Office

- Click 📊 Microsoft Excel 2010
  or 📊 Microsoft Office Excel 2007

### 🦶91   Open a new workbook in *Excel 2010*

- Click the [ File ] tab

- Click New

- Click 📄 Blank document

- Click Create

**92 Open a new workbook in *Excel 2007***

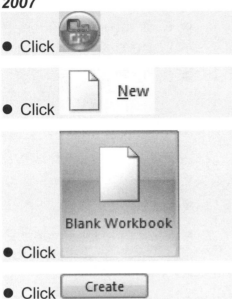

- Click

- Click New

- Click Blank Workbook

- Click Create

**93 View contents of USB stick**

- Click

- Click Computer

- Double-click the removable media

**94 Open the *Backstage* view**

- Click the File tab

**95 Sort in ascending order**

- Click a single cell in the column

- Click Sort & Filter ▾

- Click A↓ Z | Sort A to Z

**96 Sort in descending order**

- Click a single cell in the column

- Click Sort & Filter ▾

- Click Z↓ A | Sort Z to A

**97 Activate the *Filter* function**

- Click a cell in the list

- Click Sort & Filter ▾

- Click ▼= | Filter

**98 Filtering**

- In the column you want to filter, click ▼

- Uncheck the box ☑ next to (Select All)

- Check the box ☑ next to the desired category

- Click OK

**99 Display full list**

- In the filtered column, click ▼

- Check the box ☑ next to (Select All)

- Click OK

**100 Custom filter**
- By the column you want to filter, click ▼
- Click Number Filters
- Click a condition, for example Less Than...
- Enter a value
- Click OK

**101 Enter text in a table**
- Click one of the cells
- Type the text
- Press ⇥ Tab to skip to the next cell

**102 Insert Merge Field**
- Click the desired field
- Click Insert

**103 Open the *Mail Merge Wizard***
- Click the Mailings tab
- Click 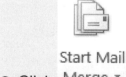 Start Mail Merge ▾
- Click 📝 Step by Step Mail Merge Wizard...

**104 Select the labels document type**
- Click the radio button ◉ by Labels
- Click ➡ Next: Starting document

**105 Select label size**
- Click 🗒 Label options...
- Click Options...
- Select the label vendor
- Select the product number

**106 Select addresses**
- Click ➡ Next: Select recipients
- If necessary, click the radio button ◉ next to Use an existing list
- Click 🖩 Browse...
- Click the desired file
- Click Open
- Click OK

**107 Insert merge fields**
- Click ➡ Next: Arrange your labels
- Click 🔢 More items...
- Click the desired field
- Click Insert

*When all fields have been inserted:*
- Click [ Close ]

**108 Arrange fields**
- Click between two fields

- Press [ Enter ↵ ]

**109 Update all labels**
- Click [ Update all labels ]

**110 Preview a label**
- Click
  ➡ Next: Preview your labels

**111 Complete the merging operation**
- Click
  ➡ Next: Complete the merg

**112 Open labels in a separate *Word* document**
- Click 🗋 Edit individual labels...

- Click [ OK ]

**113 Skip to a different slide**
*In the left side of the window:*
- If necessary, drag the scroll bar downwards or upwards

- Click the desired slide

**114 Enter a title**
- Click the title bar

- Type the title

**115 Make the text bold**
- Select the text

- Click **B**

**116 Enlarge or shrink a photo, illustration or video**
- Drag the sizing handles on the corner until you reach the desired size

**117 Save the presentation in the (*My*) *Documents* folder**
- Click the [ File ] tab

*In PowerPoint 2007:*
- Click ⊙

- Click 🖫 Save As

- If necessary, click
  🚪 Documents

- Enter an easy to identify name for the presentation

- Click [ Save ]

**118 Close the task pane**
- Click ✕

**119 Open *PowerPoint***
- Click ⊙

- Click ▶ All Programs

- Click 📁 Microsoft Office

- Click
  Ps Microsoft PowerPoint 2010
  or
  Microsoft Office PowerPoint 2007

**120 Open a recent presentation**

- Click the ▮ File ▮ tab

*In PowerPoint 2007:*

- Click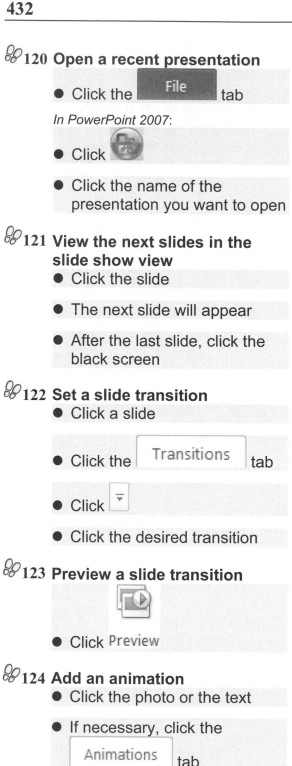

- Click the name of the presentation you want to open

**121 View the next slides in the slide show view**
- Click the slide

- The next slide will appear

- After the last slide, click the black screen

**122 Set a slide transition**
- Click a slide

- Click the ▮ Transitions ▮ tab

- Click ▾

- Click the desired transition

**123 Preview a slide transition**

- Click Preview

**124 Add an animation**
- Click the photo or the text

- If necessary, click the Animations tab

- Click Add Animation ▾

- Click the desired animation

**125 View the slide show**
- Click 🖵

**126 Insert photo album**
- Click the ▮ Insert ▮ tab

- By  click Photo Album ▾

- Click 🖼 New Photo Album...

**127 Select photos for the photo album**
- Click File/Disk...

- Click 📄 Documents

- Double-click Practice Files File folder

- Click the first photo

- Keep ⇧ Shift depressed

- Click the last photo

- Click Insert

**128 Select a layout for the photo album**
- By Picture layout: click ▾

- Click the desired layout

**129 Select a frame shape for the photo album**

- By Frame shape: click ▼
- Click the desired frame
- Click Create

**130 Select a theme**

- Click the Design tab
- Click ▼
- Click the desired theme

**131 Insert a slide**

- Click the Home tab
- By New click Slide ▼
- Click the desired format

**132 Insert a photo**

- Click the Insert tab
- Click Picture
- Click the desired photo
- Click Insert

**133 Change the picture style**
- Click the photo
- Click the Format tab

- By Picture Styles click ▼
- Click the desired style

**134 Open the slide sorter view**
- Click ▦

**135 Set a sound effect for a slide**

- By 🔊 Sound: click ▼
- Click the desired sound effect

**136 Add an audio clip to a slide**

- Click the Insert tab
- By 🔊 Audio click ▼
- Click Clip Art Audio...
- Click the desired sound clip

**137 Automatic playback of sound effect**

- Click the Playback tab
- By ⚡ Start: click ▼
- Click Automatically

**138 Insert video clip from file**

- Click the Insert tab
- By 🎞 Video click ▼
- Click 🎞 Video from File...
- Click the desired video

- Click **Insert**

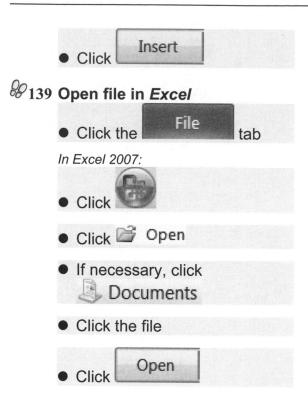

**139 Open file in *Excel***

- Click the **File** tab

*In Excel 2007:*

- Click

- Click ☞ Open

- If necessary, click
  📄 Documents

- Click the file

- Click **Open**

# Appendix C. Opening the Bonus Chapters

To download the bonus chapters from the website, follow these steps:

☞ **Surf to the www.visualsteps.com/officeseniors webpage** 🦶**60, 61**

In the left-side navigation:

☞ **Click**
**Bonus Online Chapters**

By the desired chapter:

☞ **Click**
**Start downloading** »»

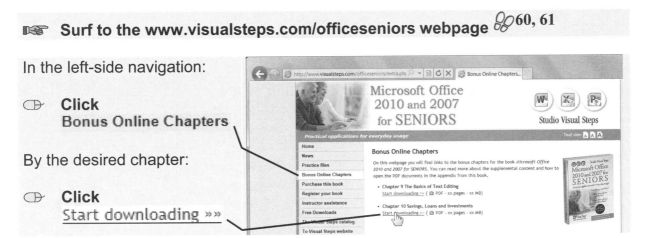

The file will be downloaded. These bonus chapters are PDF files. These PDF files have been secured with a password.

⌨ **Type:** 26725

☞ **Click** OK

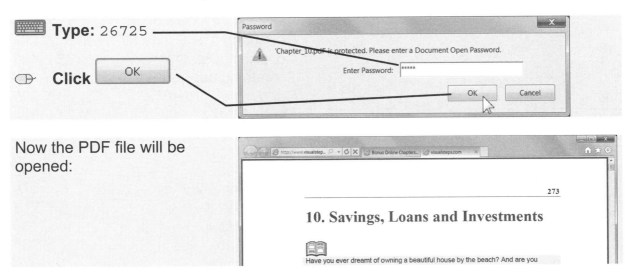

Now the PDF file will be opened:

When you move the mouse down to the bottom of the window, you will see the Adobe Reader toolbar: . Use the arrows to move up and down through the pages. You can zoom in and out on the page with the plus (+) and minus (-) signs. If you want to print the file, click the 🖨 button.

# Appendix D. Index